FROM PEONES TO POLITICOS
CLASS AND ETHNICITY IN A SOUTH TEXAS TOWN, 1900–1987

MEXICAN AMERICAN MONOGRAPH NUMBER 3
THE CENTER FOR MEXICAN AMERICAN STUDIES
THE UNIVERSITY OF TEXAS AT AUSTIN

From Peones to Politicos

Class and Ethnicity in a South Texas Town, 1900–1987

Revised and Enlarged Edition

By
Douglas E. Foley
with
Clarice Mota
Donald E. Post
Ignacio Lozano

UNIVERSITY OF TEXAS PRESS   AUSTIN

To Luisa Sanchez,
who doesn't get all the awards,
but who also touches hearts
in her own quiet way.

Copyright © 1977, 1988 by the Center for Mexican American Studies, The University of Texas at Austin

All rights reserved
Printed in the United States of America

Revised edition of *From Peones to Politicos: Ethnic Relations in a South Texas Town, 1900 to 1977*

First revised edition, 1988

Requests for permission to reproduce material from this work should be sent to Permissions, University of Texas Press, Box 7819, Austin, Texas 78713-7819.

Library of Congress Cataloging-in-Publication Data

Foley, Douglas E.
   From peones to politicos: class and ethnicity in a South Texas town, 1900–1987 /by Douglas E. Foley, with Clarice Mota, Donald E. Post, Ignacio Lozano.—1st rev. ed.
      p.   cm.—(Mexican American monograph; no. 3)
Includes index.
   1. Mexican Americans—Texas—Politics and government—Case studies. 2. Texas—Ethnic relations—Case studies. 3. Ethnicity—Texas—Case studies. I. Title. II. Series: Mexican American monographs; no. 3.
F395.M5F64   1988
976.4' 0046872073—dc 19

                                                                87-34764
                                                                CIP

ISBN 0-292-72460-8.   ISBN 0-292-72461-6 (pbk.)

CONTENTS

TABLES

INTRODUCTION TO THE REVISED EDITION

This new version of *From Peones to Politicos* updates the major political trends in North Town over the past ten years. Chapter 8 describes what has happened to the new ethnic political leaders and the "ethnic politics" of North Town's Chicano civil rights movement in the past ten years. It also discusses new comparative fieldwork from nearby Aztlán City, from a Mississippi community, and other new studies in the field. In addition, an extended theoretical discussion (Appendix B) makes explicit my views of class analysis and suggests how generalizable this case may be. I argue that class and ethnic processes as described in North Town illustrate general historical trends in the American political system and the Southwestern racial order. In effect, I now make greater knowledge claims for this study. Now that the community has been observed periodically for ten more years and considerable comparative research has been done, the meaning of the events we originally studied seems clearer. This new version of *From Peones to Politicos*, therefore, places greater emphasis on interpretation and the broader implications of the work.

We did not end the original version with extensive conceptual discussions and strong knowledge claims because we wanted to write a relatively untechnical book that North Towners might read and reflect upon. That was our response to the post-sixties criticism of abstract, ethically irresponsible social scientists working in low-income ethnic communities. We hoped to write something that contributed to an ongoing dialogue on changing American society. Consequently, people had to be able to read, use, and reflect upon the manuscript. In addition, we were experimenting with the traditional narrative forms in ethnographic writing. We wanted to write an ethnographic community study with some new forms. We included extensive oral history and ethnohistory; we used a chronological, epic form; we created a cast of contemporary characters and we published a community commentary on the book. Ethical and experimental considerations, therefore, shaped the original manuscript as much as our uncertainty about what it all meant. At the time, it seemed wise to leave the study a rich text without authoritative conclusions. That is a decision we have never regretted. The original manuscript is reasonably accessible and open to interpretation, which in a small way allowed it to become a part of this community's dialogue and struggle to change. This same quality may also have made it more useful in classroom dialogues. We now interpret the original text more extensively, however. We hope this further stimulates rather than closes off the reader's own interpretations of our data.

Finally, it must be said that the new field work involved periodic two- to three-day visits over the past ten years and a more extended six-week period of intensive interviewing in 1986–1987. The original research team no longer exists. I, as the principal investigator, carried out the follow-up study without the assistance of my able colleagues. During the intensive period of data collection, I interviewed some one hundred residents, some for several hours and some for a few minutes. As before, I tried to talk to people from all walks of life and from all political groups. I interviewed a number of new people who are the present political leaders and, of course, many of my old informants. I also attended selected community functions and reviewed the local newspaper and selected community records for the 1978–1987 period.

This follow-up study of North Town politics is not as thorough a field study as the original was. Nevertheless, my background knowledge of North Town makes cross-checking and interpreting people's accounts far easier than it was originally. Moreover, I found a number of the high school students we studied now active in local schools, businesses, and politics. This gave me an extraordinary "in" with some of the new leaders of North Town. I followed some of these people through their college careers at the University of Texas.

Many of the interviews in the restudy are, therefore, extended conversations with long-time acquaintances, confidants, or friends. The depth and duration of such relationships is the main reason I feel confident that another year of residence in the community was not needed to update the original study. In addition, I am in the process of writing a study of the schools, which involves reinterviewing a number of the students and teachers who remain in North Town. The field work is continuing where this manuscript ends, and North Town has not gotten me out of its system any more than I have gotten it out of mine.

D.E.F.
NOVEMBER 1987

INTRODUCTION TO THE FIRST EDITION

This is a study of how one small community in South Texas has been changing since 1900. This story is about how North Town Anglos and Mexicanos have dealt with the problems of economic inequality and racial discrimination. To describe the changing relations and conflict between these two groups, we have characterized the ethnic relations of North Town into three major historical periods: 1) the *Rancho* Era (1900 to 1930), 2) the *Colonia* Era (1930 to 1970), and 3) the Contemporary Period (1970 to 1977).

The *Rancho* era from roughly the late 1890's to the middle-1930's represents the traditional pattern of ethnic relations during the rise of commercial agriculture in this region. Ethnic relations during this era took place under an extremely exploitative, paternalistic sharecropper system and was supported by open racism, strict social segregation, and effective Anglo political machines. Within this oppressive and paternalistic environment an extremely poor Mexicano laboring class adapted. They created their own communities and sustained their cultural traditions in this segregated way of life.

The *Colonia* era from roughly the mid–1930's to the late 1960's is a period of rapid social change. This period is marked by major transformations in the local labor system and "Mexican Town" as an independent community. The North Town Mexicanos began developing their own economic and political leaders and ethnic political organizations. Increasingly, they began challenging the earlier patterns of economic exploitation and social segregation. Such challenges began occurring as the most extreme forms of economic exploitation, the influence of local Anglo politicians and patrons, and the beliefs about Anglo racial superiority became less important forms of control over the Mexicano people.

The Contemporary period could well include the 1960's and the 1970's, since overt Mexicano political challenges actually began around 1960. We have chosen, however, to concentrate on the years from 1972 to 1977. These years are marked by heightened Mexicano-Anglo confrontations over the control of the city, school, and county governments. The contemporary section highlights the rapid rise and decline of a Chicano third party, the *Raza Unida*, and the aggressive and conciliatory responses of local Anglos, who organized into a group called the Better Government League. The present ethnic confrontation represents to some a process of "historical retribution." To others this confrontation represents a "sickness," a "cancer" in the American way of life. To most local residents the conflict is a great source of pain and confusion, and North Towners are struggling to recapture a more harmonious community life.

Before presenting our history of North Town ethnic relations, we need to briefly describe North Town and its surrounding region, our general research methodology, and the specific responsibilities of the co-authors in this study.

North Town and the Surrounding Region

North Town was approximately 6,000 in population at the time of this study. The community is located in a South Texas region commonly characterized as a winter vegetable growing center. Such areas have a long growing season (260 days) and export large quantities of fresh vegetables to the rest of the United States. Historically, the counties of this region are part of a rather narrow strip of counties south of San Antonio and north of the Rio Grande Valley area. Developmentally, this area can be considered a transitional or frontier region that lay between the earlier Mexican society based on the Rio Grande and the developing Anglo society of Central and South-central Texas. This general geographic region did not become developed or settled to any degree until after the Civil War. The towns are generally much younger than those in the Valley or in other parts of Central Texas. Further, the major development of the towns as multi-ethnic communities of Anglos and Mexicanos, and a few blacks, did not occur until the late-1890's and early 1900's.

North county belongs to a particular contemporary sub-region of this more general historical region. This sub-region roughly includes eight counties with a populuation of 94,461 (1970 Census) centered in approximately thirty towns and settlements and scattered over 14,629 square miles. There are several ways that these counties are a functioning ecological, administrative, and economic unit. Although soil types, topology and the water table vary considerably, geographers classify this area as a common economic region with a similar set of ecological conditions. The widespread production of fresh produce vegetables links the growers, truckers, packers, and labor crews of the region, and there is considerable exchange and labor movement across the counties. Second, the local marketing system of auction barns, the cattle breeders' association and exchanges between purebred and cross-bred herds also tend to link the region together economically. Third, administratively, there are a number of ways the eight counties form a region. State welfare, agricultural research and extension, education, and health programs, with some variation, generally administer their programs to this set of counties as a region.

To a degree, then, the pattern of changing ethnic relationships described in North Town tend to hold true for this geopolitical region of South Texas. How generalizable this study is to the Rio Grande Valley or other parts of the Southwest is a subject of considerable interest, but not a question on which we can easily speculate.

A Note on Methodology

Studying a community which is deeply factionalized and mobilized for a political struggle is perhaps the most difficult of all field situations. In other writings we hope to discuss at greater length the technical methods and problems of the field work. Generally, we used all the traditional participant-observation approaches of community studies. We went to many community meetings; interviewed several hundred people; and reviewed local historical documents from the city, county, schools, two churches and the local paper. We also collected approximately fifty life histories, many from ten to forty hours of interviewing, from both men and women in various occupational roles. Finally, since a study of the local educational institutions was a major goal of the original grant, two field workers spent approximately 500 hours observing in the local elementary and secondary schools.

It is always difficult to convey the "method" of a community study to laymen, or even to professional research colleagues not experienced in or favoring such methods. Only a technical essay could communicate the empirical basis of this particular study and the value of informants, field notes, and daily participant-observation. A good descriptive and interpretive community study seeks to create a substantially accurate portrayal or characterization of the actions and feelings of local residents. We have tried to capture what seemed to be the essence of and major directions that Mexicanos and Anglo relations have been taking in North Town. How well we have portrayed life in North Town is at least partially reflected in reviews of the manuscript by North Towners in chapter seven.

Yet no matter how diligently we accomplished the field work, we undoubtedly filtered these data through our value systems. "The truth" proved to be illusive in spite of exhaustive methods and hours of cross-checking information. It was usually difficult to determine how some events *really* happened in the midst of a heated community conflict. Often North Towners themselves disagreed about conditions in their own community. Quite obviously, we have produced only an interpretation, *our interpretation*, not some ultimate truth about life in North Town. Hopefully we have communicated some of the complexity and diversity of the many realities of North Town.

Some of that complexity is reflected in the various terms used in the manuscript to identify brown Americans. The term Mexicano was generally used instead of Mexican-American or Chicano because that was how most brown North Towners referred to themselves. The term Mexicano has a connotation of racial and cultural pride but not necessarily the strong political connotation of the term Chicano. Many younger and more politically active North Towners call themselves Chicano, but many others do not use that term. The term Mexican-American is used less frequently and by more educated, less politically active Mexicanos and some Anglos. For those readers not familiar with small town life in these predominantly Mexicano, Spanish-speaking communities, the use of this Spanish term in English may seem somewhat strange, even affected. Our only defense is that it was the term most people seemed to use to refer to themselves, whether speaking Spanish or English.

The Research Team and Individual Responsibilities

One final note is also needed in the team nature of this research, and the relative contributions and responsibilities of the various co-authors. Generally, this monograph is very much the product of a team effort. All the co-authors interacted extensively and shared ideas freely, thus, it is often impossible to separate the individual contributions. These "rap sessions" or accountings were almost a weekly, even daily occurrence, and many of the manuscript's conclusions and interpretations came out of staff interactions. Sometimes notes were taken or tapes were made of these sessions to capture our collective ideas and feelings. Each person brought different concerns and insights to the situation, and invariably we all pushed and led each other to a fuller understanding.

Douglas Foley was the director and senior member of the research effort. This means that he got the initial research grants from the National Institute of Education, hired the staff, and endlessly harassed them for ideas and data from their separate research sites. He also spent twelve months in North Town and has returned there a number of weekends since the initial field work. He is responsible for the overall conception, organization, and writing of the manuscript. In this regard, he is indebted to all the listed authors and two other co-researchers, Walter Smith and Jean Meadowcroft, not listed. Some of Walter Smith's ideas on power and ethnic movements are undoubtedly a part of this manuscript. Mr. Smith collected a great deal of important comparative data during a year of field work in neighboring Aztlán City, the home of the Raza Unida Party. A portion of his field work on this controversial case was written up as a doctoral dissertation.

Clarice Mota spent nine months interviewing North Town Mexicanas on a wide range of topics, and her data on the Mexicano community and her own writings on the Mexicano family and social life have been incorporated in Chapters two and four. Some of her field work on the 1974 campaign and political leadership was also used to write chapter six. Ms. Mota, a native of Brazil, was also a key factor in collecting and understanding the various Mexicano points of view. She continued to work in North Town, particularly on the role of women in the *movimiento* and is preparing other materials on this topic.

Donald Post spent fifteen months commuting weekly to North and South Town developing a study on ethnic competition for control of schools. He also collected a great deal of demographic data on the region and wrote the sections of chapter five that describe the key political and school issues during 1972–1973. His own work on North Town greatly assisted Douglas Foley, the primary ethnographer in that community, to enter and to better understand North Town. Further, his comparative work in South Town, although not incorporated, has actually added a third reference point for interpreting events in North Town.

Ignacio Lozano, a native of this region has also played a central and varied role in this research. He collected data for the historical sections and on the Raza Unida. He spent fifteen months in the field in two communities, and his sensitivity to and connections with the South Texas Mexicano were perhaps the most important factors in collecting and understanding the various Mexicano points of view.

A final member of the research team, Jean Meadowcroft, has not been listed as a co-author. Ms. Meadowcroft spent four months in the North Town elementary schools. Her work in the schools was valuable for understanding the attitudes of Anglo teachers and how they were adapting to the new Chicano activism. These materials will be published in a subsequent monograph concentrating on education in these towns.

This is, then, a very simplified breakdown of the primary individual inputs and responsibilities. We all owe each other so much that it is hard to know where one's efforts and ideas end and where the other person's begins. This has been a collective enterprise. The sum of what has been produced would not have been possible without the variety of skills and backgrounds of the total collective. Indeed, it is clear to us that the idea of a single, all-purpose ethnographer in the multi-ethnic communities of a complex society is not altogether reasonable and methodologically defensible. There is much to be gained by having a racially and sexually diverse research group.

Further, it is important to acknowledge our gratitude for two grants, no. NE-G-0-72-3943 and no. NE-G-00-3-0117, and a great deal of patience and support from the National Institute of Education, the Anthropology Panel section. Although NIE financed this particular study, they in no way are responsible for the views and results expressed herein. The entire above staff, and particularly its senior member, Douglas Foley, bear all the responsibilities for any errors or inaccuracies.

Finally, if all of the authors listed the people who should be thanked, we would keep the reader circling in holding pattern for many pages. Several students and faculty here at the university have labored over earlier, more obscure drafts. Most importantly, hundreds of North Towners put up with us for several years. A testimony to their dedication is the many hours some spent on reviewing and correcting the manuscript. Overall, they treated "their snoopers" remarkably well. I like to think that I still have a number of personal friends there, in spite of some differences of agreement with our interpretations. I'd like to believe that North Towners and I have begun a dialogue that has been meaningful for everyone involved. This was especially true during the times when a porch, a cold beer, and an evening South Texas breeze chased away bitterness and misunderstanding.

PART I: LIFE IN THE *RANCHO* ERA, 1900 TO 1930

Chapter 1

The Political Economy of the *Ranchos*

This geographic region of South Texas was historically settled after the Mexican-American War of 1846. The area was originally on the outer fringe of a Spanish settlement in the Rio Grande Valley. The Spanish planned to develop all the land below the Nueces River to the Rio Grande Valley into a colony called Nuevo Santander.[1] Many Spanish colonial settlers were granted *porciones* (land grants), and a number of settlements and towns were established on both banks of the Rio Grande River. After the Revolution of 1824, Mexico became an independent nation, and the Mexican government administered this area as the state of Tamaulipas. During this period, a small number of Anglo settlers also began moving into the Rio Grande Valley area which the Republic of Texas sought to annex. The Texans wanted to set the boundary of Tamaulipas at the Rio Grande River. This proposed boundary was much further south than the Nueces River, thus annexing the entire area of Tamaulipas.[2] The ensuing story of annexation, the battles, disputed land titles, abandoned *haciendas*, and the flight of the original Mexicano settlers has yet to be told.

The North Town region was on the fringe of Tamaulipas and was generally much less inhabited and settled than the Valley. Several Indian tribes controlled this stretch of sparsely inhabited sandy brush land. They were hunting and gathering groups not unlike the Plains Indians that had been pushed into the area by the onslaught of Anglo settlers from North and Central Texas.[3] There were also apparently a number of *porciones* (land grants) and Mexican settlers in this fringe area. The Mexican settlers who came this far north of the Rio Grande Valley region undoubtedly encountered serious problems, first with the Indians, and later around 1848 with the influx of Anglo settlers. Further, those remaining had to re-survey and establish their lands under the state of Texas. One local history describes this "trou-

1

blesome" animosity between the remaining early Mexican settlers and the new Anglo settlers.[4]

Generally, the first Anglo settlers in the counties studied arrived from 1850 to 1860. North Town local historians indicate that there were three Anglo settlers in their county by the early 1850's.[5] In nearby Aztlán City most of the settlers came in after the Mexican-American War. Many of the original settlers were veterans of the war who had been given state land grants on the riverbottom land.[6] Most Anglo settlement came, however, after the Civil War, and by the 1880's a number of large ranches and cattle companies were established. This study did not explore precisely how these early Anglo settlers got their lands, or the extent that the original Mexican settlers resisted and were forced from their lands. Recent studies suggest that the settlement of the Southwestern United States was often a bitter struggle between organized coalitions of Anglo settlers and political officials and aggressive Mexicano resistance movements.[7]

In this marginal, poorly developed region there were, however, probably no dramatic battles or well-known, organized Anglo or Mexicano groups such as the King Ranch of the Valley or the *Las Gorras Blancas* of New Mexico. Anglos apparently had no well-organized political machines in this region. There was also no well-developed Spanish-American elite class which collaborated with the Anglo bankers, lawyers, merchants, and politicians.

The conquest tactics in this desolate, unsettled area were probably simple and relatively unspectacular. As in much of the Southwest, Mexican settlers, through a series of international wars and treaties, were left to fend for themselves against the flood of Anglo settlers. The few scattered Mexican settlers became victims of the general absence of law and community. The Anglos, with the language and laws in their favor, overwhelmed the tenuous Mexican settlements. There were undoubtedly disputes and misunderstandings over land, shootings on lonely country trails, and legalized expropriations through the Anglo county judges and sheriffs. A few of the more enterprising, politically astute Mexicans survived, some as land owners and officials,[8] but the great majority of Mexican settlers either lost their lands and retreated back to their homeland, or they stayed as landless laborers.

During the early development of this rangeland, from 1860 to 1880, many small Anglo ranchers sold small numbers of cattle to Kansas drivers. These small ranchers shared the open range and lived in tiny settlements along the main San Antonio-Mexico routes.[9] By the early

1880's two important technological innovations, the railroad and barbed-wire, had rapidly altered the entire region. The fencing changed the open-range system of cattle ranching. Many of the original homesteaders were driven out. As in other frontier areas of the great plains, the original Spanish land grants were re-surveyed and perfected. Eastern, foreign, and big city capital poured in to form large absentee cattle companies to make quick profits.[10] A few of the cattle companies and original settlers succeeded in consolidating large tracts of land (30,000 to 100,000 acres).[11]

By the 1890's this region had experienced several economic transformations. It changed from a sparsely settled territory of the Mexican state of Tamaulipas to small settlements of Anglo homesteaders. Forty years later the regional economy was dominated by large, fenced ranches and cattlemen. By this point the area had become predominately Anglo. There were, however, a number of Mexican *vaqueros* (cowboys), a few wage laborers in the settlements, and a growing number of itinerant migratory farm workers. Prior to the twentieth century the region was an excellent frontier for the expansion of commercial agriculture. It was near the growing urban area of Central Texas but was still sparsely settled enough to have cheap land. Given its cheap land and labor and mild climate, the North County region was a promising agricultural area.

In the 1890's several national trends encouraged new settlers to come into this region. First, the scourge of the boll weevil and the extension of southern and East Texas lands gradually pushed a number of cotton farmers westward in search of cheap land.[12] Second, descendants from earlier, (1830's) predominantly German settlements in Central Texas also migrated south to this less-populated area. Third, by the early 1900's the region had become the site for a number of large land promotion schemes. Several of the earlier cattle companies and other speculators from the urban areas began dividing up the huge, relatively unprofitable ranches. North Town was one of the original boom towns that survived and grew. Much of the land had been acquired for less than a dollar an acre and could be subdivided into small ten and twenty acre lots and small city lots selling for as much as one hundred dollars an acre. These companies advertised all over the United States to attract what locals called "the suckers."

The companies usually surveyed a town site and built a hotel and several stores to accommodate prospective buyers. They brought them in by the train-loads, promising cheap, fertile land, flowing artesian wells, and a growing season twice that of the Midwest. The potential

3

for a fast profit on cotton and winter vegetables attracted many poor farmers from the Midwest, as well as inexperienced greenhorns from the cities and second and third generation Central Texas settlers. The increases in farm owners and operators, tenants, and general population is reflected in the census data.[13] From 1900 to 1930 this area became a mixed economy of small farmers and ranchers. The development of larger labor forces and urban settlements soon followed.

Most of the agricultural development in cotton and vegetables was on the prime flat, river-flood plain land and on the lighter soils. The smaller (2,000 to 5,000 acres) and medium-sized (5,000 to 20,000 acres) ranches were left undisturbed by this influx of small cotton and vegetable farmers. Likewise, some of the large absentee cattle companies and most of the larger family-owned ranches (20,000 to 60,000) did not sell out or subdivide. The coming of commercial agriculture did not initially disturb or destroy the predominant place of ranching, but it ultimately made land less available and more expensive. These developments made the future expansion of ranching more dependent on modernization through innovations in breeding stock, grasses, production time, and range utilization.

Unlike, however, the days of fencing and fence cutting, ranchers and farmers were not at war with each other. Old-timers report that the ranchers, who often had more land and money, generally thought of themselves as "better than dirt farmers." They rode horses and carried guns and sometimes lived up to their reputations as hard-drinking, tough men who were also "good" with the ladies. Several of the older Mexicanos said it was common practice for ranchers to have a *querida* (a Mexican lady) whom they kept and visited on the ranch. People generally described farmers as a quieter, "less showy lot," people that "stuck to home and tended their land." Despite a number of differences in style and wealth, the transition from a ranching to ranching/farming economy was made smoothly.

The influx of hundreds of small farmers in the early 1900's and the creation of a cash crop economy quickly transformed the region. The expanded population and new economy gave rise to small, county seat market towns. These small urban centers provided the produce-packing and shipping facilities, the cattle pens, the cotton gins, and loading docks of the new economy. As the market towns developed, more merchants, bankers, and schoolmen followed to service the new settlements.

Along with this influx of Anglo farmers and townspeople came a steady stream of Mexican labor.[14] Initially, many came across to work

4

during the crop seasons, always to return home to Mexico. These temporary immigrants entered with ease. The border guards usually had lists of farmers and ranchers needing help, and the guards did not restrict the illegal entrants. Families of Mexicanos would arrive at the border, pay the guard a nickel, and get the name of a rancher. The families would then travel by mule-drawn wagons to the various *ranchos*.

There were also many other ways of entering and finding work. There was *el coyote*, the smuggler who brought the immigrants to the *enganchador* (literally, hooker) or labor contractor. These border labor contractors organized crews of cotton and vegetable pickers and took them to the local growers.[15] Often, the crews were taken North on the train to live in tent camps under armed guards. These crews moved around the area to pick crops, and then the labor contractors brought the crews back to the border towns and Mexico. Quite often these contractors gave a percentage to the border guards to assure a constant supply of labor. Others operated independently with the smuggled labor, and most used both or whatever was available.

Two factors were constantly mentioned by the old-timers as reasons for migrating. First, they were looking for a better living and more money in the growing South Texas areas. Second, many also were seeking to escape the great turmoil caused by the Mexican revolution. By the early 1900's Mexico had gone through a series of reforms and revolutions that greatly altered the relationship of the peasants to the *hacienda* land system. There were many landless peasants in Mexico seeking a better way of life.[16] Most of the immigrants emphasized the poverty and turmoil in Mexico and their hope that America would offer more opportunity. During the 1900 to 1920 period thousands of Mexican families that were temporary migrants decided to settle in the United States. Early censuses are notoriously inaccurate, due to the illegal immigrants and part-time residents, but they at least partially reflect this rapid increase.[17]

These immigrants generally settled in three different types of settings. First, some settled in the small "Mexican Towns," *las colonias*, which grew on the opposite side of the Anglo market towns. Second, a much larger percentage settled in smaller hamlets in the more distant parts of these counties, where cotton farming was extensive or where a large irrigated produce operation existed. They usually centered around a cotton gin, a general store, a small interdenominational church, and a one-room school. These tiny communities often consisted of several Anglo families and perhaps thirty to forty Mexicano families. In several cases, the store and the gin were owned by the largest farmer or rancher in the settlement. The third settlement pattern of the Mexican family was to live on the individual farms and ranches with their Anglo *patrones*. The majority of early Mexicano settlers living outside the towns were scattered throughout the isolated rural areas of the county. Every rancher and farmer had several Mexican families permanently living on their place.

The Early Agricultural Production-Labor Units

During this early boom period cotton farmers slowly trickled in from other Texas and Southern areas. They bought the land cheaply, two to ten dollars an acre, and set up small communities. The typical cotton farm was from eighty to 160 acres. Each man and mule team could generally plant and cultivate a plot of forty to fifty acres. Those Anglo farmers who had more land than they could work contracted a Mexican tenant or two to farm the rest.

There were basically two types of share-rent contracts used. Either the tenant would be a *mediero* and farm the land on the basis of a fifty/fifty split of the crop. Or, he would be a *quartero* and split the cotton crop twenty-five/seventy-five and the corn crop thirty-three/sixty-six. Under the first system the *patrones* sometimes provided some instruments for production, i.e., the animals, plow, tools. More often they provided an advance of money for living expenses and for the purchase of seeds. In most cases the sharecroppers reported having their own animals and basic tools, but they were absolutely dependent upon local merchants to advance them food and supplies on credit until the crops were harvested. Under the second system, which became somewhat more common in the late 1910's, the Anglo land owner provided only the land and, if necessary, arranged credit with local merchants. The Mexican sharecropper used his own mules, tools and seed, and ultimately shared twenty-five percent of the harvest.

This type of share-farming operation was very much of a family-based labor system. Anglo growers emphasized that the bigger the family the better the tenant. Big families provided more labor. They generally worked harder and stayed longer because they were perpetually in debt to the local merchants. Yet, even though most sharecroppers had large families, they and the owners often found it necessary to hire extra hands. Both owners and sharecroppers supplemented the family labor system by hiring younger males or landless families from nearby towns. Occasionally, even the sons of *vaqueros* (cowboys) sought to make extra money picking cotton. In other cases the sharecroppers exchanged labor with neighboring families whose crop came earlier. Several families would plan and coordinate their planting so it was staggered and labor exchanges were more possible. On larger cotton farms (500 to 1,000 acres), however, the owner generally imported crews from the border towns or the Rio Grande Valley to quickly finish the harvest. By the early 1920's an increasing number of crews were coming into the area to handle the expanded cotton acreage.

Once picked, the cotton was hauled to the local or town gin for processing and baling. The ginners kept most of the seed to pay for the ginning costs. Those farmers who had extra capital and planned ahead kept part of the seed for the next year. Once the cotton was compressed into bales, the farmers hauled it by wagon to towns or settlements with rail depots. Cotton brokers then bought the bales and sent them to large cotton brokering companies in Houston or San Antonio. Some of the larger cotton farmers occasionally tried their luck at shipping and selling their cotton in the commodity exchanges in the cities. Generally, however, the small growers, both owners and tenants, sold their cotton to local brokers at the prices given to them. Occasionally the well-to-do local farmers, ranchers or merchants speculated on purchasing, storing, and shipping the cotton.

The small dry cotton farms and the small irrigated vegetable farms were generally self-sufficient. Most farmers raised a few hogs and chickens for meat. They also planted large gardens and preserved the vegetables and fruits. Nearly every farmer had a milk cow or two, and those with brush land or extra grazing land ran small cow-calf operations. The larger cow-calf operators might have a bull and twenty-five cows. The smaller ones might have ten or fifteen cows but no breeding bull. When calves were weaned, they were sold to local ranchers with much larger grazing areas for finishing, or they were sold to brokers from large cattle companies outside the region. The small cotton farm was very difficult to operate successfully. The lack of water and weevil control, and the unpredictable cotton market often made such diversification necessary. Calves were a steady income, and there was always enough meat and vegetables "to get by in lean years."

Vegetable farming in the area varied considerably from county to county and was initially restricted to the areas with shallow flowing artesian wells or with river basin gravity irrigation.[18] In North Town only a few small truck farms existed in the early 1900's. These thirty to forty acre plots were used primarily for onions. The real regional boom in vegetables came after land speculators had drawn thousands

7

of farmers to the area from 1909 to the early 1920's.[19] A number of these land schemes quickly folded, however. Many of these new farms were poorly organized and financed. Early settlers described the problems they had learning new watering, labor, and packing techniques. They also had to clear the land and drill artesian wells, which soon had to be replaced with costly pumps. Others lacked any type of water system. Many of these small farmers were simply unable to adapt to the Southwestern brush country.

In the areas where a land scheme was promoted, most of the small farmers had already left or moved into the surrounding towns by 1917. Some of their land was bought and farmed by the larger operators who had survived, but the vast majority of the small plots and acreages remained fallow and unused or reverted back into grazing land.[20] In other counties and sections of the region, vegetable growing increased. Small truck farmers (forty to sixty acres) with favorable sites, i.e., good shallow wells and close to the rail lines, prospered. Larger, diversified farm operators (300 to 800 acres) who combined vegetable growing with dry grain farming and small cow-calf operations also succeeded. Before the 1920's, however, the region was not spectacularly successful as a major vegetable growing center.[21] These early small vegetable farmers were often at the mercy of the packers and brokers operating out of the region's market towns. Few small vegetable farmers were able to pack and ship their own produce to the primary produce market in San Antonio.

The development of vegetable farming in this region did, however, greatly stimulate the in-migration of Mexicano laborers. All the planting, cleaning, and harvesting was done by hand, and the labor-to-land ratio for vegetables was considerably higher than for cotton or cattle. Intensive vegetable farming often affected Mexicano settlement patterns. Several small North County settlements of thirty or forty Mexicano families were centered around pump or gravity irrigation systems for vegetables. Such farming operations required a number of permanent farm laborers for planting, transplanting (for onions), weeding, and maintaining the irrigation system.

Harvest labor for the vegetable industry was recruited in several ways before 1920. The large vegetable farmers with several hundred acres often brought in organized crews from the border towns. Local growers developed contacts with different border *contratistas* through the mails and occasional shopping visits to the border towns. Nearly all of these crew laborers were male immigrants who received temporary, informal permission to enter. A second source of vegetable harvesting labor was the steady stream of *mojados* (wetbacks) passing through the area on their own. The third and most frequent source for small farmers was excess local labor from the surrounding farms, hamlets, and market towns. The small but growing number of landless laborers permanently residing in the towns and with settled families in the hamlets increased rapidly during the first two decades. In addition, the sharecroppers and their sons also frequently worked the local winter vegetables.

Finally, in times of crisis, e.g., when the crop was over ripening or storms were approaching, the entire hamlet of Anglo farmers and smaller ranchers and their Mexicano laborers would help their neighbors pick the crop. Although the bulk of local labor was not yet highly organized into a crew labor system, the *patrones* knew where and when to find workers. Several old-time Anglo farmers recalled that there was always an excess of labor, that, "The Mexicans in those days were always there when you needed them." This surplus of Mexican labor was a contributing factor in keeping wages low and in stabilizing the Mexicano population into a subordinate social and economic position.

The third major type of agricultural production unit in the North Town region was the cattle ranch. This type of production unit and its labor needs are relatively easy to characterize, but it is difficult to described a "typical" ranch. With the advent of fencing and northern markets, the cattle industry of this region grew dramatically.[22] As in other range areas, urban investors bought large tracts of cheap land (one dollar an acre) and started what were initially profitable cattle companies.[23] These large tracts were often over 100,000 acres and were coordinated with other large ranching operations in Mexico. No more than one or two of these companies existed per county, but they often occupied as much as 1/7th to 1/6th of the county lands.

By the 1900's North County ranches were well-established. The large ranches (5,000 to 35,000 acres) were predominantly in the hands of original settlers and were strictly "big steer" ranches. During this period a county with a diversified farming/ranching economy would have no more than thirty or forty of these large ranches. Most of these large ranches also had several hundred acres of hay and grain land to supplement their natural grasses. But as several old-timers put it, "the real cattlemen didn't fool around with farming." Very few large ranchers had many cotton sharecroppers, and they certainly were not "fooling around with onions and spinach."

9

Large ranches generally had several Mexican *vaqueros* and their families and an assortment of young, drifting Mexican and Anglo cowboys. Usually a larger ranch (200,000 acres and 1,000 cattle) might have eight or ten permanent *vaqueros*. This labor ratio would depend upon how many sons the rancher had, the rains, the market, and many other factors. These cowboys lived in one-room houses or in the all-male bunkhouses. They were paid a dollar a day and board and generally worked year-round from sunup to sunset. These men were responsible for working cattle, rounding up, sorting, weaning, branding, doctoring, and driving them to market. They also helped produce and store the winter hay and grain crops and maintained the fencing and water systems. During round-up time or tick-dipping time the number of extra hands needed was often more than double the regular hands. Generally, *vaqueros* from other ranches or drifting cowhands were used during round-ups.

Smaller, more diversified ranchers were more prevalent in this region, however. For every large specialized ranch there were perhaps three smaller ranches (1,000–5,000 acres) that combined staple cash cropping with their cow-calf grazing operation. Such ranches were referred to as stock farms and often had 300 to 400 acres of cotton under six or eight sharecroppers. A stock farm might also have 100 to 200 acres of grazing land for 100 cows and calves run by two or three *vaqueros*.

As cotton became a big money crop and cheap labor more available in the early 1900's, ranchers began to diversify into cropping. Such ranch/farming operations were usually located on the flatter, lighter soils contiguous to the small farmers. Since these ranchers also raised crops, they often had several permanent Mexican families living on the ranch. Although these smaller ranchers made most of their profits from cotton cropping, they still considered themselves ranchers, not farmers. In early North County these small ranchers or stock farmers and the large cotton farmers (500 to 800 acres) were the most common agricultural operators.

The shipping and marketing system for all cattle ranchers was basically the same. Cattle often came into the region from East Texas or Mexico. Stocker cattle from nine months old to yearlings were brought into these counties of South Texas for grazing. Many of the larger ranching operations with extra or leased pasture supplemented their own breeding herds with these "stockers." This was especially true in wet years when the grasses were good and the brush country could support as many as one cow per ten acres. During average years the ratio was generally one cow per twenty acres and as low as one cow per thirty acres during dry years. It was not unusual for the larger cattlemen to have as many stockers as their own calves.

During the early days this area was known as "big steer" country. Ranchers generally let their cattle graze for two to four years before selling them. The common breeds, herefords and longhorn-crosses would often be well over 1200 pounds before they were marketed. The cattle were generally marketed by rail to San Antonio or Houston or sometimes farther north to Fort Worth or Kansas City. They were rounded up and brought to the stock pens in the market town. Generally, they were watered and fed overnight and shipped out the next day. Most of the cattle were bought by brokers from the big packing companies. But a few of the larger ranchers shipped their own cattle. They hoped to hit the market and make a better profit. The North Town region was, then, predominantly a cattle breeding and grazing area. There was virtually no finishing of cattle with grain and supplemental feeds. Until the thirties the retailers and consumers accepted the older, heavier animals of this "big steer" country.

All of the North County agricultural operations, in varying degrees, faced similar climatic and market problems with labor-intensive, hand and animal technology.[24] The region was potentially productive with adequate water and a good deal of management and luck.[25] As one of the early ranchers declared:

> Many people never learned how to live with this land. You got pretty good soil, if you treat it right. And you got enough water, if you sink down a good well and pump it right. You got plenty of labor, plenty of people to help clear this ole' brush country. And we Americans, the ones of us who came here in the early days, was a pretty tough lot. Fact is, I think we are a dying breed. Seems like this country is going soft nowadays. But for damn sure a lotta people who come here didn't survive. Down here you just gotta treat the land right. It ain't like back where you are from where that top soil is deep and black and it'll rain like hell during the summer. No sir, we have to fight for everything we get down here.

As he indicated, this area was productive, but the margin for mismanagement or failure was great. It was a fragile kind of relationship that the farmer and rancher had to watch and nurture well. Perhaps the most important and uncontrollable factor was the market and its highly fluctuating prices. Cotton farmers and vegetable growers were continually victims of declining prices and the problems of marketing their crops somewhere. As one farmer exclaimed, "You have to be a gambler or a damn fool to try and grow stuff for a profit." The prices for cattle also fluctuated considerably, but ranches were generally more able to weather droughts and ticks and hookworms than small farmers were. The large ranches tended to have fewer debts and lower labor costs. Cattle, despite the unstable market, were safer and easier to produce than perishable vegetables or delicate cotton plants. Although few cattlemen would disagree that ranching was an easy livelihood, this region was more suitable for a pastoral economy. The lands were basically rangeland. Farming such lands required considerable skill and luck.

Perhaps the most manipulable, controllable factor in the *rancho* economy was labor. It was abundant and cheap. This early South Texas society was built upon the first generation of Mexican immigrants. The amount and type of hand labor on these early North County farms and ranches was back-breaking. The hard, undulating clay soils were difficult to plow with mules. The hauling of crops over dirt roads was difficult. Everything was loaded, planted, cultivated, and harvested by hand in hot or cold weather. The stoop labor of cotton and vegetable pickers made the workers age quickly. The *vaqueros* frequently suffered injuries trying to rope, drive, and handle steers.

Yet one form of labor, clearing the land, was particularly burdensome and dangerous. Everyone who attempted to use these brush lands had to clear it and continually fight the mesquite brush. Soil conservationists argue that this area deteriorated into a brushland. Mismanagement and overgrazing during the boom years of the 1880's ruined this tall-grass land. When the grass cover became thin, the mesquite took over. Old-timers claim that the Mexican cattle brought into the region also helped spread the mesquite. During the long drives the cattle would eat the sweet mesquite beans and deposit them around on the open range. The more the early ranchers mismanaged the ranges, the more the area became a brushland which required constant clearing.

Clearing land during the *Rancho* period required a great deal of hand labor with crude grub hoes. The Mexicano laborers cut down, rooted, and dragged the mesquite into piles and burned it. The cactus, which was used for cattle feed, was also burned. The laborers burned the cactus thorns off with flame throwers that used large pressurized tanks of gas. Not infrequently these crude flame throwers exploded and seriously injured the workers. As one old laborer explained, "This work aged we Mexicanos very quickly. We became old men before the very eyes of our Maker." The clearing of pasture land was a never-ending battle. Even a well-cleared pasture returns to brush within five years, if the mesquite sprouts are not continuously grubbed. The intensively cultivated farmlands will, however, stay clean while in use. In a very real sense, the Mexicano laborers tamed and improved this land with their grub hoes and their flame throwers.

The Social Relationship Between Landlord and Laborers

Both Anglos and Mexicanos worked hard in these early small settlements. The early Anglos taught their children to work along with the adults in the fields. The women labored long hours to prepare meals and to keep clothes and houses clean in the hot, dusty settlements. The Anglo farmers and ranchers with small places plowed their own fields and herded their cattle while Mexicanos worked other portions of their land on shares. But these traditional American farmers and individualistic ranchers were also landlords and *patrones* in ways different from Midwestern farmers of this era.

The complex relationship between the Anglo *patrón* and his Mexicano workers reflects the class and ethnic contradictions of this early society.[26] Many of the old Mexicanos and Anglos described their relationships with *both* great hatred *and* fondness. Most *patrones* developed relationships and exchanges with their workers to bind the two groups together. Many Mexicanos were given small privileges such as permission to have chickens, a garden plot, and some free grazing land for their milk cow. Not infrequently *patrones* took their workers to town and arranged for credit with the merchants. There were also times when some of the *patrones* took their workers to a doctor or a dentist, and times when the *patron's* wife gave the workers extra fruit from the orchard, a loaf of bread, or her children's old clothes. In return, Mexicanos were expected to volunteer various forms of service to their *patrones*. The male sharecroppers were apparently often sent in the *patron's* place to serve the required five days of labor on the county roads. On other occasions the wives of sharecroppers or their children helped the owners cook and serve food during their family celebrations. The children of sharecroppers also helped clean, unload supplies, and do various chores on the farm.

To some extent Anglos and Mexicanos also socialized together on the *ranchos*. During various family celebrations the Mexicano workers invited the *patrón* to their *bailes* (dances), and sometimes he would come. Many Anglo children had Mexicano wet nurses, and most of the Anglos brought up on the *ranchos* played with Mexicano children.

13

They learned Spanish, and they ate tortillas and beans in the houses of the workers. Anglo old-timers tend to remember their relationships with workers as amiable and intimate. They frequently pointed out that during critical harvest times and crisis, e.g., an outbreak of tick infestation, "Everyone pulled to lick a common problem, to get ahead together." Judging from the reports of the Mexicano workers, some socializing and considerable exchange of daily pleasantries and small-talk certainly existed. It would be incorrect to describe the relations of Anglos and Mexicanos in the private world of the *rancho* as filled with conflict. *If* a Mexicano worker accepted his poverty, poor housing, and heavy labor, the paternalistic relations of *rancho* life had some redeeming aspects. When these isolated workers ventured out into the more impersonal, segregated towns of sheriffs, merchants, and *ricos* they apparently experienced more mistreatment than on their *ranchos*.

Yet it is also incorrect to characterize the paternalistic relationship of landlord to tenant as truly intimate and satisfying for the Mexicano sharecroppers. Whatever redeeming social qualities such relationships had, they were ultimately based on the economic needs of the *rancho*. As one old *quartero* described it, "we were *burros de la tierra*" (donkeys of the land). He went on to say:

> I worked for my *patrón* for fifteen years. Then one day the *patrón* told me to leave. He didn't need me any more. You see he bought a tractor, and it could do the work better than me. He was tired, too, of our chickens eating on his grain, and he thought our children should stay home from school and work. We weren't needed anymore, you see. So he got rid of us. . . . No, I do not think the *patrones* really liked us. Many Mexicanos believed that the *gringos* were being good to us, but I believe they used us like work animals. I know many *sembradores* who had to leave their place. We did not want to believe our *patrones* did not care. We had nothing else. We could not speak English. We had no land and no education. For many of us the *patrón* was our only hope. But we were never close, not truly *compañeros* (close companions). The *gringos* were only nice so we would work harder and stay with them until they no longer needed us. No, Mexicanos did not really like their *patrones*. And the *patrones* did not really like us. We were not bonded together like *la familia*. If we could have left we would. If the *gringos* didn't need us, they would have sent us away.

It is important to underscore that the nature of economic exploitation and social inequality in such a paternalistic, agrarian labor system is always obscured. The landlords and workers do not necessarily recognize the dehumanizing qualities of the relationships they act out.

14

The Anglo *patrones* did not openly hate and physically punish their workers. Indeed, most Anglo *patrones* remember their workers fondly and emphasize that these relationships were amiable. Many expressed the views that Mexicanos were a poor, simple, child-like group that needed guidance and close supervision. They would be appalled by the characterization that they hated their workers or were hated. Conversely, many Mexicano workers did not express open hatred and anger towards their *patrones*. Whatever they privately felt was usually not expressed; consequently, the surface reality of landlord-worker relations was usually amiable and filled with a degree of racial mixing and with a sharing of daily greetings, extra vegetables, old clothes, wet nurses, and Mexican tortillas. Both *patrón* and worker accepted the belief that the natural order of things was the superior-subordinate relationship of the *rancho*. Paternalistic kindness and the Mexicano's acceptance of Anglo superiority were far more powerful forms of control than physical violence. Force and cruelty were only necessary when the Mexicano refused to accept that *rancho* life was natural and good.

The typical Mexicano sharecropper, like sharecroppers in other tenancy systems around the world, was immobile and poor. Most sharecroppers stayed on the same plot for ten to fifteen years. A good plot might gross $500 to $700 a year, but after paying off advances and expenses there were usually no profits. Very few Mexicanos were able to become land-owners during this time. Nevertheless, sharecroppers usually perceived themselves as much better off than the landless wage laborers of the crews. The wage laborers were paid less than a dollar a day when they worked. In contrast, the *vaqueros* were perceived as somewhat better off. Although *vaqueros* had no land, they made a steady thirty dollars a month plus at least some form of minimal housing.

People in these small communities shopped at the community and ranch stores for their basic tools, canned goods, staples, and work clothes. Both Anglos and Mexicanos generally bought the major portion of their supplies from the town stores, although this depended upon the availability of transportation and credit in the rural settlements. In six North County *rancho* settlements the local store was run by the biggest rancher or farmer in the settlement. The bulk of the workers in the settlement worked for this *patrón*, and he gave them credit in his store. In other settlements with no stores, the Mexicanos borrowed from the Anglo merchants in North Town, the county seat.

In the chattel mortage records several North Town merchants had

100 to 150 names indebted to them. The same debtors often appeared for five to ten consecutive years. Judging from the population statistics for 1910 and the number of Spanish surnamed debtors, approximately seventy-five percent of the Spanish surnamed households were indebted. By the 1920's the figure had decreased to approximately sixty percent. These are, of course, crude estimates, but they bear out the verbal descriptions of the laborers that economic conditions were very bad indeed.

The interest rates charged varied from zero to fifty percent. Apparently much of the credit for food supplies was advanced without usurious interest rates. Usually, the sharecropper would get twenty-five to thirty dollars a month advances for food and supplies until their crops were harvested. The chattel mortgage records show they had to put up their *tiro*, livestock, and their cotton crop for the $150 to $200 advances. The merchants kept a record of the supplies taken and then gave the Mexicanos an accounting when they harvested their crop.

Many Mexicanos felt they were overcharged and cheated, but apparently they rarely contested the merchant because they were fearful of losing their credit. Every town seemed to have some merchants who padded their figures and others who were scrupulously honest and highly respected. The landless Mexicano laborers often relied, however, on whichever merchant that their *patrón* preferred. In many cases the workers could only borrow credit if their *patrón* signed for them. The field hands and some of the *vaqueros* were in even greater need for such credit than the sharecroppers. In this system, when the landowners suffered from the unpredictable cotton and grain market, the tenants suffered even more. The harder the times, the tighter the credit knot squeezed.

By the 1920's some Mexicanos in the cotton-producing areas of these counties had been able to buy their own *tiro* and were farming on "the quarters." Old owners and laborers estimated that perhaps fifteen to twenty-five percent of the sharecroppers in their settlements had advanced to *quartero* status. Many sharecroppers were also allowed to graze their own small cattle herds and their chickens on the *patrón's* land. In North County several old sharecroppers claimed that Anglo *patrones* became disenchanted with the *quartero* system because the Mexicanos made too much money.[27] The Anglo *patrones* were reputed to respond by forbidding poultry and by charging rents for grazing use. In several other cases, people reported that the merchants cut off advanced credit in town around 1923. Many old-timers viewed these events as part of the general anti-Mexican feeling during and after the war. Many aliens were deported and Klan activity was on the upsurge in this region. Others felt that the *patrones* feared losing control of their workers as they became less debt-ridden.

Despite such repressive activities, Mexicanos also shared in the boom years of the early 1920's. The chattel mortgage records show most Mexicanos using automobiles for security, and increasing numbers lived in the towns. But most of the life histories of old laborers and the declining crop output in the census[28] suggest that any economic spurt in the early 1920's was short-lived. By the late 1920's cotton and vegetable production spiraled downward due to soil exhaustion, boll weevil, various fungi and molds and declining market prices. As the Depression approached, most rural Mexicanos were still landless and debt-ridden. Likewise, many of the smaller Anglo *patrones* were also finding economic survival difficult.

The Early Political System

The previously described set of economic activities and relationships between Anglos and Mexicanos formed the material and social base of early life in North County on the *ranchos*. To further understand the *rancho* way of life, one must understand how local Anglos administered the public institutions and public laws. These early towns and settlements also had local government with the power to tax, deliver services, and settle disputes. Before describing the county and city governments and the early Anglo political leaders, the legal status of the Mexican immigrant must be clarified.

Perhaps the most important point of contact between the national government and these local governments has been the question of Mexican immigration. Historians have begun to explore the relationship of regional agro-business lobbies to national policies on immigration.[29] The immigration policy towards Mexicans has been intimately related to the availability of oriental, black, and Eastern European labor. Large California agro-business corporations, Midwestern sugar beet companies and Southwestern growers have consistently sought to retain their cheap Mexican labor pool. This has been particularly true when other sources of field labor were on the decline; consequently, federal immigration policies during the 1900 to 1930 period did not formally restrict Mexican labor in the manner that oriental (1884) and Eastern European (1924) immigrants were restricted.[30] By 1917 the legal Mexican immigrant with papers was left out of the quota systems established. Much of the argument for this exception centered on the fact that Mexican labor was a transitory,

17

temporary group that returned to its homeland. They would not cause a serious drag on the American economy, swell the welfare ranks of the cities, or "mongrelize the white race."

Southwestern congressmen argued that restrictive policies should not be adopted because it might affect border relations and good will towards the Latin American countries. The important aspect of the federal government's role is not, however, their formal policy. The important point is how the United States has dealt with the informal flow of Mexican immigrants through *coyotes* (smugglers) and *enganchadores* (labor contractors) and *mojados* (wetbacks). Massive numbers of Mexicans were allowed to enter through various methods, and this labor force became "invisible" in the sense that they existed without any legal status. They had no papers, and they were not citizens. They therefore had no rights against labor exploitation and arbitrary deportation.

Many of these illegal immigrants settled in the hamlets and market towns and never acquired any kind of papers. These settlers were always subject to deportation. Old-timers frequently mention this as their main fear and preoccupation. Waves of anti-Mexican feelings occurred during World War I due to the German-Mexican relationship and the increased KKK activity immediately after the war. This affected many of these first-generation immigrants. There was no way of estimating how many Mexicans were sent back between 1916 and 1926, but old-timers listed many names and said "everyone was afraid of this happening until later in the 1930's." The role of the federal government in these small communities was minimal. The government left this southern labor force to work out their own problems with local Texas Rangers, Border Patrol, and hostile Anglos.

This non-role of the federal government in protecting the rights of people is also paralleled in other areas. There were virtually no federal aid programs in health, housing, education and welfare. Nor were there any of the momentous decisions on voting and educational rights. The federal government was a distant, neutral factor in the lives of this first generation of Mexican immigrants.

Likewise, the state government had few aid or welfare programs. They did little to encourage compulsory school laws, labor unions, and county health and welfare programs. Poll tax laws and "grandfather clauses" restricting voting were also preserved. The Mexicano was left to his own ingenuity and the local *patrones* for whom he labored. If the local *patrones* wanted to get rid of their Mexicano worker, they could. They could always invoke the legal sanction that he

18

had no papers and he was here because of their goodness and willingness to overlook this fact. This remained a powerful form of control over any Mexicano, as long as even one person in his extended family was still in this status. Some old-timers contended that the problem of "papers" was the single most important "political tool that the gringos had."

Local government, prior to the early 1900's and the land boom, was almost exclusively provided by the county government. Regionally, there were only three city governments before this time. The county judge, the commissioner's court, the justices of the peace, and the sheriff and his constables provided law and order and various social and economic services to the people. The county officials were elected by a very small number of male voters through a system of county precincts. Elections were held yearly under the county's supervision in local polling places, often the settlement church or school.

Aside from holding and supervising the local, state, and national elections, the most important functions of the county were to: 1) keep all records on land transactions, and vital statistics (marriage, birth, death); 2) arbitrate in cases when people violated the state law governing property, personal safety, and community interests (community interest is a broad range of behaviors of citizens towards public buildings, public utilities, private welfare, property, and conduct in public places); 3) develop a system of bridges and roads linking the rural sectors of the county with the market town (each citizen was required to donate 5 days of free labor towards this end, and each precinct had a county road commissioner to help create and maintain the necessary roads); 4) provide social welfare payments to living ex-confederate soldiers and people declared extremely poor and indigent, as well as free burial services in a public county cemetery for destitute citizens; and 5) provide a rural school system based on large grants of state lands appropriated to each county. Initially, the county judge and later a special county superintendent, with the court of commissioner's approval, administered the schools. Each rural school also had a locally elected board that made basic decisions on personnel, building needs, and daily operating procedures.

In short, the county government was the center for all land records and the arbitrator of personal ownership, sales, mortgages and disputes; it also provided important rural services to the farmers, ranchers and their labor force such as roads, social welfare, and schooling. The county was the main governmental institution that helped sustain the relationship between the owners and the workers.

City governments in the early days were relatively less important to citizens than the county. The early South Texas city governments were either conducted by an elected council and a mayor, or an elected set of commissioners who hired a manager. Since cities also had the power to tax and to set legal boundaries, they provided basic services like water, streets, parks, lights, fuel for heating, fire protection, and a police force and municipal judge. A set of ordinances and license codes required people to minimize noise, animals, noxious smells, dirty and harmful enterprises, and hazardous use of fire arms, vehicles, foods, drink, and other human technologies and enterprises. The police and courts were responsible for punishing offenders and settling misunderstandings and disputes arising out of such activities. Unlike the county officials, the city officials were rarely paid more than token fees for meeting monthly to set ordinances and to manage the various police, inspectors, judges, tax collectors, bookkeepers, and maintenance men.

The boundary of the city government, of course, was restricted to the central market town and excluded all the local settlements. The bulk of the population only came under the city jurisdiction during shopping and social visits. Another limitation of the city was its considerably smaller tax base and lack of revenue to develop welfare projects or roads and streets. Although it dealt with many more people and the potential problems of large clusters of people, the city was a poor institution run with a make-shift leadership and a few underpaid technicians.

After the great agricultural boom and large out-migrations from the *rancho* settlements, the city government became somewhat more important. By the 1920's North Town had developed their own water, ice, gas lighting, and street systems.[31] Their services and therefore their influence over people's lives rapidly expanded. This control increased as more ordinances were passed to restrict noise and animals, the types of industry, and retail sales. As the higher level state administrative units passed progressively stricter standards for codes and licenses, the local city governments increasingly intervened in the lives of buyers and sellers.

Perhaps the most significant power difference between the county and the city was the scope and authority of the county judge and the county sheriff. As chief arbitrators and enforcers of state laws on a day-to-day basis, their potential control over people was much greater than any other government official. This became especially true because often these were virtually life-time positions. Election results from 1900 to 1974 showed that most county positions were rarely contested. One judge remained in office for thirty-two years, and several others served from twelve to twenty years. Sheriffs rotated much more frequently, apparently because of hazard and disfavor incurred with prominent local leaders. Nevertheless, a number of North Town sheriffs served from ten to fifteen years.

It is important to understand what kind of people became local sheriffs and county judges. Judging from election results and the biographies of several local officials, the large ranchers and farmers in these areas rarely ran for any of the county positions. The county officials were generally landless working class Anglos or small agricultural operators. Several growers explained it this way:

> I am too damn busy with my place to worry about what goes on up at the courthouse. I am not the kind of man who likes sitting around in meetings all day trying to decide how to spend a few dollars here and there. Don't get me wrong. I am interested in what those fellas do. I don't want them cheating or wasting my money, and I damn sure don't want the taxes to go up, and I want my roads graded. But I don't have time, and I do not want to be a boot-licker for every state senator or traveling congressman who comes wandering through here looking for votes, no sir!

This attitude was common among the big economic entrepreneurs and producers. They preferred to have a set of local political and civic leaders take care of the details while they grow and expand their businesses. A very representative view of county officials was:

> What kind of people have run the courthouse over the years? Well, some people might think they are a pretty smart lot, but if you check to see if most of them ever made it big in farming or business, you'll see that they are mostly nobodies. They never had what it takes to make it on their place, and most of them don't have no special education. So I don't see them as much of anything special. They don't know much and they ain't much. But most of them are all right. They are good ole' boys, good folks, friends and neighbors of mine.

That the county was primarily run by the non-influentials and small operators did not mean, however, that elite ideals of low taxes and minimal government were emphasized less. In early South Texas communities there was very little disagreement on the proper role of government. The less government, the better. The idea was to avoid restricting the growers and producers with burdensome taxes and duties, because their welfare was ultimately the welfare of everyone. The men who ran the county government generally controlled little of the land and labor, so they carved out their own niche in the local environment as the men who managed the infrastructure, the roads and schools and records, and who helped "order" the environment of the worker through the laws and schools and petty rewards.

The city governments were generally run by the most prominent businessmen in town. From 1900 to 1930 virtually no prominent ranchers or farmers were active in the North Town Council. Transportation was apparently very difficult until the 1920's, and most ranchers and farmers were just too isolated to get involved. Further, big producers who might have had time were not the kind of men who relished "sitting around jawing about putting a water main to someone's house." They had a great sense of their own importance in developing this land and in making a profit. They prized the ranching and farming way of life, and the ideal of "fighting the land and making something from it." Of course, "the bigger the profit, the sweeter the fight," explained one old-timer. The creation of successful farms and ranches was a time consuming affair. For many there simply was not enough time to be civic and social-minded. The smaller operators generally laughed incredulously at the suggestion that they might have been interested in being a community leader. They were "nobodies," people who had all they could do to keep their land and handle their laborers.

By default, then, the local businessmen were the civic and political leaders. The early North Town businessmen took pride in explaining that they helped the community grow as much as the ranchers and farmers. They felt that their role was to manage the basic municipal and school services, "that nobody else would." Several spoke of how being a local official changed their lives. One remarked:

I was a nobody before I got to be councilman. I had my little store and all I knew was selling my groceries. Everybody thought of me as good ole' _____. I guess they still did when I was councilman too, but I was more respected. People asked me for things, kinda looked up to me more, I think.

The storekeepers also emerged as the town leaders in other areas. Generally, they and their wives, through voluntary organizations like the Rotary and the Chamber of Commerce, participated in virtually every community-wide activity. They were also generally leaders in the local churches. This is, of course, the pattern of small town America in the early 1920's and even today.

The most intriguing and important aspect of local government, however, was how people or groups of people used the legal powers of government in greatly expanded, informal ways. Government entities become a source of independent power for enterprising people seeking to control people and things. In North Town there were a number of individuals who could be called "political entrepreneurs." They were men of relatively limited personal wealth and prestige who developed what most people called a "political machine." One of these men was a county judge for thirty-four years, and the other a city manager/marshal for twenty-six years. This pattern was typical of the region and the era. All the North Town "machines" occurred between 1916 and 1962. The present discussion will be a general description and characterization of the kinds of personalistic, political structures that controlled local government and the lives of the Mexicano laborers.[32] The discussion of these same political machines in Chapter three will focus more on why and how they declined and changed.

North County and Town had political machines that spanned the period from 1920 to 1950. Mr. Cameron, the city manager/marshal, ran the city from 1920 to 1948. He was the son of a small rancher and was perhaps the most colorful and ruthless of all the political entrepreneurs. He was a tall, handsome man who was a "good fighter" and a man who would "use the pistol he carried." He also had a penchant for women and was reputed to have frequently jailed Mexicanos so he could sleep with their wives. He had several *casa chicas* (mistresses) in "Mexican Town." He spoke fluent Spanish and knew how to mix with Mexicanos in the *cantinas*. For some North Towners Mr. Cameron had "charisma," i.e., a forceful, magnetic personality that commands a following. If people did not like his charisma, particularly Mexicanos, he had a badge and a gun and a willingness to use them. Mr. Cameron appears to have been the archtype of the rough, racist South Texas lawman of this era.

Although Mr. Cameron was not the mayor, he controlled the mayor and the city. The mayor under Mr. Cameron for twenty years was Mr. Dale, a local businessman who ran a small factory (fifty employees) that made cattle feed from cotton seeds. The mayor was older and preoccupied with his business and let the energetic Mr. Cameron run the city. Mr. Dale had been on the council since 1909 and had become one of the town's most prominent businessmen. During Mr. Cameron's regime, there were no city records kept, and some local residents were reluctant to discuss what he had done in more than general terms. His city clerk, however, and the son of the reform mayor who replaced him told how Mr. Cameron operated. Both Anglo and Mexicano old-timers described his treatment of people in "Mexican Town."

Mr. Cameron apparently made his money by underreporting collections and by keeping a percentage of the taxes collected. Mr. Cameron also used the method of not sending tax notices to Mexicanos. He then used a warrant for possessing and selling their property. He and a local rancher also had one of the first subdivisions in Mexican town, and a number of Mexican families were indebted to him for their houses. Mr. Cameron also arranged a money-making scheme with a local Mexicano carpenter and the county to bury dead Mexican indigents with county funds. There were apparently many "fake Mexicans" buried on county funds, which went to Mr. Cameron and his partners. There were apparently also payoffs from local *cantina* owners and bootleggers for selling illegal whiskey. This was reported as a common practice between Anglo law enforcement officials and Mexicano *cantina* owners. Other old-timers claimed that he got kick-backs on equipment contracts for the city, but there were no specific cases cited.

Compared to more notable South Texas political bosses, Mr. Cameron was a small-timer in terms of capital accumulation, and he ultimately drank and gambled himself into poverty. But Mr. Cameron, through various favors, intimidation, and small business deals developed a following in "Mexican Town." Anglos often said that "he ruled the Mexicans with an iron fist," which meant he frequently beat up drunks at the *cantinas*, slept with Mexican women, and inflicted several pistol whippings in public. Several Mexicanos claimed that he shot and killed at least four Mexicanos in coldblood, and they furnished detailed accounts with names and places. It was not clear whether he actually unlawfully killed Mexicanos, but he apparently did shoot at least two people. Whatever the veracity of these accounts may be, the stories have become local folklore and are passed on to the younger generations. The stories told in the barrio are that Mr. Cameron and several earlier county sheriffs killed Mexicanos for no reason and with great joy.

Mr. Cameron actually ruled through what was a common style among sheriffs, that is, to "go native" with the Mexicanos and drink and brawl in the *cantinas*. Mr. Cameron was feared, but he was also admired for his manliness and his brutality. He was as one old Mexicano put it, *"muy hombre."* He made the Mexicans laugh and could enjoy the manly pursuits of drinking and fighting. He also gave them favors like extra jobs and "breaks" when they broke the law as he defined it. Several Mexicanos told stories of how Mr. Cameron let them go for doing something illegal like trespassing, speeding, or disturbing the peace.

24

As in other cases of strong sheriffs, one of the major powers a law officer had over uninformed people was to create "pseudo-events." In other words, a law officer enhanced his power by making minor infractions seem major. He may even create situations where a citizen *seems* to have violated a law. In fact, the lawman exaggerates the infraction to threaten and intimate the lawbreaker. Then in a moment of goodness and compassion, the sheriff said: (an actual reported incident)

> Well, Pablo, I know you got a wife and kids, and I'm gonna do you a favor this time. I'm gonna let you go, but you better remember that, and I don't want to see you in trouble again.

In this case, the "offender" was grateful, and the lawman has created a debt he can collect later, possibly in the form of a vote. This was a very common way that the rough, sometimes brutal law authorities were able to control the Mexicanos. They controlled them through being a "good ole boy" and drinking and socializing with them. They gave them favors as well as occasional beatings.

Men like Mr. Cameron fit well into the rough, lawless times in early South Texas. They were well adapted to the local way of life, and they served their purpose in keeping the "dirty, brawling, immoral" working man in line and out of trouble with the better class of citizens. In this case, the Mexicanos were the ignorant, easily manipulated group, and Spanish-surnames fill the courthouse and the sheriff's records. Even more important are all those unrecorded cases that were dismissed or handled informally. They often made the victimized Mexicano seem the beneficiary, which must have made the overall system seem more bearable and fair.

In this same town, while Mr. Cameron ran the city and ruled "Mexican Town" with an iron hand, Judge Paulson ran the county and the local Democratic political machine for thirty-four years from 1920 to 1954. Judge Paulson was a very different kind of man from Mr. Cameron. He was a quiet, well-educated man whom many described as almost withdrawn. He was acknowledged as the man to know if you wanted to work for the county. He controlled the Anglo vote and that of the few Mexicanos who voted. Apparently, if one wanted to be a commissioner or official, it was only possible with the judge's blessing. People liked the way he ran the county, and no one went against him. The commissioners always ran uncontested, and the typical pattern was for a given commissioner to stay in office ten or twelve years. One individual said to be particularly close to the judge, Mr. Mason, a small farmer, served for twenty-four years, and two others served longer than ten years, and several for four to six years. The commissioners' court was described as a relatively harmonious group that got along well and followed the judge and the general wishes of the big farmers and ranchers. The judge and his commission used the typical pattern of small favors such as grading roads, loaning dump trucks, and disbursing welfare payments, county burials, and small loans. The judge also gave "breaks" on cases such as disorderly conduct, wife beating, drunkenness, petty theft, and trespassing. He operated with a very "low profile" and was quite successful in maintaining his position.

At different points in Judge Paulson's career, he was accused of taking kickbacks from machinery sales and of being inefficient, but no reform movement ever ousted him; and no one ever proved the charges. One of the major ways he apparently used his position for purposes of capital accumulation was through his connection with a large absentee landowner. Mr. Paulson's brother was the ranch manager for a portion of a major Texas banking family's large ranch holdings. A number of Anglos and Mexicanos, one a former assistant to the manager and another a large rancher, described Judge Paulson as being "in their back pocket." Evidently, this man and several other large ranchers used to run thousands of cattle in and out of the county to avoid taxation. Since the tax collector was fully aware of this, the rich landowner was receiving preferential treatment from the county officials. The most important dimension of the relationship between the large landowner and the judge developed, however, when oil was discovered in the county. Nearly all of the oil disovered during the early thirties was drilled on the big absentee landowner's holdings. Consequently, the control of taxation became considerably more important.

Local tax records confirmed that even though the properties were producing thousands of barrels of oil, this particular family was still only paying a rate that appears to be around ten percent more than other big landowners during that year.[33] It was difficult to know which taxable lands contained oil wells in order to compare the tax rates on these lands to those of other range lands. However, the small differences in the total taxes paid between these lands and other lands seems to indicate that the oil-rich ranch was under-valued for taxation purposes. How much of "a cut," if any, the judge was receiving is impossible to say. Several Anglos suggested he probably benefitted more from inside knowledge on land and investment deals than from any actual direct pay-offs. It would be difficult to prove that the judge acted illegally, but the tax rates remained low and the general

26

public was deprived of extra public revenue. While keeping the tax rates low, he personally benefitted as a private entrepreneur. He enhanced his personal knowledge and connections through his private land title office, which was housed rent-free in the courthouse. In the strictest sense, nothing illegal had been done, but the frequent collaboration between the judge and prominent ranchers generally enhanced the ability of prominent men to control more land, money, and people.

The above cases are not presented to condemn all public servants, or all Anglos. There were also stories collected about the hardworking, honest actions of local mayors, judges, and sheriffs. Even Mexicanos, who generally received the mistreatment, expressed a liking for various historical figures. Often the old Mexicanos would explain, "Those were just the way things were in the old days. You had to be pretty tough sometimes." There were city and county officials who doubtless never gained personally from their positions. Further, even though a relatively small number of people were re-elected for many years without opposition, the leadership did rotate to a degree. The leadership of the school board, the city, and the county were different groups of people. The city businessmen tended to run the city. The small farmers and ranchers and a few lawyers tended to run the county. The more active church and civic members not running the city or county tended to run the schools.

The type of person considered good at running the city water works and the daily affairs of streets, sewage, and garbage differed from the type of person concerned about the morality of the children or the football team. "Businessmen just naturally like to run the city and know how to do it better." Others claimed that "church-going people, especially the Baptists, tend to worry more about what is going on at the schools." Such people were willing to "police the schools" from their unpaid, time consuming board positions. Others simply want to get the football coach fired. In the county, the rural small time operators who needed a job or who had some aspirations to become politically active in the Democratic party often gravitated to the county jobs. Generally, perhaps no more than forty or fifty Anglo men and their wives ran all the local institutions and various other local civic groups and clubs. Further, of those key leaders there were only a few powerful political entrepreneurs. Many of the early economically influential people in the rural areas exerted their control through lesser men who ran the county, but the city and the school were of little interest to them until they began moving into the market towns.

The views of local residents and the actual distribution of leadership raise some interesting problems for characterizing local government as "elitist" or "undemocratic."[34] Of course, local leaders would stoutly deny that any small group or conspiring clique ran the town. First, there were powerful individuals, but residents would argue that such people were not usually the "real prominent" (high prestige) people in town. They would argue that people allowed them to run things as long as they didn't bother anyone. Second, while a relatively small number of people "ran everything," local people would rightly argue that "some ran one thing and some ran another." In fact, it was often difficult to get anyone to take the thankless job of being a councilman or school board member. Local Anglos would deny charges that one group controlled everything, and it is important to consider this view as being accurate in some sense. Certainly in an organizational or administrative sense, there was rotation of leadership among a small group of families, most of whom were not the wealthy, influential ranchers.

More accurately, a variety of people, predominantly from the "better class," ran local institutions in a way that generally satisfied a very minimal conception of government. They kept taxes down, provided the minimum of services, and generally kept the peace. About the only time people became concerned about replacing a local official was when he became "too big for his britches." When a councilman or board member became unapproachable and arrogant, he had violated the powers allocated to him. Things only ran smoothly *because* he did not threaten the general conception of minimal local government. When he began to act too independently and "became disagreeable," pressures and opposition invariably developed. Generally, however, differences in local ideology were so minimal that it did not matter who ran things. Organizationally, then, there was enough rotation and consensus to create at least a feeling of a democratic, caretaker local government.

On the other hand, such a system of local government did *not* act as a strong advocate for poor people, particularly the Mexicanos, nor did it *control* the rise of local political entrepreneurs who used the local government for personal enhancement. The indifferent, apathetic, or frightened Anglo voters of the early days allowed such individuals to use and intimidate and humiliate many Mexicanos. From the Mexicano point of view, all Anglos were included in these political machines built on favors and brutality. Mexicanos did not perceive the system of local government as democratic because functionally it was

28

not. To them it was irrelevant if a number of Anglos ran different institutions, since the effect was still the same. The Mexicano was unable to manipulate or control these local institutions in his own interests. This supposedly diverse set of Anglo leaders and their political entrepreneurs all operated in a very similar way toward the Mexicano.

The Mexicanos taught their children that their community was left with unpaved streets, fire hydrants for drinking water, dishonored wives, repossessed homes, and a continuing difference in wealth. That there may have been no single controlling clique or all-powerful individual (although several of the cases cited cast doubt on that) did not make local institutions function any more "democratically." These local institutions only functioned as well "as the heart of the gringo let them," as one old Mexicano put it. The early economic and political conditions that Mexicanos faced in North Town were, then, extremely harsh. To further describe life in early North Town, the next chapter will characterize how Anglos and Mexicanos privately felt about and publicly related to each other. Chapter two will also describe how the local educational and religious institutions transmitted beliefs that reinforced strict social segregation along ethnic lines.

[1] Scott, Florence J. *Historical Heritage of the Lower Rio Grande.* Rio Grande City, Texas: La Retama Press, 1965.

[2] Scott, Florence J., *Ibid.*

[3] Newcomb, William W. *The Indians of Texas.* Austin, Texas: University of Texas Press, 1961.

[4] Holdsworth, Ernest. *A History of Aztlán County, 1865-1900.* Aztlán City, Texas: unpublished manuscript, 1969.

[5] Castro, Stanley. *The Newman Strip: A Partial History of South County.* Hillsboro, Texas: Hill Junior College Press, 1969.

[6] *Historic North Country, 1871-1971.* North Town, Texas: The Centennial Commission, 1971.

[7] Acuña, Rodolfo. *Occupied America.* San Francisco, California: Canfield Press, 1972.

[8] *Historic North County, 1871–1971. Ibid.*

[9] Holdsworth, Ernest. *Ibid.*

[10] Schlebeker, John. *Cattle Raising on the Plains, 1900-1961.* Lincoln, Nebraska: University of Nebraska Press, 1963.

[11] Osgood, Ernest. *The Day of the Cattlemen.* Minneapolis, Minnesota: University of Minnesota Press, 1929.

[12] Scherer, James A. *Cotton as a World Power.* New York: Frederick States Company, 1916.

[13] See Appendix A, Table 1.1 *General Population Trends in North County, 1910 to 1970* and Table 1.2 *Farms in the North County Classified by Tenure, 1900 to 1969.*

[14] Gamio, Manuel. *The Life Story of the Mexican Immigrant.* New York: Dover Publications (reprint), 1971; and John Martínez. *Mexican Emigration to the United States, 1910-1930.* Doctoral dissertation, University of California, Berkeley, California, 1957.

[15] This analysis is based on various comments made by all of the different types of agricultural laborers and growers interviewed. The particular numbers of workers, women, ranchers and farmers are reported at other points in the discussion.

[16] Martínez, John. *Ibid.*

[17] See Appendix A, Table 1.1 *Ibid.*

[18] See Appendix A, Table 1.3 *Crop and Livestock Data for North County, 1900 to 1969.*

[19] No particular studies verify this trend. This interpretation is based on the recollections of old-timers, who judged these land schemes very successful in drawing people to their area.

[20] This analysis is based on six contributors from two major settlements. The informants were able to list and agree upon 150 names, and only twenty were still in these communities by 1915. The local land records were also consulted for these settlements, and the tax rolls show major shifts, but no statistical table was constructed to show this pattern.

[21] See Appendix A, Table 1.3, *Ibid.*

[22] Schlebeker, John, *Ibid.*

[23] We also found one original settler who kept some of the early land advertisements and his contract on the land. One contributor also had an aerial map of the entire ranch subdivision. These items, plus numerous testimonials helped develop a better description of the land booms.

[24] Tiller, James. *The Texas Winter Garden: Commercial Cool Season Vegetable Production.* Austin, Texas: Bureau of Business Research, University of Texas monograph # 33, 1971.

[25] Tiller, James. *Ibid.*

[26] Fifteen male sharecroppers and fifteen wives of sharecroppers were interviewed concerning the tenancy system. Twenty-five ranchers and farmers and various community leaders in business and the professions also made comments about the agricultural system of the North County region.

[27] Contributors generally agreed that no more than fifteen to twenty per cent of the Mexicanos in the settlements advanced to *quartero* status. It was very difficult to verify from Anglo landowners if they favored *medio* tenants as Mexicanos claimed. Several also offered reasons why tenants on the *quartero* system were better, e.g., less management problems, more dependable, less cheating.

[28] See Apepndix A, Table 1.3 *Ibid.*

[29] Acuña, Rodolfo, *Ibid.*

[30] Acuña, Rodolfo. *Ibid.*

[31] The North Town council minutes from 1907-1924 and from 1938-1974 were used to develop a general understanding of the main issues and leaders. Unfortunately, no minutes existed for the heyday of Mr. Cameron's rule. His former city clerk indicated that he avoided keeping records and claimed that he actually destroyed some as well. After becoming familiar with the issues and key leaders, a

series of interviews with old-time leaders and observers of local politics was conducted.

[32] This analysis of "political machines" is based on extensive discussions with former political leaders and political intermediaries. The local newspapers were not useful on these informal dimensions of power and political process. The election results, with the names of formal leaders, hint of conflicts and factions. The family history and occupations of those names that stood out for long service were collected. Opposition leaders and ex-clerks or retired officials were the most informative contributors. The Mexicano intermediaries for Anglo politicians were also particularly open about these relationships. Once non-leaders had revealed "the inside story" about the leaders, it was possible to cross-check this information with the leaders or surviving relatives of leaders. Gradually, a fuller, more accurate chronology of events, leaders and factions emerged.

[33] This estimate of how little the taxes of the largest absentee landlord-oilman went up was difficult to make. The tax rolls were checked at three five-year intervals after the discovery of oil. The relative increase in the taxes of this oilman were roughly compared to the relative increases in taxes for several other known large ranchers. It was reasonably clear the oilman's taxes did not dramatically increase, but a precise figure was not established since that would have required considerable work with land deeds and tax records to cover the 100,000 acre ranch. As indicated, this is a very rough estimate from scanning the records.

[34] The extensive, sometimes sterile debates in the community and power structure literature was not altogether useful in this analysis. The concepts of pluralism and of elite conspiracy are often used in such a normative sense that they misrepresent local views and political behavior in small towns. Further, both the "reputational" and the "event analysis" methodologies are seriously flawed. At least in this small setting, one does not need to, and should not, administer formal peer-ranking questionnaires to locate power holders. Nor does a full analysis of all the local political decision-making events or public rituals encompass the important power articulations or the system of power relations. This study generally used a very unstructured reputational approach with selected informants, but it also sought to locate local political behavior in historical events, historical trends and the general production and social relationships. The idea was to study "power relationships" as an aspect of other systematic relationships, not as expressly "political" behaviors or events. In this regard the notion of a "political economy" or "a culture of a political economy" provided a broader concept for thinking about asymmetry and subordination in human relationships.

Chapter 2

Cultural Institutions and
Social Life in the *Rancho*

By modern standards, life in the small North County settlements was not easy for either the Anglo *patrones* or their Mexicano laborers. There were few amenities such as running water, electricity, radio/television, or motor transportation. Most places had windmills or vacuum-suction pumps for drawing well water. Most food was canned, salted, or smoked to stay preserved without refrigeration. Every household chore, cooking, washing, cleaning, and every field task, planting, cultivating, harvesting, was done without power-driven machinery. Yet, both Anglo and Mexicano old-timers were quite sentimental about life on the *ranchos*. Rural life was physically harder but more satisfying, primarily because families and friendships were more intimate. Both the rural Anglo and Mexicano communities were family-centered. All the old-timers centered their reflections on the intimacy and solidarity of their families.

Churches in the Rancho Settlements

The social life of these tiny, Anglo-centered communities revolved around the school and the church, where Christmas plays, picnics, box socials, and weddings were held. The organized churches in most rural settlements were often interdenominational and exclusively Anglo. Traveling preachers held services, one week a Methodist, perhaps the next week a Baptist. The early Anglo settlers on the *rancho* were not described as particularly pious or spiritual, but the churches were an important community institution. Mexicanos were excluded from these Anglo churches, and they developed their own churches in the market town and their own home-centered religious practices.

In the early days Anglo Protestants made little attempt to establish missionary churches in the "Mexican Towns." However, a small group of North Town Mexicano *Metodistas* built and maintained their own church in the early 1900's. Catholic Mexicanos of North Town also built their own parish, which Anglos attended, by 1910. Before the

Mexicanos had a town church, many traveling priests from Mexicano came to their houses, gave mass, and performed baptisms and marriages. On the *rancho* there were no churches, but the Mexicanos still observed many religious celebrations. At Christmas time, a group of devoted women would perform *las pastoderas*, a ritual originating from *las posadas* of the Mexican rural villages. A few days before Christmas these women went from house to house singing about Jose and Maria's journey. During Easter, the families celebrated the resurrection of Christ with special preparations and prayers.

One farm worker described how religious beliefs blended with the love and respect that Mexicanos had for the land and people in these early communities:

> Man is born from the earth and each man is a temple of Jesus Christ. *Cristo* comes and gathers the bodies and souls of those who belong to the earth. Every one of us, like each little plant, belongs to the earth. Today the world has changed a lot. There are many things that do not belong to the earth. That is why the world is so strange today.

Religion for the Mexicano on the *rancho* was primarily home-centered. Each house had its altar, and the rosary was faithfully said. Men were generally thought to be less involved in religion than the women. Whenever possible, the children were taught the catechism, and religion played an important part in the life cycle celebrations of birth, baptism, marriage, and death.

The extent to which religious beliefs encouraged the Mexicano to accept his low social and economic position was difficult to determine. The church and early *padres* rarely acted as social advocates, and Christian beliefs tended to encourage acceptance of suffering. Nevertheless, the idea of the Mexicanos as a fatalistic, religious people has probably been greatly exaggerated. Religion in the early Mexicano settlements was primarily a set of social practices and customs which enlivened community life. Religion brought friends and relatives together socially, but few Mexicanos described themselves, or their communities, as deeply religious. Further, most old-timers located the cause of their troubles in the everyday realities of peonage, deportations, and brutal sheriffs. In short, religious beliefs did not seem to occupy the minds and lives of these early settlers nearly as much as the material questions of survival.

Schools in the Rancho Settlements

Each settlement usually had a one-room country school, and the larger settlements had from four to six teachers and more than a hundred pupils. These rural schools were under the county judge and the county commissioners' court. From 1920 to 1940 the schools had their own county superintendent. The superintendent helped each school's board of local trustees find teachers, collect school taxes, get books and supplies, and pass bonds for school building improvements. They also kept records on the general operation of all the schools. The locally elected trustees handled daily problems of maintenance and personnel and provided whatever their teachers needed. The teachers were generally recruited from San Antonio and other urban areas and were certified by the state. Most teachers had an eighth grade education. The last year of grade school consisted of a special teacher training course. This included some training on discipline, record-keeping, the psychology of children, and philosophy of education.

The classroom routine of the one-room country school was quite different from modern, specialized schools. Recitation periods for each class were generally ten minutes long, and different subjects were covered on different days. A teacher was responsible for eight classes in five subjects; consequently, lessons were done quickly, and a good deal of the work was done independently by children in workbooks. Older children were responsible for helping the younger children learn to be quiet and to work independently. Education had both a more familiar and more independent character than it does in modern schools. Most of the old-timers swore by the country schools and pointed out how successful many of their graduates were. They also felt that the long recesses, as well as the cooperative effort of putting on the Christmas play and the Easter celebration, were important experiences. Further, the communal tasks of helping the teacher haul drinking water, fetch wood, and clean up the school also taught the students practical, important values.

These small schools were primarily for Anglo children. Approximately ninety percent of the county schools were segregated, and while larger settlements generally had a Mexican school with an Anglo teacher, Mexicanos described these schools as smaller and more run-down than the Anglo schools.[1] Mexicano children rarely went beyond the first three grades; nearly all dropped out after they learned enough English to write their names. Many of those living on the more distant farms and ranches never went to school. They were needed to work in the fields, and schooling was generally considered a luxury that they could not afford. There was apparently little push by the Mexicano parents to keep their children in school, and the Anglo *patrones* did not encourage Mexicanos to stay in school. They did not value giving their workers' children a better education. It served no useful purpose to be "an over-educated cotton picker." There is no way of determining the drop-out rate or the quality of these schools, but by any standard, the county provided only very minimal public education during this period.

Conversely, most Anglo families tried very hard to keep their children in school. Only on rare occasions were the children kept at home to do farm work. Most of the small Anglo farmers realized that their children could improve through the proper educational credentials. Further, the more well-to-do ranch families often started their own ranch schools for their children. In the big ranching areas of these counties, the ranchers often hired a tutor, a young certified female teacher, to live in their house and educate their children. Two reasons were given for this practice. First, the schools were sometimes "too far away (three to six miles) for the children to walk, particularly if they were girls." Second, they felt that a tutor would provide an education that would allow their children to compete in the local high school and even go to college. Having one's own teacher also gave a family a certain amount of prestige in the community. The county eventually helped ranchers finance part of the salary of these tutors. Some of the ranch schools got at least partial aid from the county superintendent by the early 1920's.

By the twenties some of these county schools were consolidated with the town school, but others fought vigorously to maintain their rural schools for various reasons. First, people felt that when the school was gone, "the community would dry up." Second, some rural Anglos were reluctant to go to the town schools because they feared the ridicule of townspeople that they were "hicks." Others felt that since they would remain farmers, formal education was not very necessary and useful. Third, some ranchers wanted rural school districts so they could maintain greater control over their tax rates. The large ranchers from some settlements were already using private tutors, and by the 1920's they either lived in town or used private buses to send their children to the town schools. They retained their rural schools for the few Mexicanos who stayed in school and for the Anglos who could not afford tutors and private buses. The settlements of smaller Anglo farmers were also developing their own private busing system by this time so their children could attend a better junior high and/or high school. Gradually, the rural schools became a way of keeping the land taxes low and of providing the laborers with a minimal introduction to English.

Another major reason why many townspeople fought consolidation was the influx of Mexicans they feared it might bring. A crusading superintendent, who sought to consolidate the rural North County schools, described the hostility towards her plans and attempts to improve the school system. The county officials were generally indifferent, the large ranchers felt threatened, and the local businessmen were worried about the expense. She said:

> There were lots of reasons why folks didn't want to bother with the Mexicans; poor things, nobody wanted them. We started a school for them in Mexican Town in the early 1900's. Lots of Anglos criticized us for wasting money, but most of them accepted it. The Mexicans wanted their own school, too. They didn't want to come to our side and we didn't want them, I guess.

An interesting feature of the segregated schools was the strict segregation of blacks from either Mexicano or Anglo schools. The ex-teacher and superintendent's daughter went on to explain this situation:

> The coloreds were really unwanted. The Mexicans didn't want them in their schools either. They had their own colored schools. There was one in the east end of the county where a few cottonpickers lived, and there was one in Mexican Town where the rest lived. Then if the coloreds wanted to go to high school, the school district paid for them to go to Philip Wheatly colored school in San Antonio. They were given tuition, transportation, and some living expenses. I guess several took advantage of this and went there and made it good. I think some went on their own, too, and boarded with their relatives and went to schools in Houston or in San Antonio for the Nigras.

Apparently, the desire to keep blacks and whites segregated was so strong that schools were even willing to pay for sending the blacks to other communities.[2] Blacks, like Mexicanos, were generally provided with very limited, inferior "colored schools." Very few blacks or Mexicanos were able to use schooling as a way of improving their socioeconomic position. Schooling was a way of improving one's life only if non-white North Towners were able to attend city and private schools. Although there are few records that describe the quality of Mexican schools, the census illustrates dramatically the results of the educational system. The educational attainment of Mexicanos is still extremely low (4.5 years).[3] As a group, they simply were not included. The ideal of the democratic American common school for the masses did not really exist until settlement patterns and economic conditions and political changes in the thirties and forties began altering the old *rancho* system.

It is also important to understand the value orientations emphasized in these schools. There were many ways in which the schools transmitted an ideal of a rural and Anglo way of life. One of the main ways was by training in agriculture and homemaking. The early school programs in agriculture were less developed than today's, but they already had a number of youth organizations for children such as FFA (Future Farmers of America), FHA (Future Homemakers of America), and the 4-H clubs. Such organizations encouraged the children to develop projects much like those their parents competed in at fairs and stock shows. Students learned to be responsible adults through these activities. They kept records and prepared to compete and to make a profit.

Such programs placed a strong emphasis on character training, i.e., how to save money, work hard, win prizes through personal initiative, and how to be respectful, obedient, God-fearing, and loyal to community and country. A whole cluster of important traditional American values were transmitted in such programs. Only a few adults actually organized and carried out these youth programs, but most supported them for encouraging the same attitudes which they tried to teach their children at home. In the early South Texas communities and high schools, these activities were almost exclusively Anglo. The Mexicanos were the labor force, and they were not expected to learn the skills and values of the agricultural entrepreneur or community leader.

Another way that local schools transmitted values related to community leadership and the agricultural way of life was through extracurricular activities. Athletics and band programs were important ways that the schools taught individualism, competition, Anglo cultural superiority, and the subordinate role of the Mexicano. In the early days, those few Mexicanos who were in the higher grades never participated in leadership positions or in extra-curricular activities. They were never elected to class offices or asked to join teams. Mexicanos accepted the fact that such activities were for Anglos only. It was not until the late thirties and the forties that more than a handful of Mexicanos were in high school, and they did not begin participating in extra-curricular activities until after World War II. Many local people generally viewed athletics and the band as "good places to learn both teamwork and how to make something of yourself with your own hard work and effort."

Every week the youth of these small communities were given the opportunity to act out the fundamental values of hard work, cooperation, and individualism. They did this against neighboring towns, which proved that the American way of life was best exemplified by their town. Their children, and hence they themselves, could kick and catch the ball better, and play the instruments better because they worked harder. Several community leaders emphasized how much their experiences in school sports taught them about respect, responsibility, and leadership. The schools of the *rancho* period transmitted this message through their exclusion and segregation. When Mexicanos came to watch their town play other towns, they watched the Anglo children uphold their community honor and exemplify the local and national culture; they watched because they were the workers and followers and because the Anglos were the owners and leaders. In the early years, schooling was predominantly a segregated, exclusive institution, with the occasional exception of some racial mixing in a small percentage of the rural schools.

Mexicano Recollections of Schooling

Older Mexicanos vividly recall not only the general lack of schooling but the negative attitude of their parents, teachers, and Anglo *patrones*. Most reported that their parents did not "push them to go to school," and many old Mexicanos now resent the fact that they cannot read and write. One ninety-year-old woman described her feelings in the following way:

> Somebody came around to note us down to go to school, but we never did. They never came back to see if we were going to school. I guess nobody was interested in our education, not our parents, and not the school people for sure. Now we are ignorant. Nobody cared then, but we care now. We suffer much for these things. Somebody did us wrong. The school people just wanted that money from the state. We did not know what they were doing then. They took our names and got the state money. We were stupid to let them. But our parents needed us in the fields, so we never went to school. We never learned to read and write.

The few who managed to go to school for two or three years generally did not remember these schools very positively. They described how teachers used to curse at them and maintain discipline in class by using a horse whip on the children. The different grades were grouped together in one room, and the teacher could never give much attention to anyone. Most old-timers described feeling neglected and ridiculed in school. They could not understand what was being said, and the teachers took little time to explain. In retrospect, several Anglo teachers mentioned similar problems of neglect, language barriers, and overcrowding, but they did not recall cursing or horsewhipping children.

Many older Mexicanas argued that the Anglo bosses did not really want Mexicano children to go to school. Several reported various ways by which their *patrones* discouraged them from sending their children to school. If a *rancho* was far away from the bus route, the rancher, knowing the Mexicano family did not have a car, would do nothing to help them get to the bus route. A number of *patrones* also talked the parents out of sending their children to school, arguing that they did not need school learning to perform their work in the fields. Others pleaded with the parents to keep their children at home so the work would be done on time. Some Anglo *patrones* merely argued that schooling was useless for Mexicanos. Others were more harsh and threatened and criticized their workers openly. One *vaquero* interpreted the situation in these terms:

> Well, what really happened was that the Anglo boss likes a Mexicano who is not educated. An uneducated Mexicano feels inferior to the boss and lets himself be pushed around by the Anglo. What the Anglo could not stand is an educated Mexicano, a Mexicano who will rob the Anglo of his superiority image. That is why they always tried to keep us away from the schools.

The Mexicano perception of schooling is closely related to the problem of language. Since the language at home was Spanish, Mexicano children who did not go to school seldom learned to speak, read, or write English. Most of the older people regretted knowing so little English, which they considered crucial for escaping poverty and succeeding in society. The reasons given for not learning English in schools were generally the following: 1) the schools were for Mexicanos only, so peers would talk to each other in Spanish all the time, and 2) when the Mexicanos tried to speak English they made mistakes and the teachers would belittle them, which ended all efforts to speak English. One old woman had a theory that the Anglo also did not want the Mexicano to learn English because, she says, "They did not want us to become independent from them. If we knew English we would have better chances to find jobs outside."

Others reported that Anglos in those times often knew how to speak Spanish very well. They generally contended that this kept the older Mexicanos from learning English, and since the younger ones were not encouraged to stay in school, most Mexicanos during this era remained Spanish-speaking. Schooling generally had little effect upon the language competence of the Mexicano. They did not become bilingual, and their inability to use English effectively was an important restriction upon improving their chances in life.

Girls were especially discouraged from attending schools, even when people started to move into town and it was easier for children to walk to the school building. A fifty-year old woman said the following:

> My father said that I didn't need school at all. He learned how to read

and write in the private classes of a Mexicana who lived in town. Then he dropped out and taught himself vocabulary by reading the Bible. But me, he said, "No, she doesn't need to go to school. She is going to grow up and get married and have many *chamaquitos* (children). What does she need school for?"

Today, this woman is attending evening classes and working to get her high school certificate.

Other Community Institutions and Agencies

During this period there were virtually no mass media (radio came in during the late 1920's), and Anglos ran all the local newspapers. They reported Anglo social events and news about their clubs, churches, and schools. In reading old local newspapers, one scarcely realizes that there was a Mexicano population.

The major ways of transmitting the virtues of rural Anglo life were through agricultural fairs, rodeos, the local county agent, and the school-related FFA and FHA programs. The local county fairs and rodeos were showcase events for bringing people together and celebrating their way of life. Old-timers described the effort that many of the women expended to cook, sew, and preserve foods. The men and young boys also worked hard to prepare their animals for show in these contests and later for sale at the auction. In the early days there were very few rodeos, but there were many informal celebrations where the men displayed their skills in horseback riding, roping, and bull throwing. These events generally had local folk music, dancing, and entertainers from outside the county. The carnival with all its rides and games-of-chance also set up shop at the county fairs.

Other community activities such as the local businessmen's clubs, the Lions and the Rotary, and the Chamber of Commerce also transmitted community traditions and helped preserve the rural way of life. These activities were exclusively Anglo. Even in the early 1900's there were small Mexicano grocery and *cantina* (bars) owners, but none of them were asked to be in the Anglo Chamber of Commerce. When asked why, a prominent Mexicano businessman replied:

The gringos didn't want us. We were nobodies. We didn't have much money, and we were Mexicans. Those businessmen's groups were just for the rich gringos.

It was not until the contemporary period that Mexicanos either organized their own parallel organizations or were invited to join the Anglo organizations.

Socializing and shopping for both Anglos and Mexicanos occurred during Saturday visits to the market town. The town occasionally hosted carnivals or the circus and had ball teams organized into leagues. It was the place where one saw tent shows, medicine shows, and chautauquas with fiery lecturers and vaudeville actors. It was the place to gossip and swap stories, shop, and drink beer. Many of the Mexicanos related to the market town in much the same way as peasants do throughout the developing world. The women would bring their vegetables and tamales and, as one Mexicana described it, they would:

> go downtown and sell our things under the mesquite trees where we set up our *puestecitos* (little stands). *La gente pobre* (the poor people) would leave the *ranchos* at dawn to come to town to buy their groceries. When they got there, the people would walk up and down the street looking at the displays in the windows of the stores. The father would go to get his haircut, and then later in the afternoon the people went back to the *rancho*. *La gente* would come to the *crédito*. They would bring their maize, *frijoles*, their pigs, chickens to sell them in town. They would sell them to Mr. _____ who had a store and would use this money to buy things in town.

Unlike the Anglos, many of the Mexicanos emphasized the buying and selling of things, as well as the mere experience of being in town. Generally, Anglos who came to town talked about the social life which was open to and organized by them. Although the Mexicanos were not strictly excluded from these social events, they often felt out of place, and few became involved. To the Mexicano the town was primarily an economic center, a place to get credit and purchase basic necessities to feed their large families and make their small houses more liveable.

Slowly, the "Mexican Towns" grew more diverse and developed their own stores, market places, ball fields, and *cantinas*. In the late 1910's and early 1920's the *Colonia* of North Texas was a place where Mexicanos could congregate and socialize as the Anglos did in their part of town. Such developments, along with the advent of the automobile, greatly altered the extent and type of *rancho-colonia* exchanges. By the 1920's the *colonias* had developed at least a dozen of their own restaurants and outdoor plazas for dancing, meeting, and socializing. To a degree such developments in the *colonia* further institutionalized the social segregation of this era into established and restricted territories.

Ethnic Territories and Social Spaces

Segregation between Anglos and Mexicanos has already been described in various institutional settings, but racial segregation must also be understood in a broader sense as a set of social rules and territories defining all aspects of ethnic relations. Mexicanos were almost completely excluded from Anglo social life. They did not intermarry, and they had their own churches, schools, community organizations, and cultural events. There were, as described, some social and personal aspects to the economic relationship between Anglos and Mexicanos. Several Anglos reported that Anglos and Mexicanos living on the *rancho* were "one big family." They perceived these relationships as intimate and positive. Nevertheless, Mexicanos were usually supposed to stay in their own territories and were always to show a proper degree of respect during social exchanges with Anglos.

There were very few private, personal spaces that a Mexicano could consider his own, and old Mexicanos described many occasions on which their private lives were invaded. An Anglo child could come to their house, eat tortillas, and dirty the floor when company was there, but a Mexicano child could never be in an Anglo house except upon request, and certainly not when the *patrón* entertained another guest. If a Mexicano worker or wife accidentally came into an Anglo house when the wife was partially dressed, they received a severe reprimand. But if a young Anglo male saw a Mexicana dressing in the early morning, it was merely a time of embarrassment and laughter.

The Mexicano *rancho* community was not a private space if and when Anglos chose to be a part of their celebrations and social life. It was appropriate for Anglos to come to Mexicano bars, get drunk, and beat up Mexicanos. It was also appropriate for them to eat Mexican food in the little restaurants. They could go to the fiestas and *bailes* and dance and be merry, but no Mexicanos were allowed in the Anglo bars or restaurants. And if on occasion they were, they had to eat in the kitchen and leave through the back door. Nor were Mexicanos generally invited to the weddings or celebrations of the Anglo. Although a great part of the Mexicano's private and public community life was open to the Anglo, there was very little reciprocity. Instead, the Mexicano knew and adhered to the rules about where he was supposed to live, when he was supposed to be downtown, and where he could celebrate.

The Anglos in North Town built their stockyards on the Mexican side of town, and all the ranchers from all parts of the county drove their cattle through the Mexicano community. Public buildings were also Anglo territories. Mexicans were not supposed to be "hanging around" the courthouse or the city hall. They were questioned, intimidated, and asked to leave if found in these places. There was even a certain time when the Mexicana housewives were supposed to be shopping downtown. Most of the old-timers remember that their children could not always accompany them shopping because the Anglo storekeepers became angry if the children touched anything. These women had the strong sense that they were only supposed to shop in the Anglo side of town on Saturdays, preferably during the early hours when Anglos were not shopping. They were made to feel that they should pick a time to spend their money that would not interfere with Anglo customers.

Apparently, the children were particularly threating to the Anglos. A number of Mexicanos described incidents in which groups of young Anglos kept their children from crossing the tracks to shop, play, or go to the intermediate school (on the Anglo side of town). Several methods were used. One was to throw stones at the Mexicano children. The other popular one was to use sling shots and shoot dried cow dung, rocks, and sticks.

There were also times when groups of Anglo men beat up and dragged over-staying Mexicanos back to their side of town. One old-timer told how he had been watching some Anglos pitch horseshoes. He "accidentally laughed" at the misfortune of one of the players because the other Anglos were laughing. The Anglo reportedly turned to him and said:

What the hell you laughin' at, meskin? How come you're over here anyway? It's already sundown, so you'd better git your ass on home to Mexican Town. . . . Fact, I think we ought to help this smart-ass chili-pepper, don't you boys?

The Anglos then threw him in a wagon, hauled him across town, and tossed him out at his family's doorstep.

This incident suggests that not only was there a very strictly defined territory for Mexicanos, but also that Mexicanos were never supposed to act like an Anglo would towards other Anglos. There were very explicit rules of proper social etiquette for the Mexicanos to follow. Some of the more obvious rules included a deferential body posture and respectful voice tone. One also used the best polite forms of speech one could muster in English or Spanish. One laughed with Anglos but never at them. One never showed extreme anger or aggression towards an Anglo in public. Of course, the reverse of this was that Anglos could be informal with Mexicanos; they could use "*tú*" forms, "*compadre*" or "*amigo*" and shout "hey, *cabrón*" or "hey, *chingado*" (son of a bitch) in a joking, derogatory way. Anglos could slap Mexicanos on the back, joke with them at their expense, curse them out, in short, do all the things people usually do only among relatively familiar and equal people. But a Mexicano had to be very careful when, where, and to whom he expressed anger and joy. If one considers personal expression or interaction a type of private space, the Mexicano was severely restricted. Any familiarity that existed between Anglo and Mexicano was hardly based on norms of social equality and unrestricted exchanges.

The Anglo controlled much of this social space and demanded a whole set of behaviors and expressions from the Mexicano that he himself did not have to practice. Such restrictions were vividly recalled by the older Mexicanos, and they marveled at the younger generation's greater freedom of personal expression. They now wonder why they let Anglos determine where they could go and how they could express themselves. There were, of course, some Anglos who demanded less deferential behavior and territorial exclusion than others. Several older Mexicanos described how one had to "read" the wishes of each Anglo one met in public. "Some let you alone, and some seemed to want you to bow down and kiss their feet." Reminiscing in a charitable mood, one elderly lady remarked:

And I guess there were many others who just didn't pay much attention to what was going on. They didn't want to be bothered with those dirty Mexican kids, and they didn't want us in their houses, but they more or less left us alone. I guess they left things up to the sheriff and their kids. They kept us in line, anyway.

Segregation, although punctuated by personal relationships on the *rancho*, was extremely pervasive and all-encompassing. There was an Anglo world and a Mexicano world, and the main place where these worlds met was the dusty fields.

Cultural Values and Ethnic Beliefs

The description of economic, political, and social relations in early North Town shows how Mexicanos and Anglos generally related, and how one ethnic group controlled the other by a variety of means. But no pattern of unequal ethnic relationships survives without a set of underlying beliefs which justifies these relations. It is imperative, then, to understand Anglo and Mexicano perceptions of themselves and each other to understand why the inequities and oppressions of *rancho* life were accepted.

There have been many studies of American communities and the American character by historians, anthropologists, sociologists, novelists, and foreign observers.[4] Often writers merely eulogize or criticize rural, small-town culture.[5] Less frequently, studies made in the southern regions of the United States have emphasized the inequalities of racial segregation and its relationship to the American character. Likewise, there have been optimistic and pessimistic accounts of the possibility and probability of reformng the inequality and brutality of racism.[6] Several trenchant critiques of these studies point up the difficulty of generalizing about "the" American character. Nevertheless, two core values do seem to underlie life in small-town America.

Writers on American culture often point out that the two core values of equality and achievement are inevitably contradictory. On one hand there is a strong emphasis on equality. All people are created equal, and all deserve equal rights under the laws of the land. Further, it follows from this egalitarian view that no particular class, no aristocracy, should control the society. Men should appear equal in dress and manners, and they should be at least relatively equal in wealth, prestige, and power. On the other hand, Americans also place a great emphasis on individual achievement. A person proves oneself and wins the rewards of this earth and the heaven beyond through hard work and effort. From this ideal, of course, follows many actual and potential inequalities. People are considered equal in some basic sense, but they must also strive to be the best, to accomplish and acquire as much as possible, i.e., to be unequal.

Perhaps the overriding theme in the reflections of older North Town Anglos was what these writers have called a sense of manifest destiny. All of the older Anglos strongly believed that this region of the United States would never have prospered and developed in the hands of the Mexican government and the Mexicans. The Mexicans were, as a government, and as a people, inferior. They lacked the know-how and entrepreneurial drive of the hardy Anglo-American. The rich Mexicans were considered spoiled and disdainful of work. The poor Mexicans were *peones* who worked hard but were ignorant and subservient to their masters, the gods, and hence to the land they had to tame. Conversely, the rugged, hardworking Anglos who came to this area were independent and ingenious enough to master these dry lands and the problems presented by anyone or anything.

Many writers on the American character point out that this rugged individualism and optimism is based on a peculiar blend of American capitalism and Protestantism. The Protestant Ethic is based on the belief that those who work hard will be favored by God, and that those favored by God will be rewarded with material success on earth and spiritual salvation in heaven. In North Town none of the old-timers

45

seemed terribly concerned with salvation, but they did indicate a strong Calvinistic orientation towards their "ordained" role in South Texas. One of the biggest farmers in the region put it this way:

You wanna know why the whites in this area are so damn mad about this Raza Unida thing? It goes way back, you see, my father and a lot of other folks came here dirt poor. Nobody gave us nothin'. A lot of us came here with nothin' but the shirt on our backs, but we knew one thing. We knew that if we worked like hell and saved our money and used the brains that God gave us, we were going to make a go of it. . . . The Mexicans? Naw, they was already here and couldn't make it. They don't have the get-up and go that whites have. They are good at taking orders from 'ol patrón,' but they can't think for themselves. A Mexican will give you a good days labor if you treat him right, but he ain't no manager and never will be. They just don't have the know-how to run something as complicated as a farm. Now, I'm not saying they are all dumb. Don't get me wrong. I'm no racist. I don't look down on the Mexicans. They are a good bunch, some of them, especially the older ones, they still have respect, but you gotta understand that the kind of peon class that comes here didn't and never would win over the American way of doing things.

This was a world view often encountered among the Anglo entrepreneurs. They perceived themselves as representatives of a superior culture, destined to tame and make something of these dry South Texas lands. Many Anglos had a vague sense of an early history in which their ancestors simply beat the Mexicans out fair and square, as one would win a baseball game. The world is a competitive place in which one must work hard and control life as if it were a game. Anglos had succeeded where a more "servile type people" from an inferior culture had failed. In this type of world people must measure their morality or sense of honor by what they produce and what they overcome. The point is to master the environment and those in it who would not be masters. A person who becomes landed and well-to-do and powerful is a person who "has paid the price" and must be respected. It is not enough to be just a "good ole boy," a person who gets along. Sociability and neighborliness are admired too, but such behavior is not proof of a person's moral superiority. Only winning the struggle against other producers and the elements really counts. One can hardly overestimate how pervasive this world view is and how thoroughly it is passed down to North Town youth.

Along with this general sense of cultural superiority, many Anglos also expressed a number of related beliefs about the inferiority of Mexicanos. First, many Anglos feel that Mexicanos are "dirty." One former teacher gave detailed descriptions of cases where Anglo teachers had to delouse the hair of Mexicano children in school. Second, Anglos often believe that Mexicanos are basically lazy, in spite of the fact that they are good workers. Several Anglo farmers, ranchers, and businessmen told how they needed to constantly reiterate job descriptions even though their Mexicanos had worked on the same job for years. They also felt that it was hard to leave most Mexican-American workers alone on the job. The job would not get done properly. Third, many Anglos think that Mexicanos are financially irresponsible. A number of older Anglos reasoned that they stupidly waste their money on parties and drinking and having a good time. These views reinforce the notion that the Mexicano is really only suited for common labor.

Fourth, the Mexicano is not thought to be as intelligent as the Anglo. Mexicanos showed this by their failure and disinterest in school, by how poorly they spoke English, even after thirty years here, and by how they never got directions straight if they were the least bit complicated. One rancher said that it takes a long time to train them to do simple tasks, but that once they were trained, they worked out very well. Fifth, Mexicanos are hot tempered by nature and often resort to physical violence. The frequent fights, described as stabbings and shootings in the *cantinas* and wife-beating, were given as evidence of this. This kind of behavior makes them prone to disregard the law. Sixth, the Mexicanos are also viewed as clannish. They refuse to learn English; they cling to Mexican customs. They are prone to run around in gangs, and they never fight as individuals. They also can't go anywhere or do anything on their own, without their families. Related to this is the general feeling that they bring up their children in an undisciplined way, and that the whole family "spoils them rotten" with too much attention. This kind of upbringing helps to make them clannish and afraid to "go it alone." Seventh, the Mexicanos are a "sexy" people prone to heavy breeding and excessively large families that become a burden on the community.

Of course, not all North Town Anglos subscribed equally to such a negative characterization of the Mexicano people. These were, however, the prevailing sentiments or themes in the recollections of Anglo old-timers. Perhaps the major distinction that Anglos were able to make was between the better class of Mexicans and the *peón* class. Generally, most Anglos in this region are careful not to include the elite class of more "Spanish-type Mexicans" in this category. They are viewed as coming from a different, more superior culture than the Mexican *peón* who is mainly a poor Indian who worked for this Spaniard class. Many local Anglos have personally experienced contact with this more educated "Spanish *Mestizo*" class in the border towns and on their visits to old Mexico. Some Anglos described the Indian *peón* class as "the scum of Mexico, the rejects who sneak across the border." They reasoned that local Anglos, being from a better class of people, naturally do not want to associate with Mexican *peones*.

I was repeatedly asked, "Would you, an educated professor, invite your field hands over to chat about world affairs?" Many Anglos argued that it was not natural for people to mix when they were on different educational and economic levels. Interestingly, then, Anglo attitudes towards Mexicanos seem based on a number of misconceptions about their culture and customs, *and* on their class position. This, of course, is closely related to the notion of the Anglos' manifest destiny and the desire to achieve and succeed. The Mexicans were a lower class, a group that could and should fit nicely into a subordinate, working class position. They were the bottom of an unequal, stratified American society run by the superior Anglo upper or "better" class. In this case, the notions of racial, cultural, and class superiority are so intertwined that they comprise one belief system. All of these beliefs rationalize Anglo control of the workers and exploitation of the environment and, to a significant degree, contradict and negate the great American ideal of equality.

This is not to say that some notion of equality and fairness did not exist along with the pervasive emphasis on achievement and competition. In the economic struggle it was not necessary to actually destroy one's rival or dishonor him. There were rules of etiquette and certain courtesies that tempered the competitive struggle for wealth, prestige, and power. The wealthy of North Town mentioned how they tried to live inconspicuously without flaunting their wealth. Further, they felt that, to a degree, they had an obligation to share their good fortune with the poor through charity and the sponsorship of various community events. But disguising one's wealth and giving to charity did not alter the basic inequalities, nor signify that these early North Town leaders were striving for wide-spread equality.

How did the early Mexicano settlers respond to these Anglo beliefs? How did they feel about themselves and their cultural traditions? Judging from the responses of many old-timers in North Town, the Mexicanos were, given the circumstances, a remarkably grateful people. The older rural Mexicanos often said little, if anything, negative about "their" *patrones*. Yet, they described work and life as extraordinarily hard.

One elderly lady who spent all her life on the *rancho* said:

Life and the suffering of today's Mexicano is just one teardrop of what we suffered on the *ranchos*. The young of today do not understand that, no matter how much we tell them. They do not understand how it was.

These same persons would often not blame their *patrones*, feeling still grateful and perhaps still fearful. They had learned to accept their fate as a poor laboring people and were grateful for the small privileges of a few chickens, a small garden, and enough to eat. To a degree, their *patrones* took care of them, perhaps better than some circumstances they had experienced in rural Mexico. Bad sheriffs and poor harvests came and went, but life continued. Anglo *patrones* were feared and often silently disliked, but their power was respected. Whatever anger the worker had was tempered by his resignation, small paternal favors, and the sense of greater poverty in his homeland. Anger and hatred for the harshness of the *rancho* political economy were not easily or often expressed towards the person of the *patron*.

Indeed, many Mexicanos expressed admiration for how smart and well-organized the Anglos were, how successful they were in business. The older Mexicanos believed themselves inferior to the Anglo in these areas. They accepted the basic Anglo belief in his chosen position to exploit the environment. Several commented that Mexicanos could never run the city and schools as well as the Anglos do. Mexicanos lacked the know-how. They also agreed with a notion that many Anglos have—that Mexicanos cannot be leaders because they do not allow their own people to succeed and rise. Older Mexicanos expressed this Anglo belief, saying:

> Mexicanos don't make good leaders. They are too envious of each other. They will never follow one of their own kind. They will criticize him and refuse to support him because they don't like another Mexicano to be higher.

In the early days, many Mexicanos believed what Anglos thought about their own know-how and leadership abilities; consequently, they set their sights lower. Most did not seek to compete directly with the Anglo for control of the environment. This was not, however, a lack of personal ambition, as many Anglos interpreted it, but a lack of belief in the potential of the Mexicano people to change the harsh realities of *rancho* life. The Mexicano laborer aspired to be a good provider for his family and a good neighbor, but he did not aspire to control other men or large portions of the land. If he could have his *casita* and perhaps a *tiro*, or a good saddle and gun, as well as a large family of healthy children, that was enough. Generally, he did not feel himself capable of more. He learned his lesson well from the Anglos and like

49

other colonial peoples, the Mexicano accepted many of the colonizers' negative views as true.

Although the early Mexicanos often believed that Anglos were in some ways superior to them, they did not live easily with these beliefs. Nearly all the old Mexicanos also expressed a deep and unwavering bitterness toward the Anglos. They told stories of how the *patrones*, although good to them, also treated them like animals. When they could no longer work, some *patrones* let their workers go and replaced them with a new family or with a tractor. The Mexicano hated the Anglo *patrones* for not reciprocating his labor with security in his old age. If the Anglo had truly been a *patrón* in the traditional sense, he would have understood that he had a responsibility to care for his worker as a father would. The Mexicano *peones* found the American sharecropper system to be different from the feudal hacienda system of Mexico. The American *patrón*, accustomed to wage-labor and fancying himself an independent farmer, was often unable to be the intimate *patrón* he thought himself to be. The Mexicano saw the Anglos as a cold, stingy, cruel people who scarcely knew how to enjoy life or work their fields and clean their houses without the Mexicano. These negative images are, of course, not shared by all Mexicanos, but such feelings or themes stood out in the recollections of older Mexicanos.

Even more importantly, the Mexicanos, by accepting that Anglos were superior economic and political entrepreneurs, were not rejecting their own culture as somehow inferior. In fact, it was the Mexicanos' sense of pride in their culture and distinct cultural identity that made survival possible. In early Texas society, the Mexicanos responded to the Anglos' sense of superiority and control of the lands and institutions by withdrawing into their own cultural enclaves and creating their own private, Mexicano world. They fell back upon their close-knit family, neighborhood, and *colonia*, and these traditional forms of social organization served them well. They also fell back upon what anthropologists call "expressive culture," i.e., their own forms of dance, music, art, and humor. The Mexicano ballads, the *baile*, (dances) *Norteños*, (folk songs) and *chistes* (stories, jokes) all expressed their joys and sufferings and preserved their sense of humanity.[7] Confronted by a technologically superior culture with a greater rationale for exploiting the environment, the Mexicanos of this era did not assimilate and adapt to American ways. Instead, they retreated, as many North Town Anglos expressed it, "to their own clannish ways, and they wouldn't Americanize."

The Mexicanos, faced with a subordinate, segregated role in society, could not Americanize and still maintain their integrity as a people. To Americanize in a cultural sense would have been to accept the idea that a Mexicano and his ways were inferior. Most Mexicanos accepted the fact that they were not as able at exploiting the environment, but they rejected any implication that their way of self-expression and of loving and dying was somehow inferior. They chose to measure their humanity and purpose in life by more than their material achievements. This retreat into the cultural enclaves of "Mexican Towns" was more necessary than heroic, however. Their poignant *Norteños* and *Corridos* reveal that they paid a heavy price for retreating. Their *grito* symbolizes this—the joyous, heartbreaking cry of a struggling people, a people in both pain and joy, a people who make the best of the life they have. There was no attempt in this study to collect detailed psychological profiles, but the life histories of the old people express many of these contradictory feelings: the self-doubt, the hatred for Anglos, the frustration of not being able to understand, much less change things. One elderly lady puts it eloquently:

Sometimes *mi querido* (my husband) would come home tired and angry. I would talk about the *bolillos* (Anglos) and how bad they were. He wondered if maybe we Mexicans were as bad as they said. I think my husband didn't think he was much good. He thought the *bolillos* were better than us, but he never said that. He couldn't say such a thing because he hated them too much. If he said that, he would not work as good. There was just too much . . . I don't know . . . too much work I guess. It wasn't something we talked about much, you know. I guess we didn't know how to or something. But I loved my husband. He was a good man.

The core values of Anglo-American achievement and entrepreneurial ability remained, then, largely uncontested in the early years. The Mexicano adapted to his subordinate, inferior position. The ordinary Anglo probably never questioned the morality or immorality of the suffering the economic and political system inflicted upon his workers. The Anglo could fall back upon his sense of cultural superiority and could see his small favors as sufficient kindness. As indicated, the exploitive quality of this early labor system was made obscure to the ordinary Anglo landlord. Their beliefs concerning the Mexicanos' inherent racial and cultural inferiority allowed them to see the Mexicanos as objects, as beasts of burden, who needed little more than the low wages and meager future provided. Their beliefs in their destiny to exploit the environment further justified whatever was necessary to make a profit and survive economically. Within this historical context

51

the early Mexicano settlers fell back on their own resources and family system and created their own communities.

The Mexicano Family in the Rancho

Life on the *ranchos* for the Mexicano was rich and well developed, despite the lack of local institutions such as churches and schools and despite the back-breaking work and indebtedness. Oldtimers described the frequent *bailes* (dances) and celebrations. There were always weddings, baptisms, birthdays, and funerals to attend. People came together and played games of chance like *jugares* (cards) and *walchers* (washers). There were almost no public places, dance halls, plazas, or respectable restaurants for holding celebrations, so such events took place in the tiny shacks and backyards. Where the Mexicano workers lived in a cluster of houses, everyone was involved in the celebrations and shared the work, expenses, and noise. Frequently, several families would ride in their wagon or walk several miles to neighboring settlements to celebrate with their families and *compadres* (godparents).

Thus, in spite of the isolation and impermanence, many oldtimers emphasized that Mexicanos in those days were very close. They had to be in order to survive and to protect each other. Oldtimers claimed that people did not fight and envy or mistrust each other because they frequently needed a neighbor's help. They also needed the good will of other Mexicanos to help them get extra work, to get to town, and to share expenses for celebrations. Families, *compadres* (godparents), and friends formed the only social insurance the Mexicano had. There were very few cases of broken families, male desertion, or unwed mothers. The rules for marriage, courtship, and parenthood were strict, and the social pressure elders exerted upon offenders was very strong. During this period the traditional forms of social organization and the core values defining kinship roles, marriage, and respect for elders remained largely intact.

Many of these original small settlements or clusters of workers' houses around the *patrón*, however, threw unrelated families together. The influx and turnover of working was high; consequently, these early settlements were often not as family-centered as the later *colonias* in the market towns became. It was impossible to estimate how stable the population was, but some of the larger settlements apparently took on a more or less permanent character. In the surrounding settlements, as brother followed brother, and neighbor married neighbor, many families became related to each other. But *rancho* life still had a very temporary quality, and these early communities were often isolated and small. Consequently, such economic and settlement conditions made the traditional extended family a crucial institution for survival and adaptation. If the head of a small nuclear family needed help in order to work his field, he could ask his cousins, uncles, and nephews. If the nuclear family consisted of two or three sons, then the boys were able to help their fathers with harvesting, planting, clearing the land, and caring for the animals. The family was a working economic unit in which the able-bodied members—regardless of sex—were necessary and crucial.

The husband, as the main provider for the family, had little time for anything else but work. *Fiestas* (celebrations), movies, and visits were a very small part of the time he spent trying to bring food and supplies to the family. One eighty-year old man said:

> I came to this country with my uncles in 1909. I was only ten years old. Immediately I started to work in the field, earning about fifty cents a week, learning how to use the *arado* (plow) and how to plant the cotton and the *maíz* (corn). Later on, I started to work with horses, and I liked that better. But I was still a *sembrador*. Then I got married and took my wife to live on the *rancho* where I worked in the *medias* (share cropping). I had a contract and a debt of credit with the Anglos. On Christmas Eve, as we were away celebrating at our parents' houses, somehow our *casita* caught fire, and we lost everything. That was very bad luck. Then that year, the *cosecha* (harvest) wasn't any good because it didn't rain, and I lost all the cotton I had planted. I couldn't pay my credit with the *patrón*, so I had to stay another year. My wife had got sick with the *susto* (illness by fright) caused by the burned house, and the doctor was telling me I should move to another *rancho* or she would die of sorrow. But what could I do? I went on working one more year in that *rancho* and then was able to buy some horses and some tools; thus I became a *quartero*. I also worked as a *vaquero* in between planting time and harvest, when I had some free time. As a *vaquero*, I could work in several different *ranchos* and wasn't committed to anyone. It was good not to be committed to a rancher because then I could move on whenever I pleased. I also made some more money, secure money. It was very hard to make a living in those days. I was never sick, but I fell off my horse many times during my work as a *vaquero* and injured myself badly two or three times. But we made it somehow.

The wife of this particular man did not work with him in the fields, as was generally true for wives in the early settlement days. He wanted to work by himself and be able to say that he supported his family without outside help or his wife's labor. He also had told his wife that he liked her manners as a wife and, therefore, thought that she was a "true woman" of the house and should stay there. Only much later, when they moved into town, was she allowed to wash clothes for Anglo women. However, such work was only done at home in a room built by her husband especially for that purpose. Further, he did not want his children to work with him, because he thought they should go to school. He explained his philosophy in the following way:

I learned everything by myself and with some older people. I never had any *escuela* (schooling), and I am *lírico* (a natural poet). Well, then, all I knew how to do was field work, and I didn't want that for my children. That is why I never allowed them to come with me when I was planting or harvesting, even though sometimes I could use some help.

His views were unusual, however, and most boys did work with their fathers in the fields.

Life for women was spent mostly at home. Although many women did not work in the fields, women's work was still very hard and essential for family functioning and survival. The day for a wife and mother on a ranch began at four a.m. in the morning. It is described by a very old woman who lived on a *rancho* from 1915, when her relatives came from Mexico, until 1932, when she and her husband moved into the *colonia* of North Town:

I woke up first in the house and put some water to boil in a pan for the children's baths. Then I'd put some cold water in the big tub in the bedroom, plus the hot water until it was warm enough for the bath. I'd bathe all the children, one by one, and dress the smaller ones. By then my husband was also up. I'd prepare the breakfast for him and the children. He would leave by five or five-thirty in the morning. I'd then give something for the children to play with and be busy while I prepared the *masa* (dough) for the tortillas. My older daughter helped with grinding the *maíz* in the *metate* (stone bowl). That would take me about an hour or so to do. Then I'd have to start preparing lunch for my husband; if he was working in a land near the house, he would come home for lunch at about noon. He'd stay home until two or three in the afternoon because the sun was too hot at that time for him to work. Well, I was always busy at the house with one thing or the other. When I had some free time I'd go over to my *comadre*'s house by foot and visit with them for a while or then just sit and work in my *costura*, knitting and embroidering.

She had little time for relaxation. Her only sources of distraction were a few moments of conversation with her peers, and any free time usually meant other work like knitting or embroidering. She was responsible for organizing home activities, instructing her children in household chores, nursing the sick and using the family resources (food and clothing) efficiently. A proud woman was sure to have her little house always tidy and spotless, her children always dressed in clean, though old and patched garments. To have the house in disarray or the children messy was to be considered a *dejada*, a lazy woman. The self-pride of the poor working class Mexicanos often depended upon being as clean and well-dressed as possible.

Since male/female roles were generally understood and accepted, there was relatively little conflict. If there was resentment from one spouse, it was not openly expressed. Both men and women understood the importance of their tasks for family's unity and survival. A woman was supposed to obey her husband and to abide by what he said. If he said "don't go out," she did not go out; not to follow his orders was to show a lack of *cariño*, i.e., that she did not really care for him. The relationship between husband and wife was perhaps a paternalistic and authoritarian one, but also one of great mutual respect and support. Although the husband was considered "the boss," the wife had a great deal of authority over the children and family affairs. In some families, the woman was given part of the decision-making power. One woman describes the relationship between her parents, back in 1910, while they lived at the *rancho*:

> My mother *mandaba en la casa* (was the boss in the house), but decisions were made by both her and my father. If my father wanted to sell all the maiz or a cow, he first consulted with my mother. Of course, not all the couples around there were the same. There were some husbands who would lock the food in a compartment that only they could open. When the wife needed some food she'd have to ask him to open the compartment. A woman's life was very hard. We had little freedom and a lot of work. We had no horses, for instance, so we depended on the men for transportation. But it wasn't like that with my mama and papa. They were good to each other.

Most women learned and accepted that the man was the unquestioned authority at home. Usually, women attained their social identity through their men; they were always known in the community as some man's sister, daughter, wife, or mother. The older Mexicanas also wanted a man's strong hand to share the household responsibilities. They learned to think of men as stronger and better able to defend the family against outside dangers.

Many of these women do not remember the *rancho* days as particularly unhappy times. They talk a great deal about physical hardships, but what dominates their remembrances is family life. They lived in close contact with their families, surrounded by them every day, all

55

day. Even the shabbiness of a worker's shack could not obscure the feelings of love and security brought about by such close family ties. A strong-willed Señora with eight children tells her story:

> Yo nunca sufrí en la casa de mis padres (I never suffered at my parents' home) porque mi padrecito santo era tan bueno y mi mamá también. (because my saintly father was so good and my mother too). My father never gave my mother any disgusto (sorrow), never got drunk, only worked hard for all of us. We had the little house, the mules, and many other animals in the ranch, like chickens, turkeys, and pigs. When we needed butter, the whole family would get together to make butter from the pig's fat. My mother used the pig's blood to make a delicious meal. We also had a lot of eggs to eat. My mother liked to give the eggs away to relatives and friends, never selling them.

Although the woman was generally supposed to abide by the husband's words and be humilde (humble) towards him, it was obvious that the mother always held a strong, central role in the household. As an old Mexicana explained:

> La mamá era todo (The mother was everything). Without the mother there would be no family. If the mother dies, the family is disrupted; each child goes to a different household, to live with an uncle or with the grandparents or godparents. The family's unity is broken without la mamá.

The family was the main socializing agency, since schools were rare and the church was remote. The father instructed the male children, and with the mother he shared in teaching etiquette and social ideals; he taught the sons how to plant, plow, and harvest like a sembrador. A father who was a vaquero also taught his male children, traditionally the older ones, how to ride the horses. His teachings were complete and filled with the wisdom that he had obtained in his life's work. An old man recalled how his father taught him about horses:

> When I was about nine years old, my father would bring a horse to the front of the house and tell me to get on it and ride it. He did this every day, and as time passed, I improved my riding gradually until I could run the horse. He always told me that I had to think like the horse and know what he was going to do as you rode him.

Fathers also instructed their sons in how to behave as a husband and father, not only by setting an example but by exhorting them to follow certain rules of conduct. A woman told how her father instructed her brothers:

> He used to tell them that when they got married it was their obligation

to take good care of their wives and children. If they ran around with other women and neglected their wives, and for that reason their wives got sick and died, they should not come to my father for aid; they would have to find a solution for themselves because my father would not help dishonorable sons.

Daughters received their training primarily from their mothers. They were encouraged to stay home and do the domestic chores that were considered strictly female work. The boys would either follow their father to work in the field or go to school. Many girls also went to the small rural schools but would soon drop out and stay home. Girls were instructed by their mothers in sewing, knitting, embroidering, cooking, washing, ironing, and cleaning the house. These skills were an absolute necessity, if the girls were to become good wives and mothers. One woman remembers that it was her father who taught all the girls in their family how to behave towards their future husbands:

> My papa used to sit with us in front of the house, after he came from work, and talk to us about how to be a good wife. It was like a school. He'd say we always would have to abide to what our husbands say, and accept his orders and decisions, that the husband was *el jefe* (the chief). We had to have quiet manners and not argue with him. Also, we should comb our hair, put on a clean dress, and wash our face in order to wait for our husbands to come home. 'A man,' he used to say, 'doesn't like to find a wife in bad shape. Your hair doesn't have to be dirty, it should be kept clean and neat.' Your dress may be all patched up, but it must be clean. Also your face doesn't have to have makeup on, as long as it is clean and not greasy.

After women had cooked huge pots of food, washed clothes, changed diapers, and mopped the dusty floor, they still had to worry about looking nice for the man coming home from work. This same woman reports that she always tried to look nice; further, she never saw her mother arguing with her father, and also claims that she never argued with her own husband. She was married fifty years to the same man and nobody ever saw or heard them quarreling. Such reflections were common among the older women.

In the training of children, physical punishment had its place but was usually rare. When physical force was necessary to make a child obey or to punish a misdeed, the punishment was usually administered by the father. The mother was supposed to be softer in dealing with her children, and most women were proud to say that their children never required strong punishment. Apparently, they seldom misbehaved or talked back to the parents. Respect for elders was greatly emphasized within the family. Another reason that mothers were not harsh with their children is that women bear the children and therefore suffer with them. Women contended that they felt the suffering of their children more than the men. They reasoned that men, since they did not carry the child within their bodies, were unable to actually feel the suffering of a child. Consequently, men found it easier to castigate their children and cause them pain.

While children were *jóvenes* (single), they were supposed to live in the parents' home. This was especially true for the daughters. An unmarried daughter could live with a married sister or brother if her parents died, but she could never live alone or with unrelated people. Children had to be watched and cared for by the parents. Children also had to obey and follow parental advice and orders. The authority of parents could, however, be transferred to or sometimes shared with the eldest son and daughter. For example, an older brother could and often did take his younger brothers to the field where he taught them to work. An older sister often took care of the children, cooked, and washed for the older brothers in the mother's absence. The elder brother, like the father, ultimately had greater authority and responsibility.

Women traditionally also had less freedom of movement than men. Daughters were much more closely supervised than sons. Boys could go out in groups to the nearest towns and have a good time. They could ride horses and go to the movies alone. Girls could rarely go out of the home without their mothers or other trusted companions. Some women reported that they had been allowed to go out with other girls their age on a picnic. However, such outings were only possible with companions approved by their father and mother. If a girl asked why she was not allowed to do what her brothers could do, the answer would always be:

> Men are strong and they know how to defend themselves. Not women. If you are out without your *mamá* or your *papá* or your older brothers, a man can come and steal you, disgracing you forever.

When silent movies were being shown in the town nearby, a mother and her daughters or *comadres* (godmothers) were allowed to go. It was not uncommon to see a group of women driving a mule-drawn wagon to the Saturday movies. They had to go in the afternoon in order to be back home before dark. Some old women are horrified when they realize that young people today come back from the movies after midnight, "when it is already the next day." Fathers would also take their whole famliy to enjoy a movie together on a Saturday afternoon. They could not go to the movies on Sunday because it was a church day, and they had to be home early to rest for work on Monday.

The men on the *ranchos* usually went to town or went drinking with their close friends. However, the family was central to their lives, and most men were not known to neglect their families for friends or for other women. Women also formed friendships among themselves, and many reported being close with relatives, *comadres*, and women on nearby ranches. These friendships were crucial in times of need. When a woman was to give birth, not only her mother, but also her mother-in-law and other females came to her aid. A woman who lived in a settlement town said:

> You didn't have to ask for anyone's help. They would just come to you. Whenever my mother had a child, the house would be filled with other women who would take care of us children, cook for her, bathe her and the baby, help her in every possible way.

Even though the houses were far apart, they would take time to visit with each other as frequently as possible. Often, they had no transportation, or only a wagon drawn by mules; thus friends and relatives might walk several miles to see how a *comadre* was doing. If a *comadre* lived nearby and had not shown up for more than two days, one would go visiting to see whether she was sick and needed help. *Comadres* and female relatives also had a great deal of authority over each other's children. Any woman could care for the children of a related woman and expect to be obeyed and respected by them, as her own children would. Conversely, she would be expected to treat her neighbor's children as she would her own. The women emphasized how important and wide-spread these practices were. The pattern of visiting was important for maintenance of familial ties and also the solidarity of the Mexicano people. Living in a foreign, segregated society, they found comfort and aid from their own group and shared their children and their friendship.

Visits usually involved the whole family, and the traveling to another *rancho* involved a good part of the day going back and forth.

> *Mi comadre* Rosita often visited me. She was frequently coming to our house some week-ends. She'd arrive on a Saturday afternoon, coming by wagon, with everyone, all the children plus the couple. They'd stay until Sunday morning and then head back home. Her children greatly enjoyed the *columpios* (swings) that my husband had hung from the trees for our children. All our children played well together. The house was small, but there was room for everyone to stay overnight. The floors would be cov-

ered with *pura muchachada* (many young people). Of course, there was always enough food. Who feeds one, feeds ten.

People who lived in settlement towns, as well as the ones in the *ranchos*, also enjoyed having *fiestas* that took place in the backyard of a *casita* or in the "Mexican School." There was guitar and accordion music played by local people. They danced on the bare earth, under the stars, until late in the evening. Sometimes, but not frequently, Anglo *patrones* would join a partying group of Mexicanos. Nevertheless, those occasions were for enjoying themselves as Mexicanos—with their music, their language, *gritos* (cries), food, and customs. As previously described, people also enjoyed many games of cards and washers:

> There was a *rancho* famous for *los juegos* (games). People would walk a long distance to go there and would stay for a few days. They were *bienvenidos* (welcome) and a place to sleep was offered to them. In those days *la gente era muy amistosa* (people were very friendly).

Marriage was considered very important for both sexes. One simply had to get married and form another family unit in the *rancho* economy. In the *ranchos*, many marriages took place after a long, ritualized courtship that was closely supervised by the future bride's parents and older brothers. The latter were supposed to protect their sister's honor and would take great pains to supervise her. Some women resented such brotherly supervision very much and felt that the brothers interfered in their personal affairs too often. Such resentment was enhanced by the fact that the sisters had very little control over their brothers' romantic lives and other affairs. During courtship the future groom and bride would seldom see or talk to each other for any great length of time.

The ancient custom for parents to arrange the marriages of their children was no longer practiced. Young people were already making their own choice, *but* it had to be acceptable to the parents. In some cases, when the young man lived far or wanted to court his girlfriend secretly, courtship would take place through the mail. He would send her written notes or spoken messages through her relatives (usually female), and she could answer in the same manner. He could only see her at her home, under family surveillance, and usually after a formal engagement. In that way, women were protected from any "evil man" or from someone who just wanted to "play with their feelings."

It was reported by some that the ideal age for a girl to marry was around eighteen. Parents did not allow their daughter to marry earlier, fearing that they were unprepared for wifely duties. One mother of six said:

> At fifteen one is not mature enough for marriage. Besides, there is a lot more to learn from your parents at home. You shouldn't go into marriage without being prepared. That's why parents wanted you to wait until you were eighteen in order to get married.

There was some variance with respect to age. While some women report that if a girl wanted to get married at fifteen, her parents would not allow it, other women felt that they were "marrying old" at eighteen or nineteen.

Weddings were celebrated with a good deal of festivities. A typical wedding started at ten in the morning and continued until the next morning. A seventy-year old woman described her wedding:

> In my wedding, the orchestra was supposed to stay only until midnight because it was freezing cold. It was in January of 1925. But the players were my husband's friends, so they decided to stay until two in the morning. By then the grounds were so icy that nobody could go home. So we danced and had a good time until ten the next morning.

Thus, the wedding party, like other family celebrations such as baptisms or even funerals, brought together many families, friends, *comadres* and *compadres* from ranches all around; it was a grand affair, a genuine opportunity for celebration. People said that they had to go to the wedding in order "to pay their *humanidad*" (being human and friendly) to the new couple and their parents.

Marriage had to be stable and harmonious because of its important economic and social function. The nuclear family as a labor unit was essential for survival. But for many it was also based on the sacredness of life, as an old woman explained:

> A person is a *regalo del cielo* (a gift from above). You have to live a good life in order to be worthy of this gift. You have to do your best not to spoil that which was given to you by God and your parents—your own life. So you have to do a good marriage.

A big family was considered a blessing and was welcome by the parents. Women expected to bear many children. Birth control practices were largely unknown, and there was a great deal of ignorance among females about sexual reproduction. Women who wanted to stop having children had to make use of inefficient folk methods. Most women, however, accepted their fate as bearers of many children, learning to enjoy and cherish them. In fact, women who had only two or three

61

children felt slightly deprived. Such women report enjoying a visit to another woman who had many children. They enjoyed the noise and movement of a house "filled with children."

In dealing with racism, economic exploitation, and the isolated *rancho* life, the Mexican family and community were rather successful at surviving materially and spiritually. They took what was allotted them and tried to make the best of it. This is reflected in statements from old-timers who like to say that "life then wasn't as complicated or hard as life is today." Most families tried to supplement their meager income by planting a little garden of beans and potatoes and raising chickens or turkeys in order to get meat and eggs. Moreover, some women say that although work was harder and the future uncertain, everything was cheaper, and many report never lacking anything that was essential. One older woman explained:

> You had to work very hard, but at least you didn't have to worry about paying bills, such as light or water. We had no electricity, and water was brought from a well. You also didn't have school expenses, since we ate fresh, good food and had lots of natural exercise. I don't remember any of us children ever needing to go to a doctor.

Life was taken with stoicism, as something one had to endure, but also to enjoy as much as one could. They knew that lack of rain would hinder the harvest, that tempests would destroy the plants; life was often a matter of luck. It often seemed that "you either work yourself to death, or you starve to death." There was no help from the outside no federal programs, no social workers. The family was left alone, and they gathered around each other for strength, endurance, and a reason to live. They did not expect help from the outside and were often suspicious of unsolicited aid or advice. They tried to help each member of the family when possible. The rest of the world was strange and unfamiliar; therefore, it was kept at a distance.

A SUMMING UP: THE ORGANIZATION
AND POWER OF THE COMPETING ETHNIC GROUPS

It is important to conclude this discussion of Mexicano and Anglo relations in the *rancho* era with some assessment of how organized and unified each group was. The description of life during this era may have left some readers with the idea that a powerful, well-organized Anglo group consciously and willfully dominated and exploited the Mexicanos. In this superior-subordinate relationship the Mexicanos would be weak, disorganized, and passively accepting of Anglo domination. Neither of these extreme characterizations was intended. The relative power of each group, and their forms of control and exploitation were varied and complex.

To a significant degree the North Town Anglos were a dominant group that controlled the local institutions and their Mexican laborers. As a group, however, they were far from homogeneous. Socially and culturally Anglos were a hodge-podge of white ethnic groups; most of whom came to this frontier region very poor and very anxious to improve themselves. Originally, these small ranchers and farmers came in the wake of the Mexican-American War that fostered Anglo exploitation of Mexican lands and settlements. Later, big urban capital, absentee landlords, and a flock of land speculators further developed the area. Many of these settlers came from different Anglo-American ethnic groups in the Midwest, East Texas, and particularly the older German hill country communities of Central Texas. Such settlers were often small farmers who were being pushed from exhausted southern cotton lands or from more expensive midwestern lands. In their view, this South Texas region represented something of a last frontier of good, cheap farmland.

The basis of Anglo social organization in North Town was also kinship. The early Anglo families were also large, and many of the ranches/farms were father/son or brother/brother partnerships. Nearly all of a person's social life was organized around family celebrations, and elderly Anglos stressed the closeness and solidarity of their families. Frequently, the small hamlets consisted of several extended families, usually two generations deep, centered around the family head and his brothers and sisters. These ranching/farming families stressed their independendence and privacy, and community-wide organizations were minimal. In the growing market center of North Town there existed a considerably more complex Anglo community which contained the social differences so often described in small town America.

There were many religious, occupational, educational, and class differences that separated Anglos from each other. By any measure of social organization, the Anglos reflected considerable diversity for a small rural town. Further, in the management of the economy and the town, there was a degree of inter-Anglo competition. The market system for cotton, vegetables, and cattle was erratic at best, and in spite of the occasional labor exchanges and church fellowship, Anglos were forced to compete with each other. This was especially true in the fresh vegetable market. In one county a number of growers attributed the downfall of the spinach market in the early twenties to the price-cutting tactics of an organization of independent growers. Further, small cotton growers and small ranchers bitterly complained about how big ranchers, growers, shippers, and brokers were constantly taking advantage of their tenuous position. There were also cases of Anglo bankers and Anglo merchants repossessing Anglo lands. Indeed, the big economic producers, as in any other setting, often gave no quarter to the small producers. The squeeze was always on, it seemed.

Moreover, Anglos were far from united behind one political machine or one *patrón*. Old-timers revealed a very strong streak of individualism and a populist contempt for all politicians and "big shots." They were critical of the "political entrepreneurs" who helped themselves. These feelings and conflicts were reflected in the periodic factionalism in local government and school elections. The early Anglo leaders remember that during the early twenties, and the late thirties, Anglos were pitted against Anglos. Reformers wanted to get rid of "that bunch running city hall." There were occasionally "hot" county and school board elections. In most cases, it involved one Anglo angry over a particular issue, e.g., how his road was graded or who coached the football team. A person usually ran against an incumbent guilty of not grading his road. In anger he mobilized his kinship group and friends and whoever owed him a favor. These were not pervasive forms of factionalism that had long histories or were motivated by some form of blood vengeance. Nevertheless, such splits did periodically occur and at least temporarily affect the solidarity of the Anglo community.

Anglos were also divided by perceived class and status differences. Several old-timers described the differences between old families (original settlers) and new families. You were "nobody" socially unless you were one of the original families. Further, being a rancher was definitely better than being a dirt farmer. Farmers were simple, honest people who worked hard, but they lacked social graces, clothes, and manners. Ranchers tended to see themselves as rugged and better dressed, and as better fighters and lovers. They were "fancier," went to the cities more often, and knew more about the outside world. The businessmen tended to consider themselves more modern and well-informed. Those who were more prosperous were the first to have automobiles, radios, and other modern conveniences.

As in other small American communities, these status differences were also related to the churches. In North Town the Methodists tended to be the center of the civic and political leadership group, the older, better families. The same pattern of Methodist prominence was true in Aztlán City, but in other surrounding towns the Baptists were the most prominent church group. As the early civic leaders suggested, the church that became socially prominent was the one that the original ranching and business families attended. Once certain families established their prominence in the community, other aspiring new-comers tended to join the churches with prominent members.

Churches, therefore, reflected and reinforced class differences. Churches also became the basis of stereotyping among Anglos. Several civic leaders characterized the Baptists as "teetotalers and Bible thumpers." Conversely, the Methodists were thought of and thought of themselves as being less fundamentalist and conservative, or "religious" as others put it. In the Anglo *rancho* settlements religious and class differences appeared to be minimal, while life in North Town was apparently filled with more factionalism, status envy, stereotyping, and class differences. Moreover, there were always the ubiquitous effects of economic competition.

In spite of such differences and sources of disunity, most old Anglos described life as reasonably peaceful and harmonious. The Anglos of early North Town all participated in the community social life and generally cooperated to make their schools, churches, and community grow and prosper. They shared a desire to exploit the land and make a good living. To this end they sometimes shared their labor. To assure a good life for their children they maintained schools. When it was advantageous to send their children to the town school, they organized and maintained private buses. There were, then, many community activities and joint projects which brought Anglos together.

Perhaps, however, the most important source of Anglo unity was their racial feelings. Although Anglos were from many different European ethnic groups, they were white, *not* brown and Mexican. Most Anglos considered themselves superior to Mexicans, and many forms of segregation occurred because of these beliefs. The boundaries between these two ethnic groups were the most distinguishing, clearest form of social organization in these small towns. A great deal of the Anglos' energies were dedicated to maintaining this separation. It was done through laws, etiquette, schooling, and even in the practice of religion. Convincing a people of their inferiority and making it acceptable required a great deal of vigilance and effort from Anglos.

Yet, during the *rancho* era Anglos were not a highly coordinated controlling group. They were organized enough to maintain their political and economic dominance, but the ordinary North Town Anglo was probably indifferent to the affairs of local government and politics. Local citizens tacitly let their representatives—which included both vicious and benevolent sheriffs, mayors, and county judges—emerge as the key leaders and policy-makers. These officials were more dedicated to the ideal of keeping taxes low and services minimal than to using local public institutions to serve people. Instead, the pattern of paternalistic service to loyal Mexicano followers developed, and these political *patrones* or "machines" stayed in power, often for two or three decades.

These long-term Anglo community leaders also derived power to control from the absence of higher-level federal policies. The 1900 to 1930 era was a time of virtually no federal or state intervention into local affairs to aid and assist the poor. The Mexican immigrant had no legal rights and was constantly in fear of deportation. The massive flow of illegal immigrants was overlooked, leaving Mexican-American laborers less able to bargain for better wages. Further, these workers received no state or federal health, education, and welfare programs. This lack of protection and support thrust the Mexicano laborers into a more dependent, powerless position. They became easy prey for enterprising ranchers, farmers, and *politicos*. The local way of life emphasized material success, production, profit, and individualism rather than equality and human dignity. Probably not all North Town Anglos participated equally in the exploitation of the early Mexicanos. Neither were Anglos always consciously and maliciously exploiters, but the way of life they championed did not spare its working people from degradation or share with them the profits. Ironically, perhaps both owner and worker become victims of the way of life they have created.

On the other hand, how well organized and united were the Mexicanos as a group? The description of social life in the settlements demonstrates how central kinship was to the Mexicanos. To a much greater extent for Mexicanos than for Anglos, the extended family was the focal point of life. Additionally, the early Mexicano communities were a very circumscribed, defended community wherein Mexicanos had difficulty controlling their environment. The Mexicanos were so unorganized as a group that they were easily controlled. There were virtually no formal leaders in any of these communities who could weld people together for collective political action.

By 1918 North Town did have a *Sociedades de Honoríficos*. Such groups were mutual aid societies that developed to protect the Mexicanos against the Ku Klux Klan. They also asked and received advice from a Mexican border consulate upon occasion about deportation cases. Such societies created a burial insurance fund for their members (50 to 125), and in the event of a death, everyone shared the cost. These societies were a locus for various social activities in the community, and they were often active in organizing local religious celebrations. These organizations never, however, confronted or competed with the Anglos.

The other major way that these Mexicano communities became "defended communities" has already been suggested.[8] The Mexicanos were forced to withdraw into themselves and their own communities, and they responded by maintaining their cultural tradition and social life. They undoubtedly retained their sense of identity and self-worth through traditional cultural practices. All Mexicanos shared a great deal of expressive culture, a common religion, and strong traditions of sharing and cooperation. They were able to share the work, travel, extra food, and good times, and this created a high degree of cultural solidarity. In varying degrees they hated the Anglo, which further bonded them together in a common struggle.

Yet, there were also potentially disunifying class and status differences among the Mexicanos. The old-timers made the same cowboy/farmer distinction that Anglos did. *Vaqueros* thought of their profession as superior to *sembradores*. They had a horse and a gun, and they did their work off the ground. The *vaquero* lived a dangerous and manly life, and he developed a set of specialized skills in riding, roping, and handling horses and cattle that few men acquired. The old *vaqueros* were an extremely proud group, and they spoke of some envy between the cowboys and farmers.

The small market towns of this era also contained a growing merchant class. These early *negociantes* were *los ricos* (the rich) in these extremely poor communities. They became small-time money lenders and leaders in the church and the *Sociedades*. They sent their children through grade school, and they began to learn English and the Anglo ways. As these children became Anglicized, they became a source of envy for some, a new divisive element in the community. Yet social class and occupational and religious differences were not the key sources of fragmentation in these early Mexicano communities. More important, the Mexicanos were spread out geographically and isolated on the *ranchos*. Transportation and communication were poor. Mexicanos lived with their *patrones*, dependent upon them for credit and protection from the border patrol, the sheriff, and sickness. The basis of Mexicano powerlessness and disunity lay in the poverty and the dependence created by the labor and credit system.

The Mexicanos generally believed that they lacked the leadership or organization to confront the Anglo. They did not fight for their rights because the Anglo was perceived as too powerful and clever to be overcome. The Mexicano did not necessarily lose faith in himself, but he lacked any explanation for his poverty and misery. He understood that the situation was oppressive, but he reasoned that Mexico was also bad. He did not expect to attain the American ideal of equality, and he did not organize to demand it. In short, the ordinary North

Town Mexicano had no practicing ideology of self-determination, i.e., that he should control more of his own environment and make more of the decisions affecting his life.

This assessment of the Mexicano's relative powerlessness and acceptance of his lot in life should not, however, obscure the active resistance of many Mexicanos. Recent research on the Mexicanos in South Texas has revealed the existence of many community leaders with well-developed "radical" ideologies who sought to organize the people.[9] Over 300 delegates from many small South Texas towns met in Laredo in 1910 at the *Conferencia Mexicanista* and proposed such programs as labor unions, ethnic-political organizations, and bilingual education. The intent of these leaders was to go back to their communities and develop Mexicano political organizations. They were, however, subsequently crushed by the local authorities. Many of the participants were jailed, and this early attempt at a Mexicano movement was suppressed. Other recent research on early labor movements also suggests considerable "activism" and a strong sense of self-determination among some Mexicano leaders and workers.[10] It would, then, be grossly misleading to argue that Mexicanos were passive and did not actively protest their oppressive conditions.

Nevertheless, the North Town Mexicanos in the *rancho* were not a well-organized, power-seeking group. Their resistance to Anglo racism and economic exploitation took on more individual, subtle forms or were simply born stoically. Even given the harsh economic and political realities, wide-spread local rebellions did not occur. Early North Town was politically quiet. It took a series of major economic transformations and many new ideas and programs from outside North Town to set the stage for and encourage local Mexicano political activity. The period from 1930 to 1960 became crucial, then, as a prelude to the rise of organized Chicano political groups in the sixties and seventies.

[1] The discussion of the early schools is based largely on the recollections of many Mexicano students and several Anglo administrators and teachers. The county school records in this case were very incomplete and almost useless.

[2] This study concentrated little effort on the schooling problems of black Americans. How these small rural towns of South Texas dealt with their small black school populations needs to be documented, too.

[3] See Appendix A, Table 2.1 *Median Income and Median Education With Poverty Between Ethnic Groups in Three South Texas Counties.*

[4] Lipset, Seymour M. *The First New Nation.* New York: Anchor, 1963.

[5] Stein, Maurice. *The Eclipse of Community.* New York: Harper Torchbacks, 1964.

[6] Myrdal, Gunnar. *An American Dilemma*. New York: Harper and Row, 1944; and Robert Blauner. *Racial Oppression in America*. New York: Harper and Row, 1972.

[7] Paredes, Américo. *With His Pistol in His Hand*. Austin, Texas: University of Texas Press, 1971.

[8] Suttles, Gerald. *The Social Construction of Communities*. Chicago: University of Chicago Press, 1972. For the most well developed treatment of the concept of a "defended community" see this and other works by Suttles.

[9] Limon, José. "El Primer Congreso Mexicanista de 1911: A Precursor to Contemporary Chicanismo" in Aztlan, Vol. 5, #1 and #2, 1974.

[10] Zamora, Emilio. "Chicano Socialist Labor Activity in Texas, 1900–1920" in Aztlán, Vol. 6, #2, 1975.

PART II: CHANGING LIFE IN THE *COLONIA*, 1930 TO 1970

Chapter 3

The Changing Political Economy of
the *Colonia*

The early *rancho* economy gradually yet dramatically changed during the 1930 to 1960 era. Ranching and farming, the production techniques and the labor needs, were transformed; consequently, the basis of Anglo-Mexicano relations changed. This economic transformation of the North Town region involves a complex set of ecological, marketing, technological, and population changes. By the late 1920's a number of factors led to the general decline of commercial cotton and spinach production. The methods of cultivation and soil conservation were generally unscientific. Particularly the overused, unirrigated lands for cotton suffered extensive erosion and decline in humus.[1] Further, without pesticides the boll weevil destroyed larger and larger portions of the yields.[2] Finally, North Town sharecroppers reported drastically fluctuating cotton prices during the post World War I period. In the late 1920's conditions were apparently so desperate that many sharecroppers and day laborers began moving to the surrounding towns in search of new job opportunities.[3]

A somewhat similar set of circumstances also existed in the areas of the regions with a booming spinach industry. Initially, many small farmers migrated in and attempted to grow vegetables. Most of them failed, and the vegetable industry was almost nonexistent until someone discovered that the land was extraordinarily good for spinach. By 1920 a spinach boom was developing in nearby Aztlán City. Hundreds of small spinach farmers and a large contingent of Mexican labor moved into the region. In the early days, spinach was simply broadcasted, i.e., the seeds were scattered over the fields instead of drill-planted in rows for cultivation. The land was so fertile that even the simplest production methods could make high yields. Aztlán City, with its new railroad spur (1916), became the spinach capital of the world, shipping as much as eighty percent of the national supply of spinach.[4] The spinach was loose-leaf-packed and iced and sent by rail throughout the country. Spinach production boomed for approximately ten years. In the late 1920's, however, the fields were increasingly plagued with weeds and mosaic blight or "blue mold," a deadly fungus that killed spinach. The local district records show that more than half of the small spinach farmers had left by 1930, and the census indicates declining production in the late 1930's.[5]

This general decline in agricultural cash crop production in the region was greatly accelerated by the Depression of the 1930's which residents often described graphically. How many producers actually "went broke" was reconstructed from interviews of old-timers in six settlements. In settlements with heavy concentrations of small farmers, approximately half of the cotton and vegetable farmers lost their land. A few small ranchers were also affected, but the majority of older ranching and farmer/rancher families survived.[6] There were cases where the ranch or farm was sold because the family head died and the heirs were female, but the old families survived the hard times rather well. More important than the percentage who left was the general cutback in production. The prices were so low and money so scarce that local producers simply grew less. Apparently, a good deal of farmland went back into brush and open range land during this period. Some places were abandoned altogether. These trends were only partially reflected in the census data on crop production and land ownership.[7]

Others told stories of how farmers gave away crops to anyone who wanted or needed them. People from *La Colonia* would go to the farms and get the unsellable vegetables. The federal government also instituted the slaughter of cattle to control supply and raise prices. At times this meat was distributed to local people. There were also several federal government WPA and CCC projects in North Town. Local Mexicanos were employed to build a swimming pool, a library addition, and several road and street projects. Both Mexicanos and Anglos felt they suffered hardship, but they also marveled at how people helped each other and adjusted their production and consumption to survive. The most important impact of the Depression was, however, the effect it had on the labor needs and relations of an already declining agricultural system. Not as many Mexicanos were needed in the fields, and the local *patrones* were generally not wealthy enough, or paternal enough, to simply absorb huge numbers of unemployed laborers. Consequently, many Mexicano agricultural laborers in this era began finding other

71

types and places of work. To a degree these trends are reflected in the census data on migration.[8]

The second general factor underlying the economic transformation of this era was a series of technological innovations. The first tractors were reportedly used in North County around 1932 or 1933. By then the early Model-T trucks of the late 1910's had also been replaced by much larger, tandem-wheel models that carried twice as much. Somewhat later, during World War II, combines for grain and peanuts were also introduced. This trend towards much more mechanized farming was also paralleled by great increases in pump and gravity irrigation.[9] Such modernization of agriculture through mechanization significantly altered the nature of farming and ranching. The new labor needs and character of labor relations on the vegetable farms, stock farms, and ranches of this era will be described later.

A final general ecological factor which also had important economic and political implications was the changing balance of population between the two ethnic groups. Table 1.1 shows the relative growth of the region during the period of 1910–1970.[10] The Mexicano population increased regionally from forty-eight percent of the total population in 1910 to sixty-two percent of the population in 1970. The Mexicano population of North County increased by forty-four percent. In contrast, only two counties in the region reveal any population increase in Anglos. North County reveals a twenty-four percent loss in Anglo population since 1910. Presently, sixty-nine percent of the population in North County is Mexicano. In only forty years the Mexicanos have become the majority unit by a substantial margin.

Why the population balance has been changing in this direction is difficult to say precisely. Generally, demographers agree that population change for any group can come about from only two sources: 1) a natural increase (excess of births over deaths) and 2) a net migration (in-migrants minus out-migrants). Unfortunately, the historical data regarding birth and death rates and migration rates are incomplete. Table 3.3 suggests that the fertility rate of Spanish-surname population in North County is almost double that of the Anglos.[11] Further, when the difference in mortality rates is considered, Table 3.4 indicates that Spanish-surname infants have a greater chance of dying than Anglo infants.[12] Health care for the Spanish-surname population has historically been a critical problem; consequently, the large differences between Mexicano and Anglo fertility rates are even more dramatic because the higher Mexicano infant mortality rates should partially reduce such differences.

Finally, determining how much the difference in fertility rates may be due to differences in group in/out migration is difficult. Historical migration data simply do not exist. Table 3.5 suggests, however, that from 1950 to 1970 there was a steady decline in the number of foreign-born residents in this region.[13] This suggests that the North County region is becoming a more indigenous population. In-migration of Mexicanos and Anglos is becoming a less important factor in the growing differences in group population rates. The number of in-migrating Mexican nationals fell dramatically during the Depression years and rose again after World War II. There is no way to estimate the population increases due to "unrecorded" events such as marriages between citizens and illegal entrants and permanent residents without papers. Undoubtedly, illegal immigration and such marriages stimulated the increases in the Spanish-surname population to a degree, even though the quota for legal entry has remained small since 1928. Conversely, the in-migration of Anglos to the region is generally thought to be miniscule.

The other aspect of migration which may explain growing population differences is the relative out-migration of both Mexicanos and Anglos. Little data on out-migration rates exist, but a limited study of historical school mobility data suggests that both groups are leaving the North Town area at very high rates.[14] More than fifty percent of the Anglo children went on to college and prepared themselves for careers simply not available in these small towns. Anglos in the North County region have generally accepted the lack of expanding opportunity for their children and have prepared them for eventual migration. Generally, the only Anglos who stay or return are females who marry local farmers or ranchers, or the sons of local businessmen and farmers who inherit the land or form a partnership with their fathers. Given the expansion of salaried, clerical, bureaucratic, and professional jobs for Mexicanos, it would appear that a somewhat larger proportion of Mexicano youth is staying in North Town after graduation or is returning to assume skilled jobs after advanced education.

Some investigators, and many local North Towners, particularly Anglos, would argue that basic cultural differences affect the fertility rates. It is commonly thought that Mexicanos place a higher value on large families, lack birth control practices due to Catholicism, or are simply "hot-blooded" and "over-sexed." Although some differences in cultural values or in poverty may explain fertility differences, it is also important to consider economic factors. In the *rancho* production system, and later in the migrant labor stream, large Mexicano families were an absolute necessity. They were encouraged and valued by *patrones* and *contratistas*, and any poor sharecropper or migrant laborer

73

who wished to accumulate more capital could use extra hands in the family. Whatever the blend of economic needs and basic cultural differences, the high fertility rates of Mexicanos, not withstanding mortality and migration rates, have greatly outstripped Anglo growth rates in North Town. As indicated, the Mexicano is now a dominant majority, and this demographic factor will surely play an increasingly prominent role in the political struggles occurring in this region.

The general changes in the land, market, production, technology, and population fundamentally altered the old *rancho* economy. Gradually, farms and ranches emerged which used different production techniques and required different amounts and types of labor. As the local demand for labor declined, Mexicano laborers adapted and found alternative, better paying jobs in the fields and canning factories of the North. The development of this northern alternative of a migrant labor stream further undermined the traditional, paternalistic *rancho* economomy. The exploitative, paternalistic relationships between the *patrones* and their debt-ridden *sembradores* or poorly-paid *vaqueros* gradually broke down. The decline of this early North County political economy ultimately gave rise to new views of Anglo-Mexicano relations and independent Mexicano political activity. Given the central importance of such economic changes for contemporary ethnic relations, the next sections will describe, first, the changes in various types of Anglo ranches and farms, and second, the Mexicano migrant way of life.

Changing Agricultural Production Systems and Labor Needs

As mentioned, Anglo farms and ranches became increasingly consolidated, mechanized, and irrigated during this era. Moreover, there was a large turnover of land. In six settlements, long-time residents were asked to list the owners and their acreages in 1920 and in 1974. In small farming communities the turnover of land ownership often approached ninety percent. Many of these lands are presently under lease or are consolidated into larger owner-operated farms. In ranching communities, there was a seventy-five percent turnover of the lands, but there were notable exceptions; several larger (5,000 to 20,000 acres) old ranch families still operated their land. Second generation Anglo ranch families, now in their fifties and sixties, were frequently leasing their land for grazing or for crops.

There were, then, very few original owner/operators left in either farming or ranching. For produce and cotton growers, who shifted to peanuts, the percentages of original owner/operators were even smaller. Further, there has been, since the mid-fifties, a growing influx of

74

outsiders. Wealthy businessmen and professionals are buying local range land. Stories of some New York or Houston doctor "buying the old so-and-so place" passed almost daily among land agents and local farmers. The records of local soil conservation agents indicated that approximately fifty percent of the lands are in the hands of outsiders. The local tax assessor, from addresses, and land agents, from sales experience, also estimated approximately the same amount of land sales to outsiders. The price of land, from a local perspective, has become "ridiculously high." Unimproved range land that many locals purchased in the twenties for two dollars an acre and in the forties for twenty dollars an acre now sells for $400 to $500 an acre. The price is still rising fast; improved farmland is up to $700 to $800 an acre.

This tremendous inflation of land prices has encouraged many old-timers and their heirs, who no longer farm, to sell out at substantial profits. Actually working their land often brings a much lower return than urban investments. Most local ranchers figure a three to five percent return on their capital. Vegetable farmers expect a ten to twenty-five percent return. A boom year brings a much higher rate and a poor year losses. A peanut or cotton allotment provides a guaranteed income, which brings a steady ten to fifteen percent on one's investment. Unless, then, one is a gambler with fresh produce or has the security of an allotment, the local lands are considerably more valuable when sold to people seeking recreational land or tax write-offs.

Who does operate the local lands if not the original families? Generally, there has been a trend back towards tenancy and lease-operation. The present leasers are predominantly second and third generation South Texas Anglos and constitute a new class of modern businessmen. This group now includes approximately a dozen Mexicano farmers, most of whom were originally *contratistas* and *truckers* during the migrant era. One Mexicano family has become one of the world's largest watermelon shippers, and they lease several thousand acres of land, some from the original Anglo families. Generally, however, the modern rancher/farmer of this area is a middle-aged Anglo between thirty-five and fifty-five who owns a great deal of machinery, tractors, combines, trucks, and pickups, and who may have expensive irrigation equipment or purebred bulls and heifers. Most of these present-day operators own very little land because of its cost and lack of availability. Most farmers also must have substantial loans to operate on a crop-to-crop basis.[15] Such lease operators have pieces of land spread over the region and run highly mobile operations. They rent brushland or improved pasture from three to eight dollars an acre, and improved, irrigational farmland for up to fifty dollars an acre, generally on three to five year leases. The modern operator is always on the lookout for another piece of land and must compete for this scarce commodity.

Because modern agriculture is highly mobile and more diversified, perhaps ninety percent of the modern farm/ranch operators live in the market towns. This movement to the towns began when some large ranchers moved to town in the early 1920's. By the early 1950's even smaller operators were generally centered in the towns. Since many modern operators must invest large sums for machinery, land preparation, and use, the leased lands must be utilized more efficiently. Only intensive land use will bring a return from the investment and offset heavy interest rates on the loans. Consequently, modern producers practice greater diversification, which makes the distinction between ranchers and farmers increasingly unimportant. Indeed, the modern rancher's and farmer's operations are often as indistinguishable as their common western hats and boots and their pickups. However, there were differences in the crop-cattle balance of their operations, which affects the type and amount of labor they need and use.

Although there is a strong trend towards absentee owners and lease operators, there are still a number of owner-operators.[16] Several large cattle companies and large family ranches still exist. There are also some smaller owner-operated farm/ranches that have remained in the hands of original families, and there are places improved by newcomers in the last thirty years. One common kind of operation is what locals call livestock farming. Such a farm typically operates on 800 to 1500 acres of improved pastureland. The livestock farmer relies upon his cow-calf herd (fifty to a hundred heifers) and the winter feeding of Louisiana and East Texas stocker cattle for several months. The livestock farmer then sells his calves and the stocker cattle at one of many local livestock auctions that have developed since the war. Some large ranchers also purchase their cattle. Only rarely does the small stock farmer have an expensive irrigation system. In some cases irrigating a small piece of land is done to include a son in the ranching/farming operation without buying more land.

In some ways, the livestock farmer, with the emphasis on livestock, represents the modern equivalent of the early small dry crop farmer of cotton. The original small cotton farmers who survived have also developed larger, more diversified farms growing mainly peanuts and/or maize. In North County, there were approximately 150 "peanut farmers." In many ways they too were "livestock farmers," but locals categorized themselves as "peanut farmers."[17] Their primary income comes from the staple cash crop rather than their livestock. The average peanut farmer runs a very expensive operation requiring irrigation wells, machinery, and labor. A farmer typically has two irrigation wells ($30,000 apiece) that serve approximately 300 acres. A number of farmers own that much land, but as many others operate on a lease basis. This process of converting cotton lands to peanuts started in the 1930's and was a type of dry crop farming until the early fifties. At that point new irrigation techniques and government allotments made farming profitable, larger scale ventures. Originally, peanuts were harvested with binders and threshed much like oats and wheat were in the Midwest. A good deal of labor was required in bundling, loading, and threshing the crop, and local Anglo families exchanged labor and hired Mexicano day labor until the advent of combines in the early fifties. Today, peanut farming is a highly mechanized, diversified and government subsidized operation.

The typical peanut farmer with 300 acres would also lease or own enough grazing land for a herd of 50 to 150 cows and calves. Further, most peanut farmers would supplement their income by bringing in another hundred stocker cattle and grazing them on winter oats for three or four months. Finally, they are likely also to use melons or maize as a rotation crop with peanuts. They may lease the land for melons to a big grower or plant them and contract a sale with a small melon trucker. They also sell their crop in the market town to a peanut pressing company which ships the bulk oil and waste to other food and feed-processing plants. There are also several much larger peanut farmer operators with large acreages (1000 to 1500) and much larger cattle herds, but the pattern would be essentially the same.

The small farmer/rancher with 80 to 200 acres still exists, but most of these people must work in town or in nearby urban areas to supplement their income. The very small operator is generally someone who still wants to live in the country, or a city man who "keeps his hand in the land and has a few cattle." This group generally includes a growing number of Mexicanos who have made money in their trades, stores, or professions. It also includes working class Anglos who never made it into bigger farming or are trying to follow their fathers in a small way. Generally, such small places are anachronisms, or they represent recent back-to-the-country and recreational trends. The small farmer of the past has generally evolved into a fairly sizeable stock farmer or peanut farmer, or he has not survived.

The labor used by these two types of producers follows a similar pattern. The laborers who run the machines and manage their irrigation systems are usually local Mexicanos. Historically, some of these laborers represent the most unchanging relationship with Anglo *patrones* in the *rancho*. Some local Mexicano families who still live on the ranches are the second generation to work for the owners. Some present-day workers have been with their boss for twenty years or more. Modern-day owners and laborers estimate that approximately fifty percent of these workers live on the ranches, and the rest live in town and commute daily. The overall working conditions for the permanent agricultural laborers have improved considerably since the early period. Some are paid the federal minimum wage and work eight or ten hour days. Their male children often work parttime for the landowners. Those living in the *rancho* have rent-free but very modest one or two-room houses and usually a garden and some animals. Their children ride the bus to school, and all these families have cars. Even though the producer-worker relationships have become less paternalistic, many of the modern Mexicano agricultural laborers remain relatively isolated from the new social and political life in North Town.

The modern Mexicano farm hands often act as intermediaries and foremen for the Anglo producer in his relationship with *mojado* (wetback) labor. The "wets" are used for grubbing, fence mending, cleaning and moving irrigation lines, and other heavy manual labor. These "wets" are generally a highly transitory group, often staying several months and then returning to Mexico to visit their families. Many local growers indicated that those who stay several months will often return and leave periodically. Others, generally unmarried, may stay on a farm or ranch for several years. Others may only work a few days while passing through en route to Texas cities or to northern and western agricultural and industrial areas. The "wets" are paid five or six dollars a day and are given board in small houses, garage apartments, or barns. Generally, the work is very hard and the accommodations quite sparse. These modern farms and ranches generally need considerably less field labor than the early cotton farmers. The number of local Mexicanos still living or working on the *ranchos* is a fraction of what it was in the early period.

The large vegetable operator of today is also a far cry from the early small produce farmer.[18] As indicated, the produce industry went through some very hard years in the early thirties and began to revive during and after the war. Local producers attributed this revival to the coming of a major canning plant, pesticides, herbicides, and an improved market after the war. Very quickly, only a few large growers established themselves as the major operators. Those produce men who survived have generally developed highly integrated production systems that control the growing, packing, shipping, and marketing. The major produce men have their own sheds and a well-developed set of trucking and marketing contacts throughout the United States. They operate their produce business for a nine-month period from mid-October to July and deliver the bulk of this region's winter vegetables to the North.

Several of the largest operations in the region are branches of large urban-based corporations that have come in during the last twenty years. They have other operations in Florida, the Rio Grande Valley, Mexico, and other Southwestern regions. Further, there are also a few individuals who have developed prosperous lease operations. In the northern parts of this region the vegetable growers have diversified into grain and cotton farming.[19] The bulk of the local growers are, however, original families who have generally built their vegetable empires since the early forties. They are family operations with brothers or fathers and sons sharing the work. One brother or son may be the expert in bookkeeping and shipping, another in field production, and a third in sales.

Some of these operators, particularly in nearby Aztlán County, the major vegetable growing area of the region, own several thousand acres of irrigated land. Others, particularly in North County, operate largely on short-term leases and own much smaller pieces of land. The harvesting of melons, spinach, cabbage, and lettuce is still done by hand. Machines are used to dig up potatoes, carrots, and onions, and field labor sacks and loads them. A variety of irrigation systems, open canal, sprinkler, and pipe from deep wells and from rivers are being used. The most common are deep wells and the open canal or movable sprinklers, both rolling pipe and ground level tubes. The vegetables are packed and sacked in the fields and regraded and packed for shipping in sheds in the market towns.

The capital investment of vegetable operators in fertilizer, irrigation, land preparation, cultivation, and harvest labor is extensive. This varies considerably with water availability, type of fertilizer and crop, and other factors, but it is not uncommon for growers to invest more than $1,000 an acre to produce a crop. Most vegetable growers have also begun to diversify into other crop areas and into cattle ranching. The vegetable crop lands are put on a rotation system with winter oats and grasses and utilized for cattle. Likewise, soybeans, maize, and hay crops are used in land rotations and sold for cash or used for cattle feed. This allows the growers to increase greatly their land and permanent labor use and to create alternative sources of income during bad vegetable years.

The marketing of vegetables also varies considerably with each crop, season, and type of operator.[20] The large operators with sheds sell through brokers and buyers from large chain stores or wholesalers and ship freight cars or truckloads of merchandise out on well-organized schedules. The small growers and larger ones without sheds, however, often supply independent truckers and small brokers who come into the area to speculate on a few loads of melons or onions. Often the small operators fight each other to buy, and competition is keen. Conversely, sellers also compete and play off buyers and competitors against each other, fighting for the best possible price. Most transactions are verbal contracts, and a good deal of competition, luck, and disorder seem characteristic of the small vegetable marketing process. The small producer and buyer have relatively little control over the process and are much more prone to losses in spoilage, poor grading, and under-pricing.

The labor used for local vegetable growing makes up the bulk of present-day North County farm labor. The system of local labor use has gone through a number of changes since the return of vegetables in the mid-forties. From the mid-forties to the late fifties, many of the larger growers apparently relied heavily on *bracero* labor.[21] During the hey-day of the northern migrant stream, North County wages simply were not competitive with the northern sugar beet companies and fruit and vegetable growers and canneries. Most local growers were only able to hold a portion of their workers because of the loyal *contratistas*. Often growers worked out accommodations where their laborers could go north during the summer with these local *contratistas* or on their own. The major source of their harvest labor during the late spring and summer months, from late October to mid-April, was non-local.

Several local growers estimated that during the late forties over half of their labor was *bracero* or "wet" because there were not enough locals. Local *contratistas* generally described the same situation. However, as the *bracero* program became progressively more expensive and as the northern migrations began to decline (by the fifties), the local growers shifted back to a combination of "wet," green-card, and more or less permanent local labor.

The present-day crews are a relatively stable group of local Mexicanos and green-carders. They are generally under one contractor who works for one grower. The large growers in the vegetable centers have a diverse enough crop rotation to provide roughly nine months of work. The crew labor generally work by some piece rate, e.g., per basket or sack, and live in town or commute back to the border towns. If they are "wets," they live in dormitories often built originally for the *braceros*. Growers and labor contractors had difficulty estimating the relative decline in field labor needs, but roughly one half as much labor

80

is necessary for harvesting many of the vegetable crops. Since more vegetable packing is done in sheds, there are now some semi-permanent shed hands. Some pack on the piece-work system, others are paid the minimum wage.

The second part of the local grower's labor force is the permanent hands. Nearly all are locals, and they handle the machinery, fertilization, and irrigation systems. They work on an hourly basis and are paid the minimum wage and are given housing, if they wish. The amount of permanent hands needed is generally estimated at one-fifth of the number needed in the forties. This is primarily due to mechanization and vastly improved irrigation systems requiring less cleaning and moving.

The area in general has maintained a relatively stable output of produce, but the total acreage under cultivation has been declining, as has the total number of operators.[22] Most of the increase in output has been due to improved production techniques. The region is, however, generally not an expanding produce region. Most of the new crop expansion has been in feed grains such as sorghum and oats, and there is a slight shift back to ranching in some parts of the region. In the Aztlán City area, local growers attribute this to poor prices and expensive production costs and to "labor unrest." In this case, the labor unrest refers to the Raza Unida and some recent unsuccessful attempts by the United Farm Workers union to organize farm laborers.

Ranching in the North County region has also gone through a number of major changes. Today, a good-sized ranch would start at around 5,000 acres and go up to 20,000 acres. Approximately thirty-five percent of the land is still used for ranching, but perhaps no more than five to ten percent of the local operators describe themselves as strictly cattlemen. Two major trends, 1) marketing demands and organization and 2) federal programs were often cited as major influences on local ranching.

First, the finishing and marketing of cattle is now done more quickly and through local auctions. The trend towards producing lighter, younger animals started in the thirties. By the forties producers were selling 500 to 600 lb. yearlings for finishing on Oklahoma bluegrass and in midwestern feedlots. In the 1940's cattle were still finished out to 1,000 to 1,200 lbs. By the sixties producers were selling 400 to 500 lb., nine-month old steers to feedlots where the cattle were finished out to 750 to 800 lbs. in only 150 days. In marketing, cattle are no longer bought by roaming brokers or shipped by rail up north. Most locally produced cattle are sold in regional auction barns that have developed since the war. These auction barns decentralize the cattle trading business and better regulate local sales. Finally, another major development has been the growth of large feedlots that finish out 5,000 to 20,000 cattle in modern, automated facilities. These feedlots provide local ranchers another market for their calves and stockers. Few locally-produced cattle are shipped elsewhere for finishing. The local producers can now afford to finish their own cattle. This development of an integrated, cattle-finishing local economy is, of course, made possible by the growth of irrigated agriculture and grain production in the North County region.

Second, in the early forties the federal ASCA programs for land clearance and water conservation were introduced into North County. Most local ranchers built improved water tanks through these government grants. This Department of Agriculture agency also paid fifty percent of the costs for bulldozing and root-plowing the brushland. According to extension agents, this encouraged the majority of North County ranchers and farmers to clear the land and plant improved grasses such as bermuda and buffle. Such innovations have increased the carrying capacity of the range from one cow per twenty-five acres to one cow per five acres. There have also been a few ranchers who have experimented with irrigated bermuda pastures to lower the carrying ratio to one cow per acre. But the expenses and problems with disease have generally limited this intensive use of the range land. At this stage of development, ranchers prefer to clear their land and use improved dry land pasture and winter oats.

Major technological changes in ranching have also altered the nature of modern ranches. Horses are still used in the brush, but much of the working of cattle is done by pickup, and huge ranches in the area even occasionally use airplanes to roundup cattle. The use of more centralized watering and corral facilities also helps bring the cattle to points where a few men can easily work them. There even exists a few custom cow-gathering outfits who, for twenty-five or thirty dollars a day, will gather cattle with a horse and cow dog. The days of the round-up and the cattle drive as well as the work camps, line shacks, and bunkhouses are long gone. Old-time *vaqueros* contend that there are no more cowboys left, that few ranchers know anything about horses and the art of working cattle. The labor force of a modern ranch includes several local Mexicanos and "wets," who are often responsible for the crops and farming.

The Changing Social Relationships Between Owners and Laborers

Changing labor needs in all types of ranches and farms have altered the general relationship of Anglos to Mexicanos.[23] The historical importance of the Mexicano in the local agricultural economy has declined dramatically. Today, there are a few permanent wage-laborers on all of the modern types of farms and ranches. There are also a few permanent hands left as field labor for the large vegetable producers. Finally, there are new jobs related to agriculture in canning plants, feedlots, and packing sheds. Those Mexicanos still working for Anglo producers are also under a very different wage-labor system, and a good deal of the earlier paternalism and chronic indebtedness is gone. The new class of Anglo leasers and absentee landlords with ranch managers are also very different from the original Anglo landowners. They live in town, generally in a strictly segregated Anglo section. Most did not grow up with the Mexicano, and they cannot speak Spanish. They have few personal relationships with their workers and do not expect to develop them.

A few Mexicanos are still locked into paternalistic relationships between owners and workers on the *ranchos*, on the crews, and in some of the local stores. Perhaps no more than twenty-five percent of the present Mexicano labor force is involved in traditional relationships with Anglos. The majority of Mexicanos still work for Anglos, but these new relationships are more modern and impersonal wage-labor situations.

Another important consequence of the changing production system is the degree to which absentee landlords altered the structure and solidarity of the Anglo community. These new outsiders often have little association with the local community. They come to hunt and party and "to play cowboy." Some make donations to local civic activities like the FFA stock show or the local hospital. Others invite local leaders to their "exclusive" parties. But generally, the growing number of outsiders take little part in running the local community or in solving the growing conflict between the ethnic groups. As the old Anglo families and their children leave, they were increasingly replaced by outsiders.

Alternative Labor Systems: The Migrant Way of Life

The other side of the profound economic transformation which occurred from 1930 to 1960 was the rise of an alternative labor system for the Mexicanos. As previously indicated, Mexicanos began moving off the *rancho* into *la colonia* by the mid-twenties. This intracounty migration is partially reflected in the census data on rural-urban balance. In counties with extensive cotton farming, this was a response to declining cotton production. In other counties, the Mexicano population was more concentrated in the market town and worked as crew labor for the regional vegetable industry.[24] Vegetable growing areas were also affected by declining production. The trend towards falling agricultural production continued through the Depression years.

During the late twenties other important alternative labor opportunities developed to attract the North Town Mexicanos. Large sugar beet growers and companies from California, Michigan, and Colorado began recruiting Mexican labor in San Antonio and several border towns in the late twenties. Several labor contractors as well as researchers[25] report attempts by local growers to keep recruiters out of the area. Some recruiters were threatened and even had their tires slashed. By the early fifties there were also offices set up in the smaller town, and the sugar company recruiters became links between the crews or individual workers and the northern growers who began attracting local Mexicanos to the North.

After the recruiters signed up a number of people from the region, they generally contracted local *troqueros* (truckers) to haul the workers north. They were usually paid ninety-five dollars a head in advance. Their job was to organize, load, and deliver the workers and their families to the northern growers. A trucker would load anywhere from twenty-five to seventy-five people into the flat-bed trucks and drive around the clock to reach the farms. The health conditions on these voyages were eventually condemned and regulated by interstate law in 1955. Many other migrant workers with automobiles also received their advance money and went on their own. After several trips they established contacts with the northern growers and went back every year on their own. The farmers would write or call them when the crops were ready, and the workers faithfully arrived on time.

Once the truckers arrived up north, they stayed during the picking season and often hauled produce to the canneries to make extra money. They were responsible for getting their crew of people to the right farms and for maintaining their general wellbeing. The migrant workers followed many different patterns of work. When the sugar beets were thinned in May and June, they usually went on to other northern crops or returned to the West Texas cotton fields until beet harvesting in October. Some picked cherries and fruit in Michigan and Wisconsin. Others harvested vegetables in Illinois and Ohio. Most migrants returned to the sugar beets, the most profitable harvest, before returning to Texas in November to begin the winter vegetables such as onions and spinach.

As indicated, opportunities for cotton picking in West Texas also developed during this period. Local labor contractors from these communties began taking Mexicanos to join the "big swing" from Corpus

Christi to West Texas. From the early 1900's on, the more economically advanced Rio Grande Valley area spawned labor contractors and crews that served other areas of Texas. Initially, Rio Grande Valley Mexicanos provided the bulk of harvest labor. Aztlán City contractors began taking workers to the West in 1930, and North Town contractors followed in 1934. By this time a much larger pool of landless wage laborers existed in the towns.

By the early forties there were approximately thirty-five contractors with a hundred trucks hauling 2,500 laborers. Crew leaders estimated that perhaps twice as many people joined this army of cotton pickers with their own cars. Pickers from these towns usually joined this labor force during July and August and worked from the Texas coast throughout Central Texas. By September and October they were in West Texas, and some even went as far as New Mexico and Arizona. Contractors reported that nearly all of the locally organized crews in these towns followed the West Texas migrant stream rather than a northern route. Even though the money was better in the North, most local *contratistas* preferred working West Texas cotton for several reasons. The contractors had well established contacts, some feared the longer trip, and they generally profited proportionately less from the northern wages than the crew members.

When the northern and western migrants returned for the winter months, they were organized by the local contractors. In the area studied, a regional labor system developed in Aztlán City, the heart of vegetable production. Several large *contratistas,* such as Mr. Suarez, organized and hired many smaller *troqueros* from the other towns and settlements in this nine county region. During the winter season, Aztlán City became the center of activity, and hundreds of tents and shacks housed the crews and individuals coming from the North and other towns. Whole families or the males of families in other local communities spent three to four months working, first, the spinach (February to April) and then the onions (May to June).

By the thirties a new group of Mexicano entrepreneurs had developed to organize the local Mexicano labor. This network of *contratistas* and crews spread out from Aztlán City and organized all of the local winter labor and perhaps thirty to forty percent of the great migrations West and North. Historically, they developed to fulfill the new labor needs locally and organize the more informal labor recruitment system of the early 1900's. They also began joining the western cotton migrations, which were initially crews from the older valley settlements, and the northern beet migrations, which initially recruited from the valley and border towns.

Many of the early Mexicano *contratistas* began their careers in the late 1920's and early 1930's. They were originally *sembradores* who had saved their money as sharecroppers and had moved to town and bought a truck. Outside of a few small merchants in the "Mexican Towns," they were the first monied, Mexicano entrepreneurs in these local communities. Nearly all were self-made men with no education who became informal community leaders. Several became important links between the local Anglo *patrones*, sheriffs and politicians, and the Mexicano masses. Their role in local politics and the mobilization of voters will be described later in the discussion of changing political machines. By the forties some of these *contratistas* became important political brokers as well as landed farmers, merchants, and money-lenders. The most industrious and successful third generation Mexicano community leaders were often descendants of these early labor contractors. They were also the ambiguous, hated figures in the migrant experience who were the ambitious go-between for the Mexicano community and the Anglos.

In retrospect, many migrants saw *contratistas* as Mexicanos who turned on their own kind and became rich on the sweat of *La Raza*. Others pointed out that some crew leaders were honest and good to their workers. A good crew leader had to be quite a talker. He had to be able to joke with people, raise their morale, and to goad or cajole them into working harder. *Contratistas* had to pretend to hate the boss for the workers, and to hate the workers for the boss. They often pretended to do the workers favors. For example, when it rained, and there was no work, the families ate "on the tab." Sometimes the crew leader was supposed to pay for this:

> The company had given him the money, but he never told the workers. Instead, he would say, 'I fed you, and you owe me such and such, and I will pay, don't worry, I will take care of you." Other times he would pretend to find us extra-good fields because we were the best workers, but he already had his assignment, he knew, but many people believed he was doing us a favor.

The crew leader held a great deal of power over his workers. He kept track of how much they ate in his little black book, and he weighed and marked down how many baskets or boxes each person picked. Most old Mexicano field hands were sure that he cheated them on their expenses and on the time worked; presumably, the *contratistas* would work the field hands an extra half hour a day. His clock was the one everyone followed. If he said six-thirty was six o'clock, no one questioned him. Crew leaders also received a significant percentage of each hundred pounds of cotton picked. For example, around 1930 pickers were receiving thirty to thirty-five cents a hundred while crew leaders received as much as ten to twelve cents a hundred. Most workers did not question the crew leader, and the crew leader was careful not to cheat flagrantly and offend his workers. He got his percentage from piece work and from the ways he "cut corners." For example, most *contratistas* tried hard to entice the best workers in the communities. They gave some families the best housing or the best fields to keep them happy. Several old-timers claimed that most contractors liked the *bracero* labor better because they were not only harder working but also completely ignorant. One common way of extorting from the *braceros* was to arrange for them to buy from one grocer who in turn gave a kick-back to the *contratista.*

As indicated, the very early labor migration to the West and to the North was initially under either local contractors, or local *troqueros,* who were company representatives or small-time operators. However, as the Mexicano migrant families became accustomed to migrating north, some became more independent of the *contratistas* and crew system. The enterprising Mexicano migrant who owned a car and knew the growers often became a "free wheeler." As early as the mid-thirties there were Mexicano families beginning to travel to the North on their own, and this pattern grew steadily as the years passed. By the mid-fifties the vast majority of migrants had become "free wheelers," and the number of local *contratista* crews or *troqueros* hired by the company decreased.[26]

These "free wheelers" traveled in small groups of three or four families. Very often they were an entire extended family of uncles and aunts and in-laws by marriage. Other times, these small caravans were neighbors and *compadres* who followed one particularly knowledgeable, successful migrant. Usually, the more knowledgeable and successful migrants had trucks, and instead of going in cars, the people would all ride in the truck. Such small *troqueros* neither worked for the companies nor hauled people by the head. They organized and hauled *bien conocidos* (close acquaintances), often the same group for ten or fifteen years. Some families report going together in small car caravans or with these small truckers for many years. Others frequently changed migration routes and partners seeking better work and money.

The striking things, however, about the rise and extensiveness of "free wheelers" were their ingenuity and group solidarity. The Mexicanos who knew hard times on the *ranchos* were willing to take great risks to help each other succeed in the migratory stream. It can be argued that the *contratistas* historically helped local Mexicanos find these new opportunities and become more independent of local *patrones*. But this would underplay how quickly many enterprising Mexicanos adapted to the new opportunities. They organized themselves into small, highly mobile, and flexible bands that exploited the opportunities up north. Neither the *contratistas*, the growers, nor the government made many individuals prosper from the migration. The individual Mexicano and his friends and relatives were the basis of migration success.

It is important to understand how central this migration experience was in changing the Mexicano's relationship to the southwestern production system. First, those individual Mexicanos who were successful at saving money and organizing their own work experience generally built themselves better homes and sent their children through school. Some of them accumulated enough surplus capital to build little stores or to get their oldest children into stable, wage-labor jobs in local stores, canning plants, and skilled labor jobs. During the forties and fifties, many of these third generation Mexicanos helped their younger brothers and sisters through high school, and some, through college. Some extended families became settled, non-migrant families who only migrated in the summers to make extra money. In only two generations, then, the "more prominent" North Town Mexicanos had developed from the poorest *peones* to stable, lower-middle-class workers in the local market town. The migrant experience was a very important form of power for the Mexicanos, power in terms of independent wages and small business investments which further freed them from Anglo *patrones*.

The migrant experience also enabled Mexicanos to see South Texas in a different light.[27] Many of the returning migrants could not slip back into the life of North Town without new expectations. Migrants felt that they had met a different kind of Anglo up north. Many were amazed that there were few segregated places and that some young Anglos even wanted to date their children. Others had their first experience of visiting an Anglo house and eating food from their table. The northern schools, health services, and houses also were relatively better, and many of their fellow migrants settled successfully in northern towns.

The migration, they say, was a kind of adventure, something one cannot understand unless experienced. The migrants remember fondly the "big paychecks" and being able to buy their children new clothes, as well as the *chistes* that their *compañeros* and *compadres* told. They also remember the hard work, but one migrant put it eloquently:

Life wasn't so bad. It was good too. I mean, the whole family was together. We worked side-by-side. We did things together more. There was much love . . . even though we got pretty damn mad when somebody wouldn't go to sleep or something. Things were not so bad. We made pretty good money. Lots of us did, and we raised a little hell up there, man, do you know what I mean? We had a little fun, too.

Migrating was an experience which drew the family together in a struggle for survival. Countless stories were told about how children and parents were drawn together and dependent upon each other. In the labor camps people shared transportation, food, medicine, and babysitting. Particularly in the larger northern camps the migrants organized *bailes* and celebrated many occasions together. The local bands and *conjuntos* traveled north in the summers where the money flowed and hard-working people needed to celebrate, drink, and dance. To understand the migrant experience, an outsider must remember that most migrants had experienced even greater hardships, isolation, and peonage under the share-cropper system. The migrant labor system represented an entirely different type of wage-labor system. Even though the pay was still very low, people knew they were going to be paid a salary, and that the harder they worked, the more they made. On the *rancho* they were at the mercy of the weather, the *patrón*, and fluctuating crop prices. For a crew laborer, such problems were somewhat alleviated, and he was guaranteed a minimum amount of security. Entire families would still go to the fields together to work, but they were paid by the baskets and loads produced.

People developed skills for working steady and fast, stopping only a few minutes for their lunch of tortillas and dry meat or for some water. When work was done in one field, they would move to another, never missing a day's work, quite different from *rancho* days. The daughter of a *contratista* tells about a working day:

We would go to the field very early in the morning, like at five o'clock. That was the ideal time to pick cotton because it was still wet from the dew and thus heavier. We wanted to start working right away, but the owner would not let us. My father usually brought a truck load of people, families from the neighborhood that would come to work with us. He was responsible for them and would receive a proportion of what they produced. When the patron told us to start working, we would fall on those fields like busy bees. I worked as fast as I could. Sometimes my father would come over and help me in my work by filling my bag. I enjoyed that. What I didn't like was when he helped other people who did not belong to our family. I would ask him, 'Why do you help them?' And he'd say, 'Because it is good to help others; if I am good to them they will be good to me.' And it was true, those people were very loyal to my father and always came back to work with him and for no other *contratista*. About noon, we'd all stop to eat our rolled tortillas. It would take us no longer than fifteen minutes to eat lunch. My father brought fresh water in great wooden barrels, and we could drink from it once in a while. After noon, the work became slower and heavier, because the cotton was dry, and it would take us longer to make a 100-pound bag, for which we were paid.

Yet, in spite of the positive aspects of the migration, it would be incorrect to romanticize the migrant way of life. The migrants also told many depressing stories about housing and unsanitary conditions. One prominent school teacher remembered how he stayed in a huge oil storage tank which the grower had cut open and placed in it some cotton sacks for beds. Others told of leaky roofs, of corncobs for toilet paper, and of rancid drinking water. Life was bouncing in dusty trucks, cleaning up dirty shacks, and packing one's belongings. Not all Northerners treated the migrants kindly, either. Many local growers and policemen hated these outsiders. The racism of northern whites and the feelings of these migrants are eloquently expressed in recent Chicano literature.[28] The harsh working and living conditions of stoop labor was not an experience that a weak, lazy people could have survived.

It is also important to remember that many Mexicanos did not succeed economically through migration. Many remained tied to the local *contratistas* and growers. Most migrants were neither able to get out of debt nor into some independent business enterprise. Most remained locked into the migrant way of life until there was simply no more work. Indeed, the pattern of recruitment and crew composition suggests that the poor usually got poorer. The poorer, less educated Mexicanos with very large families made less progress. Exploitative crew leaders were particularly successful at keeping these workers who lacked savings and transportation under their control. It was usually the migrants with medium-sized, well-disciplined families who became "free wheelers." The more enterprising ones were able to pick and choose the more favorable work situations. Their boldness was their salvation.

By the early 1960's the entire migrant labor system had greatly changed, and the crew labor system had virtually vanished. There was much less work because machines cut the beets, shook the fruit trees, and even picked the tomatoes. Presently, a few crews still go north, but most migrants are "free wheelers" who have personal contacts with certain farmers, or who sign up through the Texas Employment Agency. Most present-day migrants are part-time migrants. Increasingly, they go for one crop or to a few places to pick up some extra money. Most wait until their children finish school in May and return in time for school in September. Others migrate to work for seven or eight months in northern factories, and they return to their winter homes in the South Texas communities. They establish their unemployment in the North and collect it during the winter months. Still others work in the fields during the summer months, find employment in the canning factory, the packing sheds, or the schools (as aides) in the winter. A small percentage come back to rejoin the local crews who work for the big growers in the area. Even Mexicano teachers who have been migrants go up north to work the beets. Some talk of it as the "Mexicano way of life" and not only seek the money but also the heritage of their parents as well as their early experiences as migrants.

The migrant life, which sustained the majority of the second generation (1920 to 1940's) and third generation (1940 to 1950's), is rapidly disappearing. The problems of resettlement and reemployment are massive. Many of the South Texas towns have hundreds of ex-migrant families who have neither been able to save money nor make the adjustment to a settled, stable job in the local economy. They cling to the small houses that they were able to buy and long for a vanishing way of life. They often devise ingenious strategies for surviving. Perhaps the grandmother receives old age assistance; the children receive free school breakfasts and lunches; and the entire family gets food stamps and other welfare benefits, or families may have the mixed blessing of an unwed daughter on AFDC money. The younger children work part-time, and the mothers may be maids or dishwashers. Everything goes into "the family pot," and somehow, many of these part-time migrants survive.

The profound changes that these economic transformations have created cannot be exaggerated. The brief descriptions presented herein are not intended to describe fully the economic histories of the local production systems or of the labor migration. Nor are they detailed portraits of any key figures or roles in this process of transformation. We wanted to present enough description to illustrate how changes in the material culture underlie the changes in political and social relations. Before discussing changes in the social and cultural life of North Town Anglos and Mexicanos, we must describe the important shifts in local politics and the forms of Anglo political control.

The Changing Local Political System

During the early part of this period, from 1930 to the late 1940's, the

91

local leadership patterns in the city, schools, and county generally changed very little.[29] Indeed, this was the heyday of the two local political machines already described. The backgrounds and orientation of local Anglo leaders remained basically the same as in the *rancho* era.

Other important aspects of the local political system also showed little change during the pre-World War II period. First, public policies in the city and school only became consciously responsive to the Mexicanos after the war. Second, the gradual Mexicanization of local bureaucracies at the lower and middle levels of management only began in earnest during the 1950's. Third, some of the most oppressive sheriffs described by the Mexicanos operated during this period. Last, there were still no major Mexicano political organizations or elected leaders until the fifties. It appears that North Town Anglo political leaders began responding only when North Town Mexicanos and the federal government began pressing for these changes after World War II. Although Anglos generally initiated few new programs, they did begin to reform local politics.

Perhaps the most independent and progressive move on the part of North Town Anglo leaders was their overthrow of *El Cameron*. By 1940 several Anglos had engineered the partial defeat of the manager/marshall, Mr. Cameron. Earlier Anglo leaders claim that they literally sneaked a new reform mayor and two councilmen into office with a surprise write-in campaign. Twenty-five or thirty prominent citizens quietly organized the take-over. They generally agreed that "Cameron was getting too big for his britches," and "was ruining the name of their town." The reformers wanted a more efficiently run city.

None of the reformers, however, mentioned overthrowing Mr. Cameron because they wanted to help Mexicanos. On the contrary, many prominent Anglos contended that the only reason Mr. Cameron had become so strong was due to his control over the "ignorant Mexican voters." Mr. Cameron, if threatened, could mobilize several hundred Mexicano votes and a fair number of Anglos; consequently, the reformers decided to wait and write in their own candidates. At that time, Mr. Cameron was in "Mexican Town" trying desperately to round up his votes, but he found out about the plan too late to keep his titular mayor and councilmen friends in office. The election was won by only fifty-five votes, yet it marked the beginning of several reforms.

Initially, the new council, led by Mayor Goodman, a prominent rancher and businessman, re-issued a bond to pay off over $100,000 in debts. This helped restore the city's credit rating. Next, they put the record keeping, the utilities, and tax collection in the hands of other people. Mr. Cameron, however, remained as city marshal for another ten years and weathered two minor election challenges. Finally, in 1948 he was defeated in a hotly contested city marshal's election (more than 700 votes) by a man with support from many anti-Cameron Anglos.

During this era, city government was marked by a few controversial issues, but signs of change were evident. By the post-war era the city government was generally moving to transform North Town to a more urban environment. Ordinances were passed to regulate fireworks, animal slaughter, beer sale, gasoline storage, outdoor toilets, vacant lot use, and garbage collection. In the 1950's street drainage, street pavement, and garbage collection in "Mexican Town" became hotly debated issues. In 1955 several prominent Mexicano businessmen requested that the council pave and light streets. For the next several years Mexicano community leaders periodically requested the council to put in curbs, gutters, and paved streets to ease their drainage problem. Lighting and paving the street leading to the Catholic church was also a major priority.

North Town city councils of the fifties and early sixties generally included several of the most prominent local businessmen, the local doctor and two prominent "modern farmers." The councils of the fifties also included "working men" and "Democrats," but they were characterized as less influential. By the mid-fifties the prominent, well-to-do Republicans ran the city hall. They generally prided themselves on continuing the progressive, fiscally responsible policies of Mayor Goodman, a Democrat. They also saw themselves as beginning to help solve the problems of disorder, lawlessness, and filth in "Mexican Town" without excessive outside federal assistance. The emerging Mexicano leaders were particularly vocal on the question of "cleaning up Mexican Town." One city councilman, a local rancher, was called "Mr. Clean, the gringo who wants to shine us all up." He reportedly gained this reputation for his vigorous campaigns to clean up vacant lots and the "shacks" (winter homes) of migrants during the fifties. On other programs the councils apparently received considerable support, but there was a growing impatience among the new Mexicano middle class.

It is important to note that the city councils of the fifties and early sixties moved to include more Mexicanos into the local government in jobs other than janitors and street sweepers. Responsible Mexican businessmen were being included on the Board of Equalization, the election boards, and various other committees by the mid-fifties.[30] They were also being hired to be assistant clerks, bookkeepers, water inspectors, deputies, and other middle-level positions. None had key leadership roles, but compared to the thirties and the forties, Mexicanos were becoming much more visible as public servants. Some Mexican-Americans had graduated from garbage collector and ditch digger, but still did not have any decision-making power.

The issue of federal assistance became more important in the late fifties when local Mexicanos began requesting some form of low-income housing. Early discussions of this issue aroused much opposition to "socialistic programs" that would undermine the American way of life. By 1962, however, the new council, which included a balance of Democrats and Republicans and the first Mexicano councilman, voted to apply for Urban Renewal. Apparently, a great deal of misunderstanding existed concerning the urban renewal program, and even many Mexicanos, including an outspoken "radical" restaurant owner, Mr. Guerra, were against it. Likewise, many of the more conservative ranchers and businessmen saw it as a federal give-away program which would "break the government." Consequently, no such programs were developed until the late sixties.

In some areas of public policy, the local Anglo leaders of the fifties were, however, slowly becoming more responsive. For example, in the early fifties the city council was discussing improvements in water, drainage, lights, and pavement for "Mexican Town." Time and again the council agreed in principle to make various improvements but invariably "backed off" because of lack of resources.[31] Small South Texas towns have very small budgets, and local people are often reluctant to raise taxes. In those times there were also fewer federal government programs, but as the early Mexicano leaders pointed out, the Anglos were reluctant to tax their side of town to help "Mexican Town." They avoided incurring the wrath of friends and neighbors.

For whatever reasons, community improvement projects were often slow in materializing. By 1964 the water tanks had been approved, and by 1967 a number of streets in the flooded area had been paved. But the major problem, drainage, despite several expensive surveys and considerable discussion, still remains unresolved. The North Town council also began discussing the possibility of subsidized federal housing projects during the mid-fifties, and they ultimately built one hundred units in 1968. The general lag time on most projects seemed to be from ten to fifteen years, which has often led to greatly inflated completion costs. It also left the increasingly active local Mexicano leaders frustrated by the slow pace of change set by Anglo-controlled councils.

The other North Town political machine under the thirty-four year guidance of Judge Paulson ended in 1954 with the judge retiring in poor health. Before retiring, he gave his support to the present judge, Mr. Ransom, a former county commissioner and drugstore clerk. Some

Anglos contend that his machine continues under the present judge, but others feel that Mr. Ransom has never developed the stature and control of Judge Paulson. Prominent Anglos often speak unfavorably of Ransom and indicate that they have been unsuccessful in "getting rid of him." In the early 1950's a prominent lawyer from one of the town's oldest families challenged him unsuccessfully. The same . group of "rich Anglos" reportedly challenged him again in the sixties, but with the strong support of rural Anglos, several hundred Mexicanos, and the Masons, Judge Ransom has held office for more than twenty years. During this entire period, the earlier pattern of commissioners and county officials holding office for ten to twenty years continued.

The major issue that most residents remembered was the loss of one rural school district which contained oil lands. Annexing this area in the early fifties could have profited the North Town school district. The judge and commissioners were frequently blamed for this oversight. The other source of concern usually mentioned was an occasional county sheriff who had become too "big for his britches" and had begun "whoring around." Others made charges that Judge Ransom and some of the commissioners were crooked, but no one substantiated such accusations. Generally, residents were critical of county officials and the judge for doing little, but the relative stability of county leadership suggests that no major issues or scandals rocked the courthouse during this era. Nor can one point to any major efforts on the part of the county government to address itself to the problems of urban or rural Mexicanos.

Local politics centering on school issues were generally quiet during the forties and fifties. Under the stimulus of new state funding, formulas based on average daily attendance (Gilmer-Akin Act, 1949), and the momentous civil rights cases (Brown vs. Topeka, 1954), the issue of improving segregated schools became an important community issue in this region of Texas. Some of the early informal political organizations, the G.I. Forum and LULAC (League of United Latin American Citizens) stressed education. They worked for scholarships and sought to raise the educational aspirations of Mexicanos. The North Town LULAC did not press the local school district for a strong desegregation program. By 1948 the North Town schools had been integrated above sixth grade, and the influx of large numbers of Mexicanos into the high school ultimately raised new issues. These conflicts over student extracurricular honors, grading, grouping, and tax bonds will be described in chapter four. The Mexicano leaders of the fifties still tended to favor a segregated Mexican Parent-Teachers Club to improve their community school. School desegregation became a sensitive issue only with increasing outside federal pressure and greater Mexicano political activity.

The Rise of Informal Mexicano Political Groups

As Mexicanos began attending council and school board meetings and demanding more and equal services, they developed their own nascent political organizations. Most of this new activity was attributed to returning war veterans and to lawyers from the San Antonio G.I. Forum and LULAC groups. These state-wide organizations helped organize a G.I. Forum chapter in 1953 and a LULAC in 1954. The G.I. Forum was for youth between sixteen and twenty-one, and they had approximately a hundred members. The organization only lasted for a year, and their meetings were mainly social and educational. They talked about local problems in town and what needed to be changed. They also had a baseball team and held various cake sales and barbecues to raise money. Many of the key members in this organization switched to the LULAC when they were organized in 1954. Two prominent Mexicano lawyers from San Antonio came to town and called a meeting of local leaders to discuss the need for education and college scholarships. They also tried to educate the Mexicanos about "how the Anglos run the schools and the city." These outsiders urged the Mexicanos to run for such offices and have representatives. This ultimately meant organizing the voters and paying their poll tax, even though these groups were formally not set up as political parties.

Initially, the North Town LULAC had 150 members, of which fifty were active.[32] They held raffles, barbecue suppers, and bingo games to raise poll tax money. They also bought groceries for poor people, gave scholarships, and donated money to widowed members. All of the members were Democrats, and there was no strategy to create a separate party, or to openly confront the Anglos. These early LULACers ran as independents, and LULAC never openly supported them, but the eight to ten key members frequently met and decided who would be the local candidates. During the elections they also led the effort to register people, sponsored rallies, and usually spent three to four Sundays before elections working the barrios for votes. Several local businessmen, county and highway employees, an insurance salesman, and a few key truckers and farmers led the group. Other local grocers participated by giving food for the rallies. One restaurant owner always gave them barbecue plates to sell for fund raising. In short, the new Mexicano middle class was the backbone of this new informal ethnic political group.

In the early sixties these Mexicano leaders began running candidates for the city council and school board. They were successful in electing and re-electing three men to the city council and two men to the school board from 1960 to 1965. For a two-year period, they actually had a majority in the city council. Several of these elections brought out 1000 voters, and the Mexicano vote reached 560. This level of political participation had been unheard of, involving twice as many voters as usual. The vote totals also clearly indicated a block or ethnic voting pattern. Each candidate from the different groups received almost identical totals.

Generally, the new Mexicano leaders were not openly aggressive towards Anglos. They were careful to use no strong references to Anglo racism or political corruption. These new leaders were seeking some minimal representation, not control of local institutions. The idea of "controlling the town" in the fifties and early sixties struck several of them as amusing, i.e., so improbable as to be laughable. Consequently, the elections were relatively calm. Anglos were generally concerned but not fearful of a "Mexican take-over." In fact, many of the earlier Anglo leaders did not seem to know of the LULAC or sense that an informal group of Mexicanos was beginning to plot and politic seriously. Nevertheless, these new developments marked a significant break with the politics of the pre-World War II era. The Mexicanos were beginning to demonstrate the potential for becoming an independent political force in North Town, and Anglo leaders began recruiting Mexicano candidates and seeking to form political coalitions.

By the early sixties, the prominent North Town Anglo leaders had invited the two most successful Mexicans, a grocer and a melon farmer, to be on the city council and the school board. These "tokens," as some Chicano activists labeled them, represent the first attempts to include a Mexican representative in elected leadership positions. This was widely perceived by the younger, more active Mexican-Americans as a diversionary tactic, and some vowed to run independently from the Anglos and to beat them. Other Mexicanos not in control of the city were approached to form an alliance. A local Anglo car dealer, described by the early Mexicano leaders as more liberal-minded and not one of those "silk stocking" type Anglos, formed a secret alliance with the newly "appointed" grocer and a local Mexicano insurance man. These two Mexicano leaders were officers in the local LULAC chapter and the Mexican Parent-Teachers Club (PTC). They had become increasingly active on the issues of local police, street paving and drainage, and a new Mexican school. This threesome swore to vote consistently with each other and to solve these problems in the Mexicano community.

This secret coalition became evident during several heated council meetings, and the Anglo car dealer came under considerable fire from the "better class" Anglos. Generally, the Anglos were split between what several people called the "Main Drive Anglos" and the "silk stocking, hilltopper Anglos." The Main Drive Anglos refers to a working class and middle income subdivision, and the hilltopper Anglos is a reference to the upper income, upper-middle-class area of town.[33] These references also roughly correspond to political party preferences. The "Main Drive" Democrat was a big spender of tax money and the "hilltopper" Republican was a fiscalizer who cuts the expenses of public institutions. Finally, this conception also refers to a tendency for working class Anglos to be less educated, more crude and rural in manners, and for upper-middle-class Anglos to be educated and more urban in lifestyle. However, since the early North Town LULAC did not provide a sustained challenge, these social differences among Anglos created only temporary conflicts, not permanent splits. Generally, both factions had representatives on the school and city boards. During the early sixties, however, the "Main Drive Anglos" and their Mexicano allies tended to control local city and school politics.

The coalition between some Main Drive Anglos and LULAC Mexicanos helped "keep out" more "radical" Mexicano organizations such as PASSO (Political Association of Spanish-Speaking Organizations). Outside organizations stayed out for several reasons, but primarily because of a split in the North Town Mexicano group between "moderates" and "radicals."[34] The members of both factions were actually indistinguishable in terms of class, ethnic, and language differences, but they did have some disagreements on proper political tactics. The more "radical" elements included several businessmen. The most active was Mr. Guerra, a restaurant owner, who was described as "crazy" and "an Anglo-hater." He was against the secret coalition with Main Drive Anglos. But when local Mexicanos were approached by PASSO organizers in 1962, they rejected "going PASSO." The moderates feared both a power play by a coalition between outsiders and radicals, and the response of local Anglos. The radical faction was also ambivalent about having outsiders come in, and they were primarily interested in criticizing the moderates for their lack of independence from Anglos.

Ideologically, there seemed to be little difference between the old LULACers who labeled themselves "radical" and "moderate." They were all committed to electoral politics, fiercely loyal to America, and generally for a gradual introduction of new federal social welfare programs such as urban renewal, migrant education, and social welfare service programs. The more radical elements seemed to place more emphasis on being Mexicano and were more distrustful of Anglos. The more moderate LULAC leaders were often criticized for "becoming too Anglo."

By the mid-sixties both Mexicano factions were represented in the city and school, but the continuing squabbling and personal conflicts eventually split the LULAC Club and the informal political group which sprang from it. The key incident which apparently ended the club was the treasurer's mishandling of some of the funds. At that point the more moderate members withdrew, accusing the radicals of mismanagement. Even before this incident, however, the outspoken Mr. Guerra had "dropped out," because he apparently suffered too much criticism about his personal affairs. He, as well as several other early Mexicano political leaders, expressed a great deal of bitterness about how ungrateful his own people were, how they turned against him. He also contended that the Anglos harassed him and several others who were active. He claimed that he was refused a loan for his business and threatened with a foreclosure on another debt. By the mid-sixties this first serious effort by Mexicanos to "play politics" had ended quietly.

Changing Informal Anglo-Mexicano Political Linkages

The challenged Anglo leaders of the post-war era sought to establish new binding relationships with the growing number of Mexicano voters. Up to the post-war days very few Mexicanos voted. There were, however, local Anglo politicians who developed blocks of several hundred Mexicano voters. They did this through a variety of favors, or apparent favors; if they needed the votes, they would call upon "their" indebted Mexicans to vote. Very frequently these local sheriffs or judges or mayors ran unopposed; consequently, there was seldom a need to mobilize "their Mexicans." Nevertheless, every good political entrepreneur "got himself a good Mexican to get out his vote."[35] Even the earlier Anglo politicians had "their man in Mexican Town" to help round up votes.

In their descriptions of "their Mexicans" a general pattern emerged. Labor contractors, *cantina* and restaurant owners, and Mexicanos working in public positions such as a city or postal clerk had natural contacts with many Mexicanos. They also had occasion to do them favors, e.g., extra work, a free beer, and a hand-delivered letter. Such men were also sometimes financially better off and occasionally made small private loans. Generally, however, the local merchants were the money lenders, and they did not usually make good go-betweens for the would-be Anglo politician. Further, some exceptional Anglos also served as the leg-men for the key Anglo political leaders. They were generally small-time businessmen or bureaucratic functionaries who dealt frequently with the Mexicano community and knew Spanish.

In North Town Marshal Cameron had operated through a local *cantina* owner and the local dance hall proprietor. He reportedly allowed both to bootleg liquor and frequently did them favors by disposing of rowdy drunks. In return, Mr. Cameron received their assistance during election time. Several old-timers described how he would ride around "Mexican Town" with these men during the week before elections. They also actively assisted him in bringing people to vote. Mr. Cameron's other major intermediary was a well-known labor contractor. He described how the Anglos always came to his house seeking advice and political assistance. He frequently advised his workers how to vote and actively campaigned for *"El Cameron,"* or the "man" as he called him. All of the ex-politicians interviewed emphasized how important it was to have such connections with the Mexican community. Without able intermediaries it became increasingly difficult to control the local Mexican vote.

One prominent political intermediary described the common feelings and type of relationship these 1940's and 1950's intermediaries had:

Ya, sure, me and _____ and _____ always used to help the gringos get Mexican votes. We worked hard to talk to those people so they would vote. Mexicanos in those days were *muy pinchones* (very tight, closed). You had a hell'uva time gettin' 'em to come out of their house and help you with a vote. They just wasn't used to such things, so the gringos needed us real bad. We all used to work for all the Democratic candidates who would come in here looking for Mexican votes. I even worked for Dolph Briscoe once. He was a young man then. He came to talk with me. The sheriff brought him over because he knew I was gettin' pretty active then. He told me about himself and how he liked Mexicans and wanted their votes. As he was walking away he put four twenties in my shirt pocket. I was so surprised; man, I worked like hell for him talking to people. After he gave me the money, me and my friends went out and had a big dinner. We drank and talked and celebrated. Then we all worked for him. Man, we thought we was in the big time with all that money. I'm ashamed to say that now, but it sure was good then.

To many aspiring Mexicano *políticos* of this era such "Anglo connections" were the most one could hope for. Such roles were the beginning of political activity.

Even though this practice of having a "Mexican contact" was important to leaders like Cameron and Paulson, the post-war era greatly increased the need for such linkages with "Mexican Town." As the landed *patrones* controlled their workers less directly and Mexicanos left the isolated life on the *rancho,* a new set of conditions emerged for Anglo politicians. The number of North Town Mexicano voters in the fifties more than doubled, due to general population increases and the LULAC voter registration drives.[41] A much smaller percentage of Mexicanos were totally dependent on local Anglo ranchers and businessmen. Many new ideas about civil rights, political activity, the ability of Mexicanos, and the injustice of Anglos stirred some segments of the Mexicano community. Mexicanos became less economically dependent, more critical of local conditions, and more aware of civil rights. New, more direct links into the Mexicano community were necessary as fear, paternalism, and voter apathy gradually declined.

This greater need for better connections in and communication with "Mexican Town" was well outlined by a very perceptive and prominent vegetable grower:

> In the old days when my father and his friends ran this town there wasn't much to it. Hardly anybody voted except your friends and your *peones.* But as time went by I think most of us woke up and realized that the Mexicans were beginning to raise a little hell and were getting harder to handle. Lots of the old Anglos moved away, there was a new bunch running city hall. Some of us, like me, have always had our ear out in the Mexican community; we let them know what is going on through our contractors, but other Anglos who want to be somebody around here have to know somebody to help them. Take ole _____ for example, he is a good businessman, a good Mexican, somebody who will help and every ambitious young buck knows that; so they ask him to help.

It was difficult to reconstruct the network of relationships that developed between local Anglo leaders and prominent Mexican-Americans. Yet from many such testimonials, it was clear that post-war Anglos recognized their growing isolation from the Mexicano community. They also recognized that they had to make such connections if they were to win local elections in the future.

This Anglo sponsorship and inclusion of influential Mexicanos into leadership positions meant more Mexicanos on appointed city committees and in elected city and school positions. Although the more extreme, "redneck" Anglos refused to accept that Mexicanos were capable of being local leaders, the more progressive Anglos reasoned that at least some Mexicans were qualified. A "qualified Mexican" was one who "thought Anglo" and was a "good businessman." Mexicanos who spoke good English, had some formal education, cooperated, and had good morals, i.e., avoided *cantinas*, were prime candidates.

Slowly, the Anglo power-holders in the post-war period began sharing at least some prestigious public positions. Along with the increasing use of political intermediaries and sporadic Anglo-Mexicano political alliances, this sponsoring of selected Mexicano candidates was intended to help Anglo leaders reestablish connections with Mexicanos no longer dependent upon *patrones* and *contratistas*. It is important to remember, however, that such new accommodations and political linkages occurred in public community affairs, *not* in the private social life of either ethnic group. The extent to which such changes affected Anglo-Mexican relations in the daily social life of key cultural institutions will be discussed in chapter four.

[1] U. S. Soil Conservation Survey for Aztlán and North County. United States Department of Labor, Washington D.C.: Government Printing Office, 1929.

[2] Hammond, M. B. *The Cotton Industry*, New York: The MacMillan Company, 1897; and James Scherer. *Cotton as a World Power*. New York: Frederick Stokes C., 1916.

[3] This historical reconstruction of the agricultural change process was based on a series of interviews with local producers. Thirty ranchers and farmers from different regions of two counties were interviewed extensively. Their interpretation of general trends and their life histories as producers and community leaders were collected.

[4] Tiller, James. *The Texas Winter Garden: Commercial Cool-Season Vegetable Production*. Austin, Texas: Bureau of Business Research, University of Texas monograph #33, 1971.

[5] See Appendix A, Table 1.3 *Crop and Livestock Production for North County, 1900 to 1969*. The analysis of the decrease in spinach farmers is based on the water district records and the reports of three of the remaining six major growers. The numbers are estimates, but the general trend is very clear.

[6] This reconstruction of changing land patterns was based on a sample of six settlements scattered throughout the two counties. Two old-timers in each settlement listed the landowners and operators in their settlements in 1920 and as of today. These original settlers and landowners were able to list quite specifically the families who made up their communities, how much land they worked, when they sold it, to whom, and where they went. The cross-check between two residents invariably turned up only minor discrepancies in their recollections. In general, a fairly accurate picture of the changing land patterns can be obtained without time-consuming work with land deeds. These recollections greatly filled out the census data on land ownership and tenancy rates in Table 1.2 *Farms in North County Classified by Tenure 1900 to 1969*.

[7] See Appendix A, Table 1.3, *Ibid*.

[8] See Appendix A, Table 3.1 *Rural-Urban Migration Rates in North County, 1930 to 1970*.

9 See Appendix A, Table 3.2 *Acreage of Irrigated Farms in North County, 1954 to 1969.*

10 See Appendix A, Table 1.1 *General Population Trends in North County, 1910 to 1970.*

11 See Appendix A, Table 3.3 *Fertility in North County by Ethnic Group 1970.*

12 See Appendix A, Table 3.4 *Infant, Neonatal and Fetal Death Rates for North County and Texas, 1970.*

13 See Appendix A, Table 3.5 *Spanish-Surname Population of North County by Nativity and Parentage*

14 See Appendix A, Table 3.6 *Out-Migration Rates and College Attendance of Mexicano and Anglo High School Graduates in Two South Texas Towns.* The pattern of return and its relationship to local community wealth and status was estimated by collecting the father's occupation of the high school graduates.

15 The financial condition of local Anglo producers was determined from the informal reports of two local bank officials. We never examined the actual loan records.

16 See Appendix A, Table 1.2, *Ibid.*

17 North County Report on Peanut Production. U.S. Department of Agricultural Extension, North Town, 1974.

18 Tiller, James, *Ibid.*

19 Tiller, James, *Ibid.*

20 Tiller, James, *Ibid.*

21 This interpretation of the federal government's role in local labor protection is based on the perceptions of twelve labor contractors. They agreed that the federal government eventually "meddled" in local labor conditions forcing them to provide better working conditions. Gradually, braceros were perceived as "too expensive" for the type work they did. Reportedly, no braceros were allowed to cut spinach. They were used primarily as fill-in labor in the crews and for special, lower-paying field labor such as staking and stringing beans. The best type of field work was given to the more permanent local Mexican workers, some of whom had worked for many years with their *patrones.* It was difficult to estimate to what degree braceros actually pushed out or replaced locals during the winter labor season. It was clear that braceros were very extensively used to pick and snap cotton in the West Texas migrant stream, and many new crews and crew leaders, predominantly from the border towns, developed in the 1940's. It would appear, however, that braceros did not disturb the set of local grower-crew labor relations which developed in the mid-thirties and forties for assuring southwestern growers dependable winter labor. Further analysis is necessary, however, to determine how local growers adapted to this federal policy, the northern migrations and gradual mechanizations. The actual role of braceros in well-established local political economies, from a local perspective of labor systems, is yet to be done.

22 See Appendix A, Table 1.2 and Table 1.3 *Ibid.*

23 The reported estimates of changing labor needs were not pursued in great detail. Clearly, much less labor was needed in all types of production systems, but to establish a more precise technical description of these labor systems would require better descriptions of the trends in mechanization and irrigation.

24 Taylor, Paul. *Mexican Labor in the United States.* New York: Arno Press and the New York Times, reprinted, 1970.

25 Taylor, Paul. *Ibid.*; and John Martínez. *Mexican Emigration to the United*

States, 1910–1930. Doctoral dissertation, University of California, Berkeley, California, 1957.

26 More recent trends of migrant labor were also obtained from the Texas Employment Commission. Very little accurate demographic information exists. The term "free wheeler" used in the text was commonly used by the officials who label the migrant workers. Local contractors and workers did not use this term, however.

27 Migrants interviewed discussed the socializing effect of the migration in very vivid terms. Most strongly believed that "going North" had a significant effect on their lives. Many also compared it to experiences that they had in the service. Teachers also occasionally reported that migrant children spoke better English and were more mature. More studies on the psychological effect of migrating would seem to be in order.

28 Rivera, Thomás. *And the Earth Did Part.* Berkeley, California: Quinto Sol Publishers, 1971.

29 This is based on an analysis of the yearly city, county, and school board minutes. All the monthly minutes were read and the occupations of all the candidates were then established. In the cases of key political figures, they were interviewed. Or more extensive biographical data was collected on them from surviving relatives, political opponents, and present-day officials. What earlier North Town politics was like was reconstructed through oral history interviews and these records.

30 The North Town city council minutes from the 1950's on clearly show this trend, if one counts Spanish surnames.

31 This pattern of policy issues and actions can be gleaned from a careful reading of the minutes.

32 Reconstruction of the early LULAC organization was done primarily with oral history interviews of the leaders in each faction. Some effort was also made to collect how the Anglo leaders of that period also perceived this new Mexicano political activity.

33 The difference between "Main Drive Anglos" and "Hilltoppers" was very difficult to precisely define. It refers to both a basic economic and a status or lifestyle difference between "prominent" and "not-quite-so prominent" Anglos. Each "group" tends to live in certain parts of town, go to different churches, dress somewhat similar, and socialize with each other. There are, however, many exceptions, and these are not very precise groups. Local people do, however, perceive and talk about these "types" of people, and at different points in local history some representatives of these "groups" battled each other for local leadership positions. During times of conflict, North Town Anglos will describe these groups as the "rich Anglos" and the "working man-type Anglo." No matter how imprecise the "groups," they have political and social significance to North Towners.

34 The terms "moderates" and "radicals" were used by North Town Mexicanos. This distinction tends to indicate the degree that Mexicanos are willing to confront, and possibly offend, local Anglos and traditional superior-subordinate patterns of ethnic relations. The terms are more related to the etiquette of power relations than to more universalistic, ideological positions.

35 Identifying who the Mexicano political intermediaries were came primarily from Anglo political leaders. In discussing their political careers, several Anglos described their "Mexican connection" without being asked. Such relationships were so basic to the political life of small South Texas towns that no one perceives this as a "bad" or manipulative thing.

Chapter 4

Changing Cultural Institutions
and Social Life in the *Colonia*

During this era there were also many other signs of change in local
ethnic relations. Some areas of life changed dramatically, while other
areas and institutions still preserved a degree of Anglo privilege. By
the mid-forties, "No Mexicans Allowed" signs in local restaurants were
gone. The spread of Mexicanos to Anglo sections of town was also
gradual but dramatic. A set of maps on ethnic housing patterns in
Aztlán City illustrates that Mexicanos were gradually moving "across
the tracks" from 1950 on.[1] As the growing Mexicano population sub-
sumed old Anglo sections, the younger, more prosperous Anglos built
new sections to move away from the encroaching Mexicanos. New
subdivisions have been added to both the Mexican and Anglo "sides"
of town, and these are exclusively ethnic subdivisions. Although no
attempt was made to replicate this study in North Town, the same residential pattern became obvious as the research staff learned where
several hundred local residents lived.

In a strict sense, contemporary North Town has an exclusively Mexicano "side of town" but lacks an exclusively Anglo side. The main
central areas and several of the old Anglo sections of town have become predominantly Mexicano. Two of the new Anglo subdivisions
also contained several middle income Mexicano families. Several upper-
income, exclusively Anglo enclaves still exist, however, on the original
"Anglo side of town." In short, the physical housing pattern of North
Town has changed rather significantly and has become rather integrated. Socially, however, neighborhood racial segregation is still intact.
The new mixed neighborhoods rarely function as social units, and
Mexicanos often go back to the barrio to socialize with their relatives.
More important, the main political leaders in the Anglo and Mexicano
community live apart in relatively more segregated sections of town.

Churches in North Town

During the post-war period local Anglos also began adapting in

105

other institutional areas. The Protestant churches, although still largely segregated, began consciously to adopt a more conciliatory, helpful posture. Before discussing specific cases, however, it is important to describe the basic difference between the Baptist and Methodist churches' administrative and financial relationship to the Mexican missionary churches. The Methodist administrative and financial organization for the region, the conference, is a highly centralized state and national organization. The conference, not unlike the regional hierarchy of the Catholic Church, collects and reallocates donations from all local parishes. They also recruit, train, and assign their ministers to local churches, with the approval of a local parish. Generally, the local parish has autonomy over its daily operations, but the minister is also directly responsible to his conference. Further, the Methodists are divided into a conference for the Anglos and a different one for the Mexicanos. The Mexicanos, unlike the blacks, did not vote to abolish their separate conferences during the mid-sixties. They have their own ministers, district administrators, and parishes that are supported from an independent fund for their conference. Although they are under the same bishop as the local Anglos, they are basically independent from the local Anglo Methodist deacons and minister.

The Baptists, however, have a much more decentralized regional administrative and financial arrangement, and they have no separate Anglo and Mexicano conferences. Each local Baptist church receives very little financial support from its regional and national organization, and it has a great deal of autonomy in selecting its minister. Qualified ministerial candidates "try out,' 'i.e., preach and interview, and the local board has complete control over who they hire and how much they will pay. Further, the local Anglo Baptist church is primarily responsible for any Mexican Baptist church that exists. Such churches are missions of a given local Anglo Baptist parish. The Anglo board of deacons selects the minister and handles the general finance and operations of these missions. Further, they often hire an assistant Mexicano pastor who works among the Mexicanos and encourages them to attend Sunday school and church with the Anglos. In either case, the local Anglo Baptists have a good deal more direct control over the Mexicanos than the local Anglo Methodists.

Historically, North Town Anglo churches, individual members, and some ministers have attempted to aid Protestant Mexicanos through various programs. In North Town the Methodists have substantially supplemented building funds for the Mexicano parsonage in 1944 and their chapel in 1950.[2] An ex-missionary teacher from a prominent Anglo Methodist family also started a kindergarten which was active from 1952 to 1965. The Anglo Methodists also established a scholarship fund which sent four Mexicanos through college from 1960 to 1972.[3] Finally, they currently supplement the local Mexicano pastor's monthly salary of $350 by $100 a month, and several prominent families have frequently given furniture and clothing to needy Mexicano Methodists. Although the minister can be a significant leader in such efforts, such aid continues as ministers come and go. Such examples of missionary aid are part of a tradition of paternalistic assistance through the church. Key local Anglo families were the prime movers behind such efforts. They reflected a general acceptance among the parishioners to "be neighborly and help their fellow Mexican brethren." Some Anglos grumbled about such "welfarism," but most rationalized it within the ideals of neighborliness and Christian charity.

There have also been conspicuous individuals who have attempted to promote new ideas about racial equality and integration. One prominent community leader, a staunch Baptist, was notable in his efforts to attract Mexicanos to the Anglo Baptist church. He was noted for attending the Catholic mass and the Baptist services, an effort perceived as an attempt to bridge the gap between Anglos and Mexicanos. He also promoted the Anglo church and Sunday school. An Anglo female Methodist missionary teacher was also noted for her commitment to improve the educational and social conditions of the Mexicano. Mexicanos described her as "different," a well-liked Anglo who lived and worked among them like no other local Anglo. She frequently helped local Mexicano families find economic aid to solve their personal problems, and she ran a well-attended kindergarten school for many years.

More recently, some Protestant ministers have initiated new ideas and programs to bring Mexicanos and Anglos together. The local North Town Methodist minister has attempted to work quietly with the more liberal Anglos in his parish to "build bridges" in the community. This has included attempts to have inter-racial youth recreational groups, a common Easter service, and increasing aid to the local Mexican parish. He has also preached several sermons that directly deal with the question of racial equality and the Christian ethic. In spite of these activities and individuals, it is difficult to argue that religious institutions have played a very central role in changing ethnic relations. The Protestant churches, which include over half the Anglo families and nearly all of the Anglo churchgoers, are still segregated. Most local residents are quick to point out that religion is "less important to people nowadays" and that the church has "failed to bring the community together."

Schools in North Town

Schools in North Town and the attitudes of many Mexicanos towards school also began changing during this era, but not without increasing confrontations. In the thirties only a handful of Mexicanos went to high school. Apparently, they literally had to fight their way across the tracks against Anglo kids, who were waiting for them with rocks and bricks. About these incidents, an old woman who had ten children and who sent most of them to high school, reflected:

We Mexicanos had to fight for everything we ever had, even the right to go to school. *Los pendejos* (the stupid) gringos would throw rocks at our children so that they didn't go to school. Now the gringos want us to forget everything and not hate them. They think that after the old people die off, that the new generation will not know about these things that they did to us in the past. But they are mistaken; for we shall tell our grandchildren and our greatgrandchildren what happened to us, and they will know about it. We shall never forget.

In the forties more Mexicanos went to high school. One Mexicano reports that the first groups of Mexicanos who went to high school were supposed to sit in the hallway and not inside the classroom, so as not to mix with the Anglos. Later on, they were allowed inside the classrooms but would sit in the back, apart from the rest of the whites. A woman who went to high school in the *rancho* describes her schooling:

We were only six Mexicanos in my class. Most families could not send their kids to high school because it cost a lot of money, like for books, clothes, etc. We Mexicano students did not participate in anything like clubs, and were not represented in anything like being class officers, queens, sweethearts, you know, all that stuff kids like so much. Well, to belong to any club or to vote in the class, one had to pay a fee. That really was a problem. Our families were already making a big sacrifice by sending us to high school. We couldn't afford the extra costs. Besides, the gringos didn't make bones about showing their dislike for us. They snubbed us at all times. We were not wanted there. We were a minority. So we just stuck together and survived as best as we could. Many would just drop out because they couldn't bear the situation. It was my children's generation that started to change all this. Blessed they be.

The Mexicano enrollments beyond the sixth grade were still very small during this period. Local enrollment records were not available, and the state records were not broken down by ethnic group. However, older teachers and administrators estimated that up to eighty percent of the Mexican-American children dropped out of school by the sixth or seventh grade. A study of the migration and advanced education of local high school graduates from the 1930's to 1974 revealed a very small percentage of Mexicano graduates until the 1950's. Even in 1939 Mexicanos were only seven percent of the graduating seniors, increasing to twenty percent in 1949 and fifty percent in 1959. Considering that Mexicanos were nearly seventy percent of the local population, this illustrates how little schools promoted the occupational advancement of Mexican Americans during this era. But even raw attendance figures do not capture the educational dilemma of earlier generations of Mexicanos. During this era perhaps more than sixty-five percent of the families were migrant farm workers who participated in the previously described western and northern migrations. Their children invariably missed three or four months of school in April and May and again during September and October. Several excellent studies of the general neglect of education for the Mexican American in the Southwest describe these same conditions that existed in North Town.[4]

In spite of these limited educational opportunities, Mexicanos had positive views of their segregated, physically run down "Mexican School." Most old students had ambivalent feelings about the segregated schooling they experienced. Not infrequently, they had felt humiliated by the Anglo discriminatory practices. Yet, they had more control over "their" school and avoided being compared to "superior" Anglo children in the classroom. The Mexicano children were among equals and did not have to prove anything to the white children from the other side of town. A fifty-year old woman described how the parents were organized around school issues in those days:

> All the parents did something to help the school and their children. We were united. Before the school was integrated with Anglo school, we had a lot of parties organized by the parents. We had dances like *jarabes*, and games, like bingo and *jamaicas*. *Las fiestas* were organized in order to get money for our school. We did all those things for our children. If the classrooms needed curtains, then we'd make fiestas to collect money and get them the curtains. It was like this.

There was an active club of Mexican parents and Anglo teachers. The parents seemed to feel at ease about going to school. The older parents who went to the school to talk with the teachers about their children say that they were well received by teachers. It was after children had to go across the tracks to the Anglo school that more problems began to arise. One local theory was that Mexicanos received a fair education in the Mexicano school because their Anglo teachers competed with the teachers in the "good" Anglo school. However, when children were put in a classroom with Anglo children, the Mexicano children often felt a sense of inferiority. A thirty-five year old woman reports on how she felt at the Anglo school:

> Well, the teacher would ask the other kids what their parents did for a living. Then, the Anglo children would say, 'Mine is a doctor,' or 'Mine owns land, has a big *rancho*,' and so forth. She'd never ask me anything, but if she did, I'd be embarrassed to say, 'Mine works in the field.' I wanted to feel proud of my family and my *papá* but was not able to among these children. I felt very stupid and was told I was a slow learner. I dropped out of 8th grade because I felt I just couldn't go on studying, that I didn't have enough brains.

The view that girls did not need as much schooling as boys was still held by many parents. According to many of the women, girls went through school mainly because they wanted to, and the parents usually gave them little argument if they decided to drop out. A woman's place was in the home, anyway, so it was acceptable for the girls to just help their mothers with household chores. They needed to learn to be good wives and mothers, since that was their destiny. The parents of some boys also felt that school wasn't really preparing them for life. An elderly man reported that when he expressed a desire to go to college, his father, a carpenter, asked him, "Are you going to learn a trade in college? Are they going to teach you how to work with your hands? If not, what good is it to spend all that money on college? What use will you make with that education?" Such views were very common prior to World War II.

Others often expressed the opinion that they did not learn anything useful in school anyway. Most told stories about the effect of migrating. In the fall they would come back when classes were already in progress. They would always feel stupid because they could not keep up with the other kids. When they got to ninth grade they were too old for the class, so they decided to drop out. In retrospect, most older Mexican Americans felt that their attitude towards school had been "foolish." Thinking that school was not very good preparation for earning a living is now seen as "immaturity" and "impatience."

In spite of low enrollment and high dropouts, after 1940 Mexicano views of schools and schooling began to change, and Mexicanos began staying in schools and pushing for improved educational opportunities.[5] The major change for most youngsters in the new *colonia* was, in

110

fact, just going to school. On the *rancho* many Mexicanos assumed that they were not able to compete with the Anglos. School was something they could not afford, and were not interested in, something that was irrelevant to their way of life. But in the *colonia* this way of life and their aspirations began to change. Not all parents were enthusiastic about sending their children to school, but the attitude of this Mexican was typical:

> I saw to it that all my ten children went to school. We made a lot of sacrifices in order to keep them in school. For the clothes, materials, books, etc. cost money which we didn't have much of. I used to get up at three or four in the morning in order to iron their school clothes and get their breakfast ready. I wanted them to go always clean and well dressed to school so that they wouldn't be ashamed of themselves or of their mother. These two rooms that you see empty now, in those days were filled with beds. At five in the morning I would start waking them up to get ready to go. They grumbled and complained, but they generally liked school, enjoyed learning new things.

Another woman reports, however, that her parents did not really encourage her to go to school, but she persevered on her own. For the most part the attitude of parents seemed to be like this, "If you want to go to school, *mi hija, bien* (my child, that is O.K.); if you don't, *tambien está bien* (also that is O.K.)" Usually, the more upwardly mobile Mexicanos, the ambitious offspring of the local entrepreneurs and businessmen, were the first to go to the Anglo schools and the first to graduate from high school.

Historically, the schools had an informal policy of allowing the "better" Mexicans to send their children to the Anglo school. Several prominent businessmen listed the names of the ten to twenty of the most wealthy and influential Mexicano families as pupils in the Anglo schools in the fifties and early sixties. Often these families spoke both English and Spanish in the homes and were anxious for their children to compete with the Anglos in high school. They reasoned that the greater exposure to English and early competition with Anglos would prepare their children for high school and even college. Anglos generally made these exceptions without serious reservations or complaints, and apparently most Mexicanos accepted these policies. Those who left the Mexicano community to go to school with the Anglos experienced a certain amount of envy and kidding about becoming *muy agringado*, (very Anglo) but this creation of a small Anglo-school educated group was apparently accepted.

Gradually, North Town Mexicanos in general began expecting their

111

children to go to school for a longer time. Many middle-aged Mexican-Americans indicated that their people came to expect that their children should finish not only grade school but also high school. Further, the well-to-do Mexicanos of the fifties began sending their children to junior college and business or trade school. The survey of high school graduates clearly shows this trend developed in the fifties.[6] By the late sixties the norm had shifted from finishing high school to finishing college, and sixty percent of the Aztlán City Mexicano seniors and fifty percent of the North Town seniors expressed a desire and plans to go to college. This increasing interest in schooling and higher credentials reflects more than a rise in the aspirations of "ambitious individuals." The Mexicanos as a group were beginning to adapt to local conditions, utilizing education as a means of self-improvement.

Nearly all of the migrant workers clearly sensed that their way of life was declining by the fifties. They spoke of getting education for their children so they could "compete with the gringos." They realized that there were very few local opportunities outside the limited business settings already mentioned. That the survival strategy of many families involved education and migration to the cities is reflected in the high outmigration rates of high school graduates.

The changes in the Mexicanos' expectations for schooling made education *the* major public issue. Poor school facilities, discriminatory retentions, and language policies became political issues. The early North Town LULAC organizations were critical of the schools. In 1960 the North Town LULAC began electing candidates to the local school board, and their major objective was to get a new school for the Mexicanos. By 1964 North Town passed a bond issue and built a modern air-conditioned elementary school to replace the old Mexicano school. They also instituted a freedom-of-choice plan, which allowed Mexicanos to go to the Anglo school, if they wished. North Town schools were not fully desegregated until 1969, however.

One of the first effects of desegregation was to destroy the Mexicano Parent-Teachers Club. According to several Mexicano leaders, when Anglos began attending their meetings discord developed. One former member described the situation:

> One could cut the air of resentment with a knife at that first meeting with the Anglos. Our Mexican president started to tell about the PTC, what we had been doing in the past and so forth. *Una Mexicana pendeja* (one stupid Mexicana) interrupted him to ask that Miss so-and-so, a gringo who was the visiting teacher, speak in his place. This gringa used to go from house to house butting into the life of the Mexicanos with the excuse that she was trying to help. The president let her speak. She said

that Mexicano children needed everyone's help because they were very poor and had no shoes to go to school. She implied that the reason they didn't have shoes to go to school was because their parents were drunks who could not support the family. I was fed up with all those offenses. I got up and interrupted her to say that if children didn't have shoes to go to school it wasn't because the parents were drunk but because the parents didn't receive decent wages from their Anglo *patrones*. That outraged the Anglo parents as well as the teacher who burst into tears. Right there and then, we were split, and the PTC folded shortly after that (two meetings more).

Another immediate consequence of the racial mixing was that Mexicano children were automatically transferred from level A (high academic section) to level B in their classes. This was done so that even slow Anglos could occupy level A. When some Mexicano parents went to the school to protest, the administration apparently said that the Mexicanos would not suffer from any change in the quality of their education. But many parents were not convinced, and they became increasingly suspicious of the Anglo administration.

Speaking Spanish was strictly forbidden. It had been forbidden in the past, but most older Mexicanos remember being able to use Spanish with each other frequently. Leaders of this era remembered that they were punished quite severely if caught speaking in Spanish even during recess. Although it is difficult to verify from the personal reports and the school records, it appears that Anglos began tightening up the standards for grading and language use during the fifties. Several of the older teachers and students claimed that Spanish was used more freely on the grounds and in the classrooms from 1930 to 1940 than during the fifties. This more lax policy towards Spanish was a continuation of the practices used in the *rancho* schools, and as one teacher said:

> It didn't make much difference then, the Mexicans weren't going to be anything but croppers anyway. I didn't worry much about them learning English. I figured most of them would go back to Mexico. Anyway, they were happy at doing their work, so I didn't see that they would need much English.

During these pre-war years the Mexicanos were not a political or economic threat to the Anglos. But as they became more independent of Anglos and began ascribing to themselves new societal roles, this new aggressiveness could be seen in the informal life of the schools. By the mid-fifties the Mexicanos were becoming the majority even in high school, and at least a small percentage of them were able to com-

113

pete academically and athletically with Anglo children. Retention rates had always been high. One Mexicano described how it was in the elementary school:

> We used to have a joke about what grade you are in. Somebody would say, 'what grade you in?' You would say, 'Zero bola con la bola,' meaning you were stuck in low zero and had not passed on to high zero. In other words, they had all these goddam grades, see. First you were in grade one, then you'd flunk or get passed to high grade one, see, because you were in low grade one before, they said. Then you'd go through low grade two and high grade two. By the time you got to junior high most of us were sixteen, so we dropped out, man, we were always *zero bola con la bola* in those days.

Undoubtedly, the rules were always strict about passing, and most Mexicanos also described being held back in the old days. But in the fifties, the Anglos devised better rationale for grouping and segregating Mexicanos from Anglos. In North Town they were able to get the Texas Education Agency to accept a plan to include at least ten to twelve Anglos in each elementary class with approximately twenty Mexicanos. The remaining 150 Mexicanos would be placed in all-Mexicano classes. They reasoned that for their social adjustment, Anglo children had the right to be with their own kind and not isolated or slowed down. The school district used such grouping devices, generally based on achievement scores and teacher recommendations.[7] Only the top Mexicano students were placed with Anglos. In high school the Mexicanos were strongly encouraged to take vocational courses while virtually all the Anglos were placed in college preparatory classes in which they were the numerical majority. To rationalize and reinforce this new form of stratification, the school teachers of the fifties and early sixties had to be tough. The retention rates were high, and the Mexicano was reminded through tough grades and strict bans on langauge that he was in the track where he belonged.

Many Mexicano students remember their teachers as this eloquent ex-student, who now runs his own small business, does:

> All I can remember about my teachers is them being on my back. It was always 'you Mexicans this and you Mexicans that.' I'll admit that I wasn't the best student. I didn't burn no midnight oil. I had a good time in school, but those teachers always had to put us in our place. They always had to make us think we were dumb Mexicans. I know they used to flunk us on purpose. We never got the breaks. They were always getting us with grades. Mrs. _____ liked to read the scores out loud so she could show how we all got the poor grades. They also got on you for

114

talking Spanish anywhere. I got put down for that lots of times. They wanted to make us feel bad, and they did, I guess.

Others invariably mentioned athletics and school honors as areas where they were discriminated against. In athletics the Mexicanos tended to excel in baseball, and the Anglos tended to excel in football. When Mexicanos did play football, apparently they were used mainly in the line on defense. Few Mexicanos were in the key leadership or offensive positions. The school annuals reflected this pattern, and several ex-players expressed bitterness that they were deprived of some extra glory in sports. Many Mexicanos claimed that the Anglo coaches tended "to give in and play the rich Anglo's son" over the Mexicano. Older Mexicanos complained that particularly the Anglos of prominent families got away with more disobedience and were more frequently given the favored assignments, seats, positions, schedules, and helpers' jobs. The Anglos' small privileges and relative immunity to disciplinary action were sore points that Mexicanos simply accepted. There were no Mexicano teachers and principals to act as advocates.

There were also stories of how Anglo teachers and administrators created ways to retain the privileges of the shrinking minority of Anglo students. They created a Señor and Señorita North Town High to go along with Mr. and Miss North High. This preserved the Anglo award by making an ethnic distinction. The cheerleaders and twirlers were also chosen by either faculty or by "an outside school/cheerleading clinic." Minimum grade levels were also set, which excluded many of the more academically marginal Mexicanos. A school activity fee of a dollar and fifty cents, in effect a poll tax, was also set as a voting prerequisite. In short, there were a great many policies that helped preserve the privilege of the Anglo minority. In the area of schooling, North Town Anglos, from 1930 to the early 1960's, were not particularly accommodating to the growing demands of Mexicanos.

Other Community Institutions and Agencies

Other major civic organizations and clubs such as the Rotary and the Chamber of Commerce remained almost exclusively Anglo. From 1930 to early 1960 there were virtually no Mexicanos invited to be a part of these organizations. Mexicanos were also noticeably absent from several civic projects such as building a local hospital, improving the local library, and celebrating the county centennial. These were all-Anglo affairs. Although a Mexicano middle class has developed, leadership roles, as in the case of the high school, were for Anglos only.

115

Likewise, the local papers continued to report primarily Anglo social events and personal items. Perhaps the major change in the newspapers was the increasing use of words such as Latin American or Spanish American or Latin instead of "Mexican man" and "Mexican Town."[8] The symbolism of American (i.e., Anglo) vs. Mexican was changing to a more hyphenated symbol for the "ethnic American."

Generally, however, civic activities remained exclusive or segregated. This trend even existed in children's programs for scouting and for little league baseball. There were Mexicano packs and teams and Anglo packs and teams. Several Mexicano scout leaders complained that they always got the old bats and balls and that their packs could not use the school buildings as easily as Anglo packs could. Again, the social fabric of daily life, the old society and its privileges, were dying hard, despite the profound economic transformations and the growing political challenge. In some ways, Anglos, in 1960, were fighting to retain these social symbols of their power in the community and in the schools. Conversely, Anglo civic leaders pointed with pride to their improvement projects such as the private county hospital and the public library. They expressed strong feelings that these projects were "for the Mexicans, too, even though some did not appreciate them."

Life in La Colonia and the Mexicano Family

As the Mexicanos moved to *la colonia* in the 1920's and 1930's they began creating an urban community. Compared to the *rancho*, the *colonia* of North Town had a variety of local institutions and organizations. There were new occupations such as selling *leña* (firewood), and working at the gin, the feed mill, or the canning plant. More women began working as maids and kitchen workers in the restaurants. The majority of people began joining the western and northern migrant streams, and a rather different way of life developed. In the market towns the Mexicanos also had their own church and plaza, a Mexican grade school and parent-teacher clubs, Benito Juarez and Miguel Hidalgo *mutualista* (mutual-aid) societies, and many new recreational spots. As the towns grew, the *cantinas*, dance halls, and grocery stores also prospered.

Many of these second generation Mexicanos were able to buy large lots, often entire blocks, when they moved from the *ranchos*. *La colonia* generally had a number of smaller sub-units called *barrios*. In early times, these hamlets were largely made up of one's extended family. In one plot the family would build the "paternal house" for the nuclear family. The surrounding plots were reserved for the children. The

116

majority of families were initially centered around the male family heads. As male children married, they settled on the lots of their father or grandfather, but a substantial number of the third generation children also settled around the wives' parents.[9] Where a new couple lived depended upon which family could give them a lot for their house. Increasingly, women preferred to remain close to their families after marriage.

Most people consider their *barrio* to include approximately one or two blocks surrounding their houses. Many of their *barrio* mates were relatives, although other new, smaller families also settled near the large extended families. Thus the community was formed around the family which continued to be the central economic and social focus of life. In the family, one could find refuge, the solace, and the care that nobody expects from outsiders. Even one's closest friends were often siblings or first cousins. The shape and organization of neighborhoods are recalled today by old timers with a great deal of nostalgia:

> There wasn't too many *disgustos* (conflicts) with your neighbors as you see today. Neighbors were like part of your family, even if not related by blood. There was more caring, more sharing. If a family had two slaughtered venison, for instance, that was a lot of meat, and they shared it with their neighbors. Besides, people were more willing to help each other without even being asked.

Even though the *barrio* was sparsely populated, people did not isolate themselves from their relatives and neighbors. All of the older Mexicanos who grew up in the *colonia* talk about the solidarity that existed in the neighborhoods. When children walked to school, for instance, a mother would feel safe about her children going alone. She knew that her children were being watched by every woman who lived between her house and the school. If anything happened to the child, a neighbor woman, whether related to her or not, would come to her child's aid or call her. Everybody knew who the children belonged to and a system of mutual care for the children of the *barrio* was informally established.

The older Mexicanos described how women from the neighborhood would drop by early in the morning every day in order to chat awhile with their mothers. Their doors were always open in order to encourage people to come in. Everyone was given *el pase* (permission to come in). Neighbors also exchanged a good deal of household help during the early days of the *colonia*. When a woman gave birth, the neighbors did all the housework without expecting any pay. When someone was sick, either the neighbors or the *mutualistas* took up a collection to help him, and women in the neighborhood helped in any way possible. During the migration numerous work-exchange and sharing patterns were necessary. One often rode with his neighbors. Those that stayed behind—the elderly, the very young, and the non-migrant—watched their neighbors' houses and cared for their relatives, plants, and animals. Visiting patterns were also much more extensive in those days. When someone arrived there was always food and drink. Most old-timers remember their neighborhoods as very real and active social groups. Some mentioned "bad" or "nosey" neighbors, but the emphasis was necessarily much more on cooperation and exchange to survive. Life during the thirties was particularly hard, and the migrations demanded a more collective and familial approach to life.

Socio-economic conditions in the *colonia* were often no better than the *rancho*. The Mexicanos of this period were generally poor, and living conditions were harsh by modern standards. Most families had *anorias* (wells), but there were also some public faucets for neighborhoods. It was women's work to go to the faucet to gather water for the household. There was always a small line of people to get water, and during washing days one could find people at the faucet until midnight. Washing clothes was an exhausting endeavor. But it usually brought together sisters and *comadres* in a common effort. First, they had to boil a great portion of water in a big tub in the backyard. Dirty clothes were rinsed, wrung out, and hung in the sun. Surprisingly, many women liked the work because they could be with other women in the family, talking and joking with each other. For a long time, most houses did not have utilities inside, thus the cooking would also be done out in the yard, as in the *rancho* days.

Most of the families that progressed and acquired some independence from the local Anglo *patrones* were characterized by a great degree of cooperation and a willingness to pursue many different kinds of labor. One Señora told her story like this:

My father was a *quartero* in the *rancho*. We all helped him in *la labor* (field work). The whole family worked, and my mother stayed home. She had her work too. She would prepare the meat, salt and dry it so that we would always have a fresh supply of meat. She canned food, sewed for the whole family, and kept our small house spotless. Then my father bought a little plot in North Town. He himself built the house which is still standing. It is not far from here. *Mi padre santo* (my saintly father) never lacked anything. He bought the plot near the *escuelita* (school) so that we children could go to school by foot. While he continued going to the *rancho* to work, my mother raised chickens and turkeys at home. Later on, after many of us were already married, my father decided to become part of crews and moved to another town where he could find more of that kind of jobs. Then he'd work everywhere in these two counties.

In town more diverse opportunities existed to improve one's condition in life. Everyone in the family did some kind of labor that would increase the family funds. Some people went to the *monte* (brushy fields) and gathered wood to sell in town. People would haul wood by wagon loads to the courthouse, the houses, and the stores. Each wagon load was worth from two to seven dollars. People also continued to raise chickens and pigs in their backyards to sell or to use as food. Eventually, however, a city ordinance (1935) declared it unsanitary, taking this source of income from many families. People also raised corn, took it to the mill to be ground, and then made bread and tortillas out of the dough. Other men set traps on the river in order to catch raccoons, and they sold the fur at the stores in town. Others would kill birds to put in the soup. There was also an ice plant and later a factory that made animal feed, employing thirty to forty people and paying two dollars for a ten-hour working day. That was an improvement over the one dollar a day paid by the ranchers. Women would also cook *tamales* by the thousands and set up *puestos* (stalls) under the mesquite trees in town to sell the tamales to shoppers from the *ranchos*.

Further, whereas in the *ranchos* no one collected Social Security, such federal programs became available in the *colonia*. People began relying upon and planning for them. For example, one lady was so interested in guaranteeing her Social Security income that she went to work as a maid and babysitter for an Anglo family. She earned nineteen dollars a week for the work but apparently had to pay twenty dollars to a woman who took care of her own children. Even though she was making no money, she persisted because she thought that Social Security would help her in the future. Several other women of this era expressed similar feelings about planning ahead with Social Security. In addition, most Mexicanos who worked in migrant crews gained Social Security benefits by the 1940's.

During the thirties and forties the traditional customs and practices of the Mexicano appear to have been substantially intact. Unlike other European immigrants, the second generation Mexicanos retained a great deal of their language and customs. Many Mexicanos in their late forties and fifties who grew up in the *colonias* during the 1930 to 1940 decade speak only very basic English. Few went to school, and their contact with the English speaking world was very minimal. They also

119

spoke the Spanish used in rural Mexico *con cariño* (affectionately) and *con respeto* (more polite, indirect, and with respect). Mexicanos of this generation also retained many of the traditional hospitality patterns, and one cannot go into an older Mexicano's house without being offered the best food and drink he has.

Many of the traditional family practices and neighborhood patterns found in the Hispanized, Catholic Mexican settlements of Northern and Central Mexico survived in second and third generation North Town Mexicanos. As in the *rancho*, the nuclear family was characterized by the presence of a husband and father who formally was the head of the household. As the main provider for the family, he made the decisions about money. The wife and mother played an important role as his partner in raising the family. She not only helped the husband provide for the family, but took care of the children and saw that they went to school and did their homework. She also instructed them in religious matters, customs, and manners. She ran the household with her daughters who would help dust and mop, make the beds, wash and iron clothes, and cook. The boys would be expected to help the fathers at work and, when needed, to fix things in the house.

Although the father was affectionate and in many families tried to be as close to his children as possible, the wife generally did not expect him to do "her chores" concerning the care of children. One wife described this common feeling:

> My husband didn't even know how to change diapers. If he would be left alone to care for the children, he wouldn't know what to do. He doesn't even like to help them go to the bathroom. But then I don't expect him to do things like that. However, when children are sick he'll stay up all night long looking over them. He is a concerned father who loves his children very much.

The way a husband showed that he cared for his family was by providing for them in the best possible way. He had to earn as much income as possible, show an interest in bettering the house, buy new furniture, and save money for the children's future. Only the younger, more modern Mexicanas expressed a desire to have their husbands help with household chores or child care. All the older (fifty to seventy years) Mexicanas expressed little doubt about what their role was as a wife and mother and what the male role was as a father and husband. They seldom questioned their roles and apparently seldom felt unduly burdened. Disciplining children was done by the mother, mainly because she was in closer contact with them. The husband would only take over when the child was being too rebellious, or when he thought that his wife was being too "soft" with them.

Thus, continuing the traditions of the *rancho* days, the man was the recognized family head. The woman typically followed his dictates, but she also had her own reserve of authority and power. The authority of the woman in family affairs also took on new subtleties in the *colonia*. Women whose husbands were upwardly mobile, successful entrepreneurs became free from field work outside the home and continued to be in full charge of the household. Their husbands wanted a wife who took care of the house and children and acknowledged their power by never making key decisions without consulting them. The wife of a successful merchant described how it worked in her home:

> I take care of the house for my husband couldn't do it. It is not only that he doesn't have the time, but also that he wouldn't know how to do it. A woman is faster at home chores and more organized. I discipline the children and watch over them. When children want to do something, they come and ask my permission first. Even if I let them do what they want, I tell them that I need to ask for their *papá's* permission for something. He looks at me, kind of tired from work, and asks, "What is your opinion?" I tell him what I think and he says, "It is all right with me then."

His role was to legitimize her authority, but informally, she often held much of the decision-making authority in family affairs. She rarely made important final decisions without consulting him, and the reverse was equally true in most stable families. Mutuality, then, was the common pattern.

The mother continued to hold a central role in the family. Even in the stable, male-headed families, she recognized herself as someone "special." Being a mother is being someone important and beautiful. This was expressed vividly by an older woman as she reacted to her son's comment that she was only a woman. She immediately perked up and said, "*No soy solamente una mujer, soy tu madre!*" (I am not only a woman, I am your *mother*). In effect she was saying that he had to listen to her or do what she was saying, even though he was a grown, married man. Her opinions were almost sacred because she was his mother. It did not matter how cruel or how uncaring the mother may have been, she was still the mother. No one could replace her. Stepmothers were generally distrusted, and stereotype of the "jealous" new wife who resents her husband's children was frequently mentioned. Being an orphan was the ultimate curse. "There is no one

121

like a mother to take care of a child," was the refrain of old and young alike. The only one who could substitute for her is perhaps the grandmother. Thus the woman could be characterized as the anchor of the household, and the man as the ship that will either take them places, loll in the same port forever, or leave them behind.

In order to fulfill herself as a human being, a woman had to marry and bear children. Women who remained single after twenty-five were considered spinsters; if they maintained their reputation as serious women who "did not run around with men," they were respected within the family and the community. They usually continued to live at their parents' homes, or in the case of their parents' death, with a married sibling. They often became an "extra" mother to sibling's children.

Married women said that they cherish having a large family and thoroughly enjoyed their children. Children were not viewed as an embarrassment or a burden. When couples went to a party, visiting, or even to an occasional movie, children usually accompanied them. One old woman explained, "If I was invited to go to a party and the children weren't to come with me, I wouldn't go. I would only go to places where I could take all my eight children with me." For the Mexicano family, the children were their wealth. Large families (seven to twelve children) were the rule. It was not until the fifties that a family planning clinic opened in the area. Until that time, women had no real information on birth control. Most women continued to bear children as long as they were capable. Cases of women having a child at the same time as one of their married daughters were still fairly common in the *colonia*.

The family continued to play a crucial role in the socialization of children, even after most children went to school and catechism class. Within the family, as well as with other people, there was a great deal of *respeto* (respect), especially from children, towards elders. Kindness and consideration towards one another were strictly valued and enforced. Of course, people were not always cheerful and loving, but nearly everyone emphasized that all behavior had to be infused with *respeto*, respect for *compadres* and *comadres*, for elders, for neighbors, for *patrones*, and for teachers. The respect that children were to show for elders was reflected in certain acts, e.g., young people could not smoke or drink liquor in front of elders, especially parents and grandparents.

Young couples during courtship could not demonstrate affection by holding hands, much less kissing or embracing, in front of their elders. A woman remembers that when she was dating her husband, they would come from school together holding hands, but when they passed in front of a relative's house they would be discreetly apart. To continue holding hands and allow an aunt or an older brother to see such behavior was to show a lack of respect. Children knew they had to kiss their grandparents' hands upon seeing them and did so readily, without being told. Failure to do so would bring great disharmony, and the child's parents would be accused of not knowing how to raise a child properly. Although such formality is remembered with nostalgia, many women also recognized that such customs impeded them from having frank and intimate relationships with their own mothers.

Children were only allowed to interrupt adults' conversations for very important reasons. When the extended family ate together, adults and children would be given separate eating areas, usually adults inside the house and children outside. Often children were served after adults, eating whatever was left over. If the adults had eaten all of a certain dish, children were not to complain or ask for that dish lest they embarrass their mother. A young woman recalls one time when she did such a thing to her mother:

> All my relatives sat down to eat before us children. My mother had fixed chicken *mole, frijoles,* rice, salad and fried potatoes. When the adults finished eating, she called us children to come in and eat. We sat down, and I realized that there was no fried potatoes left. That was my favorite dish. I made a fuss, complaining out loud that people had left nothing for us to eat. My mother almost died of embarrassment. She took the people to the other room and told me, "I am going to fix you now." Then she started peeling a mountain of potatoes right there and to fry them. She made a pile of fried potatoes and put them in front of me saying, "Now you are going to eat everything so that never again you will complain about not having what to eat." I started eating but soon was full, and there was still a lot of potatoes to eat. I cried, saying I couldn't eat anymore, and she simply said, "Go on eating, you are going to eat every single one of those potatoes." I begged my brothers to come help me eat, but she wouldn't let them do that either. Never again I complained about food in front of other people. My lesson was well taught.

Shame as a form of discipline was used in some circumstances, when other adults, especially a godmother, were present. The child could be made to feel guilty for giving the mother a *disgusto*. Adults today remember hating the times they were scolded or spanked in front of an adult not belonging to the household, especially their godparents. Therefore, they—and their mothers—tried to keep those incidents to a minimum.

Harsh physical punishment was rarely used by most mothers. One woman said that her unmarried sister, who lived with them, was the one who most often disciplined her children, since she herself was too soft to do so. Women who were known to beat their children gained a reputation as uncaring and cold-hearted. Moreover, women had to watch their children closely, keeping them inside the family compound when they were playing. If the children were seen regularly wandering around unsupervised, people would suspect the woman of having a lover and thus being unable to keep her children off the streets. To be uninterested in the welfare of one's children was a disgraceful thing on the *rancho* and in the *colonia*.

The Changing Mexicano Family

Despite a great deal of continuity in the organization and customs of the families in the *colonia*, the changing economic conditions placed new strains upon the Mexicano family system. The transient aspects of the local economy and the new opportunities opening up in other areas brought more separations and divisions within the extended and nuclear family. Families slowly started to separate, not losing their importance and centrality within the community life, but still being diminished by each man who decided to try his luck in the northern factories. All the people who grew up in the *colonia* had siblings living in California, Wisconsin, and West Texas. Many old women saw their children leave the warmth and protection of their houses to return only for occasional visits.

Moreover, life in the more urban market town placed many new pressures on every family. In the towns Mexicanos worked hard to pay for the new house, the new car, and all the material things they began to value in a semi-urban situation. Clothes became more important, since children had to go to school daily and show themselves decently to the other world. Children needed outfits for school activities, for participating in the *Diez y Seis de Septiembre* dances, shoes to wear daily in the summer and then in the winter. Life became much more demanding. Most families in the community responded to these new challenges with determination, using all their faculties to succeed and rallying around their famiiles for help and support. Other families did not fare so well and suffered new strains and problems.

During *rancho* days the social gatherings like *fiestas*, *bailes*, and games were basically family affairs. Relatively little social recreation existed outside the family. *Cantinas*, partly due to the "dry laws," did not exist. Men brewed their beer from home-grown maize or rice and drank at home with their *compadres*. But when *cantinas* were allowed

(1936), the pattern of staying home at night began to change for many family men. Several third generation women, contrasted to older Mexicanas, were bitter about *cantinas* and the consequences they brought to their homes and lives. They contended that the incidence of such family problems has greatly increased. Yet, one can neither simply blame *cantinas* and liquor, nor explain excessive male drinking with moralistic, psychological arguments about the character weakness of Mexicanos. These were men who had struggled, often quite successfully, against the elements and an unjust and uncooperative social, economic and political system. The great majority of Mexicano males in the *colonia* reportedly remained strong, faithful providers.

Nevertheless, this new life had many frustrations, many forms of humiliation imposed by the white society. Rural Mexicanos had partially escaped such problems by staying in their "place" on the *rancho*. Men soon found out that the white side of town was restricted to them, that they could go there only at certain hours and for certain purposes. Women were allowed to come over to Anglo houses as servants, where some had to eat their lunch outside in the yard. Many Mexicanos did not want their wives to clean the Anglo houses. They continued to try to play the traditional role of the sole provider and protector. But in some cases, the economic pressures were too great, and the Mexicano male with a working wife sometimes felt shame. The frustration of some males was expressed in long nights at the *cantina* getting drunk, missing work, beating their wives, and finally deserting their family.

In *rancho* days husband and wife needed each other to survive because there were no outside sources of support. They needed each other for economic and social reasons. Without a family for whom to live and on whom to rely, a person was lost, was aimless. In some cases women in the *colonia* formally became heads of the households where the male was absent. That situation, however, did not necessarily create a family "breakdown." Children of women without husbands were often different from the stereotype of disturbed, aimless, or weak personalities. Some of these families showed few sign of disaster, either financial or emotional. For every woman who failed, there was another who faced up to and overcame her family problems.

Women had traditionally been instructed to keep the family together at all costs. They had learned that the children would have to rely more on them than on anyone else, that they had an important role within the family circle, and that without them the household could turn into chaos. They considered themselves the basis for family well-being. Traditionally, women did depend on the male figure for legitimization of their authority and for some sense of strength and security. Every woman had either a husband or a brother or a father to go to in times of need. Nevertheless, the life histories of several deserted women reveal the remarkable strength of many Mexicanas forced into these circumstances. Many would fall back on their own integrity and attachment to the family ideal. They became closer to the children and more apt to take on the burdens of supporting a family. One woman who was deserted by her husband told her story:

When I got married, I was too young and knew nothing about sex. Right away I got pregnant and had children one after the other. My husband couldn't hold on to any job. We kept moving from ranch to ranch because he was always getting drunk and then fired by the *rancheros*. When I was pregnant with the sixth child, he started not to come home for days. One of my sisters-in-law told me he was having an affair. I went to talk to the woman he was seeing and begged her to leave him alone. She just said she hadn't known he was married, but she didn't stop seeing him. When I was about to have the baby he took off with this woman, leaving me with no money. The children and I had not been eating properly for months for lack of money. I sought refuge at my mother-in-law's house. She tried to help me, but she was also very poor, so there were times when there wasn't enough food for me, since I wanted my children to eat first. When the baby was born she was very tiny, malnourished. She was very ill and fifteen days later I took her to the local doctor. He said she had to be hospitalized. I told him I had no money to pay for the hospital, so he suggested that I ask the courthouse if they could help me pay the hospital. Then I was told there was no available aid. The only thing would be to apply for welfare, but it would take more than a week for the papers to be processed. I went home carrying the sick baby, and she died in my arms. My first cousin and one of my brothers-in-law took care of the funeral for I had no money, not even to bury the child. Three months later, my husband returned. At that time I was on welfare and was beginning to feel better. I had rented a small house and the children were eating better. The older ones were going to the Methodist kindergarten. I was taking odd jobs as a cleaning maid at some Anglo houses. He asked me to reconcile, and I accepted because of the children. I thought they needed their father. At the welfare, they told me I could only have two checks more while he looked for a job, but then the aid would be cut because my husband was with me again. He got a job, which was better paying, and we were doing well, except that his temperament was worse than ever. He didn't want to hear any mention of the dead baby. One day I had prepared flowers and candles to take to the angel's grave and had put them on the table. He came home in time to hear my oldest son urging me to hurry so that we could go to the cemetery right away. The man flew into a rage, threw the table on the floor, stepped on the candles and flowers. Then he grabbed me and started to beat me. My little children were the ones who interfered and made him stop. I guess it was his guilt, but what else could I do? He was guilty, and I could not relieve his conscience. Two days before Christmas, my husband disappeared again. He took off with my last welfare money and his paycheck, again leaving me totally penniless. He had gone away with the same woman. And again I was pregnant. Do you imagine what kind of Christmas I had that year? After Christmas, my mother-in-law came to ask me for his clothes. He was back but didn't want to come to the house. She was on my side but was so afraid of her son that she did whatever he told her to do. I told her that if he wanted his clothes, he had to come for them. Later, a male friend of his came to ask me for his clothes. I told him the same and the man, standing at my doorsteps, threatened to beat me if I didn't give him the clothes. I said I would defend myself as I could, but my husband had to come and face me if he wanted his clothes. So he came, filled with resentment. I told him that he owed me a child because he had killed my other one, but this baby I was carrying would live. For that baby to be able to survive, our marriage was broken once and for all. I never wanted to see him again. And I didn't. From then on it was struggle, struggle, and struggle. Little by little I was able to save money and make a life for me and my children.

Today this woman lives in a large house, and her children are leaders in the high school. The older children received scholarships to college and have families of their own.

Another woman who was left alone with nine children was unsuccessful in material terms, but she did not "break down" when her husband left. Soon after she was married, she realized that her husband was not the "dependable type" that she had dreamed of for herself. Out of a sense of morality and shame, she remained with him as long as possible, taking abuse from him, e.g., frequent beatings and stealing of the money she was earning for the family. When he left her, she reports it was a "big relief." Now her long lost husband wants to return, and she is ready to fight against him:

> I don't want to see that *cabrón* in my house even in a picture. It is funny, now that the children are grown, married and taken care of, he suddenly becomes a loving father. Where was his love when we most needed it? My older son, however, is all excited about getting to know his father. He is willing to take him in his home. He even bought a new color TV. Now I ask you, 'Is this fair?' I told my son that if he lets that *cabrón chingado* live in his house, he is never going to see his mother again.

Because of increasing desertions by husbands, drunkenness, and

127

romances with *cantineras*, women of this generation viewed marriage with a great deal of ambivalence, a mixture of desire and fear. On one hand, it was desirable and essential to get married to have stability and to become a mother of many children. To fail to do this was to fail as a woman. On the other hand, if a woman was well taken care of at home and had a warm, dependent relationship with her parents, leaving the security of the home for the uncertainties of married life was a big risk. The desire to have children, however, seemed to impel most women to marry:

> If I had known what marriage was all about, I wouldn't have married. It was all *pura batallar* (struggle). But when I married, I didn't know any better, hadn't gone to school. *Mi padrecito santo* had supported all of us, and I never even had to work with him. So until my husband's death I always lived in a *rancho*. When he died, I came to town, got the house and luckily got a job with *las costuras* (a relief program during the depression days) that enabled me to support my family. The older girls had to quit school and stay at home in order to take care of the younger ones while I worked. As soon as a child was old enough to get a job, he or she would drop out of school so as to help all of us. There was nobody for me to rely on but myself and my own children.

A woman literally had to become a fortress, a solid wall against which all of her children could lean. And fortresses many of them became.

The woman of the *colonia* was supposed to be chaste, prudish, and therefore "nice." Women who took lovers, whether they were married or not, were thoroughly despised by the other women. They had no sympathy for the "fallen woman." It was the mother's duty to teach chastity and fortitude to her daughters. Thus, an old woman proclaimed in a public meeting:

> *La mamá es la reina de la casa, la hija es la princesa.* (The mother is the queen of the house, the daughter is the princess). With her mother the daughter learns how to be a wife and a mother. She learns from her mother's *verguenza* (shame) and takes on the same qualities of meekness and softness that her mother has. The daughter is to be protected like a flower, like the precious jewel that she is.

A girl who became pregnant before marriage was a *dejada*. The ultimate accusation was *"Ella se dejó"*—she let herself slip. She was supposed to be a tower of fortitude, an example of chastity. Boys, as in any other cultural group in a sexist society, often were not blamed. After all, they were men—they were only seeking something they had a right to. If the girl gave in sexually, it was her fault. It was her duty, and hers alone, to stay away from pre-marital sex. As an unmarried mother, she was an outcast:

128

At least when women in the *rancho* had illegitimate babies, they had the decency to hide themselves, to stay home and not be seen by the other respectable people. They'd acknowledge their fall and take it. But that is past, women today do not have the same *verguenza* like women in the past.

Yet some women did have considerable compassion for unwed mothers and did not judge them harshly. They felt mainly for the children who were like outcasts; they hoped that these women would find husbands to protect them against men who consider them an "easy lay." Women who got pregnant before marrying most generally tried to marry the man who fathered the baby. If that was impossible, they looked for another man. They were anxious to regain the respectability that was taken away from them and guaranteed them a place in society. Some women were very emphatic about condemning men who made women pregnant and then abandoned them. A woman, with tears in her eyes, gave her opinion of such men:

> These men do not think of the children, of how much they are hurting their own children. Because of this, these men soil themselves and are not as dignified as they should be. I don't blame the poor girls because they are the ones who are left suffering the responsibility for the children. Women never abandon their children, they never do. Why can't men be the same way?

Women who lived alone were viewed with suspicion, unless they had already established an impeccable reputation. They also had a number of problems. For example, a motherless woman who was left childless by her husband went to live by herself in a house her father had given her. She found the situation very difficult. Men kept coming to visit, thinking that she wanted male company. She had a job as a waitress but had to quit when the cook made sexual advances towards her. She was very frightened and consequently moved her house to her sister's backyard for protection. Later on, she married a respectable man, not out of love, but to keep her reputation intact. Many unwed mothers made marriages for convenience sake to somebody else. Many women resented this "double-standard" in sex mores bitterly, especially those who "gave in" to their lovers. A woman who was pregnant before marrying and then married her baby's father put the situation in these terms:

> See, the thing is like this, parents tell their daughters to not get into sex at the same time that they tell their sons to get into sex. In this little town, there are very few *cantineras* or whores to go around. So, who are left to be seduced by the manly boys? None but the gentle daughters of other people. In this way, parents themselves bring disaster to their own

children. Take me, for instance, I knew nothing about sex. Then I started dating at thirteen and got pregnant at fourteen, and that was when my mother had a fit and almost threw me out of the house. But she had never warned me against sex or told me anything about men. I got into it almost blind, not knowing what I was doing. I was very bitter against my boyfriend, for then I had to marry him in order not to disgrace myself and my baby. But I also had to quit school, which really hurt me, since I wanted to finish high school so much.

Courtship practices in the *colonia* also underwent a number of changes. In *rancho* days courtship was so closely supervised and meetings so rare that women knew little about sex and seldom became pregnant. Most girls became women with little understanding of sexuality. One sixty-year old woman described her experience:

I was eleven years old and was at school when another girl told me that I had blood stains all over my skirt. I was terrified and ran home but found no one since they were all at the *rancho* working. I kept cleaning myself, thinking I had somehow cut myself in there. When my mother arrived, I told her what was happening in between tears, but she said that from then on I would bleed like that every month for two or three days. She didn't say why, even though I asked her so. She gave me some rags to put on and that was all. In those times we used rags and used to get a lot of infections because of that. Then my breasts started to grow, and I was very embarrassed. My mother had died by that time, and I lived with my aunt. She didn't explain to me about the breasts either. I could not understand why women had to have breasts. So I got some rags and swaddled myself to make myself flat again.

In the *rancho* girls had brothers and cousins for companions. A girl would typically meet two or three boys from a nearby family and would fall in love with the first one. Her "destiny" was to fall in love and marry. Love was not a matter of knowing somebody well and appreciating somebody's character, but a matter of economic survival. You had to marry and create an economic unit of your own, a little world for the future. Increasingly, however, the traditional customs of protecting and supervising women became more difficult to enforce. In the *colonia* young girls walked to school unescorted. They had more opportunities to go out and to meet their boyfriends secretly. There were simply more people and more chances to fall in love. Girls went to dances with their older brothers or mother, but they also met their boyfriends after school or when they went out with their girl friends.

In general, these selected stories of families, marriages, and women illustrate the kinds of troubled adaptation that some Mexicanos have experienced in this rural South Texas setting. The examples are far

130

from comprehensive, but they do suggest that the views of local Anglos, and even much of the scholarly writings on the Mexican-American family, are often overly negative caricatures. Such caricatures, when confronted with real cases of strong, successful families, with or without fathers, simply become untenable. Many Mexicano families, particularly fatherless families, did undergo difficulties. During the *colonia* era the price for adapting to American society was high, and the traditional Mexicano family system has changed.

Many Mexicano leaders expressed great personal concern for the high incidence of drinking and alcoholism.[10] Understandably, Mexicanas were nearly unanimous in their hatred for the *cantinas*. There was also increasing concern for the high incidence of separation and child desertion. Today, North Town has from 400 to 600 children of unwed or deserted mothers. Most older Mexicanos saw these problems as a development of great Americanization. Increasingly, Mexicanos have failed in getting an education and in finding steady, meaningful jobs during the 1950's and 1960's. The present rate of unemployment and under-employment was estimated at ten to twelve percent, but this appears to be a very conservative estimate.[11] The amount of welfare payments in the communities has risen dramatically in the sixties.[12] The present level of poverty as measured by health, education, income, and housing was depressingly high. The Texas survey on poverty and various other demographic tables included portray this economic disparity and stagnation vividly.[13] In the face of these conditions, it is quite understandable that some Mexicanos have been unable to cope.

The new Chicano leaders also recognized and lamented the passing of many valued traditional practices. In general cultural terms, many changes have occurred particularly in the third and fourth generations. The language has developed into a separate Chicano dialect.[14] There was little knowledge of and no practice of traditional Indian or Mariachi music forms. Most present-day Mexicano houses were American style with separate bedrooms and suburban style lots. Family residence patterns, due to expensive and scarce lots and a massive out-migration, were much more nuclear. Moreover, women no longer automatically established their houses near their husband's parents. *Compadres* (godparents) no longer have binding obligations to serve as coparents. Child-rearing and the relation of youth to their third and fourth generation parents have become increasingly Americanized, and the generation gap was very real for Mexicano students. The role of women has greatly changed. Weddings and family celebrations were more exclusive and were often held outside the homes in formal places like restaurants and clubs. Neighborhoods no longer served the same function of child-rearing and labor exchange that they once did. Second and third generation Mexicanos lamented the passing of, or gradual change of many customs and practices which sustained them in the struggle to survive. They worried about their youth becoming too American-ized, and many made real efforts to maintain their language and some of the more traditional hospitality patterns.

Given the vantage point of history, the third and fourth generation of North Town Mexicanos were clearly victims of a static, stagnating local economy. As a people, they had gone through two massive shifts in their way of life in sixty years, first, from sharecroppers to migrants, and second, from migrants to non-migrants. As a people, they had also not been passive and silent; consequently, many shifts in the power relationship between Anglos and Mexicanos have occurred.

A SUMMING UP: THE RELATIVE ORGANIZATION AND POWER OF THE COMPETING ETHNIC GROUPS

The decline in the ability of North Town Anglos to control local institutions was described as a gradual process of change in the local modes of production. The labor intensive *rancho* farming and ranching operations were gradually replaced by a more urban-based, mechan-ized agricultural production system. Even before these technological transformations occurred, however, Mexicano workers were beginning to migrate and seek better wages in northern agriculture and canning factories. The depression, better transportation, and local labor organ-ization increased the outmigrations. Increasingly, *braceros* and illegal immigrants replaced local Mexicano workers. Absentee owners and manager-lease operators replaced smaller, North Town-born *patrones*. As smaller percentages of the North Town Mexicano population were totally dependent upon traditional *patrones*, general social and power relationships between these two classes also began to change.

During the *colonia* era the nature and control of local Anglo leader-ship, the old political machines, gradually became ineffective. New Anglo leaders found it increasingly necessary to create a following among the growing number of Mexicano voters. Anglo political leaders in the post-war era had to rely more on Mexicano political brokers and new forms of political alliance which included sponsoring selected Mexicano candidates. They began to build more linkages with the increasingly unfamiliar Mexicano community through individual inter-mediaries, the sharing of symbolic public positions, and multi-racial political coalitions in the Democratic Party. To a degree local politics became somewhat more open and competitive.

In response to the internal and external changes North Town was experiencing, a new post-war generation of Anglo community leaders developed. This group included many more modern ranchers and farmers as the modernization of agriculture blurred the distinction between merchants and agri-businessmen. A group of forty to fifty younger (thirty-five to fifty) businessmen and rancher/farmers formed the leadership class of the period from 1960 to the present. By historical standards, they were significantly more urban, educated, and politically liberal than earlier Anglo leaders. Increasingly, they were forced to accept that North Town had become what could be called an administered unit. State and federal legislation and aid programs had greatly reduced local decision-making autonomy. The mass media flooded North Towners with new images of lifestyles and values. The urban areas drew greater numbers of their children away, and families became smaller and more fragmented. In some ways, it is difficult to talk about North Town as an autonomous community. Their economic, political, and cultural dependency on external state and federal institutions was prevasive. They increasingly accepted external federal and state aid programs for themselves (agricultural subsidies and loans) and for low-income Mexicanos (social welfare and compensatory education).

One important measure of the changing Anglo beliefs was the way local Mexicanos compared earlier generations with the present Anglos. For most older Mexicanos, Anglos of the sixties were a great deal more friendly and respectful. Post-war Anglos no longer physically beat up or publicly shamed Mexicanos. On a day-to-day basis, the social etiquette of ethnic relations greatly changed. No local sheriff would dare make a practice of beating up Mexicano drunks or sleeping with their wives. Such aggressive, disrespectful acts toward Mexicanos would be unthinkable and would elicit immediate counter-aggression. Most old-timers felt that "things were much better for the Mexicano. We were nothing in the early days, now we have some self-respect."

Indeed, many of the more liberal local Anglo leaders of this era were more cordial and solicitous of Mexicanos at public school and community events. Such Anglo community leaders would be offended if described as being prejudiced towards Mexicanos. They could all point to a good deal of personal missionary activities, public courtesy, and a public ideology calling for bi-racial groups and political harmony. At least publicly, the key local Anglo leaders were ready to accommo-

133

date and cooperate with the Mexicanos they considered sufficiently responsible, patriotic, and successful.

However, many North Town Anglos still did not accept their declining power positions and the new political survival tactics. The more traditional Anglos were continually "creating problems" for the more diplomatic, alliance-seeking Anglo leaders. The more liberal Anglo leaders of the sixties frequently expressed consternation with their "radical, rednecks." There were many basic cultural and class differences among Anglos that created strains in the new Anglo-Mexicano political coalitions of the 1960's. Such tendencies towards political factionalism were common among Anglos in pre-war days, and they continued during the *colonia* period.

The Changing Mexicano Group

Increasingly, North Town Mexicanos were less bound by local labor relations, patterns of indebtedness, social segregation, and general beliefs about their cultural inferiority. During this era a major cultural transformation was occurring. The ordinary Mexicano residents' view of their race and of Anglos was changing. More Mexicanos were beginning to publicly confront Anglos. Small daily acts of resistance that challenged local Anglo authority and legitimacy to rule became much more frequent from the forties on. The North Town City Council minutes indicate several incidents where local "Americans" were being beaten up in "Mexican Town." Sheriff Cameron was given the task of straightening out these problems and protecting "Americans" who ventured in the *cantinas*.

More recent law enforcement officers were often described in different terms. Police Chief Rowman, the man who replaced "El Cameron" operated differently. He drank in the *cantinas* too, but he rarely mistreated Mexicanos during arrests. Often he would take someone who had too much to drink home instead of to jail. More important, he told the local bar owners and many Mexicanos to protect themselves and to throw out any Anglos who were disorderly or disrespectful. The bars were perhaps the first public territory that Mexicans took over and re-defined as Mexicano-controlled. The recognition of local police during the late forties and early fifties was undoubtedly an important symbolic victory for the Mexicano male.

The local city minutes also show an increasing willingness of Mexicanos to complain about problems "on their side of the tracks." In North Town the Anglos live on the higher, elevated side of town, and several hundred acres of surrounding farmland and the high side of

134

town drain onto the Mexican side of town. A major portion of "Mexican Town" became flooded during heavy rains. In 1953 several local Mexicanos came to the council and complained about the drainage problem. By 1956 the local Mexicanos had created enough concern that a plan was developed to solve the problem through curbing, guttering, and paving the streets. Ultimately, the plan was abandoned because of opposition from both sides of the town. However, during the fifties increasing numbers of Mexicanos appeared before the board, demanding better drainage, more police during Saturday dances, and paved streets.

North Towners also reported that after the war more people began complaining about the school programs. A group of parents organized and vigorously complained to the school board about the mistreatment of Mexicano children in the Mexican school. They contended that their school was badly run with inferior books, broken toilets, and no bus service. Further, they claimed that their children were excessively held back and unduly punished for speaking Spanish. This early confrontation of the school board also led to the first Mexicano candidate in 1961. He was narrowly defeated, but this event was a significant break with the past when no Mexicano parents attempted to complain to teachers or the school board. The Parent Teachers Club in North Town fought for a new Mexican school and similar improvement from 1950 on. More parents were willing to demand their rights from the local schools.

By the fifties the Mexicano youth were also beginning to assert themselves. Several members described how there were "gangs" of students who "raised a lot of hell with gringos and the sheriffs." They described one group as some of the best football players in school. They wore leather jackets with the club's name on the back. Unlike big city gangs and clubs, their activities were quite tame and primarily social. They were the duck-tail, rock-and-roll Mexican *Pachuco* generation. One very important thing they did besides drink, dance, and play football was increasingly "stand up to Anglos." An ex-member expressed enormous pride in the fact that "the Anglos didn't mess around with us Mexicans anymore." The Mexicanos had a reputation for carrying knives and fighting in groups, and Anglos said they were indeed afraid of going over to "Mexican Town." There were apparently very few actual "rumbles," but the balance of power had clearly shifted.

These early Mexicano clubs were playing a historical role; even though they had no particular political ideology, they were a form of new political leadership among Mexicano youth. The Mexicano gang leaders described an incident in which the local sheriff came into one of their hang-outs to harass them. When he stopped the car, they surrounded it and began to rock it up and down until he bumped his head on the ceiling. He went back for his deputies, and they ran off. These groups also "policed" the school halls, not unlike a kind of Mexicano vigilante group. By the late fifties Mexicano youth had become the majority in the schools, and they began to "take-over" the clubs, elected offices, and the honor positions such as most popular and most handsome students.[16] By the early sixties these take-overs were well-organized, and there were informal "political leaders" for the Mexicano student body.

The rise and development of adult political leaders and resistance to exclusive Anglo leadership had its roots in the emergence of a Mexicano business class. By the thirties North Town had ten or twelve Mexicano merchants and from ten to fifteen labor contractors and truckers. This group of economic entrepreneurs were *los ricos*, and they sent their children to the Anglo schools, saved their money, and built their businesses. During the pre-war period leadership in the Mexicano community was strictly based on business acumen and not formal education. The schools had largely excluded the Mexicanos, and their main source of mobility was through capital saved from migrating north. In the post-war years the sons and daughters of these people and a number of returning veterans began finishing high school and pressing for more political change. By the mid-fifties North Town had several Mexicano professionals as teachers and nurses began returning to the area.

Mexicanos also began filling the lower level bureaucratic jobs in the city, schools, and post office from the late forties on.[15] Initially, Anglos hired the Mexicanos as county and city laborers and school janitors. In the forties Mexicanos became night watchmen and assistants to the Anglo directors of utilities and the police. By the fifties there were Mexicano postmen, policemen, assistant directors of utilities, and chief clerks. There were still no Mexicanos in administrative positions at the school, bank, or "big" local businesses (machinery, fertilizer, and chain stores). But there was a growing, stable, locally-based middle class of perhaps 100 to 150 Mexicanos for a Mexican population of 3,000 to 4,000. Many of these leading Mexicanos were active in civic programs such as scouting, the *Sociedades*, the PTA, and LULAC.

By the sixties the chain stores and the more progressive Anglo merchants also had begun encouraging this trend of a growing Mexicano middle class. By this period, there were Mexicano managers in two North Town chain stores, a bank officer, and two postal clerks. There were also several Mexicano insurance officers and building contractors.

In some cases the new Mexicano insurance officers and building contractors were men who eventually saved enough capital to become independent of local Anglos. By the late sixties this nascent Mexicano middle class had doubled in size, diversified into new occupations, and entered the local bureaucracy. There were, however, still no Mexicano principals, police chiefs, or key bank officials, and the local Anglo business and civic clubs still enrolled only two or three token Mexicanos. Further, there were still no important elected city, school, or county officials.

The political confrontations in local elections of the 1960's were, then, an outgrowth of a broader, more general economic and cultural transformation among the Mexicano people. Gradually, the Mexicano has moved out of his isolated, defended cultural enclave and has broken down many segregated, Anglo public territories. Mexicanos have forced a new set of rules for social etiquette and racial exchange upon local Anglos. The post-war era has both opened up *and* further polarized these local communities. Despite the increasing polarization, the daily public life of the Mexicano greately changed. Mexicanos were no longer submissive and confined to their segregated enclaves on the *rancho* or in the North Town *colonia*. Increasingly, Mexicanos had a new sense of their own potential. Growing numbers believed that they were capable of succeeding in schools, in business, and even in running the North Town public institutions. At least a number of the more prominent Mexicano community leaders sought to control even greater portions of their local environment.

Yet, despite the emergence of several Mexicano political leaders who had a greater sense of "ethnic politics," many Mexicanos did not share these new perspectives or aspirations. Most North Town Mexicanos still did not actively seek to politically control their community institutions. Considerable diversity still existed among the Mexicano people. Differences in basic values, political awareness, and even wealth in the Mexicano community threatened this emerging ethnic unity. Ultimately, Mexicano leaders of the sixties factionalized during their first serious attempt to organize politically.

---

[1] Aztlán City Urban Renewal Agency Report. Unpublished study, 1972.

[2] This material is based on an unpublished local history of the Methodist church and on the North Town Centennial report, *Historic North County, 1877–1971.*

[3] North Town Centennial Report, *Ibid.*

[4] United States Commission on Civil Rights Report. *Mexican-American Education Study.* Volumes I through V. Washington D.C.: United States Government

Printing, 1970–1974; Thomas Carter, *Mexican-Americans in Schools: A History of Educational Neglect.* New York: College Examination Board, 1970.

5 Smith, Walter Jr. *Chicano Resistance Against Schooled Ethnicity: A Case Study of Student Power in Historical Perspective.* Doctoral dissertation, University of Texas, Austin, Texas, 1978.

6 Mobility of high school graduates was studied in North and South Town by collecting a list of graduates at five-year-intervals, beginning in 1930 to the present. Once lists were developed, ex-principals, counselors and community leaders were consulted. The occupation of the father, post high school education completed, present residence, and present occupation were established for more than 95% of the cases. The general patterns in these data are reported in the text.

7 Smith, Walter Jr. *Ibid.* This study finds similar patterns in Aztlán City.

8 The shifts in local use of ethnic terms can also be seen in the city minutes. By the early 1950's there were no more references to "Mexican Town" and "Mexicans" as opposed to Americans.

9 The residence rules for local kinship groups were determined from approximately forty life histories of women up to ninety years old. The general discussions of Mexicano family life are based on these life histories and are supplemented with informal chats with twenty to thirty other women. Most of the life history materials were collected in two or three sessions with each woman. The time spent with each contributor ranged from four to twenty hours, the majority being from four to ten hours. Other material was also collected throughout a year of participation in community life. In all cases the material was collected by a Spanish-speaking woman.

10 The descriptions of male drinking problems and frustration are not based on any psychological testing. Most of the judgments offered in this study are, therefore, representations of the way North Town Mexicanos perceived such problems. Not infrequently, women telling these stories broke into tears, as did some males who retold stories about job discrimination.

11 The trends in unemployment appear to be greatly underestimated. These percentages are based on labor surveys by the regional government and by the Texas Employment Commission. The Employment Commission reports were dated 1970.

12 This estimate is based on interviews with social workers in Aztlán City and North Town and represent their estimates from local case records. Also see Appendix A, Table 4.1 *Welfare Assistance in Two South Texas Counties.*

13 *Poverty in Texas: A Report.* Office of Economic Opportunity, 1972. See Appendix A, Table 4.2 *Occupational Distribution* of Ethnic Groups in North and South County* and Table 2.1 *Median Income and Median Education With Poverty Between Ethnic Groups in Three South Texas Counties.*

14 Elias-Olivares, Lucia Ernestina. *Ways of Speaking in a Chicano Community: A Sociolinguistic Approach.* Doctoral dissertation, University of Texas, Austin, Texas, 1976.

15 This material is based on the city, county and school board records of North Town.

16 This material is based on a content analysis of the school annuals of Aztlán and North Town high schools from 1955 to 1970.

138

PART III: CONTEMPORARY ETHNIC POLITICAL CONFLICT, 1970 TO 1977

Chapter 5

Community Conflict and the Rise
of the Raza Unida

After the initial conflicts on the first racially mixed city council in 1964, harmony and progress seemed to earmark North Town politics. By the sixties North Towners had seen two major economic eras and a strictly segregated social life come to an end. Local Mexicanos were rising to prominence in business, community leadership positions, and even in the professions. A new, more liberal group of Anglo leaders had emerged, and the town was beginning to initiate various new federally-funded school, housing, EODC, and city programs. In the minds of at least some residents, North Town was making considerable progress in Anglo-Mexicano relations.

From 1966 to 1972 North Town politics became relatively quiet.[4] The county's largest peanut farmer, a quiet, well-liked man, was mayor, and the Anglo city council began encouraging "responsible" Mexicano businessmen to run for office. A successful local Mexicano merchant, Mr. Daniel, and a restaurant owner, Mr. Matamoros, were elected in 1969 and 1970 by Anglos in turnouts of just over a hundred voters. The school board minutes also suggest that Anglos were actively seeking young Mexicanos for Board positions. A young building contractor, Mr. Esposito, and a self-employed pest exterminator, Mr. Rápido, were elected with Anglo sponsorship and by a light voter turnout in 1968 and 1970. In all, seven different Mexican-Americans were appointed or elected to the school board and three to the city council during this period.

Meanwhile any conscious, overt Mexicano ethnic mobilization remained fragmented and sporadic. Most of the candidates elected to the city and school positions were involved in the earlier LULAC group, or were pro-Mexicano in orientation. Yet, in this era they decided to accept Anglo sponsorship. The leaders of this period described their philosophy as "working with Anglo leadership," rather than openly confronting Anglos. The young, inexperienced leaders did not attempt to develop a vigorous Mexicano organization.

During this period there were also new, external forces of change intruding into North Town. Two major federal government programs (school aid for minority students and the War on Poverty) and the civil rights movement had an increasing effect on Anglo-Mexicano relations. First, the Education Act of 1965 encouraged the local Mexicano groups and a few liberal Anglos to press for change. The funds made available by federal legislation and channeled through the Texas Education Agency clearly contributed to shifting the local school leaders' emphasis from Anglo to Mexican-American student needs. This legislation provided aid for improving the education of poverty-level children. Funds were allocated for up-grading the educational program through additional, more modern teaching aids and materials. Teacher-aides were hired to work with classroom teachers as an attempt to bridge linguistic and other cultural differences. New curricular programs were designed to meet special needs of local students defined as "educationally deprived" such as the migrant education program. Finally, the North Town elementary schools were integrated in 1970. This controversial move included building a new elementary school building in the Mexicano community for students of both races.

Second, the federal poverty programs of the sixties also provided a further source of new power for local Mexican-Americans.[2] North County is part of a regionally funded organization called the Economic Opportunities Development Corporation (EODC). The importance of this organization is manifested in several ways. First, the program represents a new economic resource for solving a multiplicity of problems—adult education, pre-school programs, health care, employment counseling, family counseling, legal aid, and a number of other services. The EODC staff in North Town understood their task to be meeting any and every need that local Mexican-Americans had. Further, the poverty program has provided local Mexican-Americans with administrative jobs and thereby the needed experience and skills in management necessary to compete with Anglos. Finally, since the local poverty program must be composed of a majority of low-income citizens, local Mexicano community members, often hand-picked by the Mexicano EODC directors, control the decision-making board.

The North Town EODC program, and the programs spawned by its activities, were viewed as a constant political threat by local Anglos. The EODC program hired local Mexicano political leaders, and its offices functioned as an informal gathering place for local and regional Chicanos active in politics. The EODC staff shared, to a degree, the political ideology of these "Chicano activists."

Third, there were other important post-civil rights movements among Mexicano students in Texas cities. Particularly San Antonio

140

witnessed numerous student walk-outs, labor strikes, and increasing attempts by Mexican-Americans to occupy political positions such as the City Council, Commissioners' Court, and School Boards. This cultural and political change spawned a variety of new organizations such as the Brown Berets, Mexican-American Student Organization (MASO), and the Mexican-American Youth Organization (MAYO). Such organizations shared a number of beliefs: that the Anglo system was oppressive; that Mexican-Americans should unite and consolidate their power to overthrow the system; and that the Mexican-American culture of the Southwest was as good as, if not superior to, the Anglo way of life.

Although this is hardly an exhaustive treatment of the Chicano movement and its ideology, it illustrates some of the key ideas of the ethnic organizations developing in the late sixties. Their basic posture was more aggressive; they were more willing to confront, harass, insult, expose, and defeat traditional Anglo political leaders, both liberal and conservative Democrats and Republicans.[3] By 1969 the influence of such urban ethnic groups, particularly the Raza Unida Party (RUP), had become apparent in several South Texas communities.

The Movimiento Comes to Town

In North Town the new RUP movement began making frequent, formal contacts with some local Mexican-American leaders during the state election campaigns of 1972. Prior to this, several younger Mexicanos of the community, some from the San Antonio colleges, had urged the traditional community leaders to take stronger stands against local Anglos. They exhorted older leaders to seize control of local institutions as RUP had in Aztlán City. Several traditional Mexicano community leaders were aware of, and sympathetic towards, the *movimiento* in San Antonio and Aztlán City. They followed the politics in these more "advanced" areas through personal contacts and newspapers such as the *Chicano Times*, *La Verdád*, and the *San Antonio Express*. By 1972, considerable diversity of views still existed among North Town Mexicanos regarding local conditions, political strategies, and the Chicano movement. However, some younger Mexicanos and older leaders of the early sixties were beginning to feel that North Town Mexicanos could replicate the Aztlán City RUP victories. They generally reasoned that Mexicanos had a large numerical majority and should rightly have at least a majority representation among local elected leaders.

In the fall of 1972 Mexicano community members described two informal groups of Mexicanos who shared much of the new Raza Unida Party ideology of ethnic relations but who were still at odds with each other. First, there was a small group called Raza Unida, which consisted primarily of the sons (some college-educated) of prominent local businessmen. There were about twelve male members who had their own bank account and baseball team. At that time the Raza Unida members were highly critical of local Mexicano leaders, many their own relatives, for not being more politically active. They accused the traditional leaders of trusting Anglos too much and of not following the example of the Aztlán City Chicano election victories in 1969. The key leaders of the other major informal group of Mexicanos, which we shall call Ciudadanos (a name they ultimately chose), consisted of a loose-knit group of fifteen to twenty young businessmen and professionals.[5] They consistently criticized the local Raza Unida group for its Anglo hatred and considered the "Raza approach" to be too "militant" and "radical" to improve effectively the North Town community. Several members illustrated this "tension" between these groups by describing a fight between members of each group at a softball game in the spring of 1972.

By the fall of 1972 many local Mexicanos recognized the less radical group as the main community leaders. Indeed, they already had two members on both the city council and the school board, but this loose-knit friendship group had no overt public political identity or set of stated goals. Because several of their members were active political and civic leaders, they expressed considerable apprehension towards the statewide Raza Unida movement. Their suspicion and criticism of the local Raza group reflected the belief that local Mexicanos could handle their own social and political relationships with the Anglos. In fact, many Ciudadanos members were convinced that an accommodation could be worked out with the local Anglos who were "good people."

Particularly those Ciudadanos leaders on the city council and school board felt that their relationships with Anglos were quite productive. Others conciliatory towards Anglos were businessmen who had many Anglo customers. Conversely, a number of people who followed these key Ciudadanos leaders—some relatives, friends, and wives—believed that any cooperative relationship with Anglos was doomed to failure. Hence, the informal Ciudadanos group of leaders and followers, a potential voting bloc of approximately 500 people, also included a variety of conflicting views concerning Anglos and political strategy.[6]

As the political competition "heated up" during the fall county elections of 1972, the informal Ciudadanos group formally identified

142

itself as Ciudadanos Mexicanos Unidos. They held several open community meetings to mobilize political votes and run candidates. By the spring election of 1973, the Ciudadanos leaders and followers had generally become openly anti-Anglo and actively sought the political advice and support of the Aztlán City RUP members.

The manner in which local Ciudadanos leaders changed their beliefs about the Anglos during the period of November 1972 through July 1973 was striking. By the late spring and early summer of 1973, Ciudadanos members had become considerably more sympathetic to the militant pro-Chicano posture of the Raza Unida movement. Conversely, Anglos formed an aggressively anti-Raza Unida organization, and the town became extremely polarized along Mexicano and Anglo lines. The chronicle of events during 1972 to 1973 will illustrate this change in the Ciudadanos organization and the growing Raza Unida influence in North Town. It will also indicate how Anglos organized and responded, and how ethnic relations escalated to higher levels of antagonism, distrust, and polarization.

The Mexicano "Takeover" of the City and Schools in 1972

In the spring of 1972 several prominent Mexicano community leaders from the informal Ciudadanos group decided to run for the city council and school board. But since there was no well-organized Mexicano effort, the candidates were not carefully screened and selected by the Ciudadanos. Several people were encouraged to run, and four candidates, two for the city and two for the school board, gradually emerged and quietly made known their intent to run. There was no open Ciudadanos organization, hence, no candidates were openly supported, and there were no formal campaign rallies or active community organizations. The candidates, with help from close family and friends, ran their own low-key, seemingly separate campaigns. They generally emphasized the needs of Mexicanos and avoided open criticism of local Anglos or the "system."

Aside from the absence of an open Mexicano organization and any overt anti-Anglo campaigning, there were other important reasons why these "unsponsored" Mexicano candidates did not arouse local Anglos. First, as previously indicated, the 1965 to 1971 period was politically calm, and Anglos and Mexicanos were cooperating on the city council and school board. Anglos felt they had adequately demonstrated their willingness to elect and appoint what they deemed as "responsible, capable Mexicans" to leadership positions. Concomitantly, a number of the influential Mexicano community leaders sincerely felt that the

143

mid-sixties period was one of considerable progress, and that Mexicanos could work with the "good," more "liberal" Anglos.

Second, the four Mexicano candidates were young (mid-thirties) and had very non-threatening backgrounds. Three were the sons or daughters of very prominent, well-respected Mexicano businessmen. One school board candidate was the eldest son of the largest melon grower. Mr. Talvez, who had served on the school board, had been in partnership with Anglos. One city council candidate, Mr. Salinas, was the son of a highly respected Mexicano grocer popular with Anglos and was one of the first Mexicanos to be in the local Chamber of Commerce. The other city candidate, Mrs. Tolivar, was the daughter of a well-liked tavern owner, and the wife of a successful, likeable civil service employee. On the other hand, the fourth candidate, an unemployed, poorly-educated woman, was not taken seriously by Anglos. They felt that she had no chance of winning; in fact, a popular joke among Anglos was that only the ignorant Mexicans would vote for her because they feared that she was a "witch." As a result of these beliefs, the voter turnout was relatively light, and all four Mexicano candidates won the election by two-to-one margins over the Anglo candidates. Their strength apparently came from a core of 400-500 Mexicano voters and approximately 200 Anglo voters.

Within a few weeks after the election, Anglos began to feel duped, and that there had been a "Chicano takeover." Much of the initial controversy and conflict centered on the actions of the Mexicano-controlled city council.[7] Many Anglos were "shocked" with the "rude" and openly "hostile" way Council business was being conducted. Some Anglos described how this new "power had gone to the Mexicans' heads." Anglos reported incidents of being interrupted, overlooked, and belittled. Mexicanos reported that they were finally beginning to "speak out" and "fight for their rights for the first time." Several open conflicts resulted between the hold-over Anglo clerks and city manager, and the new Mexicano councilmen. In one incident, the Anglo city manager reportedly told a Mexicano clerk to "shut that damn Latin music off." One of the councilmen, Mr. Matamoros, later accused the city manager of racism, which disrupted a city council meeting. In a subsequent meeting a fist-fight ensued between this councilman and the husband of an Anglo city clerk. The Mexicano councilman had reportedly offended this lady by calling her a "Mexican hater." He accused her of mistreating Mexicanos who came to pay their water bills.

Such confrontations were frequent in the city hall, and several "rash" acts further incensed local Anglo leaders. The new council raised the wages of city employees from sixty to seventy dollars to at least $150 a week. Many of these employees were reportedly nineteen to twenty-five year veterans. During this controversy the Anglo city manager was asked why these wages had not been raised in the past. He reportedly replied, "They can't read or write and are not worth more than sixty to seventy dollars per week." The pressures on the Anglo city manager of ten years grew, and he "was forced to resign" several months after the elections. In protest, the Anglo mayor and one of the hold-over Anglo councilmen also resigned. This created the need for a special election in August, 1972, and two prominent Anglos, a rancher, and a retired military officer, ran against a prominent Mexicano businessman and former LULAC leader and a young "long-haired radical." The aroused Anglo community won these hotly contested seats by a top vote total of 794 to 704.

According to local Anglos, the management of city government quickly deteriorated. Twenty to thirty Anglos began going to city meetings to "watchdog" the council. The Mexicanos considered this harassment. The council meetings became, for Anglos, "spectacles of Mexican arrogance" and for the Mexicanos, "examples of Anglo racial superiority and bigotry." Subsequently, the council hired Mr. Mata, the town's first Mexicano lawyer and the eldest son of a prominent labor contractor, as the new city manager. He reported that some Anglos refused to pay their bills, or they made a point to complain frequently. Some Anglos, such as the bank president, reportedly told him that they disliked what was happening but hoped he would run it fairly, and the bank president vowed "to go along for the good of the city." Generally, however, many local Anglos judged the actions of the new Mexicano council from the standpoint of their traditional beliefs. Mexicans, being inherently lawless and inefficient, were sure to ruin the city financially. Conversely, the Mexicanos protested that Anglos were purposely uncooperative to discredit the new Mexicano administration. Some hold-over Anglo clerks were suspected of deliberately tampering with the records to make Mexicano councilmen seem incompetent.[8]

After six months of frequent ethnic conflict during council meetings, the Anglo community was even more incensed and increasingly organized to defeat a Mexicano candidate for sheriff in the November, 1972 county elections. The husband of the newly-elected councilwoman, who became particularly outspoken and "anti-Anglo," ran for county sheriff. The Anglos launched a strongly critical campaign against Mr. Tolivar. They emphasized that he had a DWI charge against him and was a delinquent tax payer. They reasoned that anyone who had not payed his taxes should not live in a home furnished from tax money.

The Anglo opposition also hit hard on the theme that a DWI is a felony charge. Unless removed, it bars a person from graduating from law enforcement school and from being a law enforcer. Mr. Tolivar's campaign argument was that the present Anglo sheriff treated Mexicans and Anglos differently. The incumbent Anglo sheriff, a mild-mannered man who had hired several Mexicano deputies, was rarely described as anti-Mexican. One Mexicano claimed that the Anglo sheriff was a "liberal" because he had made a strong plea at the Rotary Club to admit Mexicans. But many Ciudadanos members perceived the sheriff as a weak man, "easily manipulated by the rich Anglos who made him."

The key case which many Mexicanos cited to demonstrate his favoritism was his treatment of Anglo teenagers caught with marijuana. In 1971 a team of FBI agents had uncovered a "drug ring" of Anglo high school students. It was the contention of local Mexicanos that the sheriff already knew of this ring but did nothing because the students were the sons and daughters of prominent Anglos. The subsequent arrests and trial in the county court resulted in a two-year prison term for the Anglo youth who was the "leader" and seller, and suspended sentences for twelve other Anglos.[9] Local Mexicanos pointed to this as further proof that the sheriff and the judge were "in the back pocket of the Anglo rich." In addition to this alleged favoritism towards Anglos, the sheriff was also accused of "negligence" in the case of a Mexican-American jail prisoner who reportedly hanged himself.

Mr. Tolivar was defeated in the election for sheriff, however, by a heavy Anglo voter turnout.[10] Local Mexican-Americans point to a number of Anglo election tactics to support their rationale that Anglos had no intention of "sharing control," even though the Mexicanos are in the majority. First, several Mexicanos related that elderly Mexican-Americans received phone calls threatening their loss of social security benefits if they attempted to vote. Some Mexican-Americans who worked for Anglos reported being subtly told they might lose their jobs. Again, the sheriff's deputies were reported to have been out taking pictures of the voters, which was interpreted as a means to check up on the Anglos' employees. There was the further case of a threatened arrest of a Mexican-American candidate's wife for driving voters to the polls. The arresting sheriff's deputies used the rationale that since her husband was a candidate, this type of behavior was illegal. According to the accounts, the arrest was not actually made, "because all of the other Mexican-Americans standing in line to vote demanded to be arrested as well."

Several other incidents during the elections were used to characterize the Anglos as "ruthless and oppressive."[11] First, Anglo poll-watchers were seen helping non-English speaking Mexicano voters to mark the Anglo candidates when the Mexican-American had specified preference for the Mexicano candidate. Second, Mexican-Americans were reportedly not allowed to vote if they did not have their registration cards, even though their names were on the poll lists. Yet, Anglos were reportedly allowed to vote if they had a card, even if their names were not on the poll lists. Mexicanos interpreted this as Anglo use of the rules to suit their own ends. Third, the Anglo assistant county clerk reportedly went into local nursing homes and helped even senile people vote, allegedly for the Anglo candidates.

Fourth, the election recorded 600 absentee votes, which made no sense to local Mexicanos. Most absentee voters were students and were away attending college. Several Anglo college students reported receiving periodic letters from the Anglo leaders urging them to vote. The absentee vote was also believed to include a number of "wetback" votes and elderly people in the local nursing home. Several Anglo ranchers reportedly "signed up" all their wetbacks to vote absentee for the Anglo candidates. The county clerk also reportedly sent out a number of absentee votes already notarized, which helped assure their return. Finally, one ballot box from the southern part of the county, with only sixteen votes, took four hours to count, and it was four o'clock in the morning before many of the outlying boxes were reported. The Mexicanos judged all of these acts to be illegal, and they believed that Anglos had "messed with the votes."

The Organization of the Ciudadanos Unidos

These events and the defeat of the Mexicano candidate for sheriff spurred the Mexicanos to develop a more openly aggressive political organization. The new Ciudadanos Unidos Mexicanos organization was created in December, 1973. The original thirteen members were local Mexican-American entrepreneurs, educators, and a local Catholic priest. It is important to note that nearly all of the prominent Mexicano businessmen and professionals were openly or quietly supporting this original organization. As many as thirty or forty families had a history of political involvement in the early organizations after 1960. Some of the earlier leaders were inactive but vocal supporters. Some of the younger professionals working in the Anglo schools and local offices were quiet but helped financially and organizationally. Likewise, a number of working women, many employed by Anglos, were also active opinion-makers and barrio organizers. Only a small number of the more prominent Mexicano families born in North Town were outside the Ciudadanos organization.

The group's broadly stated purpose emphasized educational, welfare, and political issues. Their basic goals were to achieve the following: paved streets, street lights, more efficient sewage system, adequate drainage, recreational parks, and an educational system more attuned to Mexicano needs. The Mexicanos compared their section of North Town with the Anglo section and concluded that Anglos would never provide the same resources for their development. The idea of a Mexican majority, as opposed to the earlier idea of representation, was espoused. But the initial Ciudadanos goals and philosophy were carefully spelled out to avoid the notion of total "Chicano control." The young Mexicano priest was particularly influential in stressing the idea that Ciudadanos was pro-Mexicano, *not* anti-Anglo.

The more moderate Ciudadanos leaders were particularly anxious to portray Ciudadanos as a "non-political" organization, not unlike a Chamber of Commerce. They sought to minimize both the Anglos' anxiety and expected retaliatory measures, e.g., firings, cancelled loans, punishment of school children, and police harassment. Indeed, in these early stages the Ciudadanos Mexicanos were very fearful of how the Anglos would react to this challenge. Ideologically, they were also much more interested in proportional representation than dominance and control, and the public image they presented was quite tame in comparison to "militant" Chicano leaders in Aztlán City or San Antonio.

Some Anglo leaders, although fearful of this new Ciudadanos, were still hopeful that Ciudadanos and its "radical Mexican priest" would listen to reason. At this stage of development, several Anglos referred to the new organization as simply a "Mexican Chamber of Commerce," but the key leaders in the Anglo organization deeply distrusted Ciudadanos.

In the early development of Ciudadanos, members held a variety of views about Anglos, the Raza Unida party, and local mobilization tactics. Some members bitterly hated all Anglos and derisively labeled them "gringos." Others, particularly the school leaders, were more prone to believe that *some* Anglos could be trusted to work for Mexicanos. They argued against any rhetoric or actions that might alienate those Anglos. Initially, many Ciudadanos members viewed their task as more educational than strictly political.

The major covert task was to "educate" Anglos to a new understanding of the Mexican-American. More moderate Ciudadanos leaders argued that traditional Anglo views of Mexicans as socially and cul-

148

turally inferior were not "inborn" and could be eliminated by education. Ciudadanos members wanted to demonstrate to Anglos that they
could follow the law and manage local institutions honestly, fairly, and
efficiently. They thought that their eventual victories would be gradual and reasonable, and that Anglos would come to accept it. Such an
orientation tended to prevail in the Ciudadanos organization until
after the spring elections of 1973.

There were many Mexican-American families who did not join the
Ciudadanos mobilization. They did not share the Ciudadanos' beliefs
about local ethnic relations and opportunities. Several families pas-
sionately described their own histories of upward economic mobility.
According to their accounts, they came from Mexico and were not
able to speak English. But they worked hard, took advantage of opportunities, and were able to finance several children's college education. Another, Mr. Luna, who campaigned with the Anglos as part of
their slate for City Hall, believed he was a special target for Ciudadanos' hostility. He decided to join the Anglos when a bullet broke a
window in his home. He assumed that the act was committed by
someone in the Ciudadanos group.

There were also many Mexicanos who tried to stay "neutral."[12]
Generally this meant staying out of any public political activities. A
variety of explanations were given for this attempted neutrality. First,
not all Mexicanos agreed that Anglo dominance was bad. Many Mexicanos spoke of being well treated by Anglos and that they "had nothing against them." Second, others shared the belief that Anglos should
share the governance with Mexicanos but were not willing to accept
the hostility and possible economic consequences of a bitter political
battle. Mexicanos taking these positions recall being constantly pres-
sured by Anglos *and* the Ciudadanos members.

These "neutral," less politicized Mexican-Americans often shared a
number of Anglo views on local ethnic relations and political mobilization. First, they contended that local Mexicanos were economically
and socially subordinate because they had not worked hard enough,
not because Anglos had kept them down. Second, they were opposed
to polarizing their community. Third, they did not feel that there was
any need to seek change in the existing structure. For example, it was
their premise that the proposed bilingual education program would
encourage local Mexican-American students to maintain their Spanish,
and thus hinder their social mobility. Fourth, they believed that Ciudadanos members were committed to violence, a belief reinforced by
reported personal conflicts between Ciudadanos members and their
opponents. Perhaps sixty-five percent of the Mexicanos fit into this

149

broad category of politically inactive or "neutral" voters. It is among this relatively inactive majority that both the Mexicano and Anglo political leaders sought additional support. For the Raza Unida these Mexicanos were the silent, colonized Mexicano mass. For the traditional Anglo leaders they represented the more reasonable, grateful, but uneducated Mexican labor force.

The Mexican-Americans described above were often perceived and labeled by "activists" as *vendidos* (sell-outs). They were described as being "used by the gringos," but "once they became aware of this they will come over to us." It was extremely difficult for a Mexicano openly active in the Anglo political organization to live in North Town. They reportedly suffered the loss of long-time friends, insults in public places, partial boycotts of their businesses, and threats of physical violence. Their children also experienced name-calling and taunts, and some *"vendidos"* received an occasional malicious phone call or letter. Several key public figures (a Mexicano councilman, the local football coach, and a sheriff's deputy), were placed in particularly difficult positions. Because of the strong social pressures placed on a few openly pro-Anglo Mexicanos, most Mexican-Americans who were either "neutral" or privately pro-Anglo led double lives. In efforts to please both sides, they judiciously avoided any public political meetings and frequent contacts with key leaders on either side. They privately promised their support to each side and became astute managers of their public images so that neither side would doubt their loyalty.

Anglo Mobilization Against the Ciudadanos Threat

The response by North Town Anglos to the "Chicano take-over" of the city council and school board led to increased ethnic mobilization and polarization. Where members of both groups had previously developed comfortable working relationships, the confrontation created intense suspicion and hostility. It became almost impossible for people from either group to maintain inter-ethnic relations. The boundaries became so clear that one Protestant minister voiced his fear at having talked with a local Catholic priest at the funeral home. It was a casual exchange of pleasantries. Yet the Protestant minister, who was trying to "keep politics out of the church" and remain neutral, became concerned about the meeting. He worried as to how his parishioners might interpret the fact that they had been talking. This Mexicano priest was viewed by Anglos as *the* leader of Ciudadanos, or *La Raza* as Anglos referred to the group.

150

As previously mentioned, North Town Anglos had observed the Chicano movement in Aztlán City with varying degrees of interest and concern. Prior to the Spring of 1973, most Anglos in North Town believed that "their Mexicans" were not like those of Aztlán City; local Mexicans were "level headed." Yet some Anglos didn't accept this idea and accounted for the Aztlán City "take over" as a result of the Anglos' failure to include Mexicanos in local governance. North Town Anglos who shared this notion were less worried about local Mexicanos mobilizing because they had been represented on the North Town council and school board. In effect, the Aztlán City experience was not expected to be replicated in North Town. A third view held by a number of Anglos was eventually responsible for Anglo countermobilization. From this perspective, Aztlán City Chicanos were "conspiring" to take over all of South Texas. The local Ciudadanos mobilization was believed to be a covert political extension of the Raza Unida Party in Aztlán City. One of the Anglo school board members had inadvertently received Raza Unida Party publications from California addressed to "the President of the Raza Unida Party school board." These materials cited North Town as one of the three future areas "most likely to fall." Further, some Aztlán City political organizers were seen in North Town.

By the summer of 1972 at least two small groups of prominent Anglos were meeting privately to discuss the "Chicano conspiracy in South Texas." One group included the ex-councilman whom the Mexicanos called "Mr. Clean," the disgruntled ex-city manager, and several other farmers and ranchers. They generally felt that it was necessary to "fight fire with fire." According to the more moderate Anglos, "Their blood ran hot. They wanted people to start firing all their Mexican-American workers and things like that." The second group of Anglos meeting was made up of a younger, more moderate group of professionals, businessmen, and ranchers. Two members of this informal group had already defeated Mexicanos in the August special city council elections. Both groups were particularly disturbed by the spectre of Aztlán City where more than fifty percent (150 families) of the Anglos had left town.[13] Given the high percentage of Mexicanos in North Town (70%), these Anglo leaders feared a similar "destruction of the North Town community."

When Ciudadanos Unidos Mexicanos was organized in December of 1972, the more moderate Anglo group took the initiative and countered with an "inclusive" bi-racial political organization. This informal group of Anglos had "done their home work." They had been in touch with other Anglo leaders in Aztlán City and South Town where the

Raza Unida Party had scored earlier election victories. They patterned their organization after a similar one developed in South Town. This move was intended "to counter any extremist Anglo organization," *and* "to expose the Ciudadanos organization as an exclusive Mexicano and racist organization." In December, 1972, the North County Better Government League was established. A statement of purpose was agreed upon and circulated throughout the county in both languages. It reads as follows:

North County Better Government League is an organization of and for the people of North County. Its primary purpose is to actively promote good, representative government which is responsive to all the people and their needs.

The organization is for supporting those candidates which are of the highest caliber, personal integrity, background and experience which qualifies them to serve.

The organization is for keeping more than one political entity available in North County to insure that all people have a true possibility to express themselves through elected representatives.

The organization is for a viable community which can prosper and grow economically for the benefit of all our citizens. We want community harmony and everyone working together to accomplish common goals.

We are for full utilization of the abilities and talents of all our local people and equal opportunity for all without regard to political beliefs.

We support the concept of local people in positions of authority which represent the interest of local people.

We are for school systems that have as their main purpose the education of children without using them as tools for political purpose. We are for respect and obedience in the home and on and off the school campus.

The organization is for sound, honest and qualified law enforcement. We support law and order with fairness to all concerned.

We are for freedom of our religious institutions from political turmoil and upheaval.

The organization is for freedom for all people to participate and express their political beliefs without fear of intimidation.

We are for sustaining our county and its communities as a good place to live and raise our families without prejudice and fear. We are for the projection of a non-controversial attitude which will cultivate respect and interest among other people in becoming a part of our area.

The statement of the BGL (Better Government League) platform reflects, in an antithetical fashion, all the traditional cultural beliefs held by some Anglos regarding Mexicanos. Such words as "good, representative, responsible, personal integrity, harmony, freedom, honesty and fairness, and experience," were intended as contrasts to what the BGL believed characterized the "*La Raza*-type Mexican." Such ideas sought to undercut the new self-concept that local Mexicanos were attempting to encourage. The idea permeating the BGL statement of purpose was that Ciudadanos governance would not represent the interests of "all" local citizens, i.e., Mexicans generally take care of their own. There was also a heavy emphasis upon local governance, which exhibited Anglo fears regarding the Aztlán City *La Raza* "taking over" North Town. The school system was believed to be an important locus for possible ethnic political confrontation, and there were fears that even the churches might be disrupted.

The BGL had approximately two hundred dues-paying members, among whom they contended were 100 Mexican-Americans. Never more than twenty Mexican-Americans attended the business meetings, however.[14] The BGL Mexican-Americans included a number of Anglo employees in local businesses and on the ranches. There were also several independent businessmen and government employees. Those Mexican-American BGLers who were dependent economically on Anglos seemed particularly anxious to communicate a pro-Anglo posture. Yet, they did not believe in dividing the town along ethnic lines. In fact, they often expressed hostility towards Ciudadanos members for "causing all this trouble." They did not believe Anglos were the cause of the depressed economic conditions experienced by most local Mexicanos. Instead, they blamed other Mexicanos for lacking initiative and willingness to work hard. Yet, some of these same Mexican-Americans appeared to be playing both sides of the political fence. Several BGL Mexican-Americans actively sought the good will of Ciudadanos members by attending Ciudadanos rallies and socializing with the leaders. Only a few North Town Mexican-Americans publicly supported the BGL and actually cut off all relationships with Ciudadanos Mexicanos. Observers in both groups estimated that approximately two hundred Mexicanos actually voted for the BGL. These estimates are not based on detailed surveys of voter preferences, but there was considerable agreement among local observers. Various leaders were able to render long lists of specific families and how each member "leaned" politically.

In general, the active BGL members numbered no more than fifty or sixty. They included the middle-aged (thirty to fifty), middle in-

153

come ($15,000-40,000), and traditionally civic-minded community members. They were the prominent young businessmen, farmers, and ranchers who would normally run the local community institutions. Several Mexican-Americans were also officers and directors, but few community members believed them to be important leaders. Some of the key Anglo leaders had been traditionally active in politics, primarily as Republicans. Most were from old North Town families, although some were recent "returnees" to the community.

Describing precisely who wielded power in the BGL is difficult since the North Town Anglos were extremely suspicious of outside "researchers" and "reporters." Nevertheless, even without access to the inner circles of the BGL, it was reasonably clear who were the most influential leaders. No one figure actually dominated the BGL leadership. The small group that initiated much of the research on *La Raza* frequently swayed the larger group on questions of tactics and policy, however. Mr. Weeks, a rancher on the city council, Mrs. Hart, a businesswoman on the school board, and the local doctors were close to the daily political battles; consequently, they became important opinion-makers and strategists. Publicly, a local electrical contractor, several merchants, the county clerk, a retired army officer, and a number of these people's spouses were active. The wives of these leaders were especially active in organizational matters during the campaigns.

The image that most local people held of the BGL leaders was that they were the rich, "silk stocking" crowd of old North Town families. Most of the highly active leaders were not, however, considered the "big money" ranchers/farmers and retired businessmen, but they were considered "well-off, socially prominent, educated, and community-minded." Behind these people was the "real money," and their role was to quietly encourage and finance these younger, more vigorous leaders. This "up-and-coming" group was highly motivated to arouse North Towners to resist any "Chicano takeover."

Organizationally, the BGL met publicly as a group once a month during the election period. The meetings were informal and generally involved discussing illegal and socially inappropriate acts of the *La Raza*; the active membership also expressed their general ideas about campaign strategy. However, most of the important tactical decisions were made among the smaller groups of leaders and not discussed at these public meetings. Several members indicated that private meetings at selected houses and extensive use of the telephone was a much safer way of making decisions and sounding out people. Generally, the intense feelings of the younger leaders appeared to hold the group

154

together, rather than any elaborate, formalized organizational structure.

Ideologically, most BGLer's would have characterized themselves as "moderates" or "conservatives" politically. In discussions of the McGovern "take over" of the Democratic party, they were appalled at his "radicalism." Most felt that the federal government had grown too big, had given away too much money to "welfare addicts," and had meddled in the lives of people excessively. Others generalized this "creeping liberalism" and big government to many other areas of life. Some saw the American way of life declining; they felt that people no longer knew how to work, save, help a neighbor, or even be patriotic and religious. Most believed strongly in the American free-enterprise system, the American form of government, strict law-and-order, and an important role for America in preserving the free world from communism. Since they considered themselves a "modern rural people," they placed primacy on land ownership, small-town community life, and progress through a blend of rural and urban life styles. What they all shared ideologically was a sense that *La Raza* did not stand for many of the values under-pinning their political and social ideals.

In mobilizing both Anglos and Mexican-Americans a central theme of the BGL was that the Aztlán City Raza Unida was a "communist conspiracy," and the North Town Ciudadanos was a part of this plot. North Town Anglos generally believed that the local Mexicanos were being "used" by outsiders in this conspiracy. Most Anglos did not mean that any of the local Mexicanos were communists, but one man did claim that "they" were trained in Cuba.

For Anglos, the behavior of local Ciudadanos Mexicanos, some of whom were long-time associates, was extremely difficult to understand. The Anglos reasoned that their local Mexicans were content, hence the origin of their discontent had to be outsiders. A "communist conspiracy" was the only logical explanation for their new, "strange" behavior. Although the conspiracy argument was not overtly used to gather public support, the idea was common in private discussions and undoubtedly stimulated some Anglos to join and vote for the BGL.

The "conspiracy" idea was particularly ascribed to a feared takeover of the public schools. A Ciudadanos school board was expected to establish an all-Chicano administration and eventually an all-Chicano faculty. This would then lead to a Chicano curriculum and the dominant use of Spanish in the classroom, i.e., a total Chicano school system which would "push out" the Anglo students. In the Anglo

155

scenario, the same events would happen in the city hall and the county courthouse, leaving a totally Chicano environment and intolerable conditions for the Anglo minority. Police protection would be non-existent, taxes raised and misused, land-owners forced to sell, immoralities condoned, and good citizens insulted and unfairly treated. Community life would be pervaded by constant conflict, hatred, vengeance, and mismanagement. Local Anglos were filled with intense fears, and many privately confided that they would sell their properties and move if conditions worsened. It became, then, a battle for the preservation of their way of life.

The Anglo political consolidation under the BGL was more difficult, however, than the preceding discussion might imply. There were a number of basic divisions among North Town Anglos that persisted from earlier eras. Further, not all Anglos initially shared the above views of Ciudadanos members, some of whom they had known and worked with for years. Some Ciudadanos members were believed to be extremely anti-Anglo and intimately connected to the Aztlán City movement; others were perceived as acting out of altruism and as "duped into joining La Raza." The idea of a "conspiracy" was initially a powerful mobilizing concept, however, and as the political rivalry escalated, BGL leaders became increasingly suspicious and critical of all Ciudadanos leaders. Events during the spring elections of 1973 further incensed BGL members and confirmed their view that La Raza was indeed a conspiratorial, criminal group.

The BGL Campaign and Election Victories of 1973

Initially, the BGL election strategy was designed to increase Anglo awareness of the Raza threat without further provoking the Ciudadanos Mexicanos. However, this backfired early in the campaign. The most dramatic event in the campaign occurred when the BGL sponsored a public meeting and invited several Anglos and Mexican-Americans from Aztlán City to explain the effects of "their Chicano take-over." The meeting was held before a packed house (approximately 500 people) in a dance hall owned by a Mexican-American BGL member. The group was roughly fifty percent Anglo and fifty percent Mexicano. The BGL chairman introduced the speakers by saying that the purpose of the meeting was to hear several Aztlán City citizens describe the results of the Chicano take-over. There was a question period after each speaker finished. The speakers emphasized the occurrence of a heavy out-migration of "good" people, losses of industry, and declining economic growth, as well as general social

156

strife. The Chicano administration was characterized as riddled with corruption and illegal acts.

After the speaker's presentations several questions were asked in a perfunctory manner. At this point a Ciudadanos leader, Mr. Alonzo, seized the floor, and according to several observers, he began "trying to incite the crowd." He argued that North Town did not need outsiders to come and tell them how to handle their problems. He was greeted with boos, hissing, and cursing from a number of the BGL members. He continued, contending that no houses were ever burnt down by Raza Unida in Aztlán City, and that Anglos were hypocrites because when Ciudadanos brought in outsiders it was "to stir up people." On the other hand, when the BGL brought in outsiders from Atzlán City, it was merely "to inform people."

The North Town Mexicano leaders were supported by a sizeable contingent of Chicanos from Aztlán City and Mr. Ramsey Muñiz, the Raza Unida Party candidate for governor. Several of this contingent also addressed the audience in increasingly angry speeches. They accused the speakers from Aztlán City of telling only one side of the story. They demanded the right to present the "whole" picture concerning the progress that the Raza Unida had initiated in Aztlán City. The BGL chairman responded by telling them that the meeting's purpose was not to present both sides of the issue. The meeting became very unruly and incoherent, and both sides appeared ready to fight with more than words. The meeting was eventually stopped when several Mexicanos and Anglos from both Ciudadanos and the BGL, fearing physical violence, restrained the most provocative speakers. The BGL chairman quickly closed the meeting and the crowd dispersed without further trouble.

This meeting was an important event in North Town history for several reasons. It was the first time that local Mexicanos had publicly challenged Anglos. It overtly symbolized what had previously existed covertly—political polarization along ethnic lines. Some Anglos, who voiced the opinion that the meeting had been a bad tactical mistake, placed the blame on "racist" BGL members. However, most Anglos believed the behavior of the Mexicanos at the meeting supported their contention that Mexicanos are disorderly, boisterous, foulmouthed, and prone to an excess of emotion, which can lead to physical violence.

On the other hand, local Mexicanos believed the meeting to be another example of Anglo chicanery. One Mexicano participant mentioned that after the meeting several Mexican-Americans attempted

157

to speak to the BGL leader regarding the one-sided presentation. The BGL leader allegedly told them that "we speak and you listen." He strongly denies these charges. The Mexicanos responded by telling the Anglos that the old days of the supposedly dumb, sleepy Mexican who passively took orders from Anglos were gone. They threatened that, "if the Anglo did not wake up and listen, his days were numbered." This incident where the Anglo BGL leader told the Mexicanos "we speak and you listen," became the Mexicano rallying cry. It was much used and quoted to symbolize how racist the Anglo BGL of North Town was.

The remainder of the spring 1973 election campaign was anticlimactic compared to the previously described meeting. Anglos sought to respond to Ciudadanos tactics wherever they appeared. Ciudadanos ran radio spots and newspaper ads. The BGL countered them with their own. It quickly became obvious in the campaign that the BGL had more money and time to devote to the campaign.

A second public meeting was attempted by the BGL about a month after the first. This was a covered dish supper with a speaker from the Governor's Office. The audience consisted of mainly BGL leaders, some Anglo supporters, and approximately two dozen Mexicanos. The members of Ciudadanos did not attend. The Governor's representative, a Mexican-American, pleased the Anglo audience by emphasizing citizenship, hard work, and the secret ballot. His discussion of citizenship stressed the need for all people to work together regardless of race; local problems could only be solved by local citizens. The stress on the work ethic stemmed from the Anglos' notion that anyone could succeed in America if they worked hard. The speaker also touched on the secret ballot because some Anglos feared that Mexican-American voters were being intimidated. The BGL contended that Mrs. Tolivar, a city councilperson, was telling Mexicano voters that they should vote for Ciudadanos because her husband, the police chief, had the key to the ballot box and could check their ballots. She strongly denied these charges. The BGL ran the following ad in the local newspaper, however:

> Has anyone ever told you that the election officials or any one else can tell you how you voted? If so, they do not understand the secret ballot.
>
> You do not identify yourself on the ballot—if you do it is thrown out as a mutilated ballot. You do sign the stub and detach it from the ballot.
>
> The stub box is sealed by the District Clerk before delivering it to the polls and remains sealed until it is returned to the District Clerk and destroyed, after time for a contest expires.

The unidentified ballots are placed in the ballot box which is kept by the election officials or their agent until destroyed.

NO ONE IS ALLOWED OR AUTHORIZED TO COMPARE THE STUBS WITH THE BALLOTS.

Therefore your ballot is SECRET.

After the meeting several Anglos said they were disappointed that the "radical Mexicans did not hear the speaker because it would have done them good." The two previously described BGL events illustrate their attempts to use external power sources to influence a larger segment of the public. Anglo visitors from Aztlán City and the Governor's Office were important symbols to promote publicly the BGL view of the conflict. The Aztlán City Anglos warned people of the "Chicano conspiracy." They stressed that the open confrontation at the BGL meeting demonstrated the lawless character of "Chicano politics." Conversely, the man from the Governor's Office symbolized the legality of the Anglo's cause, their desire for racial harmony, and the fairness of the present election system.

On several other occasions during the campaign, Anglos also used state agencies and laws to thwart the Mexicanos. They had a Mexicano police chief disqualified by using a regulation of the State Law Enforcement Officers Association. The newly appointed police chief of the Ciudadanos-controlled council was forced to relinquish his position because of a DWI violation on his record. This was ultimately a very important tactical error. In order for Mr. Tolivar to be appointed, his wife, who was the newly elected councilwoman, had to resign her two-year position. Her resignation was necessary to avoid a conflict of interest charge. Her seat had to be filled temporarily and came up for election in the following spring. Anglo councilmen openly vowed that they would "go after this appointment," but the newly elected Mexicano council felt they held the power and could do whatever they wanted. By using this state organization and a state law, the Anglos were able to force the Mexicano police chief out of office, as well as open for election a third council seat.

A second related tactical mistake that the Ciudadanos made during their first year of council control was in their choice of the mayoral candidate for the spring elections in 1973. One of the councilmen elected in 1972 decided to vacate his seat and run for the mayoral position. Consequently, this opened four of the seven council positions up for general election, instead of the two positions required for regular rotation. That made it possible for the Anglos to regain control of the council within one year, if they could get out the vote and sweep the 1973 elections. The only explanation that the Mexicano candidates had for these moves, in retrospect, was the belief that they would win anyway. They conceded that both of these moves were serious tactical errors, perhaps due to overconfidence during their first year on the council.

There were several other key tactical moves during the campaign period that illustrate the skillful uses of laws and political tactics by the more experienced Anglos. First, the hold-over Anglo councilmen were able to stall an attempt of the city council to annex a large Mexicano residential section containing more than a hundred votes. The vote on this issue was postponed several times for lack of information, technical irregularities in the survey plot, and improper procedures for annexation. When it ultimately came to a vote, the Mexicanos did not have a majority, and the issue was tabled until after the elections. Second, two Mexicano BGL members ran as third school board candidates in order to split the vote of the two Ciudadanos candidates. This tactic of having two Spanish-surname candidates was expected to split the Mexicano vote, and to a small degree it may have. Finally, and most important, the BGL worked very hard to organize their neighborhoods. Blocks were assigned to members who organized telephone committees and set up transportation facilities on election day. Many voters were called four and five times by BGL members, and supporters encouraged them to "get to the polls and beat *La Raza*."

The election campaign conducted by Ciudadanos, on the other hand, was directed exclusively toward mobilizing Mexicanos. Activity centered around educating new Mexicano voters to read and use the ballot. Radio spots in Spanish communicated the idea that the Mexicanos were in the majority, which meant that they should govern themselves. They argued that the Anglos were a minority that had governed too long, and that only Mexicano leaders would help their community acquire adequate and better streets, drainage, sewers, housing, parks, jobs and education. Several rallies were held in the park near the Catholic church and some of the more active women and candidates spent several weekends campaigning from door-to-door. Most Ciudadanos' Mexicanos acknowledged, however, that they lacked the time and money to conduct a strong and organized campaign.[15]

As a result of the intensive Anglo mobilization and the relative disorganization among the Ciudadanos Mexicanos, the Anglos swept the elections, recapturing control of the city hall and electing two Anglo incumbents to the school board. The two Anglo school board candidates polled more than 1,000 votes in a heavy turnout (forty-five percent of the registered voters). In the city election, the Ciudadanos candidate for mayor, an incumbent councilman, narrowly defeated the Anglo candidate, a retired army officer, by a vote of 1,042 to 981 (fifty percent of the registered voters). The Anglo candidates for councilman, however, narrowly defeated Ciudadanos candidates for the three vacant seats. Although Anglos regained voting control of the city council, they were still in a four-to-three minority on the school board.

Immediately following the elections, the losing candidates from each side called for a recount. Only a few votes were found to be invalidly marked, however, and the results of the election did not significantly change. Following the recount, the BGL raised $10,000 among its enraged members for a suit alleging that numerous criminal voting irregularities had occurred. In the fall a grand jury studied the lists of voters and subsequently subpoenaed more than three hundred people to determine whether they voted legally. Ultimately, the grand jury handed over thirty-two indictments of eleven people on charges of forgery, tampering with the ballot box, non-resident, alien, deceased, and felon voters, irregular absentee ballots, and irregular use of voter registration cards. The district attorney then determined to prosecute five people on eleven counts. These cases were eventually plea-bargained, and all the defendants pleaded guilty and were fined $150.

Both the BGL and Ciudadanos leaders were upset by the decision of the court. Some BGL leaders contended that the "willy-nilly, spineless district attorney and the district judge" had been extraordinarily lenient. They accused them of fearing that they "might soil their political hands," since they were running for reelection the following year. The BGL contended that a small number of Ciudadanos leaders had conspired with the two city clerks to "steal the election." They argued that there was enough evidence from the grand jury investigation to convict them of forgery, fraud, and conspiracy, charges that could imprison them for up to twenty years. The *La Raza* city clerks had purportedly forged names, obtained voter registration cards from elderly people, written in absentee votes for people that were deceased, out-of-state, or alien, and had encouraged people to vote several times.

In the view of a prominent BGL member:

"It was really disgusting the way the Mexicano *politicos* used their own people . . . It (the grand jury investigation and indictments) was not

161

the vicious thing that the majority of the Mexicano people see it as being. The reason they see it that way is because that is what the *politicos* want them to see. They knew damn well that there was every reason for another 200 or 300 indictments, and more against they themselves. When you have used your own people and have been caught with your britches down, the best thing to say is that "we didn't really do this. The gringos are just trying to brow beat our old ones into subservience and submissiveness, and they are afraid to go vote." . . . A lot of those people were ignorant and were used, but ignorance of the law is not a defense.

Anglo BGL members were also quick to point out that the issue involved in their suit was the preservation of free, democratic elections, not racial prejudice or merely an Anglo political tactic. They feared that the new Ciudadanos leaders were corrupt, and that being in control of the city elections, would continue to "steal elections." Both Anglos and Mexican-Americans in the BGL felt this way, and apparently two prominent Mexicano BGL leaders on the grand jury were central in discovering various irregularities. The Anglo grand jury members were unfamiliar with many of the Spanish-surnamed voters; consequently, the Mexican-American grand jury members were able to spot aliens, non-residents, and deceased voters. They also served as the key interviewers and interpreters for many of the older voters subpoenaed. They too were certain that these new Mexicano *politicos* were criminally involved in a conspiracy and were dismayed at the court's leniency. Perhaps more than any other single event, this alleged conspiracy rallied Anglos and anti-Ciudadanos Mexicanos around the BGL organization.

On the other hand, Ciudadanos leaders had a very different view of the BGL election suit. They contended that there was no organized conspiracy to defraud the elections. They argued that the grand jury actually found little evidence of any criminal conspiracy, and that only a few inexperienced Mexicano voters had made procedural mistakes in voting. They supported this contention by pointing out how few indictments were actually handed down, and argued that actually only two voters, felons from previous convictions, were guilty. All of the voters indicted pleaded guilty and plea bargained, they contended, to keep the felons from going to jail.

For the Ciudadanos leaders the suit was a vicious, politically motivated tactic of the BGL to frighten Mexicano voters, and hence destroy the *movimiento*. They described how several hundred Mexicano voters being called before the grand jury struck fear into the entire community. This drove many voters away from future political participation. Further, to them the grand jury was a highly illegal procedure and little more than a "kangaroo court." They pointed out that not a single Ciudadanos member was on the committee and that the twelve person jury was "really run by Anglo and Mexicano BGL members." At least by local political reputation, the grand jury was indeed made up of predominantly BGL members or political "neutrals."

The grand jury was not selected "on the spot" as some Mexicano community members believed, however. This particular grand jury was selected in the usual manner by a jury selection committee of the county commissioner's court for a one year term prior to this case. It should be pointed out, however, that research on grand jury selection indicates that disproportionate numbers of prominent, educated, well-known citizens are traditionally chosen for grand jury duty. North Town is perhaps no different from a number of American small towns in this regard; except in this case when having "representation" was critical, the new group of Mexicano *politicos* were clearly unrepresented. The Ciudadanos leaders were faced with a tradition of grand jury appointees that tend to be personally and socially connected with traditional county, city, and school leaders.

The deliberations of this grand jury became a highly significant political event. Both the BGL and the Ciudadanos leaders used the investigation to mobilize their supporters. The BGL leaders mobilized people against the "criminal *La Raza* leaders," and the Ciudadanos mobilized people against the "vicious, racist Anglos." Whether there actually was a conspiracy to defraud the elections was never proven, and that was an extremely sensitive subject upon which to query North Towners. That it greatly polarized racial and political feelings, and was a watershed in North Town ethnic relations is clear, however. Eventually, 170 voters were declared illegal, and the BGL mayoral candidate assumed office. The first elected Mexicano mayor and the Ciudadanos had suffered a bitter defeat. The BGL, feeling that a vicious, criminal attempt at "stealing the elections" had occurred, were also bitter and ready to destroy *La Raza*. In short, the community conflict escalated to new heights.

Community Leadership in a Polarized Ethnic Context

After the election defeat of the Ciudadanos in the city council, the focus of the community conflict shifted to the school board.[16] Ciudadanos still retained a tenuous but potentially controlling four-to-three majority. As noted earlier, school board members of both ethnic groups and administrative personnel had developed good working relationships prior to the bitter campaign of 1973. The Board was making decisions on regular district matters such as taxation, budget, discipline, and personnel problems. It was also beginning to study and develop an experimental bilingual program and to recruit more Mexican-American teachers. Further, both groups agreed unanimously on issues such as student discipline and the dress code. Their unity was particularly evident in the case of the Board's rejection of a textbook which the teachers' textbook committee had recommended. One Anglo board member felt that the text did not present the United States government in an appropriate manner. The Ciudadanos Mexicanos, although critical of some aspects of American society, went along with the Anglos in rejecting this "liberal" textbook. Ultimately the old classic, MacGruder's *American Government*, also judged as rather liberal, was approved. Anglo and Mexicano board members generally agreed then, on most issues. The lone exception was one Anglo rancher who usually voted against the two more "liberal" Anglos and Ciudadanos members.

During the spring of 1973, both sides were increasingly drawn into more extreme positions. Mr. Esposito and Mr. Rápido, the school board members, were active in the community-wide political organization, but they were often perceived as too moderate and conciliatory in their actions on the school board. Likewise, at least two of the Anglos were quite active in the BGL from the beginning, one being adamant and the other more moderate. The third Anglo board member never did participate in the BGL and was able to remain fairly independent. The more moderate Anglo BGL member kept a low profile in the beginning stages of the BGL, and it was not evident to the Mexicano board members that this person was active in the BGL. Active members of both the BGL and the Ciudadanos exerted considerable pressure upon all board members to be openly partisan and not to let the other side "get away with anything."

As the campaign developed, one of the Anglo board members up for re-election convinced the Mexicano board members of her neutrality and desire to represent both Anglos and Mexicanos. An understanding developed that Ciudadanos would discourage any opposition candidate from running for her position. The Ciudadanos board members had a high regard for the skill of this particular Anglo and felt that no opposition was required. Consequently, two of the Ciudadanos board members reported making a strong appeal on the Anglo's behalf at the Ciudadanos meeting when the potential slate was discussed. The issue created a lively debate among members, which continued for

164

a number of weeks. The Mexicano board members eventually persuaded Ciudadanos to go along with this Anglo candidate.

Meanwhile, the filing deadline for candidates was approaching, and some BGL leaders were increasingly suspicious of the tenuous agreement with the Ciudadanos candidates. There was considerable debate on whether to run other BGL Spanish-surname candidates in the same positions that BGL Anglos were seeking. In case the Ciudadanos tried to file late candidates to split the Anglo vote, the BGL could counter with their own vote-splitting candidates. On the final filing day the board members were scheduled to visit the Atzlán City bilingual program. Fearful that Ciudadanos was trying "to get the Anglo candidates out of town so they could file a late candidate," the BGL leaders decided to run two additional BGL Mexicano candidates to split the vote; consequently, an employee of the Anglo candidate's husband and BGL officer filed and ran. The Ciudadanos never actually filed another candidate to split the vote.

The Ciudadanos board members interpreted this act as treason because they had openly supported the "supposedly liberal gringa," despite heavy criticism from their group. The other members of Ciudadanos were now able to say, "You see, all gringos are alike, you can't trust any of them." After this event, there was a rapid movement toward separatism, and an increase in the number of Mexican-Americans who shared anti-Anglo sentiments. Suspicion toward all Anglos, including the "researchers," ran high, and those Ciudadanos members who had been "trusting," such as Mr. Esposito and Mr. Rápido, suffered a loss of face among Mexicanos. The Ciudadanos members often used this case as an illustration of the deceitful, racist character of all Anglos; consequently, a growing number of the Ciudadanos leaders, such as councilpersons Salinas and Tolivar, felt the need for a more aggressive anti-Anglo posture.

The first post-election school board meeting was devoted to reorganization. The former Anglo chairperson and the senior Ciudadanos member, Mr. Esposito, were nominated for the position of board chairperson. There were four Ciudadanos and three Anglo board members, but to everyone's amazement the Anglo candidate won. As the board meeting proceeded, Mr. Esposito and Mr. Rápido frantically passed notes to each other. After the meeting they expressed great dismay and anger. The Ciudadanos members had arranged to elect Mr. Esposito, but one member broke rank and voted for the Anglo. Much later it was learned that the Mexicano dissenter apparently had hard feelings towards Mr. Esposito which were not expressed during their planning session. This event was often interpreted as an example of how Mexicanos work against themselves and how they were intimidated by Anglos. The Mexicano leaders lamented that successful political action was still undermined by Mexicanos "who do not know how to unite and vote for their own kind."

Whereas earlier school board meetings had been marked by cordiality between the two ethnic groups, the 1973 campaign created a clear polarization among board members. During the remainder of the 1973 school year, each school board meeting was like a poker game; the competing groups revealed no emotion, and every issue called forth a series of maneuvers designed to gain control over each other. It was necessary to keep informed about the issues between meetings to understand the transactions during the meeting itself.

In response to the election of the Anglo board chairperson, the Ciudadanos members attempted to "impeach" the newly-elected Anglo in a subsequent meeting. Believing that their four votes were under control, Ciudadanos decided to unseat the Anglo chairperson. Since this was not an item of business on the agenda, the Ciudadanos leaders made a motion to amend the agenda and add this topic. They voted four to three to add the issue of impeachment, but the chairperson then declared that a two-thirds majority, not a simple majority was required in Robert's Rules and the U.S. Senate to suspend the rules. The chairperson called home and had a copy of *Robert's Rules of Order* sent to the meeting so the section specifying a two-thirds majority could be cited. The Ciudadanos were out-maneuvered again. Later they learned that the Board's operating procedures were not well specified. Informally the board had been using the Future Farmers of America school handbook, which was a condensed version of Robert's Rules. At the next meeting, with a BGL majority, the Board adopted Robert's Rules as binding. The Anglo board members contended that this was done to prevent further conflict. The Ciudadanos members contended it was to manipulate them further.

As the conflict escalated, the Ciudadanos began openly characterizing the superintendent, several other administrators, and a number of Anglo teachers as racist. The earlier public confrontations over control of the city council had shifted to the school board where Ciudadanos still had a majority. The post-election board meetings were attended by a crowd (twenty to thirty people) of BGL observers, which Mexicanos perceived as a pressure tactic. The Ciudadanos attempted to counter this tactic by getting an equal number of Mexicanos to attend the board meeting. At several of the post-election meetings members of both groups had tape recorders. Anglos reportedly expected the

166

Ciudadanos members to try to impeach the chairperson again, and they wanted to accurately document the proceedings in anticipation of a court case. The audience added tension to the meetings and apparently was effective at persuading Ciudadanos board members to stay away. One or two of the Ciudadanos members were frequently "busy" on the night of board meetings, which often left the board deadlocked.

One key event in late May illustrates the effectiveness of Anglo pressure on some of the Ciudadanos board members. The final, major act by the Ciudadanos to increase their control over the schools was to engineer the hiring of a "Chicano superintendent." By late May the Ciudadanos leaders were convinced that the Anglo superintendent was a weak "yes man," playing "both sides." They frequently said that he was more interested in "saving his skin than changing things for our Chicanitos." To bring in a "real Chicano," without arousing Anglos, they persuaded the assistant superintendent of Aztlán City to apply for a vacant federal programs director. After he was in the school system, they planned to fire the Anglo superintendent and elevate him to the top position. The Anglos were quick to see through this ploy, however; while the superintendent and the board initially expressed a positive view of the Aztlán City candidate, they were busy developing better pressure tactics to force the Mexicano board members to absent themselves. The Ciudadanos' hopes of hiring the Aztlán City administrator and firing the Anglo superintendent were dashed when the board, minus two Ciudadanos members, hired a Mexican-American candidate from Laredo. The remaining Ciudadanos members attributed this to the tension-filled meetings which made their woman board member nervous and ill. Ciudadanos was frequently unable to muster its majority membership to outvote the BGL.

By the fall one of the most controversial incidents in the troubled North Town school board occurred. One of the Ciudadanos board members, the son of Mr. Talvez, the largest melon grower, stopped attending the meetings. His absence created what appeared to be a permanent three-to-three deadlock. There were several theories why this board member stopped attending meetings. Some people contended that he was too busy with work. Others contended that he was being blackmailed economically. The board member worked in partnership with his father buying and selling produce. Their business was based on contract-buying of produce from producers in Mexico, the Rio Grande Valley, and the North Town area. Several Ciudadanos members reported that the Anglos had called one of Mr. Talvez's main Valley suppliers and had sought to persuade them to stop doing business with him.

Further, it was widely believed among Ciudadanos members that one of the Anglo board members had refused to renew a lease for a tract of land (175 acres) on which Talvez had drilled a $30,000 well. They reported that this landowner had "talked to Mr. Talvez to get his son out of politics." The Anglo board member accused of blackmailing the Ciudadanos board member strongly denied such charges and reported that the lease in question was terminated a year before the elections for forty-one different lease violations, not for any political reasons. The Ciudadanos board member in question reported that his father had requested him to pay more attention to business and less attention to politics but made no specific accusations. For whatever reason, it is noteworthy that the son became conspicuously absent from school board meetings during the last year of his term. Both Ciudadanos and other BGL members subsequently mentioned that "he had been brought into line." Whether the charges of economic blackmail were true in this particular case was not clear and most difficult to establish. The Ciudadanos board members did, however, use the incident to explain how they had lost their majority "through the economic blackmail of the gringos," which helped mobilize their followers against the BGL.

Eventually, the Mexican-American board members could not withstand what they perceived as Anglo intimidation. They countered by boycotting the meetings. Thus, the board lacked a quorum; school business that required Board action was stalled so that the emerging Anglo control of the board was blocked. On one occasion the superintendent lamented the fact that the board had not met for three months (the summer period), and business was stacked up. During the post-election period only business vitally necessary for school maintenance was accomplished. At one point late that summer the school system still needed board approval to hire some fifteen or twenty teachers. It should be noted, however, that despite these problems, the school year began relatively smoothly, and the board began to function again in the fall of 1973.

The Increasing Politicization of Mexicano Community Leaders

The change in ethnic relations stimulated by the election of 1973 led the Ciudadanos board members to redefine past board issues. An example of this was the textbook rejection case, discussed earlier. Although the Ciudadanos had supported the Anglos for a more "pa-

168

triotic" text, they now believed that Anglos were really choosing texts to keep Mexicano students ignorant. The Ciudadanos members stated that they would be suspicious the next time Anglos wanted to reject a text, for this would probably mean that the text had something that would enhance Mexican students' understanding of the Anglo system.

The school board leaders, Mr. Esposito and Mr. Rápido, became convinced that Anglo control of schools would have to be broken completely. Whereas they previously believed that the present Anglo administration was sympathetic enough to promote Mexican-American needs, they gradually came to the conclusion that a "Chicano administration" was necessary. They felt that changes would not be forthcoming *until* the school was predominantly Chicano. A Chicano superintendent would actively recruit Mexicano administrative assistants and teachers, who would produce the needed curriculum changes. They supported this line of reasoning by pointing to the proposed bilingual program. Anglos were now perceived to be procrastinating in introducing such a program. Earlier cooperation on the program was now perceived as "a trick by the Anglos to buy us off."

Although Ciudadanos members had initially discussed mobilizing the students, they did not pursue the idea, primarily at the insistence of the Mexicano priest, Father Reynaldo. The Ciudadanos school board leaders generally shared the BGL position that "politics should be kept out of the schools." Still, local political conflicts manifested themselves in student behavior, even though Ciudadanos avoided politicizing students and the schools. This traditional belief about politics in the schools began to change during the 1973–1974 school year.

The events of that year forced the Anglo superintendent, the principals, and teachers into choosing sides or making concerted efforts to avoid any public political behavior.[18] Before the elections the superintendent contended that he had open, friendly, and confidential relationships with at least three of the four Ciudadanos board members. Early interviews with the Mexicano board members as well as observations of their interaction with the superintendent substantiated his contentions. But as the ethnic conflict escalated, the superintendent gradually became estranged from the Ciudadanos board members. Leaders from both groups constantly placed the superintendent in situations where he had to choose sides. After the attempt to bring in the Aztlán City Chicano administrator, the most outspoken Ciudadanos board member, Mr. Esposito, told the superintendent that he wanted to fire him. They reportedly accused him of "siding with the gringos and dragging his feet." The separation between the superin-

169

tendent and the Ciudadanos board members widened until both believed the other to be the enemy.

The superintendent's attempt to maintain neutrality often caused him to vacillate. Teachers and other administrators interpreted this as a sign of "weakness." Administrators, staff, and teachers were nearly unanimous in their perception of the superintendent as a "puppet of the school board." There was general consensus that the superintendent could not be counted on for support in case of problems with the school board or the local citizenry. The superintendent privately described his situation as extremely delicate and demanding. He agonized over the conflict, and during the tense 1973 school year he "kept his options open" and considered leaving. The Anglo board members put considerable pressure on him to stay, however, "to help straighten this mess out." As the BGL became increasingly strong and the Mexicanos increasingly "militant," the superintendent became more openly anti-Raza Unida. He considered the past Mexicano board members to be pretty "good ole' boys" who had been "led astray by the radicals." He considered the Raza Unida of Aztlán City extremely corrupt and claimed he could see its influence locally, "because the new Ciudadanos candidates are getting worse, closer to the bottom of the barrel, the more radical they get."

The principals and faculty generally maintained a neutral public position toward the community confrontations. There were, nevertheless, a few Anglo teachers married to active BGL members, and also several Mexicano administrators and teachers who were quietly supportive of the Ciudadanos organization. However, unless a particular event called a teacher or principal to the Board's attention, most school personnel tended to keep a low public profile. Many problems in the every day life of the schools were invariably related to the local political conflicts. Principals and teachers were well aware of this and tried to avoid as many student confrontations as possible. One principal resigned at the end of the 1973 school year after he was caught between the two ethnic groups over a discipline issue. Another principal left North Town because he felt that the atmosphere created untenable working conditions.

Although the majority of teachers did not participate in the local political activities, many were quite concerned about possible consequences to themselves. Several teachers organized a local chapter of the Texas Classroom Teachers' Association (TCTA) as early as the fall of 1972. The school board interpreted this action as a "power play by teachers." The actual purpose of the local chapter's organization was two fold. First, some teachers felt that they needed greater protection in a situation where "the board is strong and the administration is weak." They generally feared that the board had become too powerful, and that the administration was unlikely to protect their rights. A case often cited was the dismissal of a teacher for "paddling students," a practice not uncommon in the schools. The TCTA organizers agreed that the teacher had acted improperly, but they questioned the decision as being too extreme. Such strong action seemed to establish a precedent for arbitrary dismissals that might require teachers with grievances to "fight for their rights through a hearing." Since TCTA provides legal resources for teachers, as does the Texas State Teachers Association (TSTA), this was one service the organizers emphasized. The second major issue was the teachers' fear of a possible "Chicano takeover." Local teachers were aware of what had taken place in Aztlán City and hoped that the state TCTA would provide defense in case Chicano candidates were elected to the school board and began to "indiscriminately" fire Anglo teachers. Many Anglo teachers shared the BGL beliefs about the Raza Unida.

The growing political conflict between Mexicanos and Anglos also affected students. The school administration and teachers recalled that during the spring elections of 1973 student discipline problems were above normal. Several examples were cited which supported this notion. First, a band concert was presented by a South Texas university. The band had a large number of Mexican-American members, some of whom played solo numbers. The solo performances were exceptionally well-done and a large number of the students responded by giving the soloist a standing ovation. However, some of the Mexicano students yelled "Viva La Raza!" and gave the Brown Power sign—a raised clinched fist. This disturbed the Anglo school leaders and local Anglo Board members. The initial reaction was a threat to cancel the remaining assemblies.

Another major conflict during the 1972–1973 school year involved the son of an Anglo rancher and several Mexican-Americans. The Anglo boy, a high school football player, initially beat up a Mexicano boy for dating an Anglo girl. The Anglo boy was disturbed that the Anglo girl was going out with a "Mexican dope freak," and he wanted to "protect her." The Mexicano youth was a popular "ladies man" who played in the band, had long hair, and "cruised around town" in his van. After several warnings, the Anglo youth beat the Mexicano youth up. This greatly angered a number of the Mexicano's friends who considered the fight unfair for several reasons. No Anglo had any business telling a Mexicano that he could not date an Anglo girl; that decision was up to the girl. Further, the fight was a mismatch because

171

the Mexicano was not a "fighter type," and the Anglo was a rugged football player. Finally, the Anglo provoked the fight because he was a "redneck bigot who hated all Mexicans, and a bully who never picked on Mexicanos his own size."

Given this reasoning, several of the Mexicano boy's buddies, who were "real *vatos*," (fighter types) jumped the Anglo in the school halls and beat him up. The Anglo student was suspended for three days. The main Mexicano offender, who had previously been suspended twice, was suspended for the remainder of the semester. The Mexicanos considered this a victory, however. They pointed out that none of the Anglo passers-by came to his rescue, which showed that Anglos really had no solidarity. The Anglos reported, however, that they considered the beating a typical "Mexican way of fighting," i.e., unfair, in gangs "like a pack of wolves." The incident apparently further crystallized the growing split between Mexicanos and Anglos, but no more fights broke out during the 1972–1973 school year.

Students from both groups were reported to be always watching to see "who was getting away with something." Both groups were constantly maneuvering for control of the school. Mexicano students reported several cases in which Anglo teachers attempted to encourage them to run for office. Mexicanos interpreted this as a traditional Anglo tactic to split the Mexicano vote. One Mexican-American teacher counseled Mexicano students to "get together" and not fall into that trap. Generally, however, it would be inaccurate to characterize daily student relations as filled with open aggression and fighting. The above incidents indicate the potential for violence and the tension that existed.

The Rise of the Raza Unida Party in the Fall of 1973

The election defeat in the spring of 1973 and the ensuing grand jury investigation of voting irregularities were bitter experiences for the Ciudadanos Mexicanos. Several hundred local citizens were subpoenaed to appear before the grand jury, which struck fear into the hearts of many Mexicano voters. Not only had they lost their newly acquired control of local institutions, but five supporters had pleaded guilty to voter irregularities. Further, the BGL had removed their only successful candidate, the first elected Mexicano mayor, Mr. Matamoros. Many Mexicanos regarded this final act as particularly ruthless and vindictive. The newly elected mayor was well-liked in the community, and it was common knowledge that his restaurant business had suffered during his attempt to win political office. The local Anglos, some of whom they had thought were friends had said, "we talk and you listen." The BGL Anglos had also used clever tactics, thus nullifying their possible control of school board policy. Above all, they had used outside agencies, speakers, and legal technicalities to defeat Mexicano candidates. By the fall of 1973 the politically inexperienced Ciudadanos had learned a number of bitter lessons in the game of politics. They expressed extreme hatred for the BGL and Anglos and vowed to fight on in the spring elections of 1974.

The mood of bitterness was, however, also colored by frustration and confusion, and the Mexicanos stood willing to fight but uncertain as to who would lead and how they were to do battle. In the face of a seemingly confident, well-organized, and well-financed BGL, some Ciudadanos members were calling for different tactics. They felt that the trickery and deception of the Anglo could only be countered by organization and a stronger stance.

During the summer and fall of 1973 no single, persuasive, effective leader emerged, and no clear plan of action was developed.[19] Ciudadanos only formally met once during the fall of 1973, and the discussion revolved around discriminatory events which happened during the elections and which were happening in the local schools. The meeting turned out to be what one member called a "bitch session, which didn't do us no good. We still don't have an organization for the elections." Many of the key male leaders in the Ciudadanos were not present, and several women active in promoting improvements in the schools and local health programs led the discussion.

Although very little formal, large group activity was occurring, a number of important realignments were taking place. As indicated, the Ciudadanos organization originally grew out of a fusion of two informal Mexicano groups, the more moderate businessmen and professionals and the younger Raza Unida. From the inception of Ciudadanos these two groups had their differences, and open arguments and personal slights and remarks were common. The first officers of the Ciudadanos were all members of the more moderate group, but the two young council candidates in 1972 were generally sympathetic to many aspects of the Raza Unida approach in Aztlán City.

The key personalities which moved Ciudadanos toward affiliating with the Raza Unida Party were Alberto Salinas, a city councilman and grocery store owner, and Noel Ramírez, a vegetable farmer. These two young men became convinced that the only way the Ciudadanos would win against the BGL was to join the Raza Unida Party and come out more forcefully. The councilwoman and her husband, an unsuccessful candidate for sheriff, as well as several other people originally considered more moderate also agreed with these emerging leaders. In effect, the smaller, less influential Raza Unida faction added some important new allies from within the larger Ciudadanos group. Paradoxically, however, the most militant, young Raza Unida members became less active in actual organizational matters. Two went back to college, two became involved with their farming activities, and the fifth, the lawyer-city manager, became disenchanted and concentrated on his managerial job with a local melon grower. Even the previously active councilwoman and her husband became less involved in planning strategy and organizing meetings.

The more active rank-and-file members, particularly several key women community workers and organizers, became, however, more vocal about Ciudadanos joining Raza Unida. The more moderate but now disenchanted school board leaders, the Mexicano priest, and several prominent businessmen and professionals grumbled and complained about this drift towards a Raza Unida affiliation. They warned that a "radical approach would turn off" the average Mexicano who believed the "gringo stories about Raza Unida." Others expressed the feeling that it was a weak organization that really could do nothing for the North Town Ciudadanos. Some felt that Raza Unida was, in fact, too philosophically radical and "socialistic." They felt that taking over the county Democratic party made more political sense. The Democratic party-oriented Mexicanos were also less enthusiastic about the Raza Unida emphasis on Chicano culture and dialect. They questioned how such practices would help their children get ahead as much as education, mastery of English, and business acumen.

The dissenting moderates expressed their views mainly in private meetings, however. They remained a disorganized, silent, somewhat confused mixture of people. They could not deny the Raza Unida advocates' charges that the gringos had "played unfairly" and had "bullied and fooled the inexperienced Mexicanos." The moderates had erred by trusting the gringos and had been "made to look like fools," hence they tended to remain silent. They grumbled about how Salinas and Ramírez were trying to "take over Ciudadanos" and "to call a secret meeting to form the Raza Unida Party." Reluctantly, the moderates began to withdraw from active leadership positions, and the energetic Mr. Salinas and Mr. Ramírez worked hard to organize sentiment for a new party.

The meeting to form the Raza Unida Party on November 15th was poorly attended (thirty-five to forty people) compared to earlier Ciudadanos meetings (a hundred plus people). Nearly all of the formerly active members of the original Raza Unida faction were present. The

174

key women community leaders active in politics and sympathetic towards Raza Unida were also there. Only six or eight of the original, more moderate school leaders and businessmen attended. The meeting began with the presentation of several speakers from the Aztlán City Raza Unida. One woman organizer gave an inspiring speech about the rights of Chicanos and the role that Raza Unida was playing in that struggle. She emphasized the need for a third party, an all-Mexican party. She was followed by two other party leaders who spoke briefly on the successes of Raza Unida statewide and in Aztlán City. They emphasized the many government grants and new programs they were able to obtain.

Finally, the leader of the party, José Angel Gutiérrez, also spoke. His entrance was very dramatic, and the North Town group clearly expressed admiration and enthusiasm for him. He spoke of the Mexicano having the *pantalones* to fight for his rights and illustrated the Raza Unida's willingness to fight the gringos with stories of victories in the courts and in the elections. The North Town Ciudadanos members asked several questions about how to organize and convince people who were still scared of the Raza Unida. Little practical advice was given, but the Aztlán City Raza leaders did encourage them to overcome such obstacles. After about one hour of discussion and speeches, the North Town Cuidadanos elected Noel Ramírez, the active young farmer, their county chairman. He proceeded to ask who was in favor of joining Raza Unida. There was no discussion, and it appeared that everyone was at least in tacit agreement. It seemed that the act of joining Raza Unida was perceived as an inevitable event, not really a question of debate. The crowd was generally optimistic about the change. After the meeting, the North Town and Aztlán City Raza groups mingled together, joked and talked for a few minutes. The North Town Ciudadanos Unidos, approximately one and one-half years later, had formally become what key Anglo leaders were labeling them since 1972, the Raza Unida Party. What importance this would have in the coming election remained the big question in the minds of many local Mexicano and Anglo leaders.

The reactions to this formal announcement of becoming Raza Unida Party were varied in the community. As indicated, the moderates and the original radicals began retreating to the political sidelines. The moderates retreated for a variety of reasons, but mainly because they felt that going openly Raza Unida was "bad politics" and "would lose votes." The original "radicals," having "converted" others to do the organizing and persuading of the masses, withdrew to their jobs and businesses. Some "radicals" expressed disillusion with local Mexicanos for being *pendejo* (stupid) or *flojo* (lazy) and afraid of fighting. It was, therefore, a waste of their energy to fight for a people who were too timid and apathetic to fight for themselves. Others expressed a satisfaction, something of an "I-told-you-so" view, with the failure of moderates who trusted gringos.

It was in this atmosphere, a time of divided leadership, confusion, and changing feelings that Ciudadanos became a chapter of the Raza Unida Party. On the one hand the Mexicanos were attempting to become more openly assertive, and on the other hand many of these same leaders were profoundly pessimistic about their chances of winning. The BGL appeared strong, united, and difficult to defeat. The Raza lacked money, experienced leaders, and unity. Born of this ambivalence and in the wake of defeat, the new Raza Unida Party vowed to carry the fight to the gringo enemy.

[1] The effect of external school programs was largely determined by frequent comments of local leaders. Anglo school leaders often expressed resentment towards federal school programs and HEW. Further, we were suspected of and labeled as "HEW spies" by some local residents.

[2] Post, Don, *Ethnic Competition for Control of Schools in Two South Texas Towns.* Doctoral dissertation, University of Texas, 1975. The South Texas case reported in this dissertation provides the most dramatic example of controversy over an EODC Center and program.

[3] Garcia, Cris (ed) *La Causa Politica: A Chicano Reader*, South Bend, Indiana: University of Notre Dame Press, 1974; Hirsch, Herbert and Armando Gutíerrez. *Learning To Be Militant: The Making of Militants in a Chicano Community.* San Francisco, California: R&E Research Associates, 1977.

[4] The general events and key personalities were reconstructed through a series of interviews with earlier LULAC leaders.

[5] As indicated in chapter 3, the terms "moderate" and "radical" are used quite loosely by local political leaders. They generally refer to stylistic differences in ethnic and social relations approaches than to major philosophical differences. The terms also do not accurately locate people in specific groups. At times people labeled were not in a given faction but were merely "sympathetic" or "acted like them."

[6] These are, of course, crude estimates based on the recollections of present-day leaders.

[7] Surprisingly, the city minutes recorded the scuffle, but this account was based on the recollections of participants. Several other council meetings were attended during the height of this controversy.

[8] During the year that Mexicanos ran the city government, there was approximately $5,000 of unaccounted receipts. In the summer of 1973, the city's bonding company paid this settlement, but a proposed suit against two Mexicana city clerks were dropped. What happened to the money purportedly lost has not been determined.

[9] It is important to note that both Mexicano and Anglo students were drug users, and many of the main dealers were Mexicanos. Anglos often perceived the drug problem to be that "Mexican pushers were getting our children hooked on

176

drugs." Conversely, Mexicano parents often complained that "Anglo kids set a bad example for our children."

[10] Approximately 90% of the 1800 registered Anglo voters went to the polls.

[11] The accusations made by both sides were not verified. The Civil Rights Commission is presently investigating the voting irregularities which occurred during these North Town elections. It seemed to us that both sides, in the heat of political battle, used whatever means necessary to win. South Texas politics can and does become "rough," and those famliar with local politics expect "irregularities."

[12] We estimated that approximately 65% of North Town Mexicanos were "neutral." This is not based on a careful survey of community political preferences, and the definition of "neutral" includes a variety of people. Some "neutral" voters are secret "Raza sympathizers," but most people who called themselves "neutral" seemed to be genuinely uncommitted. Some were tired of politics. Others wanted to avoid conflict. Others were indifferent to either side. More studies of the motives and preferences of "neutrals" are clearly needed.

[13] Shockley, John. *Revolt in a South Texas Town.* South Bend, Indiana: University of Notre Dame Press, 1974. José Angel Gutiérrez. *Toward A Theory of Community Organization In A Mexican-American Community in South Texas.* Doctoral dissertation, University of Texas, Austin, Texas, 1976.

[14] This estimate is based on discussions with leaders, the opposition, and attendance of four meetings. It became evident that the BGL had very few prominent Mexicano leaders in their organization. The parallels were strikingly similar to thé attempted Anglo-Mexican-American coalition in Aztlán City called CAASA from 1963 to 1969. For more discussion of CAASA see Smith, Walter Jr. *Ibid* and John Shockley, *Ibid.*

[15] It should be noted that only one fieldworker was present during the 1973 campaign, whereas three fieldworkers were present during the 1974 campaign. To a degree the judgments about the 1973 campaign invariably reflect the deeper experience gained in 1974.

[16] This section is based on frequent attendance of school board meetings and many hours of conversation with all members.

[17] Originally, the BGL reportedly proposed to use two candidates for the vote splitting tactic. By election time only one candidate actually ran.

[18] This judgment is based on no fieldwork in the schools during 1972–1973. We were refused entry until 1973–1974. After a year of discussion with various board members, Professor Foley was allowed to observe in the schools. This was done after a public presentation of the research to the board and a review of the research proposal. Neither Anglos nor Mexicanos were entirely comfortable with having researchers in their troubled schools and community, but they did recognize some possible utility and seemed to generally have high regard for faculty and students connected with the University of Texas.

[19] Generally we were able to gain much greater access to the Ciudadanos group than to the BGL. This was primarily due to the trust that Ciudadanos leaders had in Ms. Mota and Mr. Lorenzo, both very sensitive field workers. Conversely, Mr. Foley was less able to gain the trust of BGL leaders. Many other Anglos less actively involved in the BGL leadership such as teachers, other professionals, some old-time leaders and "marginal" Anglos were quite open and helpful, however. These differences in access are undoubtedly reflected in the emphasis in this study.

Chapter 6

Community Factionalism and the Decline
of the Raza Unida

By the fall of 1973 the conflict between the "*La Raza*" and the Better Government League intensified. As the battle for political control of North Town unfolded, many events gave the conflict continuing life. As one old-timer put it, "This thing has a kind of life of its own. Maybe we can't stop what we started 'til it just runs out of gas." A number of issues continued to engender resentments among the Mexicanos. The grand jury investigation of voters stood out as the most vivid show of Anglo force. The fate of other community improvements proposed by Ciudadanos such as a city park, improved street drainage, and a "free" health clinic were also continuing points of conflict. Other BGL moves to bar Mr. Salinas, a Raza Unida councilman, from the ballot, to petition the removal of Father Reynaldo, and to supervise the EODC Center/Head Start Program also carried the fight to *La Raza*.

Finally, other unintended events, many concerning school policies, fed the conflict. Yet, life in North Town from 1973 to 1974 is a story of both escalating *and* declining conflict.[1] No discussion of the second cycle of conflict would be complete without describing the people, events, and forces that curbed the conflict. There were times when the decisions made by BGL and Raza Unida leaders created dissension and factionalism *within* their groups. Gradually, various conciliatory moves, the internal dissension within each group, and a growing exhaustion from discord slowed the escalating conflict or "helped it run out of gas."

Key Points of Continuing Community Conflict

While the Ciudadanos controlled the city council in 1972–1973, they initiated a study for using approximately six acres of municipal land as a city park. The plan was to apply for money from the regional government council to develop this area further. Ciudadanos favored this site because it was near the Mexicano population, and it would cost less to build. They wanted a relatively large park where traditional Mexicano family reunions, outdoor barbecues, and celebrations of Mexican holidays could be held. A park big enough to hold a large number of the community could also be used for political rallies.

Although BGL Anglos opposed the park for various reasons, the main reason was ostensibly that the park site was too close to the town sewage plant. They argued that this would create an unpleasant odor on windy days. They also felt that it was too far from town (approximately one mile) to walk there. Privately, BGL leaders disliked the idea of a large park because it might be used for political rallies. They generally preferred developing several mini-parks in various sections of the Westside with the emphasis on children's recreational and playground facilities. One of the school sites was proposed, as were several other near-by private lots.

During the 1973–1974 period no specific developments occurred; however, the new BGL-controlled city council and the new city manager did begin plans to use federal revenue sharing monies for developing the school site. They planned for playground equipment and a basketball court. The city, the school board, and the county also began making plans to improve the old WPA swimming facilities at the junior high school and to build several new city tennis courts. In a related recreation program, the Little League Association, previously an Anglo-led group, fenced and improved the high school baseball field for a summer baseball program. Plans for a large park to accommodate picnickers, festivals, and political rallies were dropped, however. Among the Raza Unida leaders this remained an important issue. They realized that these Anglo programs were "good for our kids," but nevertheless, they saw the projects as "attempts to buy us off, to make us think they give a damn about us."

The second major issue which has plagued North Town leaders since the early fifties was the problem of drainage on the westside of town. The town as originally built located the eastside, the main business district and predominately Anglo section, on higher ground. "Mexican Town" was somewhat lower in elevation and was located next to a creek, originally used for water and washing. This site was also at the base of a natural watershed; consequently, more than 500 acres of surrounding farmland drained into the westside. Rainstorms sent torrents of water down more than one-third of the streets on the westside. The drainage problem was surveyed by an outside company in the mid-fifties, but the proposal for a new storm and sewer system was never acted upon due to the high cost. Periodically, Mexicano residents in that area complained to the city council, so that by 1965 another survey and plan was developed. By this time the cost had sky-rocketed, and the council was more reluctant to commit the city to heavy indebtedness and increased taxes.

In 1968 the solution of paving a large number of the streets in the poorly drained areas was proposed and acted upon. Since residents must pay for the paving costs, this method was seen as the most economical solution to the drainage problem. But as a large number of the streets were paved in this area, the problem was compounded. The concrete streets did allow the water to run off somewhat faster, but it also turned a number of streets into fast-flowing streams during the height of rain storms. Residents claimed that the water rose much higher and was more destructive after the paving.

The Ciudadanos-controlled city council began preliminary planning on the drainage problem in 1972, but no programs were initiated. In the fall of 1973 the BGL-controlled city council continued the discussion over the drainage problem. The first of two public meetings was well attended by Raza Unida supporters. A great deal of criticism was leveled at the council for not solving the problem. Several leaders made impassioned speeches, which the Anglos present labeled as political propaganda and campaigning. The meeting became rather heated and was reminiscent of school board meetings. It was subsequently announced that the engineering firm that did the second survey in 1965 would present the original plan and several feasible alternatives at a special council meeting.

Consequently, during the second meeting the engineering firm brought a Mexican-American engineer to explain the plan in English and Spanish. The meeting was sparsely attended (fifteen to twenty people), and the Raza Unida leaders purposely stayed away to express their disapproval of the plan. Several Mexicano property owners from the affected area did come to express their concerns and to ask questions. The meeting was a relatively short (one hour), simple presentation of the view that the only practical, economical solution was an open, cement run-off canal. The canal would cost approximately $400,000 and would go through thirty or forty home-owners' lots. The possibility of an underground drainage system was rejected as prohibitively expensive for such a small area. Underground facilities would have reportedly cost three to four times as much as the canal. The council further discussed the possibility of applying for regional government federal funds to cover the bulk of the construction expenses. Since North Town had not previously applied for such grants, the council was optimistic about getting up to $300,000 to finance the project. The meeting ended with very little controversy and the general agreement to explore the canal solution further.

Predictably, the Raza Unida strongly criticized the plan, not only as hazardous to Mexicano children, but also as damaging to the rights of many property owners. It was not clear how many houses would have to be completely relocated, or how many lots would lose backyards. But given the density of housing in the area, many local Mexicano leaders and residents of the area considered the canal a very poor solution. The city manager and council contended that such disruptions and relocations could be minimized, but very few Raza Unida supporters believed such optimistic predictions.

Most present BGL leaders lamented the fact that the leaders of the late forties and early fifties did not solve the problem when the city's indebtedness was low and construction costs were cheaper. Many local residents complained about the conditions, but after twenty years of flooding, they have partially accepted the periodic inconveniences. Only a dramatic turn for the worse, such as relocation and property condemnation, might rekindle the issue. Fearing such community reaction, North Town leaders were moving slowly on this issue. The drainage problem may remain unsolved, barring a major windfall of outside funds.

The third major public policy issue concerned the development of a free medical clinic. Several active Mexicanos, led by Ms. Amalia Tovar and Mr. Manuel Ramírez, planned to build a clinic and hire two National Health Corps doctors. The group, called *El Sacrificio*, held several community meetings to explain the need and benefit to local citizens. They also gathered materials about similar federal programs in the area. In 1972 they presented a proposal to the Economic Opportunity Development Corporation Board to use federal grant monies to build their clinic. Their basic argument was that local health care was expensive and woefully inadequate. They were very critical of the two local Anglo doctors, whom they considered professionally incompetent. Countless tales were told of misdiagnosis, indifference, and insensitivity to Mexicano culture.

The Ciudadanos leaders wanted Chicano doctors and a free clinic, but such programs required the approval of local health authorities, the county health officer and the county medical association. In 1972 the local doctor who served as the county health officer refused to certify such a request, and the group was unable to get a contradictory evaluation from the other doctors and pharmacists in North County. Consequently, the EODC board could not sponsor such proposals for a health clinic and National Health Corps doctors. The

Ciudadanos frequently cited this issue as an example of Anglo greed and racism and used it to arouse Mexicano voters. But by the 1973–1974 campaign the health issue and *El Sacrificio* were dead and rarely mentioned. Increasingly, local residents have taken their health problems to a new Mexicano doctor in a nearby town and to a private hospital in another town in the county.

North Town, like so many small American towns, has always had serious problems providing good medical care. In the thirties and forties they had a clinic over the city hall and a private hospital in the present-day nursing home. But when their traditional country doctor retired, the town was left without a permanent doctor and hospital facilities for several years. By the early 1950's the town was able to attract two new doctors, who along with a number of prominent business and farming families, built a small private hospital in 1960. The new doctors developed their own clinics and also periodically used the hospital. The North County Hospital has been underutilized, however, and it has gradually become a kind of nursing home, housing some patients on a semi-permanent basis.[2]

Some North Town Anglos were also privately critical of the local Anglo doctors. Stories of incorrect diagnosis were frequent, and one of the doctors was particularly criticized for his "poor bedside manner." It should be added, however, that no one has ever filed a malpractice suit against either doctor. Several prominent Anglos conceded that they "would not dream of going to a local doctor for anything serious." They confided that most Anglos who could afford it went to a nearby city. Nevertheless, many BGL Anglos felt that having these national doctors was a form of welfare socialism. Others felt that the only doctors who would join such programs were probably incompetent. A more privately held reason for rejecting the *El Sacrificio* plan was its political implications. Local BGL leaders were extremely sensitive to the Aztlán City Raza Unida plan for a health care clinic. Several of them pointed out that "this program of Gutiérrez's to give free health care to *La Raza* supporters, with his wife running the program, was a good way to win votes with federal money." The Anglo leaders were determined to block any *La Raza* accomplishments that would "dupe the poor Mexican voters into believing only *La Raza* was trying to help them."

However, by 1975 North Town had a National Health Corps doctor. A year later, after the political battle had been won and *La Raza* vanquished, the county medical official, a leader in the BGL, approved a similar program. The major difference from the *El Sacrificio* program was that the Health Corps doctors would be based at the private

North County Hospital and a new, adjacent, $70,000 clinic built by the wealthy patrons of the hospital. There would be a new public health clinic, but it would be located in a predominantly Anglo section of town.

Combating the La Raza Threat

The Better Government League continued to confront the *La Raza* movement, seeking to defeat and discredit its leaders and programs. Their most direct action during the fall of 1973 was a legal challenge to Councilman Salinas' right to run for re-election. They did not place his name on the official ballot because his residence was outside the city limits. The case was ultimately taken to the State Supreme Court by the Mexican-American Legal Defense Fund (MALDEF), and the court ruled that Councilman Salinas had filed properly for candidacy. He was reinstated on the ballot in time for the spring elections, but the case undoubtedly occupied a great deal of the time and organizational energies of the new Raza Unida leaders. This action came on the heels of indictments of illegal voters and charges of city corruption. The Raza leaders felt that the Anglos were bent on destroying them. The incumbent Ciudadanos leaders were further goaded into taking stronger stands, identifying more closely with the Aztlán City Raza Unida. This was particularly true of the fiery Salinas whose personal right to run had been challenged.

Another source of great irritation to Ciudadanos leaders in the fall of 1973 was an organized effort to "get rid of Father Reynaldo." The priest, a young liberal Mexican-American, was considered to be the "real leader" of *La Raza*. Many Anglos reasoned that Mexicanos unquestionably followed their priest. Further, Father Reynaldo had actually spoken out during church sermons about racial discrimination, inequality, and hatred in North Town. Anglo church members were incensed by this "use of the pulpit to espouse *La Raza* ideals." The priest, following the edicts of Pope John on the role of the church in social change and justice, was sympathetic to the new Ciudadanos/ Raza Unida leaders. Several of these leaders were on his advisory council. They came to run the *Diez y Seis* celebration, and there were occasions when these leaders met in the church to discuss various community problems and programs. This range of activities infuriated other Mexicano and Anglo catholics who had also been active church leaders in the sixties. The young Mexicano priest's rector, an Anglo, was not as actively involved, but he generally condoned these activities and quietly supported Father Reynaldo.

Gradually the opposition to the influence of these new Mexicano *politicos* grew. Some parishioners refused to attend services, others vowed to have this "political priest" thrown out or transferred. The most notable Anglo Catholic who opposed Father Reynaldo was a prominent doctor and former city councilman. Doctor Olson, himself married to a Puerto Rican, had personally initiated improvements of the lighting and streets near the Catholic church. The Olsons, both quietly active in the BGL, spear-headed the circulation of a petition to Bishop Flores to remove Father Reynaldo. Most Anglo Catholics had little hope that Bishop Flores, perceived as a *La Raza* supporter, would be sympathetic, but their dismay and anger moved them to try and influence him.

The efforts of Anglos to "smear the good name of Father Reynaldo" outraged many Raza Unida leaders. They also circulated a petition in support of Father Reynaldo and sought to influence higher church authorities to keep him in North Town. Many Mexicanos perceived this opposition to Father Reynaldo as the lowest and most vengeful of all Anglo political tactics. They considered their priest a restraining voice during the turbulence of 1972 and 1973. He had clearly spoken out against racism and injustice, and had encouraged Ciudadanos members to stand up for their rights and elect their own leaders. He had also worked a great deal with the youth group, encouraging similar ideals. However, none of the Ciudadanos or Raza Unida leaders considered him a part of the inner circle, a key leader or decision-maker, and neither did Father Reynaldo. That he should be labeled as such, and perhaps be forced out of town for being "too radical," seemed absurd to most Mexicanos. As one leader reasoned, "You see, you see what you get for being a moderate, for not hating and fighting, you get what Father is going to get; you get run out of town because of your goodness. We have to stop these goddamn gringos from doing this."

As the issue evolved, Father Reynaldo was indeed transferred in the spring of 1974, but apparently this decision was made long before either side sent the petitions or made him an issue. He was reassigned to a seminary in Arkansas as an instructor and trainer of other priests. He personally expressed sadness about leaving, but both he and his superiors apparently saw this as an even more important role for him. In his three years in North Town he had helped revive the youth groups and had actively supported a wide range of parish activity directed towards solving local economic, health, and educational problems. He prided himself in being a part of this process of social change and self-help in a South Texas Mexicano community similar to his own hometown. The consolation that one Raza Unida leader found in his departure was the hope that he would "train so many priests like himself that these gringos won't be able to send them all away." By the spring elections, then, Father Reynaldo was no longer an issue.

A third sequence of incidents that was widely interpreted as more Anglo vengeance centered around the federally-sponsored Head Start program. Up until the fall of 1973 all of the EODC programs were housed in a North Town elementary school complex. The building was the original segregated "Mexican school." As indicated, the various EODC programs (family planning, the credit union, Head Start, and surplus commodities) were reluctantly accepted in North Town. Gradually the director, a Mexicano and formerly an insurance salesman, gained control of the EODC board. As in many other cases, these federally-sponsored ciitzens' boards (⅓ civic leaders, ⅓ elected officials, and ⅓ low income citizens) became the site of considerable political jockeying. The former director said, "It took me four years to get the kind of people on there that would work for *La Raza*, but we finally did it."

In 1973 the EODC center employed a number of the key Ciudadanos political organizers as directors of the service programs, field workers, cooks and janitors. The director of Head Start and a portion of his staff could also be considered "pro-Ciudadanos," although none were openly active in local politics. The director was especially careful in avoiding "politics," and he prided himself in being a professonal educator. In general, however, the entire EODC program was openly and quite obviously a major site for North Town political activity. Much "political plotting" and discussion went on there, and this outside federal program was an irritating symbol of "Chicano power" and federal welfarism. Many BGL leaders expressed resentment towards the center and were frustrated by their inability to end these programs.

The EODC center never was actually a formal center or meeting place for Ciudadanos. Neither was it ever a place where the key Ciudadanos or Raza Unida leaders planned their strategy. As in the case of the BGL, most such activities went on in the homes of leaders, in some cafes, and in rented public halls. In the fall of 1973 a new director of the EODC center was appointed, and he proceeded to move the main administrative offices to his hometown in the southern part of the county. To some extent, even the informal political discussions and activities were on the decline in the fall of 1973 because of this shift in administrative offices.

However, the local school board had become increasingly disenchanted with the way Head Start was utilizing their facility. During the fall, and particularly during the spring before the elections, the school board increased their surveillance of the center. During a Head Start meeting in February the Head Start director described what he considered increasing political harassments:

Last Saturday the parents and teachers were working in the playground when Mrs. Hart (president of the school board) and Mr. Wayne (superintendent) arrived. They stayed for awhile in the car watching us from afar. Then they entered the building and started to go to each room. Graziela was making coffee for the parents; she saw them and went to tell me about it. I and the parents came into the building and asked Mr. Wayne, *"¿Qué pasó?"* (what's up?) I knew that rumors were going around that the Head Start center was a hotbed of activities for Raza Unida and that food and materials were coming out of it for the political rally. So we knew more or less why they were there. Mr. Wayne, seeing all the parents and being confronted by me, chickened out and said something about wanting to know if there were any handicapped children in the community for they were going to have a program for special education next semester. Then they left. Monday morning I received a letter from Mr. Wayne. At first it looked like a very innocent letter, but once you read between the lines, it meant more than what was really said. I was very angry and wrote a long letter in reply. But by Tuesday afternoon several Raza Unida people approached me saying they had to present this case to the school board meeting. I went to that meeting but nothing happened, since the meeting was taken up by some case of Anglo kids drinking beer and getting kicked out of school. So I sent my letter to Mr. Wayne and also a very violent letter to our director for Head Start programs so he would know of this and help fight for our program.

This is the letter that Superintendent Wayne sent to the Director of the North Town Head Start program:

As local taxes increase, as political activities intensify, and as the energy crisis worsens, our School System comes under close scrutiny from the general public. Some of the Board Members and Administrators often receive telephone calls at night, or on weekends, regarding activities going on at various schools, lights left on in certain buildings, the use of school buses, etc. The activities of the various school campuses are scheduled on the School Master Calendar so we know what is going on, where, and when.

If you will be so kind, please notify Mr. Cordova or the Superintendent's Office when you have night or weekend activities planned with your groups, so we can get the activities of our Old Westside Elementary facility on our calendar also.

I found an extra copy of the Board Policy regarding the use of all

186

school facilities and included it for your review. You may keep it for your files.

In response the director of the Head Start program wrote the following letter to the Superintendent of Schools of North Town:

I am answering your letter of February 25, 1974, a letter which on the surface appeared very innocent but which seemed to be trying to tell me something else between the lines; an accusation of misuse of my duties and responsibilities as Head of the North Town Head Start center.

I am irked, Mr. Wayne, by the fact that you did not level with me last Saturday morning when you and the lady board member came around checking our center thinking that some type of political cooking was going on. I was well aware of your reasons for being there, and as you well saw that our activities turned out to be a parent volunteer group who had someone to fix the Head Start's Children playground.

I consider the letter an insult to my intelligence, that you would actually think me so naive to allow the future and welfare of sixty poor children and ten employees to be put in jeopardy by sidestepping guidelines and policies to serve my own political interests and those of other groups interested in change. I feel no one on my staff nor I have to put ourselves in jeopardy; for change is coming whether we want to accept it or not.

My dedication has been to nothing else but the success of the North Town Head Start Center. My staff and I have labored and slaved through thick and thin; through situations such as this, in an effort to have something to offer to all the poor children of this community who don't get all the breaks that other people do.

There are a lot of people who would like to see our success terminated, for whatever selfish, egotistical or envious reasons—I don't know. Therefore, I am surprised, somewhat shocked, that a lot of board members have fallen for such wagged tongued slanderous gossip and accusations of our conducting unauthorized activities and misusing government property in our Head Start Center.

I would like to point out that our activities have never been secret, that in fact all parents of the children are made aware of any activity taking place at the center, either by notes to the parents or on the radio station. Our office is open to the people and any information wished about any activity, may be given them at their request.

Board members should be well aware, by now, that Head Start programs have to comply with stiffer rules, regulations, and demands than the school system; so it is not uncommon that the activities of the center have to go beyond the regular forty working hours of other people. We have to have more parents meetings than the school system and there are several committees that have to meet at my request, whether they be scheduled or unscheduled, and that includes Saturdays and Sundays if we need to.

As for the lights left on in our building, that has probably been me working overtime on Head Start matters, or checking the building for vandalism damage, but I guess a lot of people wouldn't understand what it is to try to keep a constant vigil on a salvaged condemned building. I am the only one who has the keys to the Head Start side of the building—so if anyone wants to question the integrity of my work or the authenticity of my story, all you need do is look around the center to see what has been done up to date in our center, or better yet, ask any parent from our community participants.

Please believe me, Mr. Wayne, and to whom it may concern, we are not trying to be a threat to you nor anyone else; just don't short change our little people justly or unjustly, for whatever reason.

After this exchange of letters, there was apparently no official action taken that charged the Head Start director with mismanagement.

Somewhat later during the year, however, the Head Start came in conflict with the administration again. This time the issue was the painting of the Head Start toilets. Upon moving into their rather dilapidated buildings, the Head Start director requested that the toilets be painted. When only one toilet was painted, the staff decided to "do the painting themselves." They selected bright yellows and greens and reds and added some flower decals and a large sun with rays, which one BGL leader perceived as the "*la Raza* sun or some Aztec sun god." During the summer of 1974 the elementary principal in charge of their building, one of the first Mexicano teachers and principals, requested them to repaint the toilets the original color. The principal told the Head Start director that the board and he felt the colors were too bright and would hurt the children's eyes. In response to these events the staff and a few parents had another heated discussion. One parent suggested that the "gringos must be dying to torture us all, even our children, if these toilets offend them." Another parent and active Raza Unida organizer delivered an impassioned speech that characterized the group's sentiment:

Do you know what that means in plain simple words? It means *que Wayne tiene la pata en el cuello de Manuel. Si él dice: brinca, Manuel, Manuel tiene que brincar* (that Wayne has his foot on Manuel's neck. If he says jump, Manuel, Manuel has to jump), not because he wants to hold on to his job but because he wants the Head Start to go on. He has to submit himself to the whims of the school board. So he needs your support. If the school board tells him to move out of here, there will be no more Head Start. So you better start doing something now. It is for your own interest.

The conflicts over the councilman, the priest, and the EODC center were, in varying degrees, conscious efforts by Anglo leaders to crush *La Raza*. There were also several other incidents that occurred in the schools which appeared to Mexicanos to be conscious aggression but were not. Rather, these incidents were oversights or unintended blunders by local officials, happenings that added unplanned fuel to the conflict.[3] Such "brushfires" caused consternation among Anglo leaders who had to scramble and explain these seeming Anglo prejudices towards "innocent Mexican students."

The first incident occurred in the fall during the student elections of class officers. Bickering broke out in the sophomore class, and the Anglo students threatened to boycott the elections because they felt that getting Anglos elected was hopeless. The teachers convinced them to participate anyway and pleaded with the general group to be fair and give everyone a chance. As in the recent past, the Mexicanos won these elections through block voting for selected Mexicanos. The great majority of the officers elected were either the children of Raza Unida leaders or were friends and members of the group. In effect, the student elections became another expression of the adult political conflict. The Raza Unida party leaders were as delighted at the outcome as the BGL leaders were dismayed. The Mexicanos pointed to their children with pride that they no longer tolerated Anglo privilege and control at the high school.

These elections aroused considerable Mexicano criticism of the school administration. The controversy centered on the removal of two popular Chicano athletes from the ballots. On election day the names of the students were missing from the ballot, but there was no explanation why. Since the Raza-oriented students had organized the student body to vote for them, it appeared that the administration had acted arbitrarily and against Raza Unida. In fact, the two students were ineligible because they had not maintained the necessary seventy grade average for being a class officer. The administration and the teachers handling the election appear to have made two errors. First, many students and parents were unaware of any eligibility rule. Second, the administration apparently did not actually check the grade averages and make their decision until just a few hours before the elections. Consequently, a great deal of miscommunication existed about why and how the two boys were removed from the ballot. Afterwards, the school board received numerous complaints, and they eventually made a public statement explaining the eligibility rule.

189

Students and parents gradually accepted the results of the election, but it became a common topic of discussion. Literally hundreds of Mexicanos used it as a symbol of Anglo disregard for their rights.

Following the student elections incident was "the homecoming affair." As is customary in most high schools, a homecoming queen and court are elected by the student body, and they are presented during a half-time ceremony. For the first time in the history of the school all the girls selected were Mexicano, except for one black, who was popular among the Mexican-American students. Traditionally, the school obtained a convertible from the local car dealers to chauffeur the girls around the field before the grandstands. This year, however, the queen and her court simply walked down the center of the field to the coronation stand.

During these ceremonies the recently deposed Mexicano mayor ran up and with tears in his eyes said:

> Do you see, Doctor, do you see what they do to our children? We are made to walk. We are not good enough to ride in their goddamn convertibles. But when those girls were white you can bet that their feet never touched the ground. Now you can understand the problem we have here.

Many other students and community members expressed similar sentiments. The story was picked up by the *Chicano Times*. They described it as an outrageous act of discrimination and urged that racist North Town schools be taken over by Chicanos.[4] This incident aroused strong feelings, and local Mexicanos quickly believed the worst about the intentions of Anglo school leaders.

The explanation of the high school principal and the teacher-sponsors was that they simply forgot to make the arrangements. The teacher in charge was extremely embarrassed. Apparently, there had been no intention to deny the Mexicano girls a car. The Anglo board members were angry that the incident happened because "the Raza Unida made some real political hay out of this one, and we got nothing but another lump on our head." Along with the unexplained removal of two Chicanos from the student elections, this incident kept students at the high school polarized and resentful. Anglo students had been denied their past privileges as officers and homecoming queens, and Mexicanos had been denied a popular leader and a convertible to ride in triumphantly.

Later in the spring one other incident at the junior high school also created considerable controversy. The question was whether or not Mexicano students had the right to wear *Raza Unida* buttons. The junior high principal thought not, and he proceeded to "crack down." Several teachers took buttons off the students, and the principal gave a long, impassioned lecture to the student council, which consisted almost entirely of children of party leaders. He compared the Raza Unida to Nazi and communistic movements that threatened freedom and the American way of life. By the next morning an angry delegation of twenty parents demanded that the superintendent either muzzle or fire this man. The school board quickly responded by rescinding this principal's unilateral action, noting that they intended to follow recent court decisions bearing on students' freedom of speech. In the process, the principal, from the perspective of many teachers, was publicly "drawn-and-quartered" in a meeting where he apologized to the Raza Unida party leaders.

None of the aforementioned conflicts entirely mobilized either group, but the cumulative effect of these aggressive acts and unintended conflicts propelled each side to more organized, militant postures. Anglos frequently saw Mexicanos as breaking the laws of voting, school building use, and student elections. Mexicanos frequently felt the vengeance of legal authority and the blunders of struggling administrators. To an extent, the conflict took on dynamics of its own. It escalated, and each side was less and less willing to tolerate any hint of impropriety or inequality. Social and political conditions they had accepted in the past became increasingly intolerable.

Conciliation Towards the La Raza Threat

Along with being more combative toward the Raza Unida, the BGL also sought, however, to be more conciliatory. As indicated, the BGL was dedicated to "breaking the back of *La Raza*," but as the BGL became stronger through superior organization, electoral victories, and their election suit, they also attempted to regulate the conflict. In effect, the BGL sought to win votes and support through more positive programs. They wanted to recruit more Mexicanos into the BGL organization while moderating their own racial extremists. These moves towards more positive programs and the inclusion of more Mexican-Americans in leadership positions began before the 1974 elections. They were even more apparent after the second straight BGL electoral victory.

Some of these pre-election moves towards conciliation have already been noted. The new city manager and the city council began seeking federal funds to solve the drainage problem. The city also initiated a day care center for children of working mothers. Finally, the city council proposed creating several recreational and park areas. From the standpoint of political strategy, the most interesting dimension of these new proposals was the BGL effort to better coordinate the Anglo-run city, school, and county agencies. Given the historic fragmentation of most small town government and school agencies, these moves were strong indications of an Anglo effort to be responsive to Mexicano demands. Past school board, city, and commissioners' court records indicated that much discussion and very little action ever occurred between these separate agencies. They were more likely to fight over how their respective lands, fire trucks, and personnel could *not* be used by the other agency. However, in the face of the *La Raza* threat, the county agreed to use revenue sharing monies for a city project to refurbish school recreational facilities.[5]

Anglo bank officials also responded to Ciudadanos demands for admitting more Mexicanos to leadership positions. A group of Ciudadanos leaders had demanded that the local bank president hire more Mexicanos. In the fall of 1973 several Mexicano tellers were hired; further, a former city councilman and highly qualified, respected community leader, Mr. Aldana, was appointed to Cashier. The cashier, a department store manager, and a postman, one of the two BGL Mexicanos on the city council, were also invited to join the Rotary Club. Although such appointments were viewed by Raza supporters as mere appeasements, the BGL leaders felt that they were seriously responding to Mexicano demands. In their mind they were including "responsible Mexican-Americans" into leadership positions. As indicated, Anglo sponsorship of selected Mexican-Americans for both appointed and elected local government positions began during the fifties. Under pressure to change even faster, the BGL leaders continued selective sponsorship and appointment of Mexican-Americans to leadership positions. It should be noted, however, that the top county, city and school administrative positions of North Town remained predominantly Anglo.

The BGL made an even more vigorous effort to recruit what they considered responsible Mexican-Americans into their organization. They were acutely aware that the BGL was largely an Anglo organization, in spite of the charter which emphasized its biracial character. Several Mexican-American businessmen and professionals who were considered "approachable" or "not hard-core *La Raza*" as one old-time Mexicano leader put it, "were courted shamelessly." He continued by illustrating what he considered Anglo courtship:

What do I mean by courtship? If you stay over here on the west side I'll tell you what you'll see. You'll see Mrs. Hart on the school board running around going to Mexican funerals. You'll see the mayor and Mr. Weeks (a city councilman) with his red face and skinny moustache being at every opening of a Mexicano business they can. When Mr. Gracias opened up his store there they were smiling. When Mr. Torres remodeled his movie house, there they were. I heard the other day that they might even start inviting us to their houses to get us into their BGL. It seems like to me some of us are getting courted. Look at Mr. Casava who they talked into running for their school board. I never knew he liked gringos, but he is a good man, a trusting man, so I guess they talked sweet to him. The gringos can talk real good when they need you for something, but it comes from their head not their heart, mark my words.

Nearly all Raza Unida supporters staunchly contended that the Anglos also either "sweet talked' or forced many of their ranch laborers or store laborers to become BGL supporters. The BGL purportedly twisted many Mexicano arms by foreclosing on loans or threatening to fire people. A few Ciudadanos Mexicanos reported cases of "political firings," but several range hands and storeworkers suggested that reports of reprisals were probably somewhat exaggerated. Several prominent Ciudadanos businessmen and farmers with large loans at the bank did not suffer foreclosures. A certain pragmatic, businesslike attitude tended to prevail that moderated excessive economic reprisal. Further, a kind of social reserve also prevailed that kept Anglo courtship from getting "too social." Several Mexicanos who were accepted as potential leaders privately admitted that they did not feel socially accepted by Anglos. They all shared a lingering sense of being isolated from both groups. It appeared, then, that some "courtship" was taking place. But the average Mexicano voter was neither wooed nor whipped into place very seriously.[6]

Conciliatory School Board Policies

Perhaps the single best place to observe the conciliatory moves of the Anglo BGL was in the North Town public schools. Indeed, local Anglo teachers and the more traditional community members rated the school board and administration as "too soft" and "wishy-washy" towards La Raza. Two descriptions of the school situation eloquently summarize how most North Town educators felt about the changes occurring in the schools. A teacher comments:

Discipline and respect in the schools has broken down. Mexican kids are not respectful the way they used to be; they are very defiant at times,

193

and their parents will complain if the kids are at all disciplined. Teachers have to be very careful now, if they don't want problems. Most of this is caused by the political thing. The Mexican kids just get promoted to avoid trouble. The parents will get angry, and these older kids will be left behind to terrorize the younger ones in their grades, especially the poor little white girls.

Closely related to this view is that of an administrator:

What we got now is a real problem. Some kids just won't get any better. They lack home influence and are just not real achievers, successful people with drive and self-discipline. There is nothing we can do, really, we need these tracks, an easy system. The kids can't do the work that we got now. The agency wants it. The people want it. We just go along any way.

Most Anglo teachers saw themselves and the schools as confronted with a very profound, far-reaching dilemma. They perceived the new influx of large numbers of lower income, Spanish-speaking children as destroying the previous quality and order of their schools. Yet even more disturbing, teachers also sensed that they were lowering the standards of work and discipline to cope with this "new intrusion." Most Anglo teachers expressed a sense of frustration and futility. Ironically, they themselves seemed to be destroying not only their schools, but the underlying values of American society. Change under these conditions was indeed painful.

From 1972 through 1974 the board initiated a series of school policies in response to the *La Raza* threat which increasingly brought them under community criticism. In the fall of 1973 the board passed a more liberal hair and dress code, which was recommended by a student-faculty committee. The board, in accepting this new policy, made clear that there was now a written, legal basis for sending offending students home. The implication was that the board would and could act now without personal, racial feelings.

Similarly, in matters of discipline the board also moved to control growing disorder at the high school. This meant replacing the previous liberal principal with a recognized authority, a former football coach and junior high school principal with a reputation for firmness and fairness. The board also replaced the school counselor and instituted a new position of vice principal. This new administrative team was mandated to "get hold of things" and "straighten out discipline [and potential racial problems] at the high school."

According to teachers, the tone and style of the high school administration did indeed change. The counselor was requested to help any and all students get into some college of their choice. The general sentiment expressed by the principal and counselor was that there was "a place for anybody and everybody." They were very careful to project the idea that no one, regardless of race, creed, and school performance should be discouraged. The counselor studiously avoided discouraging Mexicanos from going to college. He frequently expressed concern about "*La Raza* jumping down my throat with their gringos-are-racists stuff." Few students complained about discrimination in this area.

Student discipline problems were also to be handled in a "more objective, impartial manner." Disciplinary actions were generally left to the young, personable but "tough" new Anglo vice principal. He immediately established a card file on each student offender, which students referred to (with raised eyebrows) as "*the* file." Each student who had ever been sent to the central office had a "record." All of his previous unexcused tardies, detention hall sentences, and referrals from teachers were listed. His previous offenses became the basis for a discussion about his present offenses. Any tongue-lashings, "licks," (paddlings) and suspensions were based on this record. In essence, the problem of prejudicial, personal bias was eliminated by the file of evidence. The new vice principal quickly and skillfully developed this approach, and a reputation for being "strict but fair." He aroused enough hatred to have his car window smashed after a basketball game, but few seemed to think of him as racially prejudiced. Many considered him "Mr. Big Shot" and "mean," but his method of recording and handling out punishments seemed fair. Although he frequently administered some severe tongue lashings, and even occasional paddlings, the file of evidence was hard to argue against. According to a school board member, a number of Anglo and Mexicano parents did complain about him, however. The board and administration generally seemed to support him for the type of job he was doing.

Policies toward placement in classes and evaluation also projected the idea of fairness and objectivity. In this case, fairness was to be achieved by the technology of objective tests. The principal strongly defended the placement of more than fifty percent of the Mexicano student body in all Mexicano classes because their achievement test scores were extremely low. He also defended the previously mentioned policy of social promotion on egalitarian grounds, i.e., that everyone deserved a high school diploma and a chance. In order to create opportunity for "low achiever Mexicans," the objective standards were lowered. Books at the fourth and fifth grade reading level were used, and objective exams were simplified so even slow students could pass them.

Although many educators would object to such practices as "lowering standards," efforts were made to retain the form of a competitive, objective evaluation process. In practice, however, the objective evaluations were stretched to preserve them; teachers prepped students, practiced tests, and often gave re-tests. Nevertheless, teachers were careful to avoid giving the "low achievers" high enough grades to make the honor roll, so as not to cheapen the meaning of other students' achievement. With these nagging contradictions, then, the school strove to create an objective, non-racist procedure for judging the performance of an increasingly restless Mexicano student body. This is not to argue that the North Town schools were free of prejudices or that they were places that reflected Mexicano culture; the BGL-controlled school board did, however, seek to enact many conciliatory policies in the schools.

School Board Decisions and BGL Factionalism

Of all the conciliatory school board policies two stand out because they brought out old antagonisms among Anglos and threatened BGL unity. The growing disunity among Anglos centered on two school board decisions: 1) the hiring of a new high school football coach, and 2) the suspension of two Anglo boys for drinking during a school event. Although such decisions seem to have little political significance, the BGL moderates in control of the school board ran afoul of their followers on these matters.

During the fall of 1973 the North Town football team was picked to win the district championship. It was supposed to be the best team since the fifties when North Town dominated other teams in the area. North Towners, like many other Texans, take their football very seriously. The local Boosters' Club was quite active, and the townspeople prided themselves in following the team during road games more faithfully than other towns. But the football team had fallen on relatively hard times since the early sixties, and football coaches came and went with great regularity. In 1971 the board made the unprecedented move to hire a local Mexicano, a former star of the successful era. It was a controversial move because numerous people considered his appointment a way of appeasing the growing Mexican political threat. During his first two years he led a previously losing team to successive 7–3 records.

With many key players returning, he was expected to "roll over" opponents in 1973. But as the season progressed, it became clear that the North Town team was not going to roll over anyone. They were able to win four of their first five games, but never by impressive margins. Then they were upset by a small nearby town in North County, and dissension surfaced on the team. The "sideline coaches," which included many prominent local citizens, began blaming the coaching staff. Interestingly, the dissension on the team was not between Mexicanos and Anglos but among Anglo players who were jealous of each other. The players disagreed on which Anglo boy should be quarterback, and some resented a star end, who was accused of getting all the publicity but not "putting out 100%" by "being a leader."

Dissension also surfaced on the coaching staff between the head coach, Mr. Torres, and one of the Anglo assistants, Mr. Rogers, also a former star during the better years. The Mexicano head coach was receiving considerable criticism while the Anglo assistant, who coached the undefeated freshman team, was constantly praised. Near the end of the season the two men nearly had a fight after practice. Subsequently, Mr. Torres decided "for the good of the team" to apologize to his assistant. Coach Torres made a very dramatic, and to some, humiliating apology to Coach Rogers before the entire team in a show of unity.

After the season ended, there was considerable talk among the Boosters' Club about finding another coach, someone who was "tougher and would get more work out of the kids." The man most frequently mentioned was the successful assistant coach, Mr. Rogers. The Mexicano head coach felt that he should resign as athletic director and head coach. Even though he had a successful 7–3 record and finished second in the district, he had not produced champions, and he had taken a great deal of criticism from both Anglos and Mexicanos. At least one group of Anglos, twenty or thirty of the main football enthusiasts, many former players and close friends of Mr. Rogers, wanted a new head coach.

Coach Torres was also not acceptable to many local Mexicanos affiliated with the Ciudadanos and Raza Unida. His father was a prominent local businessman, who the Raza Unida labeled as a *vendido*. The party had asked him to allow a free benefit dance in his dance hall. He refused, saying that he would not do that for any political group and that everyone using his hall had to pay. The local Ciudadanos attempted to boycott his dance hall, but their boycott quickly failed. This incident was the most dramatic event they cited to prove his disloyalty, but he was known as having many Anglo friends, including an Anglo business partner. He had also been a political organizer for several Anglo politicians in an earlier era. Activist Chicanos considered his general relationships with and deferential demeanor towards Anglos offensive; nevertheless, many local Mexicanos still considered him and his son to be "good people."

Coach Torres was not active politically with the local BGL, but he did "make the mistake of going to the first BGL meeting." Further, his family and several close friends were directly or indirectly connected with key people in the BGL. The Ciudadanos group, particularly a Ciudadanos school board member who had a personal conflict with the coach, wanted to "dump this Mexican errand boy for the gringos."

The board replaced the Mexicano head coach for reasons which did not initially seem political or racial, but by the spring were. Nothing was ever publicly said against the coach as a Mexicano, but when the BGL-controlled school board selected an outsider over the Anglo assistant coach, some Anglos began publicly attacking the BGL board members. An angry committee to support the Anglo coach was formed, held several meetings, and formally protested the decision of the local board. They placed an ad of support in the local newspaper and sought a hearing with the board. Several of the leaders in the group felt the board was "playing politics with their football team." First, they felt that the board had hired a Mexican head coach to "quiet down the Mexicans." Second, they felt that the board was getting back at them for undermining "their Mexican coach" and for creating dissension through their criticisms of the head coach and praise of the freshman coach.

From their point of view the board was attempting to appease the Mexicans at the expense of the team. The board was also "letting their money go to their head," because they were putting down the working man Anglos "who were not la-de-da socialites." Those actively supporting the Anglo coach were generally working class Anglos. Some were ranch managers and farmers, several were employees in a nearby city, and one was an insurance salesman. Some were college graduates and businessmen, but most local residents did distinguish them from the "prominent citizens, the Nob Hill BGL leaders." Several of the prominent Anglos expressed frustrations with the entire issue and were incredulous that such a thing would threaten the BGL unity. A few BGL leaders considered football a minor, overemphasized aspect of school, a view with which the supporters of Coach Rogers would have violently disagreed.

While this debate raged among local Anglos, the Raza Unida leaders followed it with great interest and amusement. Their two board members had informally supported Mr. Rogers, but they lost in the spring school board elections and were not participants in the vote on the replacement of the coach. Even though they considered the Anglo coach a "redneck," they admitted that he had given Mexicanos a chance to play on the freshman team. At least several Ciudadanos leaders felt that they should "talk it up" among their people to get support for the local Anglo. During the fall when the two coaches were in conflict, they talked openly against the Mexicano coach, "to get this *vendido*." As the issues shifted, they wanted Coach Torres replaced with Coach Rogers. Many Raza Unida members signed the petition for Coach Rogers to further split the BGL. They sensed the growing antagonisms among local Anglos; they had seen this same conflict played out on other school board and council issues. The Raza Unida leaders generally perceived the split as being between the "educated, rich Anglos" and the "good ole boys," or "uneducated farmers" (i.e., less cultured, more rural, less wealthy).

The other incident that preceded and also provoked to a lesser degree the same split among Anglos was the expulsion of two Anglo youths from high school. In the spring of 1974, just prior to the coach's resignation, two Anglo senior football players were caught drinking beer during a stock show competition. The assistant agricultural teacher reported the incident to the principal, who, following the school rules, suspended the boys for the rest of the semester. One of the boys' parents appealed to the board and a hearing followed. Both boys were the sons, or friends, of leaders in the Boosters' Club who were actively campaigning for Mr. Rogers.

During the hearing many Anglo parents came and spoke in behalf of the boys. They admitted their guilt, but testified that they were good boys who needed to graduate and go on to college. The most commonly used arguments were that "boys will be boys," and that the boys generally had good records and no harm had been done. These supporters generally took the position that under the circumstances, leniency was in order. The board ultimately took what many Anglo parents considered too harsh a position. It argued that if these boys were let off, it would make future discipline at extra-curricular events impossible. Leniency would set a tone that many other students would take advantage of; therefore, the board had to do the hard, unpleasant job of setting the example.

After the meeting, which was orderly considering the intense feelings, several Anglos criticized the board's decision and blamed it on politics. They argued that the board was merely making an example of the boys to appease the Mexicans. They cited a similar incident which occurred a year earlier when two Mexicans were expelled for drinking in the school parking lot. The disgruntled Anglo parents who supported the boys saw this decision as an attempt "to prove" that this board was "fair to the Mexicans." They considered the sentence unreasonable because even the past expulsion of students was not consistent. There were other students caught drinking during school events that were not expelled. Further, none of the previous cases involved seniors with good records about to graduate and go on to college.

This incident was merely a continuation of the fall conflict over the coach and what some Anglos now perceived as a general policy of appeasement to *La Raza*. The same debate over tactics and approaches towards controversial public issues had been going on in the BGL and in the Anglo community for more than two years. These two incidents dramatically reflected the basic split between "hardline-rednecks" and "moderates" on how to conduct public relations with Mexicanos. The "moderate" position was also quite in tune with "teaching *La Raza* a lesson," but they were anxious to avoid open confrontations over relatively minor issues.

BGL–Raza Unida Perceptions of Factionalism

The key Mexicano leaders had rather vague ideas about the differences in attitudes among BGL Anglos; they were also unclear about who really held power and influence within the BGL. In their eyes the Anglos who saw themselves as moderates were considered the "worst rednecks." These Anglos were the visible leaders who had challenged them in city council, school board, and public meetings. The only Anglos who were considered moderates were those businessmen who tended to stay neutral and out of public positions such as the popular Ford car dealer, a local druggist, and several farmers and contractors who "stayed out of politics and have always been pretty good to Mexicanos." To most of the Ciudadanos and Raza leaders, any Anglo in BGL was a redneck, because the organization was dedicated to defeating them. Ciudadanos Mexicanos did make distinctions of BGL members who were "friendlier" or having "better personalities towards Mexicanos." However, they were generally not aware that Anglo moderates were having the same problems controlling their "radicals" as the Ciudadanos moderates were with their "radicals." By the spring of 1974 the Raza leaders had, however, recognized the Anglo split and sided with the "redneck" faction on the issue of hiring the coach. They sought to undermine further the BGL moderates control of the school board.

The Anglo views of Ciudadanos factionalism were no more informed than the Mexicano views of BGL factionalism. As indicated, BGL Anglos generally saw Father Reynaldo as the key leader, and for some, he became a devil figure who incited his people. He was the brains behind *La Raza*, and the Aztlán City movement was his pocketbook.

Any Mexicano who was in Ciudadanos, which was merely a front for Raza Unida, was a "radical" who hated them. The BGL Anglos did not see the ideological differences among Ciudadanos as early as 1972. They also did not realize that their own responses and actions were an important part of the "political education" of many Ciudadanos members. The Anglos explained the growing hostility of the elected Mexicano leaders as "brainwashing" by outsiders, or as some form of inherited "reverse racism." One Ciudadanos member or "Chicano militant" was as bad as another. By the spring of 1974, the BGL leaders had also, however, recognized the Mexicano split.

The Anglo BGL leaders gradually revised their view of La Raza and began applauding the actions of the "rabid types like Ramírez and Salinas." Through information from Mexicans in the BGL, they came to realize that, "the extremists are our best ally." Some Raza leaders had publicly labeled other Mexicanos vendidos and cocos (brown on the outside and white on the inside) for not enthusiastically supporting the party. This offended many Mexicanos who did not consider themselves traitors to their race for not following certain local political leaders. The BGL began to skillfully use such conflicts by approaching Mexicanos who had experienced these criticisms. For the spring elections they recruited two previously "neutral" Mexicanos to become school board candidates. The men, a gas station owner and a railroad employee, were generally against the "pressure tactics" of Raza Unida. They, like the BGL Mexicanos on the city council, resented the idea of a "party telling you how to run your life." Anglos who recruited these men emphasized the "hardline" quality of the Raza Unida leaders much in the same way that Raza leaders emphasized the racist qualities of the BGL. To some extent, the BGL appeared to be more successful at exploiting such factional differences than the Raza Unida was.[8]

The Election Campaign of 1974

In many respects the elections of 1974 marked a major change in North Town ethnic politics and general Mexicano-Anglo relations. Both the BGL and Raza Unida were entering this second cycle of conflict faced with disunity. The leaders of each side were squabbling among themselves, and the rank-and-file showed signs of weariness with "ethnic politics." The BGL generally held their 1973 vote totals and following (900 plus votes for city council candidates and 1,100 plus for school board candidates). However, they apparently made few real inroads into recruiting large numbers of new Mexicano supporters. BGL leaders contended that they picked up approximately 200 Mexicano votes, but a Raza supporter who counted all the Spanish surnames who voted (city election) and then subtracted this total from the Raza total argued differently. He reasoned that no Anglos would vote for *La Raza*, which was undoubtedly true; therefore, those Spanish surnames left (74 in this case) were the Mexicans who went over to the BGL. His point was that the BGL had not been particularly successful in wooing Mexicanos to vote for them, but the Raza Unida had beaten itself. The party had made its own followers confused, fearful, and apathetic. Although perhaps not entirely accurate, these calculations and his theory did seem to represent the general trend of the election.[9] The Raza Unida suffered an even more crushing defeat than in 1973 since their vote totals dropped to 600 plus for council candidates and 900 plus for county candidates.

Neither side ran what might be called a well-organized, active campaign. The BGL held no public rallies and sponsored only one newspaper ad and a few radio spots. As in the previous year, they effectively organized a vigorous write-in campaign and canvassed their following by phone. In spite of growing Anglo disunity, the Anglo community rallied behind the BGL for a second year, if somewhat more reluctantly. The official information of Raza Unida, the appearance of Gutiérrez and his lieutenants, several scathing *Chicano Times* articles, and the conflicts over school events kept Anglos in a fighting mood. The BGL leaders on the school board and in the city council went into this second campaign with growing confidence, despite some apprehensions. By election time it had become apparent that Raza Unida was increasingly disunited and dispirited. On the eve of the election several BGL leaders sensed that they would defeat *La Raza* even more soundly.

The Raza Unida ran a much more public campaign that included several rallies and a series of *barriadas* (block meetings). The candidates, and particularly the county chairman Ramírez and councilman Salinas, actively canvassed their community. Among the most active campaign workers were a small group of women (eight or ten) who formed the core of the Women's Auxiliary of the old Ciudadanos. Some of these women were the wives of politically active men, but several were simply strong, independent-minded women who were politically-involved. Some joked about their husbands being *vendidos*, or dead, or "run off." No more than eighteen or twenty people, then, carried the fight to the BGL. The most noticeable aspect of the campaign was the number of different factions or types of *La Raza* supporters who were, as the real organizers put it, "sideline coaches."

The reasons for different types of supporters "sitting on the sidelines" were varied and complex. Before describing the feelings of old-time Mexicano leaders, businessmen, the 1972 "radical" leaders, students, and the moderates, one key event that irrevocably split the party must be recounted. In the early fall of 1973 it was apparent to Ciudadanos leaders that the growing "radical" faction and the "moderates" disagreed on whom to support in the race for North County judge. The county had been run since 1952 by Judge Ransom. The judge, a former drug store clerk who generally had the support of Mexicanos and rural Anglos, was periodically challenged by "prominent North Town Anglos." By 1973 the Judge had clearly become vulnerable to new political organizations among young, city-oriented Anglos and among the activist Ciudadanos Mexicanos. He was generally seen as a slow-moving, unprogressive, limited leader. Indeed, the entire "court-house gang," according to some, was due for a change. None of the long-time county job holders were active leaders in the BGL, and they definitely were not sympathetic to *La Raza*. There was, then, a general mood to have a new county judge, and eventually to change the exclusively rural direction of the commissioner's court.

In the fall two new Democratic candidates emerged. One was a local Anglo lawyer who ran unsuccessfully for the county attorney's position in 1966. Random sentiment about the Anglo candidate ranged from "he is a nice fellow but not too sharp" to "he is a poor lawyer and an even worse candidate than Judge Ransom." He was generally considered a weak candidate and one who would draw just enough votes away from Judge Ransom "to let the Mexican candidate win."

The other candidate was a prominent Mexicano restaurant owner in a small town, Dobieville, in the southern part of the county. Mr. Galván was in his early thirties, had a college degree, and was active in city council and school politics in Dobieville. He, several other young Mexicano professionals, and the old and new EODC directors, had successfully gained a majority on the city council. They also eventually (1975) took control of the school board. This group, which included a young North Town educator who became their school superintendent, firmly believed that any Mexicano victory in North County was more easily accomplished through the Democratic party. They contended that taking over the existing county organization and working with progressive Anglos was the way to improve conditions in North County. The Dobieville group, which was well organized and free of factions, sought the support of the North Town Raza Ciudadanos group. Without them, it would be difficult to capture the county with the outlying, united Anglo vote against "*La Raza*."

In North Town several key members of the "moderate" faction were in favor of supporting Mr. Galván and not running any Raza Unida candidate which might split his vote. Particularly the Ciudadanos school board members sought to convince Salinas and Ramírez and others that Galván was not a *vendido* but was a strong, "Chicano-oriented" candidate. They argued that he would work for the same programs and changes that a Raza candidate would. Privately, the moderate North Town Ciudadanos leaders "talked up" the Galván candidacy, but they were not entirely sure that he really had learned his political lesson about gringos yet. They simultaneously saw him as a good man, intelligent and socially active, but politically very naive and overly optimistic about his own Anglo support. The moderates now distrusted the Democratic party strategy of coalitions with Anglos, having been "tricked" and bitterly defeated by the "gringo BGL." They favored some form of "Chicano politics" but they also felt that the quickest, most practical way of getting in the court house was through the attractive, if not entirely satisfactory, Galván.

Conversely, those Ciudadanos leaders bent on creating a strong Raza Unida Party saw Galván as a weak candidate, not unlike the "tokens," the BGL "vendidos" on the North Town city council. A formal barbeque to get the Dobieville group and North Town Raza Unida together behind Galván was organized. A good deal of private discussion among the North Town Raza factions ensued. The Raza leaders remained resolute, and Galván's advocates among the moderates gradually lost heart with his candidacy, and with the party and general election campaign.

Galván, himself, did not take his case to the Raza Unida leaders or actively campaign in the North Town barrios. Still believing that he could draw considerable progressive Anglo support, he studiously avoided being publicly seen with Raza leaders. This campaign strategy only reaffirmed the arguments of the Raza leaders, and to them, he proved himself a *vendido* and something of an "Anglo-lover." In the Democratic primaries Galván received 939 to 1,231 for Judge Ransom and 527 for the Anglo lawyer. In the run-off Judge Ransom defeated him 1,529 to 1,138 votes. Without a cross-over vote of six to seven hundred North Town Raza votes, it was impossible for Galván to defeat Ransom. In the spring elections Ransom soundly defeated what many Raza Unida supporters conceded was their weak candidate by 2,376 to 721 votes.

In retrospect, Galván realized that very few of the Anglos who claimed to support him actually did. Instead, the "progressive" Anglos ultimately supported Judge Ransom, a man for whom they generally had low regard, over a young, college-educated businessman who had a record of civic activity. The reasons for the lack of Anglo support of Galván were undoubtedly complex. The most apparent reasons mentioned during post-election gossip was that Galván sympathized with the Raza Unida or was at the least a "*La Raza*-type Mexican."

It was a bitter political lesson for Galván, who privately admitted that he had misjudged the degree of racial feelings on both sides. He blamed the *vendidos* in the BGL for turning the Anglos against him by exaggerating his actual connection with Raza Unida. But his faith in the progressiveness of Anglos was also seriously shaken, and his sense of a need for a more united, more "Chicano politics" was greater. Although one commissioner from the Dobieville Mexicano political group was elected, the opportunity to gain control of the North County court house was lost for at least four more years.[10]

As the North Town Raza Unida moved deeper into their spring campaign, the moderates became increasingly inactive. The small band of Raza Unida activists, in spite of obvious and increasing disunity, pushed forward with political rallies and *barriadas*. One major rally was held in a small park in the middle of Mexican Town. As in most Mexicano political rallies in South Texas, this one featured a series of speakers and a presentation of candidates. In the meantime, much socializing and the *comída* (eating) took place. Children were running around playing; high schoolers were flirting with each other, and everyone was eating tacos, tamales, and pinto beans. Such events are invariably family events as much as a gathering of the political clan. The men stood in bunches smoking and talking politics, pick-ups, and baseball. The women were seated around in cars or on benches, or they were scurrying after infants. The principal speaker at the rally was Señora Muzquiz, a long-time leader of the Aztlán City Raza Unida, a speaker noted for her passionate, eloquent talks: (translated from Spanish)

> Good evening, it is also a pleasure for me to be, for the first time, in a rally as beautiful as this of the "Raza Unida," in a rally of a *partido* that is beautiful because it is our *partido*. It is a party where we did not need one white to be formed. In many areas, in many communities of South Texas, we have proven, to many whites, that like them who were able to start their parties, Democratic and Republican, and have come until these times to be known like major parties, we have also seen our start, and forward we go, and we shall see each other there. Because our party has been called many names, the last one that it has been called in Aztlán County is that we are like a cancer. You know why? Because they are beginning to recognize that the *partido* of Raza Unida has been born, and that it does not care how many traps will be set, legal or illegal. *La*

Raza has risen; we have risen; and when they make us believe that we do not have dignity of position, it is going to cost them a lot. Because we know in our blood, in our Mexican blood, in our Indian blood, we know our heroic heritage. For that reason, because we have faced that reality, we are not going to be pushed again. We are going to raise our people, and we are going to place that *partido* of the Raza Unida so high that the Democrats, as the years pass, will look small. For a simple reason, we were born Raza, first appearing weak, because we have sustained ourselves on *frijóles* (beans). But we were born of a race that has learned to support hardships of our lives, in our body, ever since we were young ones. We know how to suffer the cold. We have suffered in the life of work, and our body has become strong and firm. But what we had not discovered was that we were also strong in our heart. But now we are beginning to discover this, because it was already in us. It was in our blood. But because of reasons that we were not able to explain, until now, since 1970 until the present, there have been groups of Mexicanos that have risen. We have come to recognize that, only when we get together, can we, like a family from the small ones to the older ones, we can have unity to fight for our privileges, and for our rights. This morning we participated, a group of us, in a march in Harmon. Do you know the purpose of that march? The purpose was that they have made demands to have equality in education, equality in personal treatment, because our Mexicano children are individuals, even though they are only children. They are human, and they also want to be treated in the schools with equality. Those people of Harmon have presented themselves before the school board, demanding their rights to be treated with equality, and their petition was placed aside. Their demands were not heard. They were just set aside, and that is why they began to express their opinion, and have started the march, and have started their walkout like what we have seen for the last decade in many communities. In some of this, our children, our young people, have lost their lives like it happened in Pharr; in other areas, in other states, they have died for a struggle; they have died for a cause like the one in California, in the struggle of the worker for better wages, for better treatment, and young ones have also died, and also other people. These people are asking for their rights. These people have risked their lives; and this price, brothers and sisters of *la Raza Unida*, we should consider it and notice, not only from the paper but also from our heart. Because we have arrived at this level, because those souls have died for the struggle, we can see where they are, and can say, immortals, it was not in vain.

And you here in North Town, will have a struggle not only with the Anglo, but also with our own brothers, with the same ones of our Raza. It is a pity that money has a power that we will wish at times did not exist, because money will damage some persons. But one can see here, how with the humbleness of the candidates that have appeared here in front of you, that they with that honor of accepting the responsibility of running in the *Partido de La Raza Unida*; we do have another, better alternative. The Republicans and the Democrats have proven to us, in all our lives, that there is not a chance or hope in those parties. Because we, the Mexicanos, have gone out to the streets to support them, so that they will be in strong positions, with the hope that they would help us, but the situation has continued the same. Thus, begin the protest, the *huelgas* (strikes), all kinds, because there has not been hope for us. The inequalities continue in our homes, in our housing conditions. The inequalities continue in our schools. The inequalities continue in jobs. We have run for public positions in our attempt to do something for our barrios, for our people, and they placed traps before us. When we want to run for a high position, they call us communist. And there are many that do not want to see this; there are many that are totally blind. And they do not see that the Anglo, when we try to take a position, do not want this because they do not want us to rise to a level where there is dignity. They do not think that we have dignity and that we can also serve like they have served for years and years. They have always been the special ones; they have always been over us. In Aztlán City, many Anglos moved when the Raza Unida took the positions. It was not because they were afraid or because we scare them; they could not take that a Mexicano could be in position in the city, in position in the schools, and when they saw that they could not prevent this, then they gathered their belongings and left.

That was what we expected of them, everyone in this group here will have to face that, and make within onself that peace, that feeling that you are human, that you have dignity, and that you have that right to choose whatever candidate you want. Vote for your candidate, the candidates of the Raza Unida. Show that you have dignity and that this time you will have a choice. Show them that we are also human and have dignity, and that we can also direct the government. Thank you.

In a second Raza Unida rally the day before the elections Mr. Alonzo, one of the more outspoken moderates, emerged as a peacemaker to knit the factions together. He tried to bring the Raza together by convincing the Methodist and Baptist ministers and Father Reynaldo to be key speakers. Although this tactic came too late to have much of an effect on voters, it was a surprising show of unity and sympathy for *la causa Méxicana*. Prior to this rally neither of the Protestant ministers was active politically. If anything, the Methodist minister had been considered hostile to Raza Unida. The two ministers spoke primarily about human rights and working together to make this community a better place for Mexicanos. Their message was largely religious and stressed brotherly love and Christianity. Their presence was an implicit statement against widespread criticism of Raza Unida as communistic and cruel and as a group based solely on racial hatred of Anglos. But the highlight of the evening was a speech by Father Reynaldo, his last openly "political talk" in North Town: (translated from Spanish)

Senor Alonzo—"I would like applause for the pride of the *'Colonia Méxicana,'* he is the padre of our Catholic Church. Let us now have a beautiful applause for Padre Reynaldo."

Padre Reynaldo:

There exists a pride in being here, this night especially with my brothers the Rev. Miguel Romero and Elias Tovar. Let us give a grand applause for these persons.

Señor Alonzo was speaking, and he tells us that he had some persons here, what were the words that he used? It was beautiful. And I turned to Rev. Romero and I told him, he is *madeyando* (cunning). But let us now get more serious, we those that are in charge of the spiritual life of North Town. And not only us, there are still some more that are not here. Some problems occur day after day for our people. Talking to Rev. Romero and Brother Tovar, they also let me know that the problems do exist, that our people suffer. This suffering that we see causes great pain in us. We would like to do more if possible, but the three of us cannot do it. We need the cooperation of all of you, of your families, of your relatives. One could go and pray, but remember that you are the ones that form the church. The Rev. Romero could also do the same, and brother Tovar. All three of us could be in the church praying, asking God, but you, you are the ones that form the church. Without you, we could not be successful. That is why we are here tonight with you, asking you your cooperation, talking to you Sunday after Sunday, and also in the services that we have in the churches, about the love of God and the love for those next to us. This is what all of you have listened to when one speaks. But remember if you say that we love God and at the same time we do not love those *al próximo* (next to us), Saint John tells us in the scriptures that we are liars. If we really want to love God, we have to love our fellow men. And when our fellow man is in need, we have to help him out. We see some persons that have an interest in helping the rest of the people. We see persons that have come forth as candidates for positions in the city or in the school board. And all of these persons have an interest in you. And now, you are the ones that can help them out. You can help them out in one manner or another. So that you, yourself, your families, and the people, can place these persons in a position so that they can help those people that cannot help themselves. Just one more thing that I want to say, in the scriptures and one can say many things about the scriptures. It seems as though we have all the answers for our questions, but our Father, Jesus Christ, told us once, that a house divided within itself, would fall. There is no place in our lives, there is no place in our community for division. This community should be united, helping those persons that can help us and that are going to help us, and that are going to help people that are poor and humble, those that work day after day for their bread, for the bread of their family. That is why we are here tonight, asking you, with your help, influences, can help these persons that need your help, and not only for them, but so that they, once in a position, can help the rest of the people. That is why I ask you for your help, your influences, and your prayers. With this, I would now like to present you, my friend, the brother Romero. I would like a grand applause for him. (applause) If we, if we can get together in the churches, if we can be here together, we have different theologies, but we can still sit down and talk. We are good friends. That is the way we want to see the people, united. *Amigo* (friend) (referring to Rev. Romero), if you would like to say some words. What are your desires for our city, whatever you would like to tell us. It would be an honor to listen to you. Thank you.

Another popular way that Raza Unida tried to reach its voters was through neighborhood block meetings. Approximately thirty people attended one typical meeting, which took place outdoors at one of the candidates' house. To begin, the candidates distributed their cards, and one distributed his bumper stickers. It was an informal gathering that often became emotional with people spilling out their feelings and experiences and exhorting each other to fight the gringos. The precincts were discussed, and the county chairman of the party described how Anglos had reorganized the districts to split the Mexicano vote. Then a person told of a woman who went to vote wearing her Raza Unida button and was harassed, "The gringos told her she couldn't vote with the button on, that it was in the election book." After some discussion, the wife of a prominent merchant spoke at length about what she saw as the main problems in North Town: (translated from Spanish)

Mexicanos paid city taxes, and yet all the improvements were for the Anglo side of town. Mexicanos were burdened with having to pay very highly for any improvement on their side. Mexicanos did not have to be grateful to the Anglos for anything. Some people told me that the Anglos were nice to them and how could they go against the Anglos. I said, "I don't want a pat on the head. Where are the improvements to my community? A pat on the shoulder won't pave my street." People should not vote because they like or dislike the candidate but because of what the candidate can do for the community. We are not rebels, unlawful people. We are not communists, and we are not trying to be disruptive; what we want is to fight for our rights. The struggle is one for justice, against all the injustices that the gringos had perpetrated against the Mexicanos. The priests, the bishop, and even the pope are for justice and are fighting for the same cause as theirs. We need to do this for our children's future and the community welfare. The children needed better education, but if candidates right now are not the better educated people, that doesn't mean they shouldn't be elected because what counts is their *voluntad* (good will) and what they want to do for the community. Wayne may have diplomas, but he won't do anything for the Mexicano. There are Mexicanos who are in official positions who won't do anything for the Mexicanos either because they are running for another party and are under the gringos' orders. That is why the Mexicanos need a third party to be completely independent from the gringos. Salinas for instance doesn't have to give account of what he does to any gringo because he doesn't run with them, so he can serve the community as a Mexicano. We are Chicanos and should be proud of it. There are in South Texas eighty-five Chicanos for fifteen gringos. Yet the school in North Town has 125 teachers but only ten are Mexicanos. Why is that? We need Mexicano teachers who will give classes in both languages, so that kids who only know Spanish won't get lost and will learn better.

As the meeting continued several other people described incidents at the schools, how Anglo teachers humiliate the children in front of their peers by cleaning their heads of lice. Another woman told how she was a certified teacher but was denied a job in the North Town schools because her husband was a Raza Unida leader. Others told horror stories about the schools and about denied opportunities. The meeting finally closed with some discussion of Councilman Salinas' trial in Austin and the victory that had been salvaged.

In retrospect, many of the Raza Unida leaders felt that the *barriadas* were generally not very effective because they reached mainly those who were already committed. Others criticized the campaign efforts for not having enough big rallies. Others wanted more block workers to get out the vote. Outside of a few active women and the candidates themselves, no one else did the tedious, day-to-day, door-to-door or phone canvassing. Unlike the computerized block lists and the hordes of student and party workers in Aztlán City elections, the North Town leaders ran a very limited campaign.[11] Of all the problems they encountered, however, perhaps the most debilitating was the number of non-participating sympathizers.

Raza Supporters "Sitting on the Sidelines"

The largest group to withdraw from the movement was the "moderates." In actual fact those moderates who were candidates and those who sought to be peacemakers did attend *barriadas* and rallies and were "active." But there were many others who stayed away from any involvement. Some, like the deposed mayoral candidate, were deeply in debt from the previous election. They stayed home to build up their businesses. Others like the cashier and an outspoken principal minimized any public activity because of their positions in the Anglo bank and the Anglo school system. Others were simply tired of the fighting among their own people, as well as against the Anglos. At this point a number of the moderates had become disgusted with the "dictatorial" and "hard-headed" approach of the new Raza Unida leaders. They felt that it was useless to talk to them about not calling people *vendidos* and *pendejos*, or about not formally becoming Raza Unida, a label which they felt confused and scared many Mexicanos.

Gradually, the moderates developed the strategy of strategic withdrawal, in effect, to destroy the Raza Unida party. They did not seek to destroy Chicano politics, only a Chicano politics led by Chicanos whom they felt were out of touch with the people. Rather than openly fighting the "radicals," they chose to "let them beat themselves" in future elections. The moderates generally felt that it may take several election defeats for the most stubborn radicals to understand that they did not have the people's support, but the moderates were willing to wait. They felt that there would come a time when, they, "a more reasonable, respected group in the community," could begin to reorganize under a new political banner, or perhaps under the Democratic Party banner. Several moderates had intimate knowledge of how open, warring factions had developed and torn the party apart in Aztlán City. They were anxious to avoid this. Though they would make lasting enemies of the Raza Unida leaders for this withdrawal, they felt that it was the best way of avoiding a permanent split along family and friendship lines in the entire community. It was time to cool politics off for a while, and only a withdrawal could do this.

Another type of Raza supporter that seemed to be on the sidelines was the "ex-radical." Several of the original activists of 1972, the ex-city manager, his brothers, the ex-councilwoman, and some young college students seemed to be exhausted by the struggle and disgusted with the lack of support they had received. They felt that they had worked very hard for the party and the people for nothing. Mrs. Toliver, the former councilwoman, expressed her disillusionment in the following way:

> When we started the whole thing there were more people involved. About 1300 people voted for us. Then the gringos cut us down by taking people to court, things like that. Now people are basically afraid of going out to vote. Even the ones who are legal, who would have no problem of being penalized, don't want to go because they don't want any trouble for themselves. The gringos have the power, the money, everything. It is hard to go against them. Like the gringas who have Mexicanas as maids, tell them who to vote for. They even come here to pick their maids to go

211

and vote, and they give them the sample ballot. So the Mexicanas, of course, vote for gringos. It is very difficult to make people aware of political problems because of the gringo power over the financial lives of the Mexicanos. Besides, the Mexicanos here don't care too much about politics, about the community. "*Se nos da la fregada*" (they blamed us, gave us no credit) when we are working hard for them. Like when we were in the city council or school board, these people tell us that we aren't doing anything and start saying bad things about us. After a while, a lot of good people naturally don't want to work in politics any more if they are going to be hurt and abused by the community. It is discouraging.

The ex-city manager, who was often criticized for "selling out" by taking a job with the largest Mexicano vegetable farmer in the region, expressed similar feelings. He also added that they had made too many tactical errors:

> Raza Unida is too disorganized and not in control of themselves. The Anglos are shrewder about over-reacting. They are controlling their rednecks pretty good and keeping their cool better. We blew it . . . The people don't care about politics. My boss doesn't care about politics. It is very hard to educate people to be interested in politics . . . But we are getting what we wanted anyway. The gringos have to respond. They have to do more, get in more programs, improve things. This thing has forced some changes in this town. Things are starting to get a little better because we started something . . . Raza won't last here . . . I don't know how things will turn out in the future. The Mexicanos aren't going anywhere, though.

Another type of supporter who seemed to head for the sidelines as defeat appeared imminent was the Mexicano businessman. Initially a number of the most prominent Mexicano businessmen openly supported Ciudadanos; but as "Chicano politics" became less popular and more disruptive in the community, some feared for their businesses. Several of the leaders in Ciudadanos and Raza had suffered serious business losses. They had neglected their businesses and had lost customers for political reasons. The community was still not sufficiently politicized and organized to carry out a successful economic boycott against non-Raza stores, nor were they able to successfully support businesses that were openly pro-Raza. The survival instincts of most successful Mexicano merchants and farmers prompted them to tone down whatever political fervor they initially had. Only a few "hard core *La Raza* types," as one Anglo merchant put it, "tried to make their politics and business mix." That the monied Mexicanos ultimately did not actively support Raza Unida proved to be a serious problem for the financially weak party.

212

A final type of Mexicano supporter that was curiously supportive in spirit but inactive in body was the old-time political leader. One thing which became apparent about the nature of small-town, local politics, Mexicano or Anglo, was that leadership was very generational. When an older, earlier generation or era of leaders suffered defeat, there were no triumphant returns to the center stage to lead again. Losing a local election apparently discredits one thoroughly because local politics is a very personal thing. When a candidate who lives in close proximity to the voters is rejected, it is at least in part a personal rejection. Unlike national politics where voters really do not know the candidates, to lose among one's friends and neighbors is a greater loss of honor. Consequently, the old Mexicano political leaders such as Mr. Guerra, the fiery ex-city councilman of the sixties, were particularly bitter. They really were not able to actively join the new wave of leaders. A barrier of fallen reputation stood between the old and the new generation that neither could overcome. Mr. Guerra described his political career and views:

> I ran independently for the Mexicano people. I was the first elected Mexicano. The others were just put in there by the gringos. They tried to buy me off too. The mayor invited me to his home to talk . . . People ten years ago were *muy pinchones* (uncommitted, unsupportive), now that we are getting in power, they are beginning to come out. They know they will get it. It will take five more years. People have been overpowered. Now we have lots of votes, and they'll feel the pain, and we're gonna beat them. We have been under their feet quite a bit of time. I don't have anything against gringos, though, but lots here are very much prejudiced; they think we are underrated people, but the majority are beginning to understand to meet us between the goal lines . . . No, I am not active anymore. I have too many skeletons in my closet. When things were hot, they accused me of many things. They say I drank too much and had too many women. No, my day is past . . . I am still a Democrat. I think the Republicans created this Raza Unida to split the Democrats . . . No, they don't come here to get my advice. I am not involved anymore. I got put out to pasture early, but I am still a good man, you better believe that . . ."

And if the old leaders were on the sidelines because of missed opportunities, the young high school students were there because they were given few opportunities to participate. There were many different student groups, some were against Raza Unida, some were "neutral." Those students whose parents were active in the movement were particularly pro-Raza. These students were generally the ones who organized Mexicano students "to beat the gringos" in student elections.

Some of these organizers were outstanding students, some were the *vatos locos* (poor students, clowns, hipsters) who went along with Chicano power or any power that could challenge the boredom and seeming arbitrariness of school and school rules. One of the pro-Raza honor students attempted to organize the eighteen-year-old vote at the high school. He succeeded in registering eighteen of fifty-three students, of which only half voted. Another popular student leader, the niece of the former councilwoman, made a short speech at one of the Raza Unida rallies. Other than this, the students were uninvolved. The party leaders generally perceived the students as too young and immature to be an active part of the movement.

It was generally true that Mexicano students were not well informed about local politics, but many had strong feelings and very high motivation to be involved. Generally, however, they never approached the level of involvement that youth in Aztlán City did during their school walkout of 1969.[12] Although the administration worried about a similar student walkout, there were no forceful student leaders, and the adults tended to shy away from including the youth in politics, or from "playing politics too much with the schools." This ethic, one frequently expressed in the youth work of Father Reynaldo, was perhaps the single most important reason that students were generally on the political sidelines.

A Final Outburst of Conflict

On election day both sides were primed to find any irregularities or "cheating." Particularly the Raza Unida, facing what seemed imminent defeat, were frustrated and ready to salvage some honor from another election defeat.[13] The party set up a table in front of the library to watch whoever came to vote. The precinct lists of registered voters were used to check who was not voting. Meanwhile, individual BGL leaders were also driving around, observing the flow of voters into the polling places and setting up pollwatchers' tables. Generally, the election went on smoothly and peacefully. However, later in the day two Raza leaders, Mr. Alonzo and Mr. Matamoros, vented their frustration towards the BGL. The first incident occurred at the Catholic church when Mr. Matamoros attempted to frighten an Anglo pollwatcher, the wife of Dr. Weldon, a prominent BGL leader.

Mrs. Weldon had the reputation of being the "chief spy" for the BGL. She regularly attended school board meetings, city council meetings, and district court proceedings and always took extensive written notes on her observations. As one of the Raza leaders said,

"She was everywhere, always writing down everything." On the day of elections Mrs. Weldon, who was accompanied by her housekeeper, parked near the Catholic Church and was observing the polling place. Mr. Matamoros reportedly went up to her and asked, "What are you doing snooping around here? Who is that Mexican with you?" After being told she was her maid, Mr. Matamoros asked, "Don't you know how to clean house? I bet you don't even know how to cook." He then told her, "You better get the hell out of here if you know what is good for you." Since he appeared drunk and attempted to open the car door, Mrs. Weldon was reportedly terrified and left. Mr. Matamoros apparently did not intend to physically harm Mrs. Weldon, but he was offended that she had brought her spying activities to the doorsteps of his church in the heart of the Mexicano community.

Later in the day several other incidents occurred which involved Mr. Alonzo. He reportedly took a BGL pollwatcher's checklist away from her near the high school polling place on the Anglo side of town. A little later he allegedly tried to swerve in front of another Anglo lady who had been a pollwatcher, at the same time hurling insults at her for spying on the Mexicanos. Both men were charged in the local Justice of the Peace Court with disorderly conduct, abusive language, and intent to assault. This action led to a protest march on the court house and considerable private grumbling. Eventually the more serious criminal charges were dropped, and both men pleaded guilty to the disorderly conduct charges and paid $150 fines. In retrospect both admitted that they had "gotten hot" and "had gone a little too far," but believed that they had been provoked. They also admitted that "putting Mrs. Weldon in her place" may have been worth the fine.

A SUMMING UP: THE ESCALATION AND DE-ESCALATION OF CONFLICT

The disunity and decline of the Raza Unida, then, was a very complex phenomenon. As the struggle continued, many different types of people withdrew for different reasons. Others had been on the "sidelines" from the beginning. The splits between the leaders were personal and ideological, and most often, simply a lack of organized group communication. Ex-leaders reported being called "drunkards," "whores," "greedy," "sell-outs." Present leaders reported being called "dictators," "fanatics," and "racists." Some leaders called the people *flojos*, and *pendejos*. As the movement suffered defeat, the leaders and followers blamed each other as much as the hated "gringos." In the face of such intensive personal conflict and criticism, a kind of exhaustion and disillusionment affected even the most ardent leaders and supporters. The same sort of feelings and reactions were also apparent in Anglo disunity, but they had staved off defeat and with that had avoided, at least momentarily, widespread disillusionment, hence serious disunity.

Organizationally and psychologically, the BGL came out of the 1974 elections much stronger. Their strategy of punitive and conciliatory moves had been successful. Many Anglos expressed great relief following the elections. Some thought *La Raza* had been broken. Others said they would be back. The Anglos discontent with the BGL school board continued to criticize them and even made overtures to Mr. Alonzo and Mr. Matamoros about joining forces to oust the BGL! Further, even in victory the BGL leaders were also exhausted, tired of conflict, and the heavy obligations of being political leaders. Their personal lives and businesses suffered from neglect. Some BGL leaders talked about disbanding the organization, and several new leaders replaced the most active leaders of the 1972 to 1974 period.

In retrospect, perhaps the height of the conflict was during the fall of 1973 at the time of the BGL election suit. With that defeat, the Ciudadanos organization began to collapse. The then deposed Mayor Matamoros dropped out of politics to concentrate on his business. The school board leaders and several others who considered themselves more moderate became increasingly inactive. Of the once united and active city officials, only Councilman Salinas fought on. As the Ciudadanos organization became Raza Unida, rumors swept the community that this was a desperate rather than decisive and strong move. A small band of active women and several men close to Mr. Ramírez were enraged and wanted to avenge their series of losses to the hated BGL. They still sought to continue the Raza Unida-BGL rivalry and escalate the conflict further. The Ciudadanos leaders, by their withdrawal, sought to de-escalate the conflict and end the election competition and rivalry. In a sense, their moves signaled to the BGL leaders that they had less reason to continue fighting the *La Raza* threat and some reasons to seek conciliation.

As the BGL became progressively stronger and realized that the Raza Unida was no longer a serious threat, they began de-escalating the conflict. Sporadic conflict, some intended and some unintended, occurred during 1973–74, but enough conciliatory moves were made in response to the Mexicano withdrawal to slowly wind down the general community conflict.

The reasons for a gradual de-escalation of community conflict are complex, but the previously mentioned factionalism and the psycho-

216

logical exhaustion with "political fighting" were surely important factors. Further, as one group became less able to compete and the other more dominant, each side began seeking conciliation, one from strength, the other from weakness. In effect the rivalry between relatively equal warring political parties changed to a less conflictful relationship among relatively unequal parties.[14] As earlier historical patterns of superior-subordinate relationships reoccurred, a degree of community harmony was restored. However, the question on everyone's mind was how long would the decline in organized political competion and rivalry last?

If, as the historical analysis suggested, major economic and cultural changes had occurred, some Mexicanos will seek to be political rivals again. They believe themselves to be equal, and they seek equal or dominant relationships with Anglos, not subordinate ones; consequently, when some group of aggrieved Mexicanos is relatively united and strong enough to compete, it is very likely that community conflict will escalate again. Conflict may occur again, regardless of what the peacemakers in both groups do to appease those seeking a rivalry through political competition. This is not to argue that no peace and harmony is possible in North Town, but it is to say that a powerful dynamics exists for ethnic political conflict. Factors such as organization, leadership, communication, and controversial issues may engender future conflicts. Most importantly, new leaders seem likely to arise from old, bitter resentments.[15]

[1] Following the political battle between Mexicanos and Anglos on a daily basis involved attending many public meetings and frequent informal, "off the record" discussions with leaders from each group. In some sense the major way data was collected was to be "plugged into" the gossip networks of each group. Since many opinions collected were indeed slanted, constant checking and cross-checking of the materials occurred. In the text some of these "opinions" are simply reported to illustrate how different residents perceived community events. At other times we attempt to report a community event "as it really happened." In this part of the narrative we have "combined" the reports of different points of view with our own and come up with a single description or interpretation of "what really happened." Of course, considerable judgment comes into play when trying to give one account of a community event.

[2] Although some residents would debate this characterization, even the administrative director of the center expressed such sentiments.

[3] The judgment rendered here is based on considerable informal observation of the administrators and teachers involved. If they were as culpable as the *Chicano Times* indicated, that judgment was not based on any discussion with or observation of their reactions to the reported events. They acted more embarrassed and dumbfounded than guilty.

[4] In order to disguise the town, the exact article will not be cited. Serious re-

searchers can obtain this information from Professor Foley at the University of Texas.

5 The parallels in this case towards a unified leadership and the Aztlán case are striking. In both cases the existing leadership group, when seriously threatened, were able to unify local services to a degree under one policy-making group, thereby making local government more "planned" and complimentary.

6 This judgment was, of course, very difficult to make. Neither side was above arm-twisting, threats, and intimidation. It should be noted that one Raza Unida leader, Mr. Alonzo, apparently lost his job as a labor contractor for his political activities. Several other Mexicano businessmen were reportedly "talked to" about losing loans and business, but apparently nothing happened to them.

7 A much more detailed discussion of life in the North Town schools will be presented in subsequent publications. This discussion is a general characterization of the BGL response to the La Raza threat. Since the old rationales for Anglo authority, i.e., Anglo cultural superiority, were no longer acceptable to many Mexicanos, the BGL school board had to find a new basis for being the accepted, legitimate authority over the communities' schools. They had to convince Mexicanos that they could rule fairly and objectively, hence many school policies were instituted that more traditional Anglos objected to. In some ways the school board could satisfy neither the Mexicanos nor the Anglos.

8 It might be noted that although each side appeared to have much misinformation about the leaders of the other side, they were very good at finding each others' hypocricies and contradictions. For example, it was amusing to Anglos that some of the most ardent Raza Unida supporters had gotten their start in business because of Anglo sponsorship. In one case a strong party member's father had apparently been the local bootlegger under the hated Sheriff Cameron. Conversely, some BGL leaders who often tried to publicly express their fondness for Mexicanos were often described as hypocrites in regard to the manner in which they treated their maids or in their fondness for Mexicana mistresses and cantina life. No doubt, many local Mexicanos and Anglos were not above self-deception, contradiction, and impropriety. Fortunately, they were quite human and fallible. It is important to understand, however, how each side rationalized their own public political behavior with the sins of the other's private behavior. This most surely fed the conflict and justified heightened hostility. All of this misinformation and rationalization also made locating who were the "real" leaders exceedingly difficult if one was to rely on the simplistic approaches in the literature called "reputational" and "key decisions/events" analysis.

9 It sould be noted that we never seriously pursued this question with careful data analysis of the shifts in voting trends.

10 The Dobieville Mexicanos have, however, continued to organize and have apparently avoided the factionalism of Aztlán City and of North Town. Interestingly, they are now considered a "communist threat," too, since they have been able to take-over the city council and school board.

11 Smith, Walter, Jr. Ibid.

12 Smith, Walter, Jr. Ibid.

13 Investigations by the Civil Rights Commission will undoubtedly find irregularities under the Voting Rights Act. Both sides justified "cheating" to stop the other sides cheating. In most cases, we did not witness the actual irregular acts.

218

The reports presented were reconstructed from interviews with the participants and members of both Ciudadanos and the BGL.

14 Bateson, Gregory. *Towards An Ecology of the Mind.* New York: Ballentine, 1972. This explanation of conflict resolution is based on Bateson's general concept of schismogenesis in human relations.

15 For a more extended conceptual discussion of the decolonization process in this region see Douglas E. Foley "Decolonization and Mental Health in South Texas." In Sally Jones Andrade (edited) *Chicano Mental Health: The Case of Crystal.* Austin: Hogg Foundation for Mental Health Publications, University of Texas, 1978.

Chapter 7

An Epilogue: North Town from 1974 to 1977

Politics from 1974 to 1977

In the 1974 elections, the Raza Unida party polled a high of 745 in the city council and 831 in the school board. In contrast the top BGL candidates polled 990 in the city and 1395 in the school elections. In 1975 the top Raza Unida candidates polled only 384 in the city and 478 in the school elections. In contrast the top BGL candidates polled 920 in the city and 1073 in the school elections. In 1976 there were no Raza school board candidates, and those in the city council elections polled only 319 votes. The total for the top city candidates of the BGL was also down dramatically (628), but they still won by a 2-to-1 majority. By this point only the more active members and supporters of each organization were still doing battle in local elections. Now that the *"La Raza* takeover" had been broken, both Anglos and Mexicanos stayed away from the polls in large numbers.

During this period when local electoral politics seems to have "settled down," the political organizations of each side have evolved in different directions. The BGL, although now less mobilized and active, remains strong. Some of the most active leaders, the former party chairman, the mayor, the school board president and a key board member, have "retired" from active roles. New faces, although always active, have emerged at public meetings and during recent community conflicts. Interestingly, the wives of several prominent businessmen/professionals and the county clerk, also a woman, are now perceived by the Mexicanos as the key leaders. As in the past, a number of prominent Anglo ranchers, farmers, and businessmen still support the BGL. It should be noted that BGL supported candidates currently control all the city council positions and all but one of the school board positions. The present BGL city and school leaders are fifty percent Mexicano and fifty percent Anglo.

The factionalism among Mexicano *politicos* that began in 1972 and culminated with the 1974 withdrawal of the Ciudadanos "moderates" has deepened in 1977. A number of the original Raza Unida and Ciudadanos leaders remain politically inactive. Some attempted to run for political office under the Democratic Party. Others began to re-organize through new ethnic and social organizations. Several of the original LULAC/Ciudadanos organizers belong to a social club of ten or twelve prominent families called the *El Sarape*. Just how political this club is has become a much debated topic. Both the BGL leaders and the Raza Unida leaders generally perceive it as a group with po-litical aspirations, one that quietly supported a candidate for county commissioner and for the school board. Raza Unida leaders contended that the most significant thing about *El Sarape* was that it combined two anti-Raza cliques. One clique represented the personal followings of several of the moderate Ciudadanos leaders, who withdrew their support in 1974. This included some prominent Mexicano business families which Mr. Ramírez, the Raza Unida chairman, considered "exploiters of the Mexicanos." The other clique was the personal fol-lowing of the largest Mexicano melon grower, who Mr. Ramírez ac-cused of getting "his men" into city council and the county commis-sioner's court positions. When this prominent grower recently joined the *El Sarape*, the alliance, according to Mr. Ramírez, was now official. Some local people consider this grower a potential "king-maker" or man-behind-the-political-scenes. Others contend that he had little interest in politics and a great deal of interest in his business.

The *El Sarape* Club was often criticized for its limited, exclusive membership. To restrict membership any new proposed member must be accepted by all other members. Consequently, the actual member-ship, for whatever reason, has been purposely kept small and includes only prominent businessmen and professionals, many of whom were formerly politically active. Most *El Sarape* members would dismiss Mr. Ramírez's charges that they are *los ricos* who think of themselves as somehow higher and better. They contend that he talks nonsense and is "just sour grapes about losing the election." *El Sarape* members stress that their group is merely a social club of people who enjoy each other's company. They would strongly deny any pretensions of setting themselves above the Mexican people as superior. This was, however, a view that a number of non-leaders and non-Raza Unida Mexicanos also expressed. The emergence of *El Sarape* appears to have created a more formalized class difference within the Mexicano community. In this sense, the previous splits among Mexicano *politicos* has deepened and taken on new connotations.

In the meantime, the Raza Unida party has clearly lost its following and credibility with Mexicano voters. As the election statistics indi-cate, even the key party leaders now have no more than 200-300 fol-lowers. That hard core of followers represents more of a personal, family, and friendship following than it does a broad-based group. In local North Town politics almost any serious candidate for public office can usually muster up this large a following from personal rather than philosophical commitment. However, the ideas advocated by Raza Unida have had a real impact, as the comments by reviews of this manuscript reveal. The concept of Mexicano self-determination and a more active ethnic politics is now advocated by many people who no longer support the party. The party organization was unable to mobilize voters to follow its chosen candidates, but North Town politics will never be the same.

Continuing Ethnic Conflict in the Church and the County

Although North Town electoral politics has "cooled down," the battle between various Raza Unida and BGL leaders continues. To a degree, the electoral conflicts of the 1972–1974 era have shifted to the Catholic church and to a proposed multi-county, federally-funded health program. The recent conflict in the North Town Catholic church between the Raza Unida leaders and the new parish priests has most directly affected the Mexicano community. The rector of the parish, feeling that this type of study might revive the conflict, preferred not to discuss the matter, but several pro and anti-Raza community members and the rector's associate did describe the events that have occurred since the fall of 1975.

When the two priests arrived in the fall of 1975 they began familiarizing themselves with the needs and problems of the North Town parish. They found a troubled parish divided by differing political alignments. The prominent Anglo parishioners and a number of Mexican-Americans were disgruntled with the influence of "radical," Raza Unida leaders in church affairs. For example, since 1970 Mr. Ramírez and his followers had been organizing the major religious/social celebration, *Diez y Seis*. Politically active Mexicanos ran the most successful eating booths, the bingo games, the parking concession, and several other money-making ventures for the church. Mr. Ramírez has records indicating that his committee had made more than $30,000 for the church in seven years, thus paying off much of the construction debt for the church building. He contends that their celebrations were better attended and bigger money-makers than those of the sixties.

Various Anglo and anti-Raza Mexicanos contend that Ramírez takes too much credit, has mismanaged the committee, actually lost money, and is primarily interested in using the celebration to recruit voters.

During the dances there were political speeches extolling the pride, beauty, and unity of *La Raza*. There were also "Raza candidates" in the competition for the queen of the celebration. Moreover, anti-Raza parishioners cite that Raza Unida was using the church in other ways. Party leaders have held several meetings in the recreational rooms, and the church was used during a Raza Unida primary election as well as during the regular local school elections.

During the first six months relationships were apparently cooperative between Mr. Ramírez, other party members, and the new priests. In retrospect, Mr Ramírez felt "used" because he took one of the priests to meet the MALDEF lawyers, revealed the party's various activities and law suits, and introduced him throughout the community as a friend. Conversely, the priests also felt that Ramírez was trying to "use them for his political purposes" as he had done with earlier priests. Increasingly each sides' suspicions grew. By spring the important new policies which undercut the activeness of Raza Unida leaders in church affairs were initiated.

One of the first changes made was to replace the old parish advisory board with new members. In a letter to the former board members, which included a majority of Raza sympathizers, the new rector stated that he would appoint an interim council to get "new blood and other people involved." The reason given for having an appointed council was that his advisory board committee for the preparation of by-laws was taking a great deal of time. The letter reassured Mr. Alonzo that this decision was not due to any adverse feelings but merely was a needed change. Mr. Alonzo and other Raza Unida leaders felt that the change was unnecessary and that not having these positions elected was undemocratic. They reasoned that prominent Anglo BGL Catholics now "had the priests in their pockets."

During this period the new rector and the new advisory board instituted several new policies that further irritated the Raza Unida leaders. First, all meetings in parish buildings by any organized group, even private baptismal and wedding parties, were prohibited. This policy was initiated to avoid any personal, therefore, possible political use of the church facilities. One test of this rule was the exclusion of a group of individuals who were seeking to develop a rural health program. The priests, as did most other North Town residents, perceived this program as a "Raza Unida-sponsored health program." This was indeed a program long-sponsored by various Raza Unida members and began with the *El Sacrificio* organization mentioned earlier. Raza leaders saw this policy as directly seeking to destroy their following and even more critically, as a way to disrupt the social life and social relations of the Mexicano community. Much of the important friendship and family exchanges take place through church-centered celebrations; consequently, such policies were the most important way that disunity could be created in the Mexicano community.

Second, the site for the fiesta committee was to be changed to the grounds and the street between the rectory and the church. This moved the *Diez y Seis* celebration from the traditional site, a large open field donated by a prominent Anglo parishioner. The priests felt that the old site was poorly drained and dirty and that the temporary booths used for restaurants were unsanitary. They contended that the church site, although somewhat smaller, had much better facilities. The Raza leaders, who had run the celebration for seven years, saw this as a move to eliminate their role and influence in the celebration.

Third, the rector was criticized for spending $7,000 for remodeling the rectory. Some parishioners argued that he spent their hard-earned money for his comfort. Meanwhile he reportedly refused to spend the money on a new center with class and meeting rooms. He was also criticized for his policies on first communion classes, which reportedly allowed Anglo children to have their own separate class and did not require the Anglo parents to attend the weekly orientation meeting for parents.

In general during the spring of 1976 a group called The Committee of Concerned Parishioners openly criticized the new priests. This group was predominantly Raza Unida members, but it also included some ex-Raza, Ciudadanos, and *El Sarape* Club members. The group discussed their grievances with the administrative assistant of the archbishop. They wrote the archbishop a letter strongly critical of the rector. Further, one evening, at approximately 10:30 pm, a group of fifty-five people went to request an audience with the rector. He refused to meet with the large, agitated group and suggested that they select a few representatives and meet with the advisory council and him during the day. The following day the group, incensed by the rector's refusal to meet, requested him by letter to meet on the church grounds. More than 100 people went to confront the rector, but he did not attend the meeting. Eventually, a committee of five parishioners met with the rector and the advisory council in the afternoon. From the parishioners' perspective the meeting was unproductive, i.e., none of the new policies were rescinded. Further, they became even more incensed after the meeting upon discovering a police car parked near the rectory. They reasoned that the priests, fearing violence, called the police to observe the meeting. To them this showed that "he must think we are a bunch of animals or something." However, other parishioners sympathetic to the new priests considered all these meetings and the protests excessive harassment "by a bunch of sore losers who can't have their way anymore."

Another concurrent incident, the appointment of Mr. Alonzo to the EODC board, further embroiled the priests and the church in the ongoing conflicts between Raza and BGL leaders. Apparently, Mr. Alonzo requested the rector to write him a general letter of recommendation attesting to his activeness in the church and general good character. He subsequently presented that letter to the EODC board, claiming that he was the Catholic Church's representative. He was instated and began to serve on the board until several outraged members of the church protested to the rector. The rector informed the EODC board that he had not written the letter with any intent of having Mr. Alonzo appointed on the board as a representative of the church. This incident proved to many non-Raza Unida parishioners and the new priests that the Raza leaders were indeed devious and were only out to manipulate the church for political purposes. Mr. Alonzo subsequently resigned his EODC position as a church representative and rejoined the board as the representative of the reactivated LULAC organization.

As the criticisms, letters, phone calls, publicity on T.V., and meetings increased, so did mutual suspicion between the priests and the group called the Committee of Concerned Parishioners. The new priests were "victorious" in the sense that the archbishop did not investigate, and he reassured them that they should continue as they were. But the priests let it be known to their parishioners that such events were intolerable. There were rumors that the priests were "fed up," that they "might ask for a transfer because their efforts were unappreciated." Consequently, in April another group of parishioners organized a meeting of "all concerned citizens to voice support for what the priests were doing." Approximately 250 North Towners met in the church as described by one of the priests:

The meeting didn't last more than fifteen minutes. They assembled in the church, sang a hymn and said a prayer, and a couple of people read statements that they didn't want us to leave, and they appreciated what we had been doing and how we had made an effort to unify the community. In the meantime the Raza Unida was outside and taking pictures and cursing the people and being as trashy as only they can be. It opened the eyes of a lot of people, and now they can see exactly, and they know now. They get better service than they have ever had, and we don't involve ourselves in politics one way or another . . . (on the BGL's possible political use of that meeting) . . . That is ridiculous because the ones that started the whole thing were Mexicans who decided that they were going to have this show, to give us a vote of confidence. So the fact that they were there, they came as individuals, not as members of the BGL or anything else, people that we know on the other side, people who were friends of ours and so forth . . . There were no political overtones in that thing whatsoever. I don't care what anyone says, there were no political overtones whatsoever. We had Baptist, we had Methodist, Presbyterians, Masons, and everything else . . .

The priest further commented on what he considered the effect of that meeting on the church and the community, and on what he felt was the general cause of the initial conflicts:

When they (Raza Unida) saw the Anglos, not only the Catholic Anglos but the non-Catholics, that there were representatives from every aspect of the community and certainly on this side of the tracks, many of the people realized. You see Raza leaders had been rather successful in convincing all the people here, the older Mexicanos, that the Raza Unida and the Catholic church were one in the same thing. And when the people saw that we no longer participated, that we didn't want any part of it, they had their eyes opened, it literally was a thing that broke them . . . I think we have been very successful and the Mexicans themselves feel that. I hear more from this side than from the other side how grateful they are that we have finally put the church in a position and given the church the prestige that it's supposed to have in their own minds, to remove from it the whole idea of politics, that we are not supporting this group or that group, and that politics is your own personal business . . . The whole thing is, if we were tomorrow to say, "No matter what you do, we are going to back you all up. We are with you 100%. We are going to get into this business. We are going to join the hate outfit. We are going to hate the Anglos." You could go around tomorrow morning, and you would find out that everything was just magnificent . . . Those who lead the Raza Unida did not go to church before. They came because we had a couple of priests here who sort of didn't care one way or the other what happened and gave them free reign in the situation, and then we came. They saw that we weren't going to do it. In other words, see they are unable to distinguish between politics and religion . . . One of the things they (Raza Unida) have all got to learn is, they never learned how to see a person. They have no concept of this at all. In other words, I look at you and the only thing I can see in you is an Anglo and possibly a potential enemy . . . Outside of a few little radical groups, most people are not that concerned with anything. They take people for what they are . . . (on the controversy in the parish) . . . That has really all died down, now. It has all died down because people know where we stand;

there is not a question of any controversy any more. They know where we stand, how we think, and that is it . . .

The Raza Unida leaders' explanation for taking pictures at the meeting was to document how hypocritical the protestant BGL Anglos were. They reported that one BGL leader circulated a petition among the group to elect a candidate for a position on the EODC board, for which the priest publicly apologized. Further, several "BGL leaders were kneeling in prayer like Catholics, trying to convince the Mexicanos that they were religious." After this series of events, approximately twenty to thirty Mexicano families no longer attended church. In the fall of 1976 Mr. Ramírez and a number of other disgruntled parishioners organized their own *Diez y Seis* celebration which competed with the one held by the church on the church grounds. Both sides reported huge successes, but according to several less-aligned observers, the attendance, and probably the profits, at the church-sponsored fiesta were down considerably. The Raza Unida-sponsored fiesta drew at least as many participants and probably more than the church-sponsored fiesta. Although the priests contend that all the controversy has died down, Mexicano *politicos* are still plotting different ways to get the priests transferred. The North Town Catholic church remains a troubled, divided parish; now Anglos have returned to a more active participation in church affairs, while some of the politically active Mexicanos have become inactive. In many ways the church has come full circle from the days of Father Reynaldo and the Anglo rector who sympathized with his activities.

The other major non-electoral battle that seemed to occupy various Raza Unida and BGL leaders during 1976–77 centered on a controversial proposal to establish a multi-county rural health program through HEW funds. A small group, led by the former Raza Unida mayor of nearby South Town, created a non-profit organization called the South Texas Health Services. In the spring of 1976 they presented a preliminary proposal to the local advisory committees of the Regional Government Agency. This proposal called for a regional rural health agency that would coordinate existing health personnel and facilities and institute three local clinics to provide basic ambulatory, out-patient treatment and preventative medical services. The key idea in this proposal was that the existing private health system does not cover a large number of low-income people that do not qualify for welfare or Medicare benefits. They argued that what is needed was not simply more private physicians but federally-funded local clinics to screen, refer, and educate people. All these services would be provided on a sliding fee scale. These centers were to ultimately have a full staff of a doctor, a nurse, medical technician, and enough medical facilities to treat common medical and dental problems. The program was to be "an entry point for families to other health care institutions by referral and would serve immediate needs."

The first presentation of this proposal was hastily prepared, and it aroused a storm of local protest from existing health professionals and various political and civic leaders through which the proposal had to pass. Critics of the program pointed out a variety of serious weaknesses in the program. First, the qualifications and representativeness of the South Texas Health Services Corporation were questioned. Only two of the members were experienced or connected with local health care professions. The board was not accountable to any local authority such as the county judge, mayor, or city manager. The board also included two people from Aztlán County, which had its own clinic, and North County had only two of sixteen positions. Numerous observers felt that the organization was not representative of the various communities it served. It was unrepresentative in the sense that the program was made up of various Raza Unida leaders in all of these communities.

Second, the lack of coordination between existing health programs was evident in the proposal. Not even the National Health Corps doctor who was listed as a key personnel knew about the proposal. Other private doctors wrote scathing criticisms of the program for the lack of coordination and the possible duplication of services. For a program expressly designed to enhance cooperation, communication, and coordinated local efforts, the initial proposal was a testimony of the opposite. That the Raza leaders had not sought out and contacted various local health officials was also understandable in North Town, since they had been their most bitter political enemies for the past four years. Nevertheless, the concept that these Raza leaders would be able to coordinate a wide variety of local people often in opposition to them seemed overly optimistic to even relatively unaligned local observers.

Third, the proposal was criticized for its excessive cost ratio for administration. The program included an executive director, a medical director, clinic director, accountant and several personnel, a social worker, nurse and physician who were assigned to a region, not a local clinic. The organizational flow chart and the elaborate monthly objectives statements conjured up images of bureaucrats leisurely driving back and forth between the counties while patients waited. Critics

228

argued that the programs would neither provide good coverage and immediate care nor an efficient administration that used a large percentage of the federal dollars on actual care. Generally, critics perceived of this as one more government give-away program ($1,284,276 over three years) that could not ultimately become self-supporting. They contended that more efficient, privately-run clinics, if anything, were needed.

Finally, various local critics also sought to discredit the proposal's statement of the problem. The statistics used in the proposal and the federal definitions of health problems, e.g., "high infant mortality area," "high migrant impact area," "medically under-served region" were all vigorously attacked. Critics argued that the health problems of the North County region were really not that serious and that the report misused census data and greatly exaggerated the problems. They contended that the proposal also underestimated the existing local health care facilities. None of the critics provided any new evidence from systematic surveys or home observation, however, that low income families were, in fact, being adequately served. Neither side actually demonstrated much serious evidence as to the true nature of local health problems and the effectiveness of existing programs. Demographic statistics are only simplistic, indirect measures of the actual health problems. Each side, depending upon whether it was defending or attacking a private, profit-making medical system, chose to use the statistics in a manner that suited their view of social and political reality. Any local community worker can testify to the pattern of underutilization of medical facilities. Most people simply cannot afford to be sick. They have come to expect medical care only in crisis circumstances. This fact seemed lost in the rhetoric over the correctness of the program's supporting statistics.

Having fielded all the initial criticisms, the regional government agency requested a revision of the proposed program. In the spring of 1977 the rural health program was re-submitted through the North County Goals committee and was again rejected. Advocates of the program contend that the committee continued to block the proposal for purely political reasons. They point out that the county goals committee is appointed by the county judge and a committee of representatives of member governments in the county. The goals committee was initially chartered with a majority of members sympathetic to the BGL. Subsequently, a number of Raza Unida supporters went to these meetings and attempted to become voting members through regular attendance. When the controversial health proposal came before the group, the chairman restricted voting members to the original fifteen appointees. They were apparently the only ones officially listed as present on the minutes. After much heated debate, the proposal was rejected for a number of previously stated reasons.

This decision was subsequently overruled at the regional government meeting. They agreed to sponsor the proposal with the conditions that the HEW should closely monitor the grant, give the applicants considerable technical assistance, and require the applicants to demonstrate much closer coordination with local medical personnel and the entire community. They also recommended that the plan to create new clinic facilities in North Town be carefully analyzed in light of the existing North Town Clinic and Hospital location. The final evaluation did, however, accept that there was a serious need and gave a cautious voice of approval to the proposed Rural Health program.

In a subsequent meeting the North County Goals committee approved what they considered a superior medical assistance program, a $70,000 screening and referral clinic sponsored by the Southwest Migrant Association. This clinic was scheduled to be located in the remodeled EODC Center building and would operate five days a week; consequently, if both of these programs are funded, North Town may soon have two new clinics to serve the health care problems of low income families. Raza Unida leaders consider this another major victory over gringo opposition to all programs for Chicanos. BGL leaders skeptically await what they consider more federally-funded Raza Unida political activities disguised as social and public service. It would be inaccurate to dismiss all the criticisms of the health program as purely political and racial. Further, it remains to be seen if the inexperienced Raza Unida leaders can develop an effective, efficient rural health program. It also remains to be seen to what extent BGL leaders will now cooperate to make the programs successful.

Contrasting Mexicano Leaders: The Diplomat and the Militant

Perhaps, however, the most interesting development in the recent politics of North Town has been the careers of two controversial Mexicano political leaders. Each has been extolled and vilified by his people for varying reasons. On one hand there is a local federal government employee, Benito Luna, who became the highly successful BGL Mayor. To some, Mayor Luna is the only hope for a peaceful, biracial community. To others he is a *vendido*, a puppet and mouthpiece of the "real gringo leaders." On the other hand there is a vegetable farmer,

230

Manuel Ramírez, who became the outspoken leader of the unsuccessful Raza Unida party. To some Mr. Ramírez is the only hope for a real change in a racist, gringo society. To others he is a "radical and a communist agitator" bent on destroying the community. These two men, often judged as good or evil by their fellow North Towners, represent two different political and ethnic relations approaches.

Actually, many North Towners who know these men hold more complex views of them than as incarnate good or evil. Most residents of this troubled community would agree that they have been central actors, but there is little consensus that they represent ideal philosophies/approaches or are even important "leaders." Most BGL members would argue that Mayor Luna has been the ideal type of leader, "a true moderate" seeking progressive programs and racial harmony. For some Mexicanos, Mr. Ramírez represents the ideal philosophy and has been a strong leader, but as indicated, many other "moderate" Mexicano *politicos* are searching for a "less radical" political organization and style. These brief vignettes of two key political actors in North Town politics from 1972 to 1977 are not meant to suggest any future political directions. These descriptions should further clarify the complex, sometimes confusing politics of North Town.

Benito Luna: The Diplomat

During this consolidation of BGL control over various local institutions, several new Mexicano leaders have emerged. Of the three new city and three school board members one stands out, the present mayor, Benito Luna. A high school graduate with one year of college, the soft-spoken Luna, in his late thirties, was not active in politics until 1973. His major community activity prior to the Raza Unida threat had been Little League baseball. He reported becoming involved during 1973 after several conflicts with the new Ciudadanos leaders. First, his father-in-law and his family suffered considerable criticism and were called *vendidos*. Second, a businessman in the Ciudadanos denied Mr. Luna and his baseball team a lease to continue playing on their field. Third, Mr. Luna contends that a disgruntled Raza Unida Party member shot a pellet gun through his study window late one evening. This series of events convinced Luna that some "more level-headed Mexicanos" had to get invovled in politics. His friend the local sheriff urged him to run, and he decided that the BGL, despite the presence of "some rednecks," was "the most sensible group." He won a seat on the city council in the hotly contested 1973 election and then became the first elected Mexicano mayor in 1975, polling 920 votes.

He was one of the original, key members in the BGL, and according to other prominent Anglo members, has grown in influence within the organization.

Most recently, some of Mr. Luna's major accomplishments as mayor have been to work with the dynamic new Mexican-American city manager to solve the city's street and drainage problems. Since 1974 the new BGL council has moved swiftly to obtain a variety of federal funds through HUD, the Army Engineers' Corps, and Parks and Recreation programs. The North Town City Council received a $160,000 grant to remodel the old "Mexican School" (EODC Center) in the barrio. This will centralize their child-care program and will rent spaces to the various state and federal social service programs such as social welfare, social security, and food stamps. The city received an additional $250,000 from HUD to pave another large section of streets in the barrio. The earlier controversy over a new park has also been settled, and a $100,000 grant will be used to develop approximately one square block directly behind the old Mexican school. The park will have picnic tables, barbeque facilities, basketball courts, and children's play equipment. It is neither the large park proposed by Raza Unida leaders, nor the mini-park proposed by earlier BGL leaders. Finally, and most important, North Town has a commitment from the Army Engineers' Corps to develop a $4,000,000 underground drainage system in the next three-to-five years. This plan avoids both increased taxation and the controversial open canal system and may solve one of the major problems Mexicano residents have faced since the fifties. Although Mayor Luna has certainly not done this single-handedly, his administration has made some important progress in the past few years.

Another dimension to Benito Luna's political leadership role is the extent that he appears to be a moderate, mediating force within the BGL. The moderates of this organization see him as being the single most influential peacemaker. He, along with several other young Anglo leaders, reportedly have convinced the more conservative, "redneck" elements in the organization to select and recruit more Mexican-American leaders. Since many of the Anglo BGLers are personally unfamiliar with these potential candidates, they rely heavily on information from Luna and other Mexicano BGL members. When Mr. Luna says that this Mexican-American can be trusted politically, he can speak from daily contact with people in the barrio. He prides himself on being able to mix well with ordinary people in the barrio, without airs:

232

I will go out to the ballgame and sit down with everybody, regardless of who they are, and I will be just one of the guys. I have always been just one of the guys, and I always will be. I know what I am, and I don't try to change myself. I am proud, and no one is going to tell me that they are better than I am, and I am not going to say that I am either. That is what hurts some of these guys (Raza Unida *politicos*). That is why I don't like some of them because they don't go around and mingle with these people. I guess you could say the poor people.

Further, Mayor Luna feels that his ability to be a source of information, good judgment, and a decision-making leader is very important to the BGL.

Let me put it this way, if I was to get out of politics right now, or if I was to switch sides, it would be, it would change the whole picture. Not that I am smart or anything, but I do think that I have some common sense, and I think that I have a lot of backing in this town. Just by dropping out and not becoming involved any more would create a lot of suspicion as far as my backers were concerned. (on his decision-making role) . . . I have had more decision-making than people realize. I have always been here to decide who was going to run. They wanted a really good man in there, and they want to know if I would support them, and I have always tried to get somebody to do the job right . . . If it was a Mexicano, or even an Anglo, I would always have a say so in it. Everyone that has run before, I was always the person that told him whether he should run or not.

Some of the following comments will indicate different aspects of his views of ethnic relations and local politics:

Myself, I wasn't fighting for one side or the other. I told them, I can get a lot of things done, and I am going to do it. But I am going to do it my way. I am going to try to negotiate. As long as I keep doing what I have been able to do, I think I can stay there as long as I want to because I am not trying to put the shaft on anybody. I am trying to better the town as a whole. I don't want one side to be on top. I really want to try and make this town a better place to live in and provide more jobs for people . . . I just think it's a big problem that has to be worked out by both sides working together, and I would much rather sit down and talk to my enemy than to fight him, right? Let's sit down and try to work something out, no use taking punches at each other and not accomplishing anything . . . Well, I can't go all the way to the other side of town and punch out a guy just because his daddy beat up my daddy, for no reason at all. You have to look ahead. You can't live in the past. If you ever intend on progressing or bettering yourself, you have to look ahead. You can't keep looking back over your shoulder. And that's what these people are doing. They are fighting a fight that is long gone . . . By the middle sixties things were changing quite a bit. Mexicanos were getting better educated and doing a lot of their own thinking. They had the opportunity to progress whether they wanted to or not, depending on them . . . Lately, there are so many ways. You can go get all kinds of help to educate yourself, get a college degree or whatever you want . . . Yes, you have your majority, and I guess you have to do with the majority of the business people and the large land owners, ranchers, or farmers, whether they are Anglos or Mexicanos. They can do their job, and there are not many Mexicanos that can provide that for the people . . . There are people that are discriminated against, not because of their coloring but because of their character. I mean, if you go into a place and act like you own the damn thing and do what you want to, and that place belongs to somebody and it cost them money to build, you can't just go in and destroy things and do as you damn well please in a place that doesn't belong to you. If the people that own it throw you out, that doesn't mean that they are discriminating against you . . .

Manuel Ramírez: The Militant

During the rapid decline of the North Town Raza Unida, Manuel Ramírez has emerged into a controversial, enigmatic figure. Until politics "got hot" in North Town, Mr. Ramírez, a high school graduate in his early thirties, was a small melon farmer. He had served in the army and was active in various civic activities such as chairman of the *Diez y Seis* celebration and vice president of a community health organization. In 1973 he was instrumental in changing the Ciudadanos organization into a chapter of the Raza Unida Party. His political activities intensified and took on new directions, however, after he was "sold out" by the moderates in 1974 and after he was severely beaten up in a local bar by two Alcoholics Beverage Commission Agents in 1975. In retrospect, such events convinced Ramírez that this would be a long, hard, sometimes lonely struggle. Increasingly, he has become more active, and ironically, the more politically active he has become, the less he has been able to build a following of voters and win elections.

A full description of Ramírez's political activities from 1974 on would require more than a brief vignette, but generally he began to use legal and media resources external to the community in his political struggles. He filed numerous complaints in federal and state courts concerning the structure and process of local elections such as apportionments of voting districts, voter registration, and bilingual ballots. Such election procedures were covered in the 1965 Voting Rights Act.

Further, he testified before various Congressional subcommittees for the need to extend the Voting Rights Act to cover Texas and the Mexican American minority. He also testified in the Texas House of Representatives on similar problems of election procedure and general racial discrimination in Texas.

These testimonies were extremely strong accusations that North Town Anglos had willfully and maliciously manipulated Mexicano voters through the following devices: annexing Anglo city voters and excluding Mexicano voters; gerrymandering county voting precincts; changing voting hours and restricting polling places; intimidating voters economically, i.e., Anglos threatening employees with loss of jobs; intimidating voters through "swaggering sheriffs with billy clubs;" challenging election results whereby the signed ballot stub becomes public and voters traced and intimidated. Needless to say, some North Town Anglos and Mexicanos found these testimonies exaggerated and outrageous. Mr. Ramírez felt, however, that he had to publicize these concerns and involve federal observers and extend federal voting laws to North Town. He had little faith that local Anglos would ever reform electoral procedures that benefited them. Chapters five and six described these events in terms that are perhaps not entirely acceptable to either side.

Mr. Ramírez is not the only local leader who shared these views or sought these reforms. He also did not single-handedly bring about the extension of the Voting Rights Act to Texas, or the subsequent Justice Department plan on the redistricting of North County voting precincts. Many other citizens throughout the state and country also testified before these congressional committees, and the Mexican American Legal Defense and Education Fund (MALDEF) lawyers actually directed the complicated battles on redistricting the North County voting precincts. This involved the Department of Justice delaying the 1976 elections, a series of appeals, and finally a 1977 Supreme Court decision upholding the Justice Department plan. Mr. Ramírez's role in all this was to get MALDEF involved, to assist the investigators, and to continually follow the progress of the long legal battles. He was an important local contact that facilitated their work. How influential his congressional testimonies actually were is difficult to say. He did, however, as a number of his followers point out, "stand up and fight for these things when everybody else had given up and was sitting on their butts bitching about 'damn radicals' and losing the election." Undoubtedly, his persistence in raising and publicizing these issues and in obtaining the legal aid for court battles has brought about a number of changes.

Mr. Ramírez himself would emphasize that seeking reforms in local election procedures, although a major activity, was not his only preoccupation. He was also instrumental in helping some people, e.g., a school employee and a county constable, get cases of job dismissals and salary inequities investigated. Further, he was active in the long series of proposals, program revisions, testimonies, and meetings leading to the regional government agencies' approval of the South Texas Rural Health program. Likewise, Ramírez was central in the previously described attempts to have the new priests transferred and has been an outspoken member of the politically-active EODC program.

More recently, Ramírez seems to have broadened his criticisms of local programs to even those run by former Ciudadanos/Raza leaders. He recently initiated an outside investigation of how Mr. Rápido ran his Migrant Aid program, and he personally investigated how Mrs. Tolivar ran her EODC-Sponsored Credit Union program. He contends that these programs were not properly or fully serving the people and says, "I don't give a damn who is running these programs. If a Mexicano isn't doing his job, I'm going to get on his case just as much as I get on the Gringo's case." According to Mr. Ramírez, these investigations, which the program administrators see as groundless charges and harrassment, have "made these people get on the ball more."

Further, a number of people come to Ramírez seeking advice and assistance on various matters concerning the school, the welfare office, health problems, jobs, and even personal matters. He lives a somewhat hermit-like existence in his trailer-house which is equipped with a Xerox machine and his files. To an extent, he has become an all-purpose community social worker and mini-*patron*. Recently he received a $25,000 grant from an eastern foundation to further institutionalize his role. His brothers presently do virtually all the farm work, and he now devotes his full energies to this wide range of nonelectoral activities. The community service agency that he is attempting to initiate is generally dedicated to serving as an intermediary or spokesman for local people. In some sense he sees all local programs and agencies, irrespective of who runs them, as being unresponsive to poor people; consequently, a community service organization "should be the conscience of the community"; it "should squeeze more service out of the lazy, corrupt bureaucrats."

Many local people would see this new service agency and his activities in general as "crazy" and "self-serving." Some would say he is merely trying to "get more votes," or "cause trouble," or "get-back at his political enemies." Many people question the sincerity of his motives. They also dislike his abrasive confrontation style and his tendency towards rhetoric and exaggeration. As Mr. Ramírez says:

Since I have become active in politics, I have been called *puto* (sexually promiscuous), *joto* (homosexual) and *aratero* (a thief). They have hurt me deeply; they have got to the stage where they beat me unconscious for two days. The people advised me to stop, but I understand from the scriptures that somebody has to be a martyr. I'm single. I have nobody to cry for me, nothing to leave behind. They will just bury me. I'd rather fight for equality. I believe, like Emiliano Zapata, that the land belongs to those who work it. But here in Texas the Chicanos work the lands, but they are administered by the Anglos. I'd rather fight injustices than to say I didn't in this world because they got away with it. In the Bible it says Christ freed men. He broke chains of slavery. Christ said, "I am the light, follow it." I'm trying to do that, but the rich and the educated still take advantage and abuse us. In today's democratic government we must take advantage . . . I wanna be better than them (the *politicos*), people have to learn to respect me for that, I won't give in, they have to. It's dangerous to say that if you want to be a politician, but if I really want to be the solution to my problem, our problem, I have to be an example. I knew when they beat the shit out of me and I almost died, I knew that I lived to do something more . . . We must realize that the Raza Unida is in its infant stage, it still can't walk, the Chicanos of North County. The politicians are Democrats, and they have been for a long time; they aren't sure. Once economic reprisals start they want to play it on the safe side. They wanna be with winners. Earlier leaders made a lot of noise but not much follow through. Mexicanos aren't politicized for a party. They don't know what it stands for, what is Chairman, conventions, precincts, the role of leaders; they don't feel that personal esteem for this; they are undecided. Things had not crystallized. They think they are ready, but they don't know the laws and the power of the opposition, how hard the struggle will be . . . I have tasted the bitterness of Anglo society. They thought I was wrong. They said we can win as Democrats, and I said that you'll find out. They said that Raza Unida was bad and that being Democrats would keep the Anglos from overreacting. But you see what has happened in Dobieville? To whites the color is the difference. Race is the key. I told these people. Now they are being called communists, too. Now they are being dragged into court. People are being threatened if they vote. They will lose their jobs. It is the same thing, and these wishy-washy Democrats could not understand. They said *"ya ganamos"* (now we will win) just like we did, but the people did not show up. Mexicanos can stand up for their rights, but losing your job is different. It will take time, my friend, but that is one thing that Chicanos have got, *time*. We got no money but we damn sure got plenty of time.

How prominent will either of these current political figures be in future North Town politics? Or for that matter, will any of the existing political groups be prominent in the future? This is unclear because the key to electoral politics in North Town, the "neutral" Mexicano voter, remains somewhat of a mystery to both sides. The BGL leaders contend that their sensible, bi-racial approach to community leadership and community relations has had a calming effect on the community. They point to their successful Mexicano mayor and the school board president as proof of this. They claim that these "level-headed, competent Mexicanos" have won a considerable following among Mexicano voters who became disgusted with the racial hatred generated by Raza Unida. Conversely, the Raza Unida leaders claim to have awakened the conscience of the Mexicano people. Since, however, voter turn-outs are fifty percent lower than during the peak years of 1973–1974, it seems equally plausible that the "typical" Mexicano voter may be more confused, indifferent, frightened, preoccupied or disgusted with politics than convinced by any particular group. From numerous comments one hears, most voters believe that *all politicos* are up to no good, and that being active in politics increases, not solves, one's personal problems.

A SUMMING UP: ETHNIC RELATIONS IN NORTH TOWN, 1977

In spite of all the political confrontations described, it would be an exaggeration to characterize the daily life of North Town as rife with open conflict and hostility. Although there was much organized competition between Anglos and Mexicanos for control of local government and schooling agencies, local life was generally peaceful. There were no open fights or extreme forms of aggression and violence. Sentiment ran high among both Anglos and Mexicanos, but most people were able to control their feelings and avoid open confrontations. A great deal of people's aggression towards each other seemed to be channeled into private "bitch" sessions. We had occasion to participate in numerous private discussions over coffee or beer in public places and private residences. The conversation would invariably drift to heated discussion of the latest atrocity committed by the opposing group.

People also worked out their aggressions towards each other by isolating themselves from the other group. Anglos stopped going to the Mexican celebrations of *Diez y Seis* and *Cinco de Mayo*. Only the bravest Anglo would also venture into the Mexican *cantinas*, and each group had their own restaurants, bars, and public meeting places. A high degree of social segregation has always existed in North Town, but the recent conflict has clearly driven Mexicanos and Anglos apart. The North Towners with mixed marriages complained that they had become virtually isolated and had lost friends on both sides. Ultimately, they had to limit relations and become publicly identified with one group socially and politically. Generally, however, such couples and people on both sides who sought to be "in the middle" were forced to avoid all social relationships. Perhaps the majority of people in town sought to maintain polite public relations with any and all people from the opposite ethnic group.

Such patterns of public avoidance of conflict were very evident in the sometimes elaborate efforts of local businessmen, educators, civic leaders and churchmen to "be friendly." It is, of course, traditional in most small American towns to be "neighborly" and "friendly" in public, but many Mexicanos noted that Anglos had clearly changed their public behavior. Some Raza Unida leaders interpreted this as "phony," as crude attempts to influence gullible Mexicanos into voting for them. Other Mexicanos felt that Anglos were sincerely trying to change, and their evidence of this was the better treatment of all Mexicanos in public places. Yet, others reported a continuing pattern of preferential treatment of Anglos in the waiting rooms of doctors' offices and in grocery store lines. Anglos were still served first. Poor Mexicans were still publicly embarrassed for using food stamps or for cashing welfare checks. Prominent Mexicans still felt socially excluded from Anglo "high society."

As indicated in the earlier discussion of changing economic and political conditions during the 1940 to 1960 era, North Town had already undergone some very profound changes in local relations between Anglos and Mexicanos. For the old-timers in the community the modern-day Mexicanos had come a long way. Both old Anglos and Mexicanos marveled at the way Mexicanos as a group had risen from peonage to higher levels of education and prosperity. Earlier forms of brutality, open killings, deportation, and physical whippings were largely a thing of the past. Many older Mexicanos, however, still cautioned their youth to be constantly vigilant of Anglos, lest they return to their old ways. There was considerable agreement among local Mexicanos which Anglos were "rednecks" who hated them, and which Anglos were trying to be fairer and more friendly.

Among the Mexicanos one could also find a good deal of bitterness and hatred for all Anglos. The vivid testimonials reported in earlier chapters represented what many North Town Mexicanos still carry in their hearts and minds. There are, of course, many other Mexican-Americans who have made peace with the past and present forms of discrimination, and who seek to live without hating Anglos. Some are indeed examples of what the Raza Unida called "colonized Mexicans"; they were still overly fearful and deferential to Anglos as *patrones* and superior people. They still believed more in whiteness than in their own brownness. Other "quiet Mexicanos" or "neutrals" were simply people who wanted to live peacefully without fear and strife. They wanted to stay out of politics and raise their family in the quiet of their home. To them much of this political struggle and the labeling of people as gringos, *vendidos*, and Chicanos was a form of madness. They believed more in the simple pleasures of life and were perhaps indifferent to the ideal of "standing up for their *raza*." Despite all these differences, however, it is safe to say that the post-war changes have brought to North Town Mexicanos a new posture and perspective. North Town Mexicanos, whether militantly Chicano, colonized, or indifferent will never be the same. The west side of town, and particularly the youth, generally share a new sensibility and ethnic pride that will prompt them to fight for their individual rights. Anglo racism will be met with "Chicano pride," and increasingly Chicanos will demand full economic, political, and racial equality.

Local Anglos were extremely sensitive to any and all charges that they might be "racists" or discriminating against Mexicanos. Some were bitter about the way outsiders from government agencies and newspapers came and stereotyped them. We are included in this category, and some local Anglos refused to talk with us for fear of being misquoted and misunderstood. Other Anglo leaders were convinced that we had already written our conclusions, which included picturing them as hateful racists and the local Chicanos as the heroic, downtrodden masses. The local Anglo leaders felt completely misunderstood and in a sense "sold out" by their country. One prominent local farmer put it quite succinctly:

> Our family came here and made something out of this land and here I am, the fourth generation, and I'm still here fighting it out to make a living. I feel like a dying breed, I really do. It seems like the whole thing is going wrong. People up in Washington don't understand, neither do the politicians in Texas. Nobody seems to care if these *La Raza* types come in here and destroy everything a lot of good folks have worked pretty hard to build up. I can't figure it out anymore. I thought I was being a good American, and now we got all these damn bureaucrats from everywhere comin' in here and telling us to give the Mexicans this and that. They act as if we are killing them in the streets or something. I tell you this, there are good Mexicans and bad ones. It makes me sick to see so many on those food stamps and welfare, but I know some of them are fine people. I don't give a damn about politics, and I am sick as hell of being called a gringo when I don't even know what I have done.

There is in this testimonial, and in others collected, a great paradox for most Anglos. To them they have been model citizens doing what they were brought up to do. They saw themselves as hard working, honest, fair-minded people who make America the great country that it is. They hold many of the traditional values of rugged individualism that, to them, epitomize American society. But things have changed, and they sense being out-of-step with the times. They feel that their life-long attempts to live up to the ideals of American society are now misunderstood by many other Anglos who they label "outsiders," "liberals," "bureaucrats," and "bleeding hearts."

Yet, the old rationales as being the chosen people, those destined to lead and develop this land, were hardly believable. Anglos had come to see Mexicanos run successful businesses, make important school and city council decisions, be on the honor roll in school, and generally achieve all the forms of success that only a supposedly superior people could obtain. Clearly, at least some Mexicanos were as talented or more talented, hard working, and successful than Anglos, and it has become increasingly hard to use the arguments of Anglo genetic or cultural superiority. Many Anglos privately admitted that much mistreatment and inequality had marked Anglo-Mexicano relations. For some this sense of guilt was difficult to live with.

A few of the more liberal Anglos in the leadership group and a few teachers were increasingly more accepting of the Mexicano people in general, but little direct socializing or genuine exchanges and friendship seemed to exist. Anglos did not shop and socialize in the Mexicano side of town, and they generally knew very little about the personal lives of the Mexicano. The stereotypes of the lazy, drunken, dirty, sexually promiscuous, mentally slow Mexican were still common. A distinction was made between the "better class" Mexican and the average Mexican, but many Anglos expressed resentment for the Mexicano. Many saw the average Mexicano as on welfare and as "sponging off of their taxes" and using various "tricks" to get free money. They feared that the large number of Mexicanos in the schools was bringing down the quality of education for their children which affected their own chances of competing in the larger world.

In short, the Mexicanos were often blamed for the high levels of unemployment and the stagnated economy. The new group of Anglo leaders have inherited the third and fourth generations of the original sharecropper and cheap migrant labor. At one point in history they needed these people. Today, however, the Anglos do not have the wherewithal to create a new economy that will employ and absorb this fast-growing Mexicano labor force. Most Anglos subscribe to a theory that somehow the present "problem" they have inherited is the

241

fault of the local Mexicano. Many would prefer to assign the blame to the character and cultural inferiority of the Mexicanos. Anglos feel that economic opportunities are there, if the local Mexicanos would discipline themselves and work as the Anglos have. Those Mexicanos that remain poor and ignorant are simply reflections of their inherent inferiority or present character. Many Anglos still have a rather ingenuous, narrow view of the Mexicano people, a view that overlooks the historical roots of the present situation.

Yet, no outsider could live in North Town without being struck by the numerous attempts to redefine everyday ethnic relations. Particularly the youth of North Town were struggling to redefine how to relate to each other. There were a dozen cases of secret Anglo-Mexican dating. One clique of interracial students studied the Bible together, while another group smoked marijuana and got drunk together. Many students expressed disgust with the quarrels of their parents, with "all this stupid politics." They could not "wait to get out of this town." Many others spoke and acted exactly like their warring parents about "Meskins" and "gavachos." The Anglo youth generally feared and hated *La Raza*, and the more politically-oriented Mexicano youth hated the BGL. Socially, Anglos went their way and Mexicanos went theirs. But in general the youth of North Town were forced to cooperate and "get along."

In some of the youth there was a good deal more doubt and uncertainty about the negative views they held of each other. As in the case of adults, each group could identify who were the "rednecks" and "brownnecks" and who were the "live-and-let-live ones." Although organized attempts by the Methodist minister failed to bring church youth groups together, and sports and band activities did not magically wipe out racial feelings, there were changes. Under the circumstances, each group avoided conflict remarkably well. To a degree, it could be said that there was a growing amount of mutual respect. One particular irony that many people noted was the marriage of the son of a prominent BGL leader and the daughter of a prominent Ciudadanos leader. To some, this seemed to be some kind of poetic statement about youth to the adults. To others, this, like the previous six years of conflict, could only raise perplexing questions. North Towners were asking, "Has anything really changed? What will happen in the near political future of North Town?"

Community Responses to FROM PEONES TO POLITICOS

Part of the community's answer to these perplexing questions can be seen in their reflections over an earlier draft of this book, which was reviewed by twenty-five people. The majority of the reviewers were key leaders from all the various political groups and factions. A few of the reviewers were less politically involved residents. Approximately half of sixty hours of interviewing was taped, and a sample of these respondents and their views will be presented. These views should give the non-North Town reader some sense of how North Towners felt about the study. This should give a reader unfamiliar with South Texas and with community studies methodology another basis for evaluating the study. In a very real sense these interviews were a dialogue between the researchers and North Town residents. Many times local readers challenged our facts and interpretations. Many times I challenged their interpretations of their own community. This procedure elicited much new data and improved the original manuscript. It also provoked considerable feeling and reflection which add a new dimension to the original manuscript. It is important for the reader to study carefully this marvelous, honest, and complex text of North Towners' views.

A Long Time Resident, Professional and Rancher:

Here's my thinking on this type of study. When you go to a person and ask him to complain, you're going to get far more negative, 90%, than affirmative. Sure there were some injustices; had it been the other way it would have been the same thing; had the other people, the Anglos, been here first and the poor people, it would have been the same thing. Now this you may not like because I know you worked hard on this, spent a couple years at it, but what *good* is gonna come of this long study that you made? . . . Well I'm still up in the air. Have you revealed something that wasn't already known, or is it important that it be brought out? Will it help the Mexican people? Will it bring people closer together? . . . Since I have read it I'm thinking a little deeper, course I'm not saying this because I have a world of friends that are Mexican people. My daddy had too . . . This kind of makes you think of *Roots* a little bit. Now how much good all that does is it make Negroes hate whites. They say, "I just wanna get out and cut white throats when I see that." I'm not sure, maybe the Mexicans here will feel the same way . . . I thought it was pretty good. I was impressed with all the work that had gone into it. It was interesting to read . . . Sometimes I wish I could get about ten miles up above this community until the east side and the west side got so small that you could barely see them. I'd like to be able to understand all this trouble we're having. Sometimes I'd like to write a book . . . It would have to be an outsider. Nobody here could do what you did. We are all too close to it to figure it all out . . . I learned quite a bit from it, but I think that in book form that if it hits this community, the Anglos wouldn't like it at all . . . It would have been much worse if you'd have used the names. You'd get run out of the state. This is bad enough . . . I don't think it would be good for them (students). It would cause all kind of confrontations. The amazing thing to me, and you pointed it out, that on these elections that some people haven't been shot or there wasn't more violence . . . Like I said, it is written for the benefit of the Latins rather than us; its not quite objective enough. But to be a 100% fair, it would have to be so objective that it probably wouldn't be interesting, ain't that right, Doc? Of course I noticed you went into things each time, and sometimes you came back and made some good points too about all Anglos not being bad . . . Maybe you could put a better summary which would try to not lay the blame on either side. You see, that's the way it was. You couldn't blame either. You did, of course, get into the work ethic which was the spirit that the early pioneers were. You worked from sun up to sunset, and that's the way that you saved your pennies and got rich. You didn't pay anybody anymore than you had to who worked for you, and you kept those under your thumb. Well that *was*, but that was success, that was the way it was. You couldn't blame anybody for wanting to make money, and as you illustrated in here too, very well, the Latin gang boss, the *troquero*, there was nobody any harder on his underlings than those people, a lot harder than Anglos over the Latins. But a summary trying to show that it was just kind of the way things were, it would kind of soften it in both directions . . . You might have given the patrons a little more credit. Most of them were good to their workers. There weren't too many real mean ones. Of course they expected you to work long hours. If you pay 'em too much money they would get spoiled and leave. If you didn't pay them enough they'd leave. You had to reach a happy medium.

A *Businessperson and Farmer*:

Well, I told you that when I went over this *rancho* era that I felt like that it was slanted. Just because of nothing else, the quotes you give from old timers, Anglos and Mexicanos . . . From these quotes the Anglos come out with an image pretty consistently of being arrogant, self-assured, loud, insensitive, and uneducated, but because they choose to be. This is what I am assuming because of the grammar you quote, the kind of person who takes advantage of others, male or female, young or old if it pleases them, and they don't work very hard, and there is no mention that they suffer any very real hardships, and they have only a kind of vague sense of loyalty to family, friends, employees, church, and community. You know, they don't serve on community things, just get the dummies to do it and act for them. And then all of the quotes from old timer Mexicanos seem to reflect an image of a humble, quiet, uneducated, but not

244

by choice, loving, docile, clean people that take advantage of no one, work together harmoniously from sun up to sunset, suffer extreme hardships, and have an intense loyalty to their family and God with their home worship . . . Your assumptions or deductions, as you pass through these eras to the contemporary time become more slanted. Possibly an explanation for this, as I told you, is after it was apparent that you and Mr. Post had changed the purpose of your study, its format, we assumed that you had intentionally been deceitful about what you were going to do all the time, we quit talking to you . . . I suspect, too, that you were also cut off from certain elements of the Mexicano population, because the further you go through this analysis the more the ideas that are quoted here begin to zero in and circle down to a fairly small group of *politicos*. It does a very good job of expressing their feelings. It almost reads at the end like a personal diary of Esposito and Rápido and a few others thrown in on the side that were active politically . . . One thing you left out in the *rancho* era was, if there was one Anglo family and five Mexicano families, the six families melted in a family type unit. The five Mexicano families may have related in a more intimate and closer way, I am sure they did. Nevertheless, it was really one family unit . . . I could not recall ever hearing from my grandparents or my great-grandparents ever any statement that was prejudiced or hateful or hostile toward the Mexicano as a race. They may have singled out one they felt hostile toward, like you would single out Anglos . . . The remarks that come to mind was a positive type of remark like, "I don't know what I would have done without Maria when the last two babies were born." . . . That they felt locked in, I don't doubt. But the fact of the matter was that they were only locked in insofar as they were limited themselves to do something else. I mean it wasn't like the slavery system. The *patron* didn't own them, and they could leave, except that I can recognize their plight too. Where were they going to go? By the same token, too, where was the *patron* going to go? He was locked in, too. . . We don't talk about what happened to those anglos *patrones* that lost everything, their homes and everything in the depression, or the *patrones* that before mechanization and irrigation could compete with dry land farming and hand labor. He didn't have enough land or enough capital to irrigate and buy this equipment so he was displaced . . . The whole story of what happened to the small Anglo farmer is simply not there . . . Also, I think that the description of the Mexicano family is very good, but it was not brought out that both Anglos and Mexicanos have an intense loyalty to the family structure but that the structure is different . . . You have plenty of good examples in here where the Mexicano is free to be who they are . . . One mother told her daughter that it was alright if she didn't want to go to school . . . This is a basic difference because it wasn't okay if I didn't want to go to school, I'll tell you for sure . . . I think a basic difference of the two races is that the Mexicanos tend to accept themselves individually, whatever they are, for what they are (their weaknesses and bad habits), and I

245

think generally Anglos are not that well acquainted with themselves. They have more of tendency to become something they are not. That's this inner drive or motivation to achieve, to what did you say, discipline themselves and work to do things that maybe they really don't want to do . . . In that era Anglos on the *rancho* didn't care how progressive the county judge or the sheriff was. They were somebody who lived in town. How they managed really didn't make that much difference, as long as "you don't step on my toes." Now if they had started abusing or mistreating Anglos the way they apparently did Mexicans, that would have been a different story, and they would have been hung quick . . . I would dare say they (Mexicans) could have done as much the Anglos. They had a vote. I would bet you that the voter turn out wasn't even ten percent . . . Politics at the local level just wasn't that important . . . Anglos could turn around and say that they ought to control guys like Ramsey Muñiz that are running for the highest office in the state and selling marijuana at the same time. Why didn't they get rid of him? They knew he was a crook and a dope peddler. . . . The description of the farming and ranching was pretty accurate, but it leaves out one significant factor, the reason why Mexicanos became more active during the late 1950's and early 1960's. The new leaders of this period knew each other before. They had already lived together during the *rancho* era and grown up in this close-knit family situation. The Anglo leaders had gone to school with them, played with them, and worked in the fields with them . . . I am not saying that overall they respected and loved the Mexicano man that they grew up with on the ranch. But there were some areas where they recognized their good qualities . . . I don't think it was a speed-up, hurry-up effort of "let's involve the Mexicano because he's getting restless" . . . You would expect that they would appoint these men that they knew personally to these positions because they knew their capabilities . . . They did this for personal reasons, not just political or racial ones . . . I think you overplayed the significance of the LULAC or the GI Forum, and especially these lawyers from San Antonio and other places that came down. I think the significant thing is these returning veterans and the changing image they had of themselves when they returned. They no longer saw themselves as hyphenated Americans or some lower kind of semi-quasi-American. They came home from that war, and they were Americans. *That* is significant. Along with this change in self-image was this concomitant change in aspirations and goals. It almost Anglicized them. Then after this change in image, they were a lot more motivated to achieve and had Anglo-type aspirations for their children and community and the world they lived in. . . . I think emphasis on the depresssion, and the sharing that went on at the *Rancho* between the two races, and WW II and the sharing and the pain of that experience is highly significant because these are two bad experiences that had a tendency to unite people. Here in the end, this end thing, has anything really changed? Is the town really better for all this? I think that the answer is an emphatic *NO*. Lots of things have changed. Many material or surface things have changed, but the quality of life between the two races has not changed for the good . . . After all this political stuff for two or three years, the question I would ask, "Is the mere avoidance of conflict all that's resulted?" This is where we were when it all started, Dr. Foley. When it all started there was more mutual respect and less suspicion among those who wanted to see some change than after it was over with . . . When this thing blew up, old and bitter and buried prejudices and hatreds surfaced again . . . I will not be a bit surprised to see more extreme prejudicial feelings come out of our children . . . It wasn't for nothing; there has got to be some bigger issues than local politics. And that contested election was a bigger issue. That is where you have many factual errors in your report . . . What is scarey about that is that it takes away a free election . . . That incited people because it was a bigger threat . . .

A BGL Political leader and wife:

When you came here people were afraid to be interviewed because they were apprehensive about the Aztlán City experience. Some people said that you were funded by the Ford Foundation to do a hatchet job, that you came to write something derogatory to make interesting reading. If we would have known your intentions, you would have gotten more information from us. I don't think you were, I don't question your integrity. But some of your sources were not reliable, but I don't feel that you deliberately did it. You tried to be objective . . . No I don't think it was nearly as bad as some of the newspaper reporting I've read . . .. Well the first part, the historical part, I didn't have much quarrel with, except that it was, it seemed like it was written by a Mexicano and that nothing was done wrong on the part of the Mexicans, and that nearly all of the gringos were reprobates and trying to take advantage. And granted there were a lot. Some gringos were that way, but everybody was having a hard time. They depended on each other a lot more than is reflected in this part . . . We had sharecropper farmers on the ranch who farmed on halves, and it would come time that the trucks were heading west to migrate and if there was still work to be done, a possible second crop or something, there is no way they would stay. And they always came back broke without any money, and we had to carry them on until the next crop. It was more like a vacation for them it seems. None of that is shown. Kind of like the Mexican Waltons, everything is beautiful, and everybody is doing his part . . . They didn't feel any responsibility when there was work to be done if there was an opportunity to jump on the truck . . . They came back broke, because their own people, who were the truckers, gouged them . . . I also felt that by far the best teachers were in the westside schools . . . I thought that was a very accurate account of Miss Larson and her show, but the Parent-Teachers' Club didn't dissolve because of her (i.e. her racist statements) but because, in my opinion, their president would get up and endlessly describe nothing and then insist that it all be translated in Spanish . . . After two meetings most people just quit coming . . . As for throwing out these political machines, well, people didn't have the leisure time, they didn't have the communications and what have you to stay on top of what was going on . . . The thing that really got me the most of all about the whole thing, and I really don't understand it, because in my mind it is probably the *most* significant thing that happened in North Town, and it wasn't mentioned. I don't understand why our Mexicano mayor is not even *mentioned*. He doesn't even have a pseudonym! The fact that he polled more votes than anybody ever had in North Town, the fact that he is the first Mexican-American mayor is not mentioned . . . I think that he stuck to his middle ground, and I think some of us climbed on his middle ground. I think that the whole thing is focused around his acts. I don't see us pulling it off without his Christian attitude, ignoring insults, still level-headed, still trying to make a better community. Anglos are not really afraid of Mexicano representation, if they could run it without running us out like in Aztlán City . . . The whole tone of the entire thing seems to be the stress on the Anglos being so afraid that they are going wild to buck this Raza Unida. This is what I didn't like about it. I don't see things in the last eight years like that book portrays them. I see things as really good, and this whole thing sees things as really bad . . . I don't think there are very many who are afraid of the racial thing. I don't think it was the thing at all. I think it was the political thing they were afraid of . . . This book doesn't portray the vengeful quality of Raza Unida, the ugliness of the way they acted when they took over the city . . .

A Long-Time Resident/Businessperson:

It's pretty good. It's their side of it. It's an economic situation like you point out. If we had enough good jobs around here there probably wouldn't be much politics. Things kind of went down-hill over the years, I guess . . . I thought it was pretty much like I figured, being an outsider, you were for the down trodden. They should eat it up on the other side . . . I learned quite a bit about the town from it that I didn't exactly know. For example, I never realized that the Anglo councilman in the fifties had a deal with those Mexican councilmen. I knew they were close and it figures that they did, but I had no idea at the time. And your portrayals of the sheriff and the county judge and the courthouse bunch were real accurate. That is the way it was, and that is the way people really look at that bunch at the courthouse . . . My only criticism is that you checked mostly with them. They didn't live well, and they were taken advantage of, that is for sure, but it is slanted some. I guess there is not much to write about us. They would stay here if they could do better, but they left the farmers and ranchers to get ahead . . . The old-timers here will resent it . . . You know, the thing that I will never understand is why the *La Raza*, especially the young smart ones, like their lawyer and some of the other ones, blew their big chance. They got in there in the city and acted terrible to everyone. Then they lost all that money and messed with the election. It was their chance to show everybody that they could do it, but it fell apart on them. Their own people got disgusted with how they were running things. I think you do a pretty good job of pointing out all this, but you don't bring out enough of our side of it . . . No, I don't think it is over. It is pretty quiet now, but they will probably try again. You are right, they were put down in the past. There is a lot of hate in some of them. It's true, there is no use denying it, but we can't live in the past either if we are ever going to have a community again.

Local Official and Farmer:

I didn't experience the hate for the Anglo. If this was true, they certainly disguised their feelings. We had good relationships with all the people that I knew and grew up with. We're still good friends . . . Maybe where I was raised was a different set up . . . It kind of glorifies the Mexican-American, but that is all right. I think Mexican-Americans have made a big contribution, helped build the country. I don't really know what the abuses were, and no doubt there were abuses. You get racists on one side and the other, and I think the majority of people are more moderate, are kind of in the middle, the mainstream, and they don't really have that much hate. I find some radicals on both sides, and you can't talk to either side; so I think maybe the negative was over exaggerated. I didn't see the extremes of it. There are good and bad Mexicans and Anglos, and probably the same proportion. If we can't work together, well we just have to if we are going to get anything done . . .

A Young Professional and New Resident:

I was familiar with the political aspect, the things that occurred within the last few years. It was made more interesting to me by the historical background . . . The story of the migrants and the effect that it had as far as gaining independence, a feeling of independence, was interesting. Also I never stopped to think that there wasn't always a barrio here in town. I never thought back before that when people were living out on ranches and there wasn't as much communication and common bond. When they moved into town that probably *did* have a dramatic effect on the life style . . . I wasn't aware of the raw discrimination. I thought it would probably be a little bit more sophisticated than that, but apparently it wasn't. What is hard to understand is why these people didn't react more than they did, but I guess there's a lot of other factors . . . I guess somebody has been a super salesman. They made a certain part

249

of the Mexican-American population believe that any kind of dissent is un-American or unpatriotic. I don't know how to say it, but they have actually brainwashed that part of the population to actually believe it and go along; and if they open their mouths or try to rock the boat at all, it is un-American. That I don't understand . . . I don't think it (the book) would cause trouble, I really don't think so. I don't think that any time that you increase the communication and understanding of people about each other that it is bad. But I think that those who are really firm in their beliefs, it's not going to do much of anything. They will figure out a way to rationalize their actions and make it be the way they want it to be, unless they are fairly broad-minded . . . The more I stay here the more I realize it's just going to be grinding the stone down . . . My first reaction was that this (the book) is good, this will expose this situation to the outside world. I got the feeling here that this was isolated from the rest of the United States, and we had the federal government and everything else but there was no hope. We were just at the mercy of the so-called local establishment, but I think that I have become more pessimistic and less hopeful that the book would cause a fairy book ending where the feds would eventually come in and straighten this thing out . . . There is a sort of balanced and cautious tone to the book. Based on my emotional feeling, I wish that it was told in a more emotional way. It would be more interesting if it were more subjective. I think that if somebody was to read it from here, there would probably be more nerves stepped on that way . . . But I think that the way that you presented it is stated in an unsensational way, and it would tend to put the reader more at ease and be prepared to believe some of the things that you have put down on paper. If you go with some of the more sensational things that have actually occurred recently, then the reader may tend to think that the author is putting too much subjective material in . . .

A Community Worker/Professional:

I think that the book is very much slanted. I feel that it spends a great deal of time portraying the rise of the Raza Unida Party. I think that there are two sides to every story, and I don't know if both sides, I have heard from the Anglo side and I have heard from this side, and I feel, personally, that this book is just for one particular purpose, and that is the glorification of the Raza Unida Party . . . And now they have no power whatsoever. There is only a small group of them, a couple of families I think . . . The only time that we have had any problems, difficulties, was when the Raza Unida came to town . . . I thoroughly enjoyed what you say about the life as it's described on the ranches. I thought that was well done. I don't know how well versed you are with the situation, when you talk, for example, about culture. I want to know what that is. I have worked among the Mexicans for thirty-seven years, and I want to know what it is because these people have neither the culture of the country nor the culture of the other country. They are people, as far as I am concerned, devoid of any culture. It is not really their fault. They come from the northern part of Mexico which is very sparsely populated . . . But that portrait of Mexican-American life doesn't hold up today. I enjoyed it there, but it doesn't hold up today. I don't think that there is that much family life. There is no Christian family life at all in an area like this . . . That there was discrimination and things like that in the early days, I am sure, just like your family and my family and other families. I don't believe that we have to constantly keep bringing up the discrimination of the past. Every other nationality had picked themselves up by their bootstraps and got going . . . I think that it (the book) is going to have no impact on the youth. I think more and more that the youth of North Town, like the youth of the world today, don't much care what your color is. They have learned to respect the human person; so we have the Mexicans dating the Anglos and the Anglos dating the Mexicans, and the kids will tell you, they aren't the least bit interested . . . I don't think that it would be a dangerous thing for the manuscript to be read here, but I don't think that there is that much reading going on in this town, I will be honest with you . . . I don't think that it should be used in schools . . . I think it's having, well right now from those I know who have read it, it's had a very negative impact. Everybody seems to think that it's bringing up a lot of the stuff, and I think people are seeing a lot of the stuff very subjectively . . . A lot of those things are past, there is no use bringing it up again.

A Community Worker, Democrat:

I think that you did pretty well. I think you touched on a lot, not just one point of view . . . I think that you made a good point on your title from one thing to another. It's for people to change. It has taken quite a while, but we have changed. I can't *imagine* us being that way. I can't . . . I haven't read too many books like that. There aren't too many books out on it. I have never had access to anything like that. If it ever comes out, I will buy it, and what I will do is I will put the names of the people that I think are in that book for my children to read. It is just something to pass on and say that I was in this era, and I helped bring about some change . . . Like I said, I am astonished at the way you wrote it in every aspect the way that I know that it is, the situation, pretty accurate. In fact I was amazed that you could have gotten that much from just talking to people . . . I thought it was going to be more one-sided, I guess. I thought it was mostly going to give us credit, I think. But you showed their side too, but I feel that not enough credit is given to Mr. Ramírez. People have not given Ramírez enough credit. I don't particularly like his way of doing things, the way he talks. I think he is very smart. He is not very educated, but I think that he is self-taught. I also think you should try to show more of our victories, the redistricting, the health program, the job discrimination cases . . . There were a lot of conflicts, personality conflicts. Some people wanted to do it a lot faster, and we had different ways of going about it. Mr. Ramírez's ideas are very definite, and he is not going to give an inch. I think that this is where they made their mistake. I think you described it exactly the way it happened . . . No, I didn't realize that they were having problems, too. They have always taught us that we have within ourselves, that we can't help another Mexican, that we have to lower him. And I said, well, we are the only ones having this problem. But we are no different. People fight. We have fights in this house just like our Anglo neighbors have in theirs. They are not that united. They are having the same problems; only we are having more. That is going to help us in the long run . . . Right, the ending is just left up in the air, fifty-fifty maybe, and we don't know where we are going. We are all up in the mid-air, and of course there is a lot of people who have stayed out of it. But I don't think that North Town will ever be the same again. I think that they know what they have to do. I know what side they are going to have to take. It isn't that I hate Anglos. I never did. It is just that in order for us to progress, our children, we have to take charge. There is no other way. I feel like in this town that if you don't, they are never going to let you do it. . . . Whether we are victorious under Raza Unida, it makes no difference because we will have victories under the Democratic party, like we do now. Of course there is a lot of people, their views are not as drastic or radical as ours. . . . There is no doubt in my mind that change is coming, and there is no way you can stop it. I think we will get together again, but it will take time . . . I wouldn't put my trust in Anglos because they don't know what we need. We know what we need. We know what our problems are . . . We don't know whether it is ever going to clear up. Maybe with our children, but I don't think even with our children because they are telling their kids things that we are telling ours to be on the defensive, watch out, don't trust them, I told you so, don't let them do what they did to us. I think the book shows the way each side has reacted to the other. One reaction causes another. One action causes a reaction. It shows people why we act the way we do, the feelings that we do have, why we mistrust a public official, why we mistrust each other . . . Maybe it will become a best seller and you will become rich. Maybe you will, you don't think so? I think that this is the time for a book like that. There aren't too many books like that. There is no access to these books. They weren't at school. They banned them . . . All these others, I can't recall their names, but they are writing books. That Elizabeth is going to get quite a bit, so I figure that everybody that writes a book will . . . I think that we are going to get more out of it because our view points have never been presented before. Like in the paper, there is nothing about it unless an obituary when we die. It is a onesided newspaper, and it always has been. We are the mean ones, the dirty ones; that is the way that it comes out in the newspaper, only when we are arrested or prosecuted, negative for us, and I think that maybe this book, it isn't 100% for us, but it presents both sides, both views . . . I wish I could buy a copy of it. If I had a lot of money I'd buy one for everyone I knew, not just on my side but send it to the judge and the mayor and the newspaper editor . . . Will it be translated into Spanish so more people can read it?

BGL *Community Leader:*

As far as the information in it going way back, some of the things are almost the things I have heard from old people and even my parents; so I thought a lot of it was true facts, I don't know to what extent. I think that the contemporary part is true to a certain point. There was a lot of hatred on both sides and distrust. The feeling now is still that, even though things are getting a lot better . . . Some of the incidents, I guess it all depends on who you heard it from, because not all of them I was aware of. Some of the things in the book aren't exactly like I heard it, but then again, maybe what I heard wasn't what happened. . . . I think that the Mexicano side or version of it is probably exaggerated a little bit more than what was really there. They were really out looking for blood. I can see to a certain point that we have had discrimination for years and years, but I never had it done to me so I wasn't looking for it. Maybe it was going on, but I didn't pay attention to it because I wasn't treated that way. Now, even minor things that have happened in the schools gets turned into political stuff . . . I think in general the focus was mostly pro-Mexicano. I don't really think that the Anglo point of view was very well represented. I guess I would have to take that back because it is true, some of the things, they were aware of some of the things going on. Since they had control, they did not have to worry about doing anything. Now this is *one thing* that all this mess has done. It has started people thinking about what they are doing before they do it. There are a lot of good people on both sides of the tracks. There is just a small handful of people creating all the problems on both sides. We have some radicals on both sides. It is kind of hard to live with. I think that most of the people will probably laugh at this book because they know, like myself, they know there were a lot of things that went on, that the information that you got is not true. That is why they never won an election because they knew that they were lying about other things. If they were saying what was true then they would be winning elections . . . It would be okay for my kids to read it. I wouldn't keep it away from them, but I wouldn't put it on my bookshelf for them either. I wouldn't make a point of having them read it because I don't think anything said is any thing that either side should be proud of. I think it is something that should be forgotten . . . On the contemporary part, they can give you the information that they weren't Raza Unida from the beginning, but we knew better because they had been seen together in Atzlán City and here. They would meet over there, about two houses down from me, every night and you had Muñiz and these other people out there; and then they claim they are not Raza Unida . . . They split because there were too many people who really wanted to be in power in the party. They had too many chiefs trying to run their own show . . . And thank goodness the wrong kind of people got it. If the right kind of people had gotten hold of the party they could have really torn this town apart . . . The Anglo minority that was creating the problems were not very important. Most of those creating problems did not belong to the BGL. They really stick together as far as an election is concerned, or even where a man is concerned, they help each other out regardless of what their views are . . . Some of the so-called big shots on the Mexicano side of town have been used to having some say-so in some of the decision-making on either the school board or the city council, and once we got in they could no longer do this. That is what created a little problem . . . Apparently the Anglos did not vote for Mr. Galván. A lot of BGL people voted for him at first, but after the run-off they went against him because they were worried about him to begin with, that he was in Raza Unida, but he lost more on the Mexican side . . . I think Father Reynaldo was an important key to that organization. He did get involved quite a bit, that is what I had against him. I don't think the priests or ministers should be in politics. They can to a certain point, but they shouldn't carry it to extremes. He encouraged a lot of it. They try to protect him because, you know of his position . . .

Businessman/Ciudadanos Leader:

After reading the book, I don't have any gripes pertaining to our part. I think most of the thing is fairly accurate from what my experiences were at the time . . . Now as far as 1940 on back, I didn't experience it, but just in talking to other people, I think that most of what's in there holds up to my conversations with older folks that lived through that era . . . One thing that I found was of real interest to me was when you're out here doing something, well, a lot of times you don't see your motives as clearly as when you come back and see them later. We made a helluva lot of mistakes, looking back . . . Some people who may not have understood our motives, we didn't come out looking worth a *damn*, but I think that it made better individuals out of us even though we made a lot of mistakes. I know that had we known at the time what's written in this book now, we would have approached things a helluva lot differently . . . I think we were very reluctant in standing up and speaking our own minds . . . The book points out specifically the fact that a lot of us could have stood up at the time and could have said this is not the way we wanna do things . . . They (BGL) kept a better grasp of what the hell was going on, and by doing that they kept more of their people together. It portrays them as a good coalition and as being more, at the time, I would say, way ahead of us as far as what constitutes politics . . . I think that this book is gonna make an impact. What it will tend to do is create an awareness of what the hell is going on. I don't think that there is even one Mexicano kid in this town, or in South Texas, that after reading this book and opening up his mind and eyes to his surroundings and going back into history, into his own personal history, he can't help but relate to all this . . . When they look back and see where they came from and where they are in this stage of life, I think that it would make them feel, I would say more proud of their achievements. I'm not talking about their personal achievements but those of their people, where they came from and where they are trying to go in this stage of the game. Will it also raise the consciousness of the Anglos? It might in a small way, but they aren't going to do an about face, maybe some of your more moderate ones, but I think that your die-hards, I don't think its gonna make much difference to them. I think that their way of life and upbringing is pretty much reflected in this book, and I don't know if these people could be any different than they are. From the crib to the grave these people had it in their minds that they are superior to the Mexicano race . . . I don't know if these people know how to act different toward Mexicanos, as far as the Mexicano is concerned. This damn thing is bred into them. I think that it may be like an act of God. They may not even know that they are being unfair. It's just like the Mexicanos saying, hell I'm superior to Los Negros, and I'm good to that damn nigger 'cause I give him work, and I give him something to eat and a place to stay, hell I'm good to him! I'm fair . . . If they feel that they have been portrayed unfairly in this book, I think that this is something that they brought upon themselves. It would be the same way if I would treat someone unfairly. That guy would think of me as an unfair person, and I would have created that myself . . . Some of the reservations that we had about the research was that we've been researched to no end, and it looks like the gringos learn more about us than we do about them. I can't look at this book from the standpoint of research but as more of what transpired. I can only associate it with what our mistakes were and why the whole thing came about. I can see why things came to a head, but it does not point out things that we would be afraid of. It does not point to Mexicano people, and maybe myself too, as being very vulnerable to legends and hearsay and sentiments. There is nothing in there that says my family is very religious, and if you mention the Virgin mother, well, we are all gonna kneel . . . The way some of these researchers see it, hell it seems like they think that if you show a Mexicano a crucifix they start sweating or something. A lot of these books that I've seen talk about witches and all this bull shit, which I don't believe in. I believe in religion, and I am religious, though, but not like in those books . . . I think it points out the contribution that the Mexicano made to this community. The gringos may not be willing to accept them, but it really doesn't sterotype the Mexicano as being irresponsible, or lazy, or negligent. The books show that we have made some gains, that we were all inexperienced in politics, and our reluctance for total involve-

255

ment. Not all of us were totally committed to one purpose because there wasn't a good sound policy that everyone could adhere to. Not everyone wanted to associate with a bunch of *locos* calling everybody *vendidos* . . . It's a pretty broad view of things that happened. One thing that might make it better would be more in-depth descriptions of the characters. It would fictionalize it more. This way maybe a bigger segment of the community could relate to it . . . No, it is real easy to read. I think most people here can read and understand it. It was very interesting. But, that might make it even more interesting.

Former Raza Unida Organizer:

Well, in the first place it is gonna shock 'em like me because there are things, as I said, that I had not known before. It will make them realize what is *really* going on. They are going to see a different view of what is what, school system, political, they'll see it, you know. People who take the time to read the book will find out something surprising . . . What really shocked me was this way you say the education was . . . Now I know why my parents were not educated. It wasn't really because they were poor. It was only because the school system didn't give a heck about giving the Mexicano an education. And about crossing the railroad tracks, that's true because it happened to my brothers when they were young, and that is the reason they didn't continue . . . I feel that if we could go back to that respect, to that obedience to parents that we had, we wouldn't have the problems that we have right now. I admire that part. I liked that because I feel that that's one thing that we don't have, and I don't think that we will ever have it again. That's lost . . . It all started with the *rancheros* wanting to keep large families in the *ranchos* so they would have more hands. That's the way it had to be in those times, you know. The largest gap there was between the *patron* and the *trabajadores*. I felt that all of it was the truth. I don't like it, because I feel right now that I am as good as anybody else. I feel that if you make yourself that humble and you think somebody else, because of the color, is better than you, something is wrong with you because nobody is better than you are . . . Yes, you will see a lot of people migrating to better themselves. These migrants are, they are not treated over there as they are here. They really like it over there. It's another world for them. But they go for one purpose, to earn money, to improve themselves. It was that way then and still is now . . . I used to work, I used to work in getting the Mexican-Americans to go vote for the Anglos. All of that is true. Even I was fool enough to believe that. I took those people to the polls. They even gave me their cars so I could take their people . . . We never realized that they were paying the judge and the visiting teacher to do that. We were that *dumb*. And the clothes she gave wasn't even *hers*. She was like me, a working person, and yet she never bothered to explain to people that, "I am only workin' here. I'm only doin' what my job requires." Heck there was nothing attached to it, nothing personal. It is the same thing for the judge, even today . . . If you don't know anything about law and the court itself, really you don't know nothing, and that is not very easy to understand. We still don't understand. We still don't understand the educational system here . . . Well there was a lot of it in there, but Mr. Ramírez has done so much. You could practically fill out this book on him alone. He's still working more deeply into the political matter, and he's trying his best to help . . . He is sort of giving them guts to stand up for what they should believe in. What he is doing is he is telling these young people, "Look out for yourself. You are as good as anybody else" . . . I think the split between the Mexicanos was described fairly accurately. I may be wrong, but I think what we need now is a reconciliation. Somebody has to give a little on these matters . . . No, it's hard to believe that such a thing could happen with the Anglos. Because what we see might be something different than what is going on. For example, when I go to meetings, what I see is they always stick together. I'd say one thing though, it's only a small group that is *really* fighting us, that is *really* trying not to let the Mexicanos improve. But no I couldn't believe they were having the same problems . . . The way I see it the Mexicano now expresses himself more. More and more Mexicanos believe in themselves. They don't think they are nothing like they used to. More Mexicanos are getting education . . . We know a little bit more about political life than we used to . . . No, they'll never change. If they're showing in some ways that they are changing or if they are planning or doing something, it's only another strategy that they are using. It has not changed, nothing has changed . . . You don't see Mexicanos in the court house. That is the most important place. You don't see Mexicanos in the important positions, the lawyers, the clerks, the judges . . . No, the bank is neutral like you said. I don't know Briscoe. I never met the man, but from what I read of him, he's a businessman. I'd say he's a businessman, and if hiring two Mexicanos for a whole bank is something to convince the rest of the Mexicanos, I would do it, too. I really would . . . I'd like it to be used in the schools because for example my kids, the ones who are in college, have seen that book and one of them said "Is this the life of North Town? Is this the life that you went through? Heck with it!" They didn't like it. They didn't really know about it. My dad has told them a lot of stories but they simply cannot believe us. They think we are just exaggerating, but you could have put a lot worse things in that book, I know.

Prominent Mexicano Professional:

It would take a book five times that size to get a complete story, but in general, I don't have too many criticisms. It covers things pretty good

. . . I got really involved in the history part. It is pretty much the way I've heard it. You go into detail more about a lot of things, but it's really just about the way I've heard it, the old sheriff and the county judge . . . The descriptions about the ranch life and our families was pretty good. A lot of that material, it is interesting to read. I'd like my kids to know what happened in the early times as to what people went through. My kids have never had hard times. They've always had it fairly good, and some of the other kids have gone and migrated. I want them to understand their hardships and what it means to be poor. They also need to understand why a lot of these people are raising a big cane. But one thing that I don't like is that some of the Raza people are not letting their kids form their own opinion. I'd like my kids to form their own opinions as to which way to go. Friendship is one thing and politics is another. That is one thing that a lot of the kids seem to understand better than the adults around here . . . The contemporary parts that I read seemed alright. In my case, I've thought about it a lot. They've probably used me in a way. Like I don't agree with what they are trying to do, yet they try to include me in just about everything that can happen. I'd say a lot of them, I've told them, if they think because I'm included in their meetings, that doesn't mean that I'm siding with their way of thinking. I'll support my race anytime there is anybody who knows what he's doing. I don't support any Mexicano, but some times they have to take sides too. I've thought about it a lot that maybe my people are thinking that I might be a gringo lover, or whatever they want to call me. But I can mingle with any of them. I'm not taking sides when it comes down to who I'm supporting. The Anglos can see me in public with Mr. Alonzo or anyone, I don't care. It's a free country, I can do whatever I want to . . . I think that if you have a community that you want to work together, it's gonna take more people to get involved in these organizations. But I still don't feel comfortable in going to some of these things. Sometimes I kind of feel out of place . . . There are good people on both sides working for the betterment of this community. It is only a few that cause the trouble . . . Some of the things that happened, you can sympathize, even me. It angered me sometimes to know the things that some of the Anglo people did. There were several occasions that the Anglo people would talk to me, talk about my people, and they were talking to me like they were talking to one of them. I think that somebody that talks to you like that is stupid because he should know better than to talk to a Mexicano as maybe not being a Mexicano and being an Anglo. I think the same thing happened to my kids in school. They tell you things about your own people which make you more aware and maybe sympathize more with Mexicanos, but my kids stayed level-headed too and tried to have friends on all sides . . . I think it is probably a good idea if people read this book. A lot of people I know want to read it. I don't think it would hurt anything.

From chapter one to five is pretty well the way I understand it to be in that time. The only thing that I saw there was several incidents in chapter five and six that were not exactly the way I experienced them. It doesn't change the meaning. You get the picture. It gets close to what happened. It's really something to look at that, the way that we did things, I had never thought about it that way. Yet I know what was going on. I don't know, having the whole thing, all these years, put together like that in a story is really something to see that way . . . I was talking to this fellow the other day, an Anglo, and he said there is a lot of racial stuff there to antagonize people. But the thing is, what is there *happened.* There's no two ifs about it, and you know it's not that it was made to look that way. It was what was actually happening. What they did you can never erase. Regardless of how many flowers they put on it, it will always be the same. Anytime you twist somebody's arm, it hurts the other guy, but it doesn't hurt you; so it's natural for them not to understand how they have hurt us. It's natural for them not to believe our complaints. They still don't really see what has happened . . . It makes us look bad because we didn't know a lot of things that were going on. We didn't know a lot of things that we wanted to do, even though we knew they were right . . . As for the splits, their side was pretty accurate to what I knew and our side was pretty accurate to what I felt was going on, too. I never gave any thought about that while everything was coming all at once. As for the split with Dobieville, I think that was pretty close to the truth. That was the way the Mexicanos saw it and what happened . . . The big meeting where the gringos came from Aztlán City? Well that was pretty close to what I experienced. Everything that they did there were lies. That's the reason the opposition was from the Mexicanos, but they never proved that such incidents like houses being burned were true. You didn't put in there about them being unable to answer back how many houses Raza Unida really burned in Aztlán. Those were just speeches to arouse people. That is what we objected to. But you should end that book with what is happening to the Mexicanos in Dobieville. You know those Mexicanos are full-blooded Democrats, and they are being called all kinds of names, too. It doesn't matter what label you have here, if you are a Mexican and you are trying to change things . . . I think this book can work either way, looking at it the way I did, anybody can take it and interpret it the way they want. And if they want to use it against the Mexicano, I guess they will. I guess if they want to use it against the gringos, I guess they will . . . What is there, the political lessons, maybe not as it was, because the lesson was taught to everybody, what it shows there is if any radical gringo wanted to do the same things again, they may try. They may not do it, but they will try. And the

Mexicano, well, it depends on how they use it . . . People from the outside would probably think that we were foolish, that we were dumb. Maybe the gringos were foolish, and maybe they were dumb, too. You can second-guess anybody, but I'll be damned if they would have done something different if they were in our day and age . . . I think that I would love for everybody here in North Town to have the book. I would *love* to see that. Maybe we'll have some unity. Maybe something good would come out of it. When I was reading, I was hoping that everybody would have learned their lesson because it will come. I don't know when, but I know that it will come. It's better to be working together than to be the way people have always done here . . . I've always been level-headed, and I've been fair with everybody, but my remarks and my ideas have never been accepted by gringos and neither have those of other Mexicanos . . . The state agency wouldn't accept it, and it wouldn't be recommended, then it wouldn't be used because of that. A lot of books don't tell you the facts. They don't tell you a lot of things like the politics and local or municipal government. You have to go to college to learn that. I don't think that kids could be educated by reading that book, in the sense of what we call education; and yet they read a lot of junk that is not true in history, and I don't approve of that . . . Maybe they would learn from it, too. I've never seen something like that in a school, but I know for a fact that they never will approve it . . . That is not a complete book. You left out a *lot* of things, you get the picture, but it would take several volumes to tell all the things that really happen here.

Author's Response to the Community Reviews

As any reader can see, there are some real differences of opinion regarding the veracity and utility of this book. The manuscript also seems to have stimulated some reflections and reaction among North Towners. Since it has yet to circulate widely, there still is no community-wide response, but I suspect that the sentiments expressed in the reviews will be a good sample of future responses. We are anxious to see it more widely read and debated. We think it will do more good than harm. If we didn't hope that someone would learn and profit from this work, we never would have begun. Yet, it is hard to say specifically what good this book or any book does. One can throw out all the cliches about increasing communication and provoking a search for new ideas, but considering how subjectively everyone reads and reacts to the manuscript, one wonders. To me, the most striking thing about all these reviews is the extent that each person tends to reaffirm what they already believe and to rationalize away what they dislike. On the other hand, a number of reviewers were clearly forced to look at some aspects of their experience differently. I got the sense that the

260

reviewers were also learning something from the manuscript. As I indicated, I was generally impressed with the depth and quality of the reviews.

There is no way to answer each and every criticism in the reviews. That probably would serve little purpose. Many specific changes have been made in this version of the manuscript which were stimulated by North Towners and other reviewers. The summaries at the end of chapters two, four, and six pretty well spell out the main arguments, which did not substantially change. One major point might be made again, however. The first reviewer, a long-time resident, professional/ rancher, inadvertantly says it all, "You didn't pay anybody anymore than you had to who worked for you, and you kept those under your thumb. Well that *was*, but that was success. That was the way it was. You couldn't blame anybody for wanting to make money . . ." This is precisely the system or way of life we describe, except he generally accepts it as natural, "the way things are." We generally argue that this way of life has done too many unacceptable things to many people, Mexicanos *and* Anglos, in the holy quest for material success. If the descriptions of stoop labor, Mr. Cameron, humiliated women and children, and hateful, bitter people on both sides are even partially true, one wonders if our society can't do better, if North Towners can't do better.

Some North Town readers will surely say that we have exaggerated the negative aspects of life in North Town. To be sure, many people there, as in other small American communities, have comfortable, pleasant lives. North Town really isn't such a bad place to live, and most people there would probably tell you that. Moreover, if this book has portrayed North Town Anglos as villains, it should be added that they are like people everywhere, on the whole a good, decent people. The book never sought to or intended to denigrate North Town as a community or North Towners as individuals. We would agree with the old-timer, "If it would have been the other way around, it would have been the same." That is a pretty chilling, pessimistic thought, but I believe that to be true. If there is something fundamentally wrong with the system that people try to create, it is unlikely that one race can run it any more or less humanely than another. Mexicanos are probably equally capable of inventing dehumanizing, racist beliefs if they had to protect and justify their profits and investments. If brown businessmen and ranchers replaced white ones, would they operate less like businessmen and land owners? Are Mexicano *patrones*, moneylenders, and contractors any less willing to squeeze their workers and renters?

An epic struggle began between the "haves" and the "have nots" of North Town, but that struggle has sputtered to a stop under the confused leadership of prominent Mexicanos. A new, more moderate group of Anglos emerged to "stamp out" this political threat and to be more responsive to the growing demands of Mexicanos for greater equality, but many traditional racial and class prejudices remain. A number of other important factors external to the community have also altered and circumscribed this confrontation such as: the competition from the northern agricultural region; the development of agro-business; the role of the traditional political parties; the increase of federal control and programs; and the political influence of the new state regional governmental agencies. Fundamental change in the political economy of North Town has not occurred because of these various political responses and adaptations. Inequality is still as plain as the one-room paper-thin houses that dot the west side of town. One wonders how much human energy and conflict it takes to light the fires of change.

All of this is to say to North Towners that it wasn't always clear who the heroes and the villains were. As one reader suggested, I was probably for the underdog, but I would hasten to add that I would be the first to write a denunciation of Mexicano *patrones* and *politicos* if they came to power and abused it too. As many readers have suggested, race really is only a coincidental issue here. The real problem is a way of life that allows even one human being to be degraded and used. I would prefer to think of this interpretation as pro-human rather than pro-Mexicano or pro-Anglo. It might be added that a similar story could probably be written about almost any American community; and this is not to say that America is such a bad place when compared to various poverty-stricken, fascist regimes around the world. But we still have a long, painful way to go before creating a just society. The story of North Town is a remarkable example of this process. As critical as this may seem of North Towners, I cannot help but admire the confusion and pathos of their struggle.

PART IV: FOLLOW-UP STUDY, 1978 TO 1987

Chapter 8

The Legacy of the Civil Rights Movement

North Town Politics and Politicians from 1978 to 1987

When we left North Town in 1978, the intense political and racial conflict of the early 1970's had subsided. The Raza Unida Party had lost nearly all its supporters, and only Mr. Ramírez, the dedicated militant, struggled on to assure voting rights legislation and a free health clinic. Various members of the original Ciudadanos organization had revived the LULAC civic organization and founded *El Sarape* social club.

By 1979 Mayor Luna, formerly considered the *vendido* of the biracial BGL political coalition, found himself in trouble with his Anglo supporters. He was reluctant to fire his city manager, a long-time civil rights activist and talented federal grantsman. The city manager was widely criticized for a drinking problem and lax administrative practices. The mayor had been able to maintain the support of his most loyal BGL supporter, County Judge Warren, but a number of other Anglos were encouraging a recent arrival in town to run against the mayor.

This turn of events created a temporary reunification of the Mexican-American community. The mayor's faction, approximately four hundred to five hundred Mexicano voters, ran a slate of city council candidates that beat a slate of Anglo-sponsored candidates by several hundred votes. Most observers felt that the BGL candidate would have defeated the mayor easily without the new support of the old Ciudadanos faction. Apparently several leaders in LULAC convinced others that the mayor was no longer a *vendido* and could be trusted. At least some local Anglos reported suspecting a new *La Raza* plot. Rumors abounded that the "radical" Ciudadanos faction and the "moderate" mayor and his faction had formed an alliance.

By the spring of 1979 several new Mexicano leaders had also emerged on the school board. Soon after the city elections, the new, tenuous alliance between the two Mexicano factions had elected three more Mexicanos to the school board. Mayor Luna stayed on the sidelines and did not actively work against the Ciudadanos-type slate. He, therefore, tacitly supported the move toward an all-Mexicano school board. By the spring of 1980, North Town politics appeared remarkably similar to the earlier Mexicano political revolt in 1972. The more activist Ciudadanos-type Mexicanos regained a majority on the school board, as well as influence over the city council and presumably the mayor himself.

From 1977 to 1980 the old Ciudadanos group picked up several new, energetic professionals, some native North Towners back from college and some outsiders. On the school board a strong alliance formed between Mr. Ramos, the former board president and a government worker, and Mrs. Serrano, the new president and a former educator. Both the Ramos and Serrano families have long been active in civil rights and social service activities. The new North Town school board of 1980 shifted to a much more active, reformist orientation. The board felt that the local schools needed major changes in administrative leadership, teacher evaluation, and curriculum. They hired the first Mexican-American school superintendent and a Mexican-American athletic director from the Rio Grande Valley. Various teachers interviewed saw the board as "meddling," "autocratic," and "racist." The board quickly became involved in conflict with the new Mexican-American superintendent.

The superintendent was ultimately charged with twelve major deficiencies, the main ones being managerial and fiscal incompetence. He was also considered insubordinate for failing to provide information and failing to institute curriculum and evaluation reforms. Various opponents of the board characterized the charges as political. They reported that the real conflict was over the superintendent's unwillingness to fire Anglo teachers and generally go along with a *La Raza* type takeover of the schools.

The conflict built to a crisis in 1981, when the board, after a series of heated, late-night meetings, fired the superintendent. The board conducted a hearing, piped to the community by closed-circuit television. During the hearing approximately six hundred angry citizens heard lawyers grill the superintendent on anomalies in his employment record. Approximately fifty students, many of them graduating seniors, then staged a one-day boycott and protest at the high school in support of the superintendent. They were led by the daughter of a Mexicano school board member and by several children of prominent Anglo families. This brought in the San Antonio media, which played up the irony of Anglos supporting the first Mexicano superintendent against an all-Mexicano school board.

The local newspaper carried strongly worded editorials calling the board "Aztlán City Clones" (referring to the "radical Chicano/Raza Unida Party takeover" of the nearby Aztlán City schools, which led to Anglos leaving the Aztlán City schools). The board was portrayed as seeking to ruin the schools the way *La Raza* did in Aztlán City. Rumors also swirled among students that the Texas Education Agency would censure the district and make their degrees worthless. The local newspaper ridiculed the four Ciudadanos-type board members as the "fabulous four." They were portrayed as setting themselves up as dictators to rule over Anglos. Several Anglos reported that many Anglos were threatening to leave town if the school board was not thrown out of office.

From all reports, North Town was once again embroiled in a bitter political and racial battle that was as intense as the ones we personally experienced in the early seventies. The "fabulous four" were not labeled communists and criminals the way the original Ciudadanos leaders were, but they were branded as racists bent on destroying the schools. Conversely, the "fabulous four" saw such charges as politically inspired. They accused Anglos of supporting an incompetent Mexicano superintendent to discredit the emerging independent-minded Mexicano leaders.

The actual issue of the superintendent's competency will probably never be clear, although a recent TEA report on his appeal does uphold eleven of the twelve charges. What is clear from the recollections of both Anglos and Mexicanos is the role this superintendent had in stirring up old, bitter racial feelings. The superintendent, when unable to work with the all-Mexicano board, apparently leaked a good deal of information/misinformation from executive meetings to Anglos. He accused the board of being generally anti-Anglo and reported that board members were making inflammatory, anti-Anglo remarks. He portrayed the board as plotting to fire Anglo teachers and showing preferential treatment toward Mexicano students in academics and in sports. The new Mexicano athletic director/football coach, a close friend and drinking buddy of one of the board members, apparently offered a good deal of visible evidence to support the superintendent's claims. The coach reportedly made disparaging racial remarks, was arrested in a drunken brawl, and occasionally showed up late for practice. In addition, one of the Mexicano board members was perceived as frequently visiting the schools and spying on teachers. Several teachers reported that they thought he was out to get them, which confirmed rumors emanating from the central office. Finally, the Mexicano director of federal programs was accused of inflating the migrant education rolls with nonmigrant children. This is a common practice in South Texas schools which conservative ranchers and businessmen look upon as a corrupt "giveaway program."

The school board controversy ended in 1981, when the remnants of the old BGL group and others organized a slate of moderate Anglo candidates to regain control from the "radical Mexicans." At this point Ramos decided not to run for reelection to the board, and a poorly organized slate of more openly militant candidates lost by 2-to-1. Just as in the early 1970's, Anglos and the moderate bloc of Mayor Luna mobilized to crush a "racial" Ciudadanos-type ethnic political threat. And as before, the more extreme the Anglos became, the more it provoked the most militant Ciudadanos types to run an outspoken but hopeless campaign. As before, the more moderate of the Ciudadanos types retreated to the sidelines to let local politics "cool off."

In the meantime, North Town city hall politics had become relatively peaceful with the reelection of Mayor Luna in 1978. He subsequently replaced the controversial city manager with a native North Town Mexicano who had an M.A. in city planning. The present all-Mexicano city council, which consists of several local educators and prominent businessmen, is generally regarded as relatively independent of the mayor. It has worked hard to continue obtaining federal and state grants. The council is proud of paving the majority of the streets in the Mexicano barrio as well as some in racially mixed parts of town. Since 1978 the council has also continued to encourage outside businesses, principally Wal-Mart, to locate in North Town. This policy aroused considerable opposition from downtown Anglo merchants and the Chamber of Commerce. Sales revenues for the city are up 40 percent, but as in other small towns, the Wal-Mart chain appears to be driving out several long-time merchants. The council, and particularly the mayor, have not escaped criticism.

In addition, the mayor became involved in controversies with the school superintendent, with Mr. Alonzo over zoning changes, with his sister over personal matters, and with a local group seeking city support of proposed recreational programs. One hears many rumors in North Town that the mayor has become "too independent, stubborn, and arrogant." Talk about his personal indiscretions, a sure sign of disfavor in small-town politics, has also surfaced. In spite of the criticism, however, most people seem to think the mayor and the council have been active and successful. Except for the 1982 mayoral race, when a young Mexicano school administrator ran against him, city elections have been noncontroversial. This opposition candidate was strongly supported by Mr. Alonzo, which signaled the final rupture of the tenuous alliance between Ciudadanos types and the mayor's more moderate followers.

The other major area of political controversy has centered on the county elections. Former BGL leader Judge Warren and former Ciudadanos leader Mr. Alonzo have alternately held a 3-2 majority on the Commissioners' Court since 1980. Judge Warren has emerged as the strongest North Town Anglo politician through his close alliance with Mayor Luna and his general support in the Anglo and Mexicano communities. His eight years as county judge are free of scandal and are marked by his work in social service and the juvenile court. He considers his decisions toward youthful offenders a sign of caring and liberalism. His detractors in the Mexicano community accuse him of excessive leniency to avoid conflict and to win votes. In spite of detractors in both communities, some old Ciudadanos activists privately admit that the judge has supported various community health, recreational, and social programs that benefit Mexicanos.

Judge Warren has also proven to be a fierce opponent of Mexicano politicians whom he perceives as racial extremists. He has been active in investigations into Commissioner Alonzo's alleged misuse of road equipment and was involved in the proposed investigation and a boycott of the local radio station. The judge is also actively trying to institute a unitary system of road maintenance equipment under a county engineer. He claims this is a "modernization" program. Commissioner Alonzo sees it as another political attack on his road-paving activities.

Judge Warren's standing in the Anglo community still seems strong, but as in the early seventies, some describe him as "too educated, too liberal, and too lazy." Despite conflicts with various Anglo factions, he retains a solid vote in that community as well as in the Mexicano community through Mayor Luna's bloc and his own efforts.

The major basis for Commissioner Alonzo's rise to power has been the general efforts of the old Ciudadanos leaders to become prominent in the local Democratic Party. They have abandoned any idea of a separatist ethnic politics or political party. Mr. Alonzo's family and other North Town Mexicanos worked extremely hard for the election of Democratic Governor Mark White, and they now have state-level connections that no North Town Mexicano ever had. Alonzo was subsequently appointed chairman of the regional government council, which oversees all grant applications from local counties. In addition, he was elected to the executive committee of the state Democratic Party. Locally, he has won reelection as a county commissioner and has solidified the old Ciudadanos vote, although not without detractors. He accuses the judge and other political opponents of harassing him over a liquor license for his son's store, alleged misuse of county road funds, libelous newspaper ads, and a variety of other incidents involving his family.

The local media give extensive coverage to the conflict between Judge Warren and Commissioner Alonzo. The local paper, which led an editorial charge against the "fabulous four," generally runs anti-Alonzo commentary, and the radio generally runs news coverage that casts Alonzo in a more favorable light. The local paper has been quick to cover alleged misuse of road-grading equipment and county workers on the private driveways of *cantina* owners in Commissioner Alonzo's district. Conversely, the radio station ran an impassioned speech against the Anglo power elite, without mentioning specific names, for its treatment of the embattled school board president. Everyone I interviewed agrees that when racial tempers flared, each side has a media organ that will put the best face on its particular cause or champions.

Amidst this swirl of opinion, Judge Warren and Commissioner Alonzo have developed into enduring political enemies. Of course, each minimizes the importance and ability of the other, but they are worthy adversaries who have their own followings. More militant types in each ethnic group see this conflict as symbolizing the Anglo–*La Raza* confrontation of earlier years, but, increasingly, others see this conflict as a personal feud that is sometimes entertaining and at other times detrimental to the community.

Rumors abound that Commissioner Alonzo will ultimately attempt to defeat Judge Warren, or will encourage his eldest son, now a lawyer in the U.S. Army, to become the first Mexicano county judge. This seems to be the one still-unattained political goal of activist North Town Mexicanos. Periodically, Mexicanos have held all the major local leadership positions, and Commissioner Alonzo has had the majority vote at the Commissioners' Court for several years. In addition, the old Ciudadanos activists have become the most influential local politicians in the Democratic Party. They have minimized the traditional Anglo connection between county judge/courthouse and the state party in power. Nevertheless, the county judgeship seems to remain that last elusive symbolic victory for Mexicanos. Mr. Rápido, a former Ciudadanos leader and now a justice of the peace, recently challenged Judge Warren in a strong campaign and lost by fewer than eighty votes. This represents a substantial gain over previous Mexicano candidates for county judge. It may also represent a decline in Judge Warren's power and influence.

Some Mexicano leaders, such as Commissioner Alonzo, believe that only a better-mobilized Mexicano vote (only 25 percent of the registered Mexicanos vote) will elect a Mexicano to the last bastion of Anglo power. Mr. Alonzo continues to advocate a more ethnic political approach. Others, such as Judge Rápido and former board members Mrs. Serrano and Mr. Ramos, believe that moderate Mexicanos and Anglos will cross over and vote for strong ex-Ciudadanos types who have proven their commitment to community public service and professionalism. These are, of course, expressions of views that were around in the early seventies. The main change, however, seems to be that a growing number of Mexicano professionals and business leaders believe that emphasizing "the community" over *La Raza* is the only way to maintain a peaceful, improving community. They argue that when Anglos are too threatened, extreme racial polarization occurs, and the misunderstandings that result set the community back in its gradual evolution away from a redneck South Texas town. They deemphasize ethnicity and ethnic causes and advocate building political bridges with more moderate Anglos and Mexicanos.

In summary, North Town politics 1988-style has an old, familiar ring, even though the formal political organizations of the early seventies, Ciudadanos Unidos, Raza Unida Party, and the Better Government League, are now defunct. North Towners see today's politics as less ideological and even more factionalized than in the days of *La Raza* versus the BGL. New alliances are being made within and across racial lines. Leaders in both ethnic groups talk of crossover votes and which Anglo is liberal enough to get Mexicano votes and which Mexicano is reasonable enough to get Anglo votes. In the 1986 county elections, there was some evidence of Anglos, one hundred to two hundred, voting for Judge Rápido and for the controversial former school board president, Mrs. Serrano. Both of these candidates were considered "radicals" in the past. This represents a definite break with earlier bloc voting. In the election aftermath, Judge Rápido attributed his defeat to the low Mexicano turnout and a former Ciudadanos member's small but active campaign against him. He was encouraged by the crossover votes, however, and by the absence of racial rhetoric on either side.

Some of the original leaders of the old organizations have retired. Others have developed strong followings based on the original groups. New leaders have emerged. Some new leaders were students in the high school when we did the original research. The present-day groupings might best be characterized as personal political networks. The one enduring alliance across ethnic groups has been between Judge Warren and Mayor Luna. Neither man could probably win without the other, and anyone who wants to defeat Warren or Luna must come up with an alliance that cuts across ethnic groups or that mobilizes far more Mexicanos to vote. Given the calculus of the above relatively stable personal followings, everyone with political ambition is jockeying to find new alliances to increase his or her following.

Electoral politics in North Town has entered a transitional, unstable period. No one seems quite sure whom to trust or what alliance to make. Deep personal conflicts and images of people as "radicals" and "vendidos" remain, but the idea of local businessmen and professionals being "radical" is hard to sustain after years of community public service. There are new signs of greater acceptance by Anglos and moderate Mexicanos of the new Mexicano middle class as legitimate political leaders. Their image as "radicals" is dying in spite of the racial flare-up in 1980. As political competition becomes less racial, North Town politics will undoubtedly return to the classic American pattern of low voter participation and a few leaders, most of them Mexicanos, running things for many years.

Racial tensions will continue to flare up, however, because long-time political enemies such as Alonzo, Warren, and Luna will do battle again before they retire, and their struggles will embroil many other partisans. The patterns we have traced in detail since the fifties will undoubtedly continue for several more generations and will, at times, take on racial overtones.

The Impact of the Chicano Movement on American Politics

It strains the logic of causality to argue that events in one small South Texas town directly alter the American political system. However, the structures and processes of race, class, and politics described in this case are likely to be found in other towns in South Texas and possibly in the Southwest. This case suggests by illustration how American society, at a given historical moment, is evolving and changing. In a sense, North Towners are making American history as they make their own local history. From the ethnographic perspective, to

270

really understand broad societal processes or phenomena such as race and class, one must know the small, everyday world of peace and their communities.

What then was the impact of the Chicano movement on American politics? The Raza Unida Party itself died quickly, but sometimes ideas live much longer than people and their organizations. In this case, the ideas of "self-determination/self-rule" and of ethnic pride live on in North Town. The idea of Mexicanos being politically and culturally equal to Anglos is a deep and profound legacy of the original *movimiento*. No self-respecting Mexicano leader would downplay these ideas, even though most now express ethnic pride more moderately than in the seventies. The new generation of ethnic political leaders are generally a more assertive, independent type of politicians. The old role of being dependent brokers for Anglos evokes derision and criticism from many Mexicanos. This corroborates the pattern that De la Garza and Vaughn find in recent Mexican-American political activities.[1] There are still Mexicano politicians called *vendidos* and accused of being weak and the puppets of Anglos, but such charges are increasingly difficult to sustain. Most Mexicano politicians now strive to be perceived as independent of Anglo influence. A new ethnic pride is now a widespread cultural norm in North Town.

Another important effect of the *movimiento* has been to dramatically increase the numbers of educated, professional local leaders. A whole new political generation of young college-educated locals are returning to North Town to be its teachers, social workers, city council members, and local business people. These new leaders are predominantly Mexicano, but also include some Anglos. This generation experienced the *movimiento* of the late sixties and early seventies in the local schools, and some report having the *movimiento* explained to them in Chicano studies programs at various state universities. Their younger brothers and sisters are going to higher education institutions in increasing numbers, and North Town is now full of what psychologists call "role models of success." Those Mexicano families already positioned to take advantage of desegregation and the new political gains are definitely the economic, political, and educational equals of established middle-class Anglo families. The emerging Mexicano middle class is the big gainer from the civil rights movement, a finding that has parallels in the black civil rights movement.[2]

More political competition has ultimately made the American political system of distributing state aid work better in the entire region. North Town has gotten a great deal more of the pork barrel for its schools, streets, and health clinics. The political competition from this new generation of Mexicano *políticos* has also shattered the old moralistic states-rights view of small government. The federal aid programs flow into this poor rural community in a much bigger way than in the past, and, increasingly, local Anglos accept this as something other than "welfare handouts" and "federal control." The movement has made conservative ideologues and moralists more pragmatic, and they now reluctantly accept federal aid for their low-income populations. Moreover, it is the old Ciudadanos leaders who now deliver the vote and get the recognition of Anglo state Democratic political leaders. The personal patronage networks between local brown politicians and state and national brown and white politicians is growing. This will assure the flow of future aid to North Town.

The rise of this generation of ethnic politicians has also broken the monopoly of a do-nothing landed-merchant class over the local political process. The pre-war period of politics in North Town was marked by two small-time "political machines" and high levels of civic inactivity. The present-day county government and city council have accomplished far more public improvement projects than the pre-war leaders. Voter participation rates have more than doubled, and general civic participation in schools, churches, health, and welfare projects is higher. A group of young professionals and business people from both races has developed to lead civic and political activities. It would seem that the general educational level of the new leaders is considerably higher than that of earlier leaders. If education, technical expertise, and the relative youth of local leadership are good measures of quality, one could argue that the quality of local leadership is higher than in earlier days.

The revolt has also increased the general level of information, debate, and political campaigning. The media coverage of elections is definitely more extensive than in the days of no active radio station and newspaper. Moreover, both Mexicano and Anglo politicians agree that Mexicano voters are more experienced and informed than in the past. The level of voter participation and awareness seems higher than in other communities. Twenty-five percent of the registered Mexicano voters and 50 percent of the registered Anglo voters participate, but the level of voter awareness is impossible to establish without attitudinal surveys. My impression is that the ongoing political competition has undoubtedly had an educational effect. Some voters are more concerned, some more cynical, and involvement is generally higher than in the past. Only more research could actually determine the impact on voter knowledge, attitude, and participation.

Most political scientists who subscribe to a pluralistic view of American politics would use this case as a classic example of how interest group politics and the American party system work.[3] As in the case of other third-party challenges to the system, the dissent and the dissenters were incorporated and absorbed into the two-party system. By absorbing new "radical" ideas, the political system reformed and improved as a system of distribution and representation. Although it may sound outrageous to North Town Anglos who consider the *La Raza* movement evil, the rise of ethnic populations has improved and has actually made American democracy work. Having looked carefully at the type of democracy that existed in North Town before World War II, I would have to agree strongly with the pluralists. The North Town case seems to prove that the American political system is resilient, reformable, and evolving toward a fairer, more responsive government. Moreover, one has to admire the long struggle and real gains won by Mexicanos in North Town. There is, however, another, more revealing point of view or theory for interpreting what this case of political reform means.

The Class Character of the Chicano Political Movement

The pluralist view of American politics has an element of truth to it, but such a model always underplays the class character of grassroots political struggles. Deeper historical class formations are always conceptualized as ephemeral, ad hoc interest groups detached from capitalist economic development. The early chapters described in great detail the region's economic transformation from a semifeudal cotton sharecropping economy to a wage economy based on migrant labor. As agriculture in North Town became fully capitalist in character, a recomposition of the old semifeudal relationships of *patrones* and their *peones* into a modern, impersonal, more antagonistic wage-labor relationship occurred. As tenant farmers turned into a rural wage-labor proletariat of vegetable and fruit pickers, they forced the local landed gentry to accommodate to their Northern migrations. Local growers ultimately constructed a labor system using some local Mexicanos as a kind of labor aristocracy of permanent field hands, managers, machinery operators, and contractors. They helped manage a broader base of illegal, *bracero*, and less-fortunate local Mexicanos. These Mexicanos also became key actors in a pattern of "sponsored political enfranchisement."

Various small-time Anglo politicians, county judges, and sheriffs developed "political machines" of loyal Mexicano brokers and voters. As the local political economy evolved in the *colonia* era, class relations went through a major recomposition. Unlike in the earlier *rancho* era, the landed gentry controlled labor through Mexicano contractors. Small-time Anglo politicians and their loyal Mexicano brokers ran carefully orchestrated low voter turnouts. Local politics and labor organization were left, therefore, to the emerging middle class or petty bourgeoisie of both races. By the post–World War II era, a gradual process of political incorporation, sponsored upward economic mobility, and even selective school and residential desegregation was occurring. Local Anglos were responding to the early civil rights movement and were slowly dismantling the racial order.

Historically, ethnic working-class struggles have occurred in South Texas since the early 1900's.[4] In the postwar years new civil rights leaders and organizations emerged to articulate the growing demands of the Mexicano people. I would emphasize, however, that the Mexicano rural proletariat, not the various formal civil rights organizations, was the basis of change. The proletariat's struggle for dignity and justice grew stronger by the early fifties. Its new assertiveness was daily expressed in work stoppages, wage thefts, confrontations in bars, complaints at schools, and fights between youth. As its collective anger built into a series of small, periodic defiances, and as its desire for change grew, various local community leaders emerged. A new group of post-war Mexicano *políticos* organized this general pattern of resistance and self-assertion into electoral challenges.

Ideologically, the leadership of the ethnic political revolt in the Winter Garden region has varied during the post-war era. The latest and most "radical" expression of this movement is the cultural-nationalist perspective of the Raza Unida Party (RUP) in Aztlán City. RUP emerged in the late sixties and had strong affinities with campus leftist thought and the black power perspective of SNCC activists in the deep South.[5] Its nationalist perspective stressed the positive character of Mexicano language and culture and the negative character of Anglo racial oppression. In its strongest version expressed in Aztlán City, cultural nationalism advocated local control of all government institutions and schools through a separate political party. The party was to run local governments in a unified way that better coordinated the powers of taxation, federal aid, and county-generated industry to serve low-income Mexicanos. The schools were to advocate strong programs to preserve and express the local language and culture of Tejanos.

South Texas Mexicanos consider themselves distinct from either Mexican or Anglo culture. They are the historical product both of traditional Mexican culture and of the economic and political struggles against the racial barriers of American society.

In this view of ethnic culture, politics and culture are inseparable. The character and shape of everyday Tejano culture spring from its political struggle for a positive identity in a racist society. Nationalists sought to reverse the negative identity of Mexicano language and culture as a prelude to or part of political enfranchisement and local political control. Cultural pride and directly confronting the cultural imperialism of the dominant Anglo society were fundamental to their ideology. Many North Town Mexicano leaders did not subscribe to strong versions of cultural nationalism, but all emphasized ethnic cultural pride far more than pre-war Mexicano leaders did. They generally shared the concepts of self-rule and ethnic pride and sought a new measure of cultural, political, and economic equality. The ideological legacy of the *Raza Unida,* although moderated, is still strong among many class sectors of Mexicanos in this region.

The Chicano movement in South Texas spawned at least two models of social and political change. The more "leftist" model was in Aztlán City.[6] Shockley's political history, our follow-up studies, and various other works describe this much-studied case.[7] Shockley's generally reliable account overestimates the uniqueness of the Aztlán City revolt, however. He mistakenly concludes that Aztlán City will not happen elsewhere in South Texas without the extraordinary leadership patterns found in both Aztlán City revolts. *Los Cinco,* the leaders of the sixties, were the traditional entrepreneurial of petty bourgeoisie (a business agent, real estate salesman, photographer, store clerk, trucker). The Raza Unida leaders of the seventies were primarily a "new" petty bourgeois class of professionals, technicians, and small businessmen.[8] Some were holdovers from *los Cinco,* some were fresh from campus movements. The architect of the revolt, José Angel Gutiérrez, successfully blended these two elements for a brief time. The factionalism that ensued and helped destroy the experiment is a story in itself. In a general sense, what happened in Aztlán City is happening everywhere in South Texas. The entire region has the same underlying class dynamic of a proletarian struggle, and the same class actors, the petty bourgeoisie, are leading other political revolts. What was unique about Aztlán City was its curious, eclectic ideology of cultural nationalism, county socialism, and brown capitalism and its militant rhetoric and style of race relations.

The model of local politics that ultimately developed in the heyday of the Raza Unida Party might best be characterized as a Chicano social welfare state. Party members themselves advocated "brown capitalism" and owned land, a restaurant, and a beer distributorship in Aztlán City. In addition, they advocated creating a county mode of production based on land appropriated through taxation. They envisioned a variety of useful, money-making industries such as a piggery, a farm, and a hollow block plant. None of these proposals was initiated, however. Further, since the party perceived itself as a separate underdeveloped nation within a nation-state, it had its own foreign policy and sought economic and cultural aid and exchanges from the third world, e.g., Mexico and Cuba. Such radical ideas evoked extremely hostile responses from the landed gentry of the area, one of whom was the governor and leader of the conservative wing of the state Democratic Party. The Texas ruling class and the state apparatus it controlled sought to destroy the RUP through various investigations, lawsuits, bad press, and subterfuge.

In the face of these threats, the party organized itself into a highly skilled grant-writing/grant-getting operation. By using a cadre of imported professionals in all the human services fields, the party generally tapped the War on Poverty flow of federal tax monies for health, education, social welfare, and housing. Party leaders skillfully played on the guilty-conscience liberalism of federal functionaries and on the competition among Republican and Democratic administrations for the "minority vote." These tactics greatly increased what some class theorists now call the "social wage" of the national welfare state.[9] The party distributed this social wage in the form of jobs at the schools, construction contracts, new houses, free medical care, special school programs, and a host of other real benefits. All the new social welfarism was accompanied by numerous political rallies and a very extensive effort to resocialize youth in the schools with a *"chicanismo"* worldview.[10] The extent of political patronage distributed and the extensiveness of the efforts at political socialization were indeed unique to South Texas.

The real impact of Aztlán City in the Winter Garden region was not that anyone replicated much of its ideology or modus operandi, but rather that "Aztlán" hung like a spectre over the entire region. The revolt stimulated a great deal of reform to avoid "another Aztlán City." Mexicano leaders in North Town did learn to go after more federal monies and to demand more respect for their language and culture, which forced traditional Anglo leaders to respond. North Town Anglo leaders carefully studied the Aztlán City case, and those who were less racist and more liberal learned to make concessions. They advocated various social welfare programs and expressions of cultural pride, e.g., bilingual education. They also sought to restrain and reeducate the most extreme white racists to live with and share political power with a "responsible" Mexicano middle class. At least in nearby North Town, the spectre of Anglos packing up and leaving Aztlán City with the Raza Unida advocating "killing the gringo" (economically and metaphorically) evoked both a desire to change and a fear of *La Raza*. To some Anglos *La Raza* meant an anti-white lust for revenge and the domination and humiliation of Anglos. "Aztlán" has made it both easier and more difficult to be an assertive Mexicano leader in the region.

In other towns, like North Town, one encounters a second model of change that is far less dramatic and publicized and more characteristic of the political process of American pluralism. The role of campus radicals was far more ephemeral. The North Town "radicals," the Ciudadanos Unidos, were predominantly small businessmen and growers. As in Aztlán, few working-class leaders ever emerged, nor were there any "theoreticians" with the stature of Gutiérrez; consequently, little formal ideology ever developed. North Town leaders only partially responded to the cultural nationalist ideology of the Raza Unida and were never enthusiastic about county socialism, trips to Cuba, or foreign aid from Mexico. Nor were they ever able to organize the type of federal grant–getting operation so basic to the party's economic base in Aztlán City. The Ciudadanos have ultimately reconstituted themselves as Democrats, and those individuals of particular tenacity and personableness have developed into prominent, successful community/civic leaders. In Kornblum's study of Chicago ethnic politics, the middle class runs electoral politics, and the working class, if there are labor unions, runs labor union politics.[11] In the case of South Texas, there is no active farm workers' movement in the Winter Garden region. Politics has become, therefore, a competition between the brown and white petty bourgeoisie. As time passes, interracial alliances will probably increase in this highly personalized world of local politics. As political competition declines, so will voting and general voter awareness. North Town is probably a more representative model of how the ethnic political revolt is incorporated as the racial order slowly disintegrates. The spectre of "county socialism" and massive "white flight" from various towns in South Texas seems highly improbable.

This ethnic political revolt has been directed at winning elected positions of power. Many of these small businessmen and professionals come from working-class backgrounds themselves, but in the eyes of the Mexicano proletariat, they are now well-off, established *ricos*. In any grand scheme of classes, almost none of them are bourgeois or own the means of production, but in the community class structure, they are well above workers in education, income, and status.

Culturally, this emerging Mexicano petty bourgeoisie is invariably bilingual and bicultural. The Mexicano middle class shares many mainstream values—e.g., hard work, entrepreneurship, cleanliness, and thrift—with Anglos. Its expressive ethnic cultural practices (e.g., speech, music, folklore, dance, and food) retain a distinctly Mexican-American style, however. In this sense, middle-class North Town Mexicanos are still culturally quite similar to the working-class North Town Mexicanos.

What has the Mexicano proletariat learned from all of this? Among some Mexicanos there is now a sharper understanding of class exploitation. A young working-class Mexicano put it to me this way: "These politicians are all in it for the money. The Mexicanos are the same as the Anglos. I don't give a damn. They don't make things any better for me. I still gotta find a job and survive. Nothing has really changed for me that my father and his father before him didn't see."

What one finds in talking to Mexicanos who have not made it economically is a view that they have been oppressed by the rich. Ultimately, the civil rights movement was the liberal, "bourgeois revolution" or revolt that created a greater class consciousness among the Mexicano workers left behind. As the American political system successfully incorporates the civil rights movement's leaders, it also unmasks their theory of racial oppression as only part of the story. While pluralists may celebrate the present durability of bourgeois democracy, leftists will take heart in the fact that a general condition of political rule has been established where the brown elite now acts out of the same class interests that the white elite acted out of in the old racial order. This clarifies the class interests, and class exploitation remains after racial exploitation has been dismantled and reduced. Although not necessarily an intended effect of the Mexicano civil rights movement, this may prove to be its most lasting accomplishment.

The Impact of the Chicano Movement on the
Southwestern Racial Order

What are racial orders and what does this case teach us about the decline of racial orders and racial attitudes in the Southwest and in general? From a class perspective, capitalist racial orders in the heart of the world's most advanced capitalist society are actually archaic systems of organizing labor and social life. Such systems are best characterized as dual systems of exploitation organized by a particular ruling class, whites in this case, to preserve and protect their position of privilege.

Racial orders that privilege one group over another are actually irrational, inefficient ways of organizing a capitalist production system. Organizing labor markets and production by race wastes the talent of the oppressed group and promotes corruption and incompetence in the privileged group. Such a practice also reduces the distribution of wealth, hence the rates of consumption in the oppressed group. Moreover, such dual systems of oppression can become politically unstable when oppressed groups demand that irrational racial privilege be abolished. At some point, capitalists themselves, particularly the national ruling class, and even some local and regional capitalists, may move to modernize or abolish these archaic forms of organizing labor and social life. The political privilege of various regional groups is not necessary for the general development of American capitalism.

Greenberg's comparative study of capitalist racial orders provides us with some important theorizing on how racial orders generally persist and change as capitalist societies develop.[12] He suggests three fundamental factors that determine how such racial orders persist: (1) the strength of the dominant business challenge to traditional racial hegemony; (2) the resources and coherence of the racial state; and (3) the strength of the subordinate sector challenged (i.e., the working class). Greenberg emphasizes studying specific class actors by studying the ideology and actions of their major organizations, the chambers of commerce, labor unions, formal political parties.

Several important historical descriptions of the Southwestern region's racial system as an internal colony document the patterns of economic and racial inequality and exploitation.[13] Finally, a colleague of Greenberg's, David Montejano, has begun to conceptualize how racial orders in South Texas vary and work at the community level.[14] Montejano labels the racial pattern he finds in South Texas "frustrated apartheid." He suggests that different types of communities, ranching versus farming, had different systems of labor control. He contends that until the 1940's agricultural communities used the most repressive systems of labor management. He also suggests that the most extreme forms of repression were not very successful, which our description of the post-thirties labor migrations confirms.

279

Although Montejano does not explicitly compare racial orders in the Southwest to those in the Deep South, one is left with the feeling that "apartheid" South Texas–style was not very enduring or effective. I would like to pick up on that theme and elaborate a number of factors that made South Texas racial orders easier to dismantle than those in the Deep South.

Generally, race relations in the Southwest lacked the historical depth of the Deep South's apartheid-like race relations, i.e., the progression of slavery, Northern-led Reconstruction, the white Southern reaction to Reconstruction, and the ultimate creation of a ruthless system of segregation. The Southern system was marked by near total social segregation, complete political disenfranchisement, and considerable organized violence and terror by the Ku Klux Klan and the White Citizens' Councils. Moreover, the racial ideology of white superiority was rooted in biblical texts and the pseudo-science of social Darwinism. The history of the Winter Garden region records Klan activity in the 1920's, and the Texas Rangers have always been a para-military group marked by racial and class bias toward Mexicanos.[15] Moreover, nineteenth-century Texas history clearly records a number of lynchings and brutal racist attitudes toward Mexicanos.[16] None of this amounts to the same sort of organized, state-supported system of intimidation, lynching, and terror to maintain racial segregation found in the Deep South, however.

Present-day North Town Anglos do not evoke biblical rationales or crude versions of Social Darwinism to justify their racial superiority, whereas many whites I interviewed in Mississippi were still very devout segregationists.[17] However, North Town Anglos do express a belief in the cultural superiority of Protestant Anglo-Saxon culture to Catholic Hispanic culture. They emphasize the superiority of Anglo practices of child rearing, marriage, family life, food, economic entrepreneurship, and general leadership. There is little doubt that Anglos still stereotype brown people as a lower class that tends to be less moral, dirtier, louder, and more drunken and undisciplined. These are, of course, the same class biases that the white bourgeoisie usually expresses about the white working class. The prejudices expressed are usually a mixture of racial and class biases, which discourage intimate social contact, deep friendships, and marriage. Racist ideology against "darker races" has never been as fanatically subscribed to in the Southwest as in the Deep South, De León's and Montejano's fine works notwithstanding.[18]

From a class perspective, the historical composition and recomposition of class relationships in the Southwestern rural economies would appear to have several distinct features that have hastened the decline

280

of its racial order. In the South Texas case, it is impossible to understand the underlying class character of the Chicano civil rights movement and the more rapid decline of the racial order without some concept of a reserve labor army. In this case, the permeable U.S.-Mexican border is a crucial factor in the historical recomposition of classes. The possibility of continually reconstructing the Mexican working class with a reserve army of third world labor set up a sixty-year class dialectic that spawned a more conciliatory class pattern than that found in the Deep South.

As Montejano suggests and our description of the patterns of labor migration shows, the Mexicano rural proletariat, although lacking any organized farm workers' union, was difficult to control.[10] Montejano finds a few patterns of legal controls of labor, but the major factor has always been the citizenship status of Mexicanos and their family members. The history of the Southwest is marked by periodic deportations, repatriation movements, and reprisals in the Mexicano communities. The repressive side of life near the border has been well documented and is, no doubt, one of the major forms of social control of the Mexicano working class.

The other side of that story, however, is the extraordinary capacity of the Mexicano labor migrants from South Texas to organize themselves to find relatively better work in the North, thus playing the Northern capitalists off against Southern *patrones*. From the 1930's on, the Southern farmers and ranchers were forced to lobby for an open border and a *bracero* program so that they might reconstruct a cheap, controllable labor force based on third world labor. In addition, they had to make major concessions to many of the settled, local Mexicano citizens to assure fall and winter laborers. Many North Town Mexicanos became a kind of labor aristocracy that managed the illegals, *braceros*, and less fortunate locals, and the machinery and irrigation systems for the local *patrones*. A rigid system of legal controls or pass system was impossible to impose on these enterprising Mexicanos. Ultimately, the final solution of capitalist agriculture was to mechanize as much of the production process as possible, to replace living labor with machine labor.

Apparently, the same sort of massive migration occurred among rural blacks, but they appear to have stayed up North in much larger numbers, and the agriculture of the Deep South did not convert into large mechanized feedlots and vegetable farms the way the Winter Garden did.[20] Moreover, some heavy industry and textiles relocated in the Deep South and provided a measure of secondary industrialization for some areas. The proximity of the border and the strong pull among Mexicanos to stay in their Southwest homeland forced local *patrones* into greater accommodations. These accommodations spawned a class of assertive brown entrepreneurs that was missing in similar rural black communities.[21]

The enormous pressure of this aggressive, relatively successful Mexican-American proletariat led, therefore, to a pattern of class accommodations and alliances among the Anglo and Mexicano elites. One can see early, unique class mediations of the color line in various Southwestern communities. The curious ideology of a "Hispanic mythology," which is shared by both Anglo, and Mexicano elites, developed in older rural and urban communities and apparently much of the state of New Mexico.[22] Anglo and Mexicano elites constructed a myth of cultural origin that emphasized the Mexicano elite's European high culture origins. Unlike Afro-Americans, Mexican-Americans can claim a connection with white Western European civilization. Hispanics, sometimes regarded as "colored" and sometimes as "white" in the Southwest, are descendants of a Mediterranean, Christian civilization. De León's study of nineteenth-century Tejano society argues that Anglos in this period considered the Spanish high culture connection negative and inferior to Anglo-Saxon culture.

In the twentieth century, however, this high culture connection is evoked to distinguish the Mexicano elite from Mexican *peones* and their more Indian peasant culture. In this view of culture, the Mexicano proletariat becomes a "low-status ethnic group" and the more Hispanic Mexicano, supposedly with lighter skin, more correct Spanish, more formal education, and a more European penchant for entrepreneurship and business, becomes a "high-status ethnic group." This fusion of cultural and class factors into a kind of "high-status ethnic" makes possible a sharing of political power and racial intermarriage, at least in older border towns and cities. Concessions and incorporation of the Mexicano elite occur without the wholesale dismantling of the old racial order or racial prejudices toward the more "Indian" Mexicano proletariat.

This fusion of an interracial elite makes possible the general practice of "sponsored political enfranchisment," a practice more common in South Texas politics than in Southern politics. The classic political machines of the lower Rio Grande Valley have long included important Mexicano lieutenants as well as organized groups of Mexicano voters.[23] I found similar patterns in the Winter Garden region. As the petty bourgeoisie of these small towns develops, it too becomes a political intermediary for Anglos. This segment of the Mexicano community is also sponsored in a variety of ways, e.g., loans for their businesses, transfers for their children into the Anglo schools, and appointments to various local government committees and boards.

Unlike in the border towns, however, social segregation remained in North Town, and racial intermarriage and extensive socializing were never encouraged. The class alliances of elites in North Town apparently preserved the racial distinctions to a higher degree than in border towns. The Hispanic myth of origin was rarely evoked; consequently, the early North Town Mexicano elite, although often politically aligned with the Anglo ruling class, never perceived itself as culturally superior to the people. This more partial class mediation of political incorporation and racial segregation made the Winter Garden region far more responsive to the cultural nationalism of the Raza Unida Party. In the lower Rio Grande Valley where the well-to-do Mexicanos were more structurally assimilated and accepted as a "high-status ethnic group," the party was far less successful in mobilizing the Mexicano people. Both Valley and Winter Garden Mexicano elites were far more politically and culturally incorporated, however, than the black elite of the Deep South.

Comparing the recomposition of classes in the developing agricultural economy of North Town to a small rural Mississippi town, a rather different pattern emerges.[24] The rural economy of a comparable small cotton-producing Mississippi town was never transformed into a productive commercial agricultural region like the South Texas Winter Garden. Consequently, the local white ruling class never had to make the kinds of political concessions that were made to the emerging petty bourgeoisie of North Town. The black petty bourgeoisie of this small Mississippi town was less needed as an intermediary class to control the labor and votes of the black proletariat. In a stagnant economic situation the black proletariat was politically weaker and more disorganized. Consequently, until the sixties civil rights movement, blacks were completely disenfranchised in this town. They outmigrated in proportionately greater numbers and were not constantly infused with new third world proletarians. After cotton collapsed, local blacks became a surplus population that was managed through a ruthless system of terror run by the local White Citizens' Council and the Ku Klux Klan. As Greenberg demonstrates in several cases, without any real economic development, the most extreme white racists control the political state at all administrative levels.[25] They do not need to make any class concessions.

Such was clearly not the case in North Town, and other studies of this region and the lower Rio Grande Valley suggest a rate of evolutionary change and class concessions absent in rural Mississippi. Ultimately, the violent confrontations of the sixties and the force of the national state have dismantled the legal dimensions of the Deep South's racial order and have enfranchised blacks. This has not led to the breakdown of racial segregation or to the softening of racial attitudes that one sees in the everyday cultural practices of North Town, however.

This thesis about the role of a strong proletariat in the dismantling of the racial order in a developing capitalist agricultural region needs further testing, however. Deep South communities that are developing rather than declining must also be compared with the Southwestern communities. The recomposition of classes and the emergence of a more enfranchised, integrated, local black petty bourgeoisie should also occur in such communities, as it has in North Town. Over a period of time, such class mediations should also undermine the caste-like character of everyday black-white race relations. Of course, the extreme racial ideology in Mississippi and the power of white segregationists in the state to preserve a racial order, as Greenberg suggests, are factors that can slow the effect of capitalist development and a strong proletariat to force change.

This study merely suggests that the American racial orders of the rural South and Southwest are changing at different rates, and that the rate of change in the Southwest may be much greater than observers realize. The Chicano civil rights movement, although less dramatic and publicized than the black civil rights movement, has nevertheless engendered considerable evolutionary change. Although it has never been explicitly a working-class movement, the underlying dynamic of class conflict is undermining the existing racial order. A more class-conscious group of political actors may ultimately emerge in the Southwest because of its more extended process of class conflict and agricultural development.

But what of the racial attitudes of people in this region? As the legal structures of racism have tumbled, how do Mexicanos and Anglos feel about each other? On my return visits to North Town, I made an effort to talk to as many people as possible about their general views of race relations. A variety of feelings were expressed, but generally North Towners believe the racial confrontations of the early seventies and again in 1980 were an educational process that eroded racist feelings and stereotypes. Most North Towners say the worst excesses of racism are gone and that the main problem is a small number of "rednecks" and "brownnecks" in each community. Anglos, particularly the younger, educated ones, more readily admit that the town's racist past leaves much to be desired. Few of them angrily defend the past or talk of

284

La Raza as a communist plot or criminal conspiracy. Most North Town Anglos now say that it is inevitable that Mexicanos must hold the majority of the leadership positions, and most no longer expect to be able to control Mexicano voters through brokers. They know Mexicano *políticos* seek to be and are autonomous actors, not sponsored, subordinate leaders.

The issue for many Anglos is finding Mexicanos who will be "reasonable" toward Anglo interests and rights and not "anti-Anglo." The fear of retribution and revenge for the past still concerns many North Town Anglos, and their trust of Mexicano leaders is still a fragile thing. One can also find Anglos who have not changed much in their racial views. Some younger Anglos back from college say North Town is still a "redneck town" and describe their relatives' prejudice toward not only *La Raza*, the political movement, but Mexicanos in general. Outspokenly liberal Anglos express deep frustration with their own people and say the older generation will never change, that the best one can hope for is more tolerance and acceptance of rule by law. I was impressed with what younger Anglos had to say, however, about the racial situation. Some have real friends in the Mexicano community, a sense of past inequalities, and a greater willingness to live together peacefully and equally.

Mexicanos also express a variety of opinions about race relations. The majority feel that things are changing for the better. The most commonly mentioned sign of this is the way youths from both races openly hang out together at drive-ins and openly date one another. Others mention the greater respect shown to them in public by Anglos. One Mexicano educator put it particularly well:

> It's more comfortable now to be a Mexican. It's all right to eat Mexican food and listen to Mexican music and speak like a Mexican. It's kind of like coming out of a closet, or some dark place. This little redneck place still isn't Laredo or San Antonio, but it's just more comfortable now. I don't have to give a damn what some *bolillo* thinks anymore.

Many of the emerging middle-class professionals also express disinterest in making a racial fight out of politics. They talk about improving life in North Town for the "community" not for *la raza*. A prominent Mexicano leader put it this way:

> We, and I, have come full circle. I grew up in South Texas accepting racism. I went off to college and joined the *movimiento* and rallied against racism. Now I find myself working hard to improve this community for

285

both Anglos and Mexicanos. There isn't any other way. We all have to learn to live together.

Some prominent Ciudadanos leaders are now busy running their businesses and sending their children to college. They describe their interest in politics as still there but more accommodating to a slower, gradual process of change. They express optimism about the future for themselves and their children. Others, working-class Mexicanos, say the gringos do not "pick on people much anymore," but that life is still hard.

Many Mexicanos also portray the present racial harmony as easily disrupted. No one seems to believe that old personal and racial animosities have magically died. Most people believe that racial attitudes have "mellowed" and that there is a greater willingness to cooperate, but they say that extremists on both sides will never change. All North Towners hope no one will stir up old, bitter resentments, but most do expect more trouble. After so many years of listening to North Towners, they strike me as grizzled veterans, warriors in the slowly ebbing battles of a war already lost but still to be fought. So-called experts on racial orders and racial prejudice, to my knowledge, have no theories to explain how long it takes for ingrained racial attitudes to be transformed. My best guess is what North Towners tell me. It will probably take several more generations of people from both ethnic groups asserting their right to be treated with respect and dignity. Such a dialogue will gradually reduce irrational group prejudice. A real beginning has been made, however, and perhaps a hundred years from now North Towners will read this tale as a curious and strange chapter in American history.

[1] De la Garza, Rodolfo, and David Vaughn. "The Political Socialization of Chicano Elites: A Generational Approach." *Social Science Quarterly* 65, no. 2 (June 1984): 290–307.

[2] Piven, Francis Fox, and Richard A. Cloward. *Poor People's Movements: Why They Succeed, How They Fail.* New York: Vintage Press, 1977. Marable, Manning. *Race, Reform and Rebellion: The Second Reconstruction in Black America, 1945–1982.* Jackson: University Press of Mississippi, 1984.

[3] Dahl, Robert. *Pluralistic Democracy in the United States.* Chicago: Rand McNally, 1967.

[4] Zamora, Emilio. "Chicano Socialist Labor Activity in Texas, 1900–1920." *Aztlán* 6, no. 2 (Summer 1975): 221–236. Nelson-Cisneros, Víctor. "La clase trabajadora en Tejas, 1920–1940." *Aztlán* 6, no. 2 (Summer 1975): 239–265.

[5] Marable, Manning. *Ibid.* Carson, Clayborne. *In Struggle: SNCC and the Black Awakening of the 1960's.* Cambridge: Harvard University Press, 1981.

6 Trujillo, Larry. "Race, Class, Labor and Community: A Local History of Capitalist Development." *Review* 4, no. 3 (Winter 1981): 371–396.

7 Shockley, John S. *Chicano Revolt in a Texas Town.* Notre Dame: University of Notre Dame Press, 1974. Smith, W. Elwood. "Mexicano Resistance to Schooled Ethnicity: Ethnic Student Power in South Texas, 1930–1970." Ph.D. dissertation, University of Texas at Austin, 1978. Smith, W. Elwood, and Douglas Foley. "Mexicano Resistance to Schooling in a South Texas Colony." *Education and Urban Society* 10, no. 2 (February 1978): 47–61. O'Brennan, Junius, and Nopal Smith. *The Crystal Icon.* Austin: Galahad Press, 1981. Gutiérrez, José Angel. "Toward a Theory of Community Organization in a Mexican-American Community in South Texas." Ph.D. dissertation, University of Texas at Austin, 1976. Navarro, Armando. "The Evolution of Chicano Politics." *Aztlán* 5, nos. 1 & 2 (1974): 57–83. Andrade, Sally (ed.). *Chicano Mental Health: The Case of Crystal.* Hogg Foundation for Mental Health. Austin: University of Texas, 1978.

8 Poulantzas, Nicos. *Classes in Contemporary Society.* London: Verso, 1978.

9 O'Connor, James. *The Fiscal Crises of the State.* New York: St. Martin's Press, 1973.

10 Smith, W. Elwood. *Ibid.*

11 Kornblum, William. *Blue Collar Community.* Chicago: University of Chicago Press, 1974.

12 Greenberg, Stanley B. *Race and Class in Capitalist Development: Comparative Perspectives.* New Haven: Yale University Press, 1980.

13 Acuña, Rodolfo. *Occupied America: A History of Chicanos.* 3d ed. New York: Harper & Row, 1986. Barrera, Mario. *Race and Class in the Southwest: A Theory of Racial Inequality.* Notre Dame: University of Notre Dame Press, 1979.

14 Montejano, David. *Anglos and Mexicans in the Making of Texas, 1836–1986.* Austin: University of Texas Press, 1987.

15 Paredes, Américo. *With His Pistol in His Hand: A Border Ballard and Its Hero.* Austin: University of Texas Press, 1958; reprint, 1971.

16 De León, Arnoldo. *The Tejano Community, 1836–1900.* Albuquerque: University of New Mexico Press, 1982. De León, Arnoldo. *They Called Them Greasers: Anglo Attitudes toward Mexicans in Texas, 1821–1900.* Austin: University of Texas Press, 1983.

17 Foley, Douglas. "Notes from a Field Study of Fayette, Mississippi, and Mayor Charles Evers." 1981.

18 De León, Arnoldo. *The Tejano Community.* Montejano, David. *Ibid.*

19 Montejano, David. *Ibid.*

20 Marable, Manning. *Ibid.* Raper, Theodore. *Rape of the Peasantry.* New York: Atheneum, 1968.

21 Foley, Douglas. *Ibid.*

22 Juárez, Anna. "The Historical Development of Social and Ethnic Stratification in Laredo, Texas, 1750–1900." M.A. report, Department of Anthropology, University of Texas at Austin, 1983. García, Richard. "Class, Consciousness, and Ideology: The Mexican American Community of San Antonio, Texas, 1930–1940." *Aztlán* 9 (1978): 23–69. Sánchez, George. *Forgotten People: A Study of New Mexicans.* Albuquerque: University of New Mexico Press, 1940. Taylor, Paul S. *An American-Mexican Frontier: Nueces County, Texas.* New York: Russell & Russell, 1971.

(Originally published by University of North Carolina Press, 1934.)

23 Shelton, Edgar. "Political Conditions among Texas Mexicans along the Rio Grande." M.A. thesis, University of Texas at Austin, 1946. Anders, Evan. *Boss Rule in South Texas: The Progressive Era*. Austin: University of Texas Press, 1982.

24 Foley, Douglas. *Ibid*.

25 Greenberg, Stanley B. *Ibid*.

288

APPENDIX A

Data Tables

Table 1.1

General Population Trends in North County
1910 to 1970

Year	Mexican-American	Anglo American	% Mex.	All Total
1910	4,320	4,575	48.6	8,895
1920	5,244	4,052	56.4	9,296
1930	5,869	3,542	62.4	9,411
1940	NA	NA	NA	NA
1950	6,250	4,107	60.3	10,351
1960	6,250	3,862	61.8	10,112
1970	7,711	3,448	69.1	11,159

1910–1970 Trends Summarized

% Population Chg. Mexican-American	% Population Chg. Anglo-American	% Population Chg. All — Net Migration
44.0%	−24.6%	20.3%

Source: U.S. Census

TABLE 1.2

Farms in North County
Classified by Tenure: 1900 to 1969*

Year	Owner-Operated†		Manager	Farm Tenants				
				Share††	Cropper	Share-Cash	Cash	Unspecified
1900	294		16	60	—		24	—
1910	337		14	538	—	6	7	—
1920	1981		4	829	192	—	16	5
	Full	*Part*		(All Tenancy Combined)**				
1954	269	145	3		124			
1959	181	151	4		88			
1964	194	122	—		50			
1969	268	149	—		101			

* Data not available for intervening years.

** Tables for these years (1964, 1969) list all types of tenancy together, and divide ownership into "full" and "part."

† 1900 Category of "part-owner" is included under category of "owner."

†† Category of "standing renter" is close to "share-tenant" and so is included there.

SOURCES: 1900—12th Census of U. S., 1900, Vol. 5 Agriculture, Pt. 1, Farms, Livestock, and Animal Products, Table 10.
1910—13th Census of U. S., 1910, Vol. VII, Agriculture, Reports by States, with Statistics for Counties, Table 2.
1920—14th Census of U. S., 1920, Vol. VI, Part 2, Agriculture.
1954—United States Census of Agriculture, Texas, Vol. I, Part 26, 1955.
1959—United States Census of Agriculture, Texas, Vol. I, Part 37, 1960.
1964—United States Census of Agriculture, Texas, Vol. I, Part 37 (?) 1965.
1969—United States Census of Agriculture, Texas

TABLE 1.3

Crop and Livestock Data for North County
1900 to 1969

COUNTY	Staple Cash Crops			Perishable Cash Crops			FORAGES	LIVESTOCK		
	Cotton	Peanuts	Grains	Vegetables *($Value)	Fruits & Nuts[1]	Potatoes	Hay, Feed	Cattle (#) (number head)	All Other (#) (number head)	$ Value all Livestock
North	(Bales)	(lbs)	(tons)	($Value)	(tons)	(tons)	(tons)			
1900—output	2,616	115	709	$ 3,045	—	13	6,539	53,927	15,263	$ 1,089,786
acreage	13,764a	2a	5,600a	74a	—	8a	3,606a			
1910—output	6,822	11	132	$ 6,498	3	—	3,158	13,335	3,656	$ 352,337[2]
acreage	52,057a	27a	3,123a	330a	—	—	3,909a			
1920—output	4,303	11	8,667	$ 208,222	20	332	16,304	33,172	5,310	$ 2,776,275
acreage	55,349a	60a	15,210a	762a	—	218a	11,323a			
1935—output	713	1,330	5,690	$ 6,315	7	27	9,353	45,522	12,481	no figures
acreage	6,056a	8,975a	5,097a	2,894a	292a	18a	16,207a			
1945—output	—	4,325	5,992	$ 633,193	35	—	1,601	45,857	9,388	$ 2,567,979
acreage	—	19,395a	16,306a	11,500a	337a	—	6,800a			
1954—output	3,002	2,114	5,343	$ 195,880	30	994	14,474	46,074	10,469	$ 2,048,953
acreage	5,539a	10,961a	9,569a	5,093a	52a	154a	13,032a			
1950—output	3,260	7,641	29,534	$ 505,904	83	862	8,602	38,354	7,998	$ 3,351,227
acreage	5,539a	13,444a	25,451a	6,178a	114a	226a	3,712a			
1964—output	3,772	19,064	15,256	$1,134,099	8	1,813	24,975	48,686	3,874	$ 3,379,741
acreage	3,134a	16,707a	15,017a	8,698a	32a	203a	10,550a			
1969—output	2,084	21,960	415,989	$1,527,844	22	2,557	9,375	68,424	8,692	$11,621,715[3]
acreage	2,573a	17,596	22,462a	10,193a	338a	397a	6,090a			

1 "Acres" for Fruits and Nuts = "Land in fruit and nut trees"
2 "Sale of all live animals" as opposed to $value of animals in other years
3 Figure includes poultry sales for this year.

SOURCES: Table 1.3 Crop and Livestock Data for North County, 1900 to 1969

1. 1900: Agricultural Census Report, Vol. VI, Pt. 2, Crops & Irrigation, Sections I–VI, Tables 10, 15, 22. Livestock, Vol. V, Pt. 1, Table 35.

2. 1910: Department of Commerce, Bureau of the Census-Agriculture. Vol. VII, Table 4. Livestock, County Table 2.

3. 1920: Department of Commerce, Bureau of the Census-Agriculture. Vol. VI, Part 2. County Table 2, 4.

4. 1935: Census of Agriculture, Vol. I, II, Pt. 2. County Table 2, 3, 4, 6.

5. 1945: Census of Agriculture, Vol. I, Pt. 26, Table II, Part 1, 2, 3.

6. 1954: United States Census of Agriculture, Texas, Vol. I, Pt. 26, County Table 7, 9.

7. 1959: United State Census of Agriculture, Texas, Vol. I, Pt. 37, County Table 4, 7, 8, 13, 24, 11.

8. 1964: U.S. Department of Commerce, Social and Economic Statistics Administration, Bureau of the Census. Vol. 1, Part 37, Sec. 2. Table #4, 8, 7, 13, 24.

9. 1969: U.S. Department of Commerce, Social and Economic Statistics Administration, Bureau of the Census, Vol. 1, Part 37, Sec. 2, Table #4, 8, 7, 13, 24.

DEFINITIONS:

GRAINS: includes corn, sorghum grain, oats, kafir corn & milo maize, broom corn, wheat (add in 1945), barley and flaxseed (add in 1959).

VEGETABLES: garden variety.

FRUITS & NUTS: apples, peaches & nectarines, pears, plums & prunes, grapes, figs, oranges & grapefruits (add in 1934)*, pecans.

POTATOES: Irish, sweet, plain, yams (add in 1920).

* In 1934 oranges and grapefruits were reported in "Boxes" for which we could find no conversion to Tons, so they were not included in that year.

TABLE 2.1

Median Family Income and Median Education, With Poverty[1] Between Ethnic Groups in Three South Texas Counties

Counties	Median School yrs. complete (25 years and over)		Median Family Income (dollars)		Percent of all families less than poverty threshold
	Spanish	Total	Spanish	Total	Spanish
North 1960	2.3	6.5	1666	2676	80.7
1970	4.5	8.8	3724	4926	51.6
South 1960	1.4	4.8	1585	2296	80.1
1970	3.5	7.0	3000	4056	65.2
Aztlán 1960	2.3	4.6	1732	2314	82.3
1970	3.1	5.2	3984	4981	52.7

Poverty level threshold is measured by the U.S. Census at $3888. The computation used here is a more conservative threshold of $2999. This has made the computation easier and probably accounts for regional variation.

Source: U.S. Bureau of the Census. 1970, General Social and Economic Characteristics, Texas, PC(1) C-45, Tables 133, 124, 120. 1960, Characteristics of the Population, Vol. 1, Part 45, Tables 83, 86; Selected Reports, Persons of Spanish Surname, Texas, Table 14.

TABLE 3.1

Rural-Urban Migration Rates
for North County, 1930 to 1970

	Rural	Urban	Percentage Change
1930	72.7	27.3	
1940	65.6	34.4	7.1
1950	56.8	43.2	8.8
1960	51.1	48.9	5.7
1970	48.7	51.3	2.4

Total percent of change from 1930 to 1970: 24%.

Source:
> 1940 U.S. Population Census.
> 1950 U.S. Population Census, Vol. II, Characteristics of the Population, part 43, Texas, Table 5.
> 1960 U.S. Population Census, Vol. II, Characteristics of the Population, part 43, Texas, Table 6.
> 1970 U.S. Population Census, General Social and Economic Characteristics, Texas PC(1)—C45, Table 43.

TABLE 3.2

Number and Acreage of Irrigated Farms
in North County
1954 to 1969

Years	Number of Irrigated Farms	Proportion of all farms (%)	Land in Irrigated Farms (acres)	Average Size of Farm (acres)
1954	41	7.6	69,371	1692.0
1959	91	21.5	142,265	1563.4
1964	not given	not given	not given	not given
1969	129	24.9	212,855	1650.0

Source: U.S. Department of Agriculture, U.S. Bureau of the Census.

TABLE 3.3

Fertility in North County by Ethnic Group, 1970

CHILDREN BORN	Spanish-Surname	Anglo
women 35–44, ever married	331	209
children born	1,865	588
per 1,000 women ever married (%)	5.6%	2.8%

SOURCE: U.S. Bureau of the Census. General Social and Economic Characteristics, Texas PC(1)–C45, Tables 120, 130.

[1] Anglo figures computed by subtracting Spanish-Surname (table 130) from County total (table 120).

TABLE 3.4

Infant, Neonatal and Fetal Death Rates for North County and Texas, 1970.

	Infant	Neonatal	Fetal
North County	27.2	13.6	23.8
Texas	20.8	14.0	15.9

SOURCE: Unpublished data on live births, infant, neonatal, maternal and fetal death rates and ratios per 1,000 live births by county and city of residence. Texas Health Department. Austin, Texas, 1970.

TABLE 3.5

Spanish-Surname Population of North County by Nativity and Parentage*
1950–1970

Nativity and Parentage	Population 1950	Population 1960	1970	1950	Population 1960	1970	% Gain loss	Absolute Change 1950–1970
Natives of Native Parentage	5542	5614	7711	88.7	89.9	92.2	3.5	1569
Natives of Foreign or Mixed Parentage	0	17	0	0.0	0.3	0.0	0.0	0
Foreign Born	708	619	600	11.3	9.9	7.8	−3.5	108
Total	6250	6250	7711	100.0	100.0	100.0		

* Census data is not specified in each category, especially "natives of foreign or mixed parentage." However, the data does present a "crude" indication of migratory changes.

SOURCE: U.S. Bureau of the Census. (1) 1950, Special Report, P.E. #3c, Persons of Spanish Surname, Texas, table 7; (2) 1960, Special Report, Persons of Spanish Surname, Texas, table 15; (3) 1970, General Social and Economic Characteristics, Texas, PC(1)–C45, table 130.

TABLE 3.6

Out-Migrating Rates and College Attendance of Mexicano and Anglo High School Graduates in Two South Texas Towns.

Year & Ethnic Unit	Total all	Never left	Left			% Leaving
			came back	came back & left again	Left & Never Came back	
1940 Class	27	4	2	6	15	77.8%
Anglos	25	4	2	5	14	76.0
Mexican-American	2	0	0	1	1	100.0
1948 Class	24	3	1	6	14	83.3
Anglo	21	2	1	5	13	85.7
Mexican-American	3	1	0	1	1	66.6
1955 Class	30	4	0	4	22	86.7
Anglo	19	2	0	2	15	89.5
Mexican-American	11	2	0	2	7	81.8
1958 Class	38	4	3	4	27	81.6
Anglo	23	0	1	4	17	91.3
Mexican-American	15	4	2	0	10	66.6
1964 Class	46	6	1	4	35	84.8
Anglo	25	4	0	4	17	84.0
Mexican-American	21	2	1	0	18	85.7
1969 Class	43	11	2	4	26	69.8
Anglo	22	5	1	2	13	68.2
Mexican-American	21	6	1	2	13	71.4

Source: primary research, Don E. Post.

TABLE 4.1

Welfare Assistance in Two South Texas Counties

County	Total $	Old Age Assistance	Number Families	Aid to Families with Dependent Children	Number Families	Number Children	Aid to Blind	Number Blind	Aid to Permanently & Totally Disabled	Number Disabled
North										
1972	662,487	339,719	522	275,912	230	600	6,343	7	40,513	51
1971	660,043	383,661	521	232,266	183	523	5,932	5	38,184	47
1970	576,909	371,846	492	165,362	146	444	6,314	7	33,387	46
1969	453,461	331,793	477	84,409	87	269	7,728	9	29,531	44
1965	319,838	264,302	369	36,363	33	122	7,189	10	11,984	17
1960	281,268	198,143	310	51,625	49	150	4,927	8	6,573	11
1955	195,984	128,627	276	63,051	85	252	4,306	11	—	—
1950	9,799.26	7,228.50	231	2,325.76	51	138	245.00	9	—	—
South										
1972	439,639	218,275	307	172,374	124	347	7,162	8	41,828	63
1971	453,881	249,143	310	161,440	120	374	7,333	7	35,965	49
1970	406,182	246,362	302	120,690	93	287	8,320	8	30,810	48
1969	323,953	226,563	302	68,282	64	199	6,936	8	22,082	37
1965	210,168	139,903	201	56,162	55	151	7,097	9	7,006	11
1960	181,125	128,606	200	44,292	49	127	5,872	8	2,355	4
1955	137,525	83,400	179	49,288.50	66	188	4,837	10	—	—
1950	7,606.32	4,918	154	2,381.82	55	144	306.50	9	—	—

[1] Source: Annual Report of the State Department of Public Welfare, To the Governor of Texas, Fiscal year September 1, 1971–August 31, 1972.

TABLE 4.2

Occupational Distribution* of Ethnic Groups in North
and South Counties, 1970

Occupations	North County		South County	
	Spanish Surname	Anglo	Spanish Surname	Anglo
Professional & technical	3.1	21.2	2.9	25.8
Managers & Adm.	5.0	10.3	4.9	18.0
Clerical & Sales	10.1	23.7	10.9	13.0
Craftsmen & foremen	13.8	11.4	11.1	13.0
Semi-skilled	17.4	10.1	26.2	1.9
Farmers & farm managers	5.9	15.9	2.0	13.2
Farm workers	23.7	4.6	16.5	3.0
Service workers	14.8	2.8	15.5	11.9
Private household workers	6.0	0	10.0	0.2
TOTAL	100.0	100.0	100.0	100.0
	(1998)	(1353)	(889)	(462)

* distribution occupationally of all employed 16 years and over.

Source: U.S. Bureau of the Census. 1970, General Social and Economic Characteristics, PC(1)–C45, Tables 122, 132.

APPENDIX B
A COMMENTARY ON CULTURAL NATIONALISM
AND CLASS THEORY

In this appendix I would like to indicate what kind of class analysis this study represents. An extensive debate over dependency theory as a model for explaining Chicano history and politics has been waged.[1] Numerous Chicano scholars now argue that an inadequate understanding of class theory has led cultural nationalists of the Chicano movement into a number of uncritical political practices. These political practices were flawed because their model of an internal colony of racial oppression is flawed. Class theorists contend that this model provides too limited an understanding of how class societies work. Several scholars have sought to retain the internal colony metaphor but substantially revise it with class segmentation, world systems, and developing capitalist racial orders theories.[2] Finally, Acuña, one of the original Chicano scholars advocating an internal colonial model now frames his analysis in more conventional class categories.[3] As the culturally nationalistic Chicano movement has declined, so, it seems, has the influence of its theory of racial oppression and ethnic politics.

This brief essay cannot do justice to the complexity of these debates, but I would like to indicate what the general weaknesses and strengths of a cultural nationalist view of race and class are. This discussion will indicate what I learned from the cultural nationalist perspective that enriches class analysis. Having explored the internal colony perspective, I will then contrast my perspective on studying capitalist racial orders with David Montejano's history of South Texas. Our community study of North Town has a great affinity with Montejano's ambitious, excellent historical account, but we also differ on some points worth noting. Our differences suggest variations in ways of doing class analysis. That such theoretical differences exist suggests that the study of Mexican American history is a healthy, emerging field with many new perspectives.

Before critiquing the cultural nationalist perspective on internal colonies, I must define whose perspective I am reviewing. A careful outline of the cultural nationalist currents of thought in Chicano letters would require an intellectual history project well beyond this essay. When I refer to the cultural nationalist view of race and class, I mean the one frequently encountered during fieldwork in the Texas Winter Garden region. José Angel Gutiérrez and Raza Unida Party members frequently articulated this view in Aztlán City. The academic and literary expressions that they most admired were Acuña's original view in *Occupied America* and the poetry of Alurista. My understanding of cultural nationalist thought and the internal colonial model of racial oppression comes largely from fieldwork in the Winter Garden. This might best be read, therefore, as a class critique of the Raza Unida Party's notion of the American capitalist racial order.

The major deficiency in the internal colony metaphor is its lack of any explicit concept of capitalist development and class struggle. Unlike class theory, this version of dependency theory has no value theory of exploitation; therefore, class struggle is not the motor of historical change The internal colony theory's concept of exploitation is one of conquest empires rather than of capitalist production systems organized into antagonistic classes. The colonialism model emphasizes military occupation, force, local elites collaborating with foreign invaders, and racial and cultural prejudice toward the conquered populations. A colony is a kind of spatial, geographical metaphor that suggests "outsiders" conquering a simpler, stable, peaceful people. In this view, local ethnic communities make up a nation-within-a-nation, a ghetto or internal colony largely ruled by outsiders and their lackeys, the acculturated, collaborating local elite. This theory describes the power structure of elites and various general patterns of economic exploitation, but it does not focus enough on the development of the society's mode of production and the resulting class formation.

As previously indicated, our description of North Town as an agricultural hinterland or "internal colony" in a capitalist racial order focuses the analysis around the idea of an organic, ongoing class contradiction or struggle as the motor of historical change. Consequently, we included exhaustive descriptions of how various types of farming and ranching modes of production and their systems of labor control evolved. As previously indicated, the evolution of capitalist agriculture from a semifeudal sharecropper system constructs a restless Mexicano proletariat and a new brown petty bourgeoisie.

In this type of analysis, the idea of an underlying organic process of class conflict postulates an "objective" process of history that class actors "inherit." Their actions, therefore, are always partly conditioned by this past, but they in turn develop an understanding of the structures that determine and bind them and consciously create their own history and culture. In this perspective there are no "great men" of history, only determining historical structures and group processes that break and make new social orders. Cultural nationalists tend to lose sight of the dialectical relationship between determining historical structures and groups of people who reshape the historical circumstances they inherit. Nationalist writings that celebrate cultural heroes and ethnic achievements tend to exaggerate the accomplishments of individuals and groups. They may also confuse reformism with fundamental change of historical social structures.

Extreme versions of cultural nationalism also overemphasize the acculturated, Anglicized character of the Mexicano middle class. The nationalists, a new emerging elite themselves, are competing with the traditional elite for a proletarian following. Their rhetorical criticism of the so-called acculturated middle class obscures their common class interest. It also leads to all sorts of contradictory political practices and miscommunication within Mexicano communities. As I have indicated, at least in expressive cultural terms, the Mexicano middle class and the proletariat are still more similar than different. The process of cultural assimilation *is* generally more advanced in the Mexicano middle class. Ironically, the new petty bourgeois, the cultural nationalists, are more culturally assimilated than are traditional petty bourgeois often labeled *agringados* or *vendidos*. The nationalists' excessive emphasis on acculturation differences ultimately obscures the entire question.

Moreover, the heavy emphasis on elites also tends to highlight the unity, control, and power of the rulers to be oppressive. Focusing on the Anglo ruling class's ruthless, clever use of state powers tends to convey the idea that change flows down from a powerful elite. Acuña's second edition avoids this by stressing working-class resistance, especially as an organized labor movement. The connection, however, between an organic class contradiction and a constantly reconstructed class formation of proletariat, petty bourgeoisie, and bourgeoisie is never quite spelled out. One is left with more of a populist view of classes that tends to romanticize working-class resistance but obscures the political meaning of class developments. This type of class analysis in labor history has been forcefully criticized by Green.[4]

In addition, the internal colonial model also places heavy emphasis on Anglos as a monolithic, invading group of outsiders. This emphasis makes a class analysis of politics and the role of the state impossible. The cultural nationalists view the state as a repressive instrument. In an advanced capitalist democracy the state is a complex welfare bureaucracy subject to class struggle.[5] Anglos running political parties and the bureaucracy of the state may act out of bourgeois liberalism to reform and moderate class and racial interests and capitalism itself, thus creating many moral, fiscal, and legitimacy crises within the state. These are openings that the new ethnic politicians have used skillfully to the advantage of their followers and themselves. None of this complex process can be discussed if one starts with the notion of Anglos as an oppressive group and of the state as their instrument of repression. This undifferentiated, unsubtle model of politics as competing racial groups also tends to glorify the *movimiento* and underplay the class interests of the new ethnic political leaders. It also completely misses the point of how politics works in a pluralistic, bourgeois democracy.

What the welter of new ethnic political organizations across America has done is extremely important, but one must put that in perspective with the longer, more sober perspective of historical class formations. A class analysis describes the "modernizing role" or reactionary role of both the brown and the more liberal white petty bourgeoisie. Contemporary political leaders from *both* ethnic groups have used external state welfare programs to begin dismantling the racial order. Many class mediations and interethnic alliances, from the fifties on, mark this general process of political incorporation and class compromise.

On the other hand, cultural nationalists, both academic theorists and local practitioners, have something to teach class theorists about capitalist societies with archaic racial orders. Their theory reintroduces notions of caste-like ethnic relations, cultural imperialism, and a cultural identity struggle that is lacking in most traditional class theory. The American system of caste-like racial relations specifies numerous rules for everyday intergroup relations outside of work relationships.[6] Beliefs about racial/ethnic superiority dictate rules of marriage, residence, civic participation, use of public space, and a host of everyday social activities. These forms of dominance are not present in all systems of class dominance, and the notion of exploitation in the labor theory of value does not include any historically specific concept of the cultural domination and cultural resistance so characteristic of ethnic national movements.

The major reason for this blind spot in class theory seems to be what some call the "homogenization" thesis. The idea of a universal proletariat, the inevitable proletarianization of all populations under capitalism, is a powerful, sweeping idea. Class theorists often underestimate the durability and utility of particularistic proletarian cultural systems and ideologies. Anthropological works on working-class cultures suggest that even well developed proletarian classes use elements of their traditional, everyday culture to wage their struggles for dignity and group identity and solidarity.[7] Work by Chicano anthropologists also dramatically illustrates such practices as counter-hegemony, resistance, and the strategic use of ethnic cultural forms and practices.[8]

Conventional class theory also usually characterizes proletarian culture as an ideology, i.e., a correct socialist consciousness, a class theory of history. More recent class theorists emphasize, however, that the working class has a culture in the anthropological sense of daily life practices and expressions.[9] The proletariat of the world actually has many forms of historical cultural practice and expression, which reflect different stages of world capitalist development.[10] The culture and dialect of South Texas Mexicanos is partly a product of their struggle against the conditions of poverty and racism in their poor, segregated *barrios*. Their culture is a blend of Mexican tradition and what they construct during their struggle to survive in a hostile American society. The insight in cultural nationalist thought is that the proletariat of a capitalist racial order is subjected to a hegemonic ideology emphasizing *both* the class and the racial superiority of the predominantly white ruling class. This creates an ethnic/racial struggle not only over labor and wages but also over cultural identity.

Cultural nationalists in Aztlán City urge people to resist the ghettoization and stigmatization of the Mexicano way of life and language. They advocated reversing the negative connotations placed on many expressive cultural practices that mark identity, e.g., music, food, dress, dance, and lore. These daily cultural practices of working class or "barrio" culture give meaning to life by locating one in time and space. The struggle was as much over beans, *conjunto* music, code-switching Spanish, and brownness as it was over political power and better wages. The activists of Aztlán City and North Town live in and use this expressive culture. They are able to articulate a very concrete, existential expression of their people's sense of oppression. Cultural nationalism, because it is a much less abstract, less internationalist theory, expresses the Mexicano people's commonsense understanding of their oppression.

With very little political education and consciousness raising, South

304

Texas activists were able to inspire, embolden, and mobilize many Mexicanos to reject public intimidation and political disenfranchisement. We tried to capture this subjective side of the struggle by reporting Mexicanos' feelings about the daily racial degradations of *patrones*, sheriffs, teachers, and storekeepers. A narrower class analysis of production systems, rates of exploitation, and political events simply would not leave a rich enough record of the intense identity struggle that was waged against this capitalist racial order.

Finally, cultural nationalists of the Winter Garden had insights into historically specific contradictions and mediations of the ruling class not found in general class theory. They characterize their own ethnic elite quite negatively as collaborators, traitors to the people. This is partly in response to their use of mainstream consumer culture status symbols to create a distinction between themselves and the working-class culture of the *barrios*. Such practices divide the Mexicano community socially. The Mexicano elite may, therefore, become a model and agent of the dominant society's stigmatization of *barrio* culture. Consequently, this segment of predominantly proletarian communities becomes a part of the cultural imperialism for controlling the people. Conventional class theory's emphasis on control of the production system underplays the importance of such cultural hegemony and the cultural resistance of the working class.

In our community study of a class struggle, we generally included the "cultural" by emphasizing how rooted the struggle was in community institutions such as family, religion, and education. The family was a haven of dignity and the base of economic, spiritual, and political survival. Many observers have made such a case, but we also tried to show how the urbanization of rural families, a direct effect of capitalist agricultural development, engendered new group solidarities and new assertiveness in women and youth. The old patriarchal family underwent many changes as Mexicanos broke down segregation and became politically incorporated. Of course, many traditional beliefs about female domesticity, the value of children, female-centered homes, the importance of extended kin, and male privilege remained.

The emphasis in our class analysis of "cultural politics" was not on particular acculturation rates. We focused on the family as the basis for a cultural and political struggle against a capitalist racial order. Strong family unity was the basis of proletarian dignity and self-worth as well as the basis of upward mobility among the petty bourgeois class. Especially the women struggled against the dominant society's cultural imperialism in the schools and streets long before any males were elected

to political office. Women also have organized a great many of the recent political mobilizations and have fought for new health and social
welfare programs—always in the name of the family and their children.
This emphasis on *la familia* as the basis of the Chicano struggle was, of
course, a key element in Raza Unida's cultural nationalist ideology.
Traditional class theory would underplay such cultural factors.

As indicated, our community study of North Town has a great affinity
with David Montejano's ambitious new history of South Texas.[11] In
many ways his regional study subsumes our history of one community
and illustrates the need for more studies on all levels. Montejano's excellent study retains the notion of conquest or annexation, but he stresses
that an uneven, varied pattern of racial oppression and accommodation
occurred throughout South Texas. He links this uneven transformation
of South Texas racial orders to capitalist agricultural development more
closely than internal colonial theorists do, thus tying racial oppression
more directly to economic changes and the recomposition of social
classes. Montejano phrases this underlying economic transformation of
South Texas in a manner different from conventional class theory, however. He develops a stage theory of ideal types (in the Weberian sense)
of rural societies. He periodizes South Texas history as a succession of
four types of societies: the Mexican hacienda, the Anglo-Mexican ranching, the segregated farm, and the pluralistic urban-industrial. His ty-
pology of rural societies replaces class theories' notion of successive
modes of production: feudal, Asiatic, capitalist, and socialist.

Montejano draws a sharp distinction between nineteenth-century
ranching and twentieth-century farming societies as racial orders. He
emphasizes a common theme in the study of American frontier societies,
the battle between ranchers and farmers over land and labor. However,
in his account, unlike other American historians' treatment of this classic
battle, commercial farmers construct a rigid, repressive racially segregated society to control the Mexicano proletariat. He follows Greenberg's[12] thesis that the early stages of capital development or modernization are often marked by an intensification of racial discrimination.

Montejano notes that some regions of South Texas such as North
Town apparently experienced a smoother, more gradual assimilation of
farmers and merchants into paternalistic Texas ranch societies. He
characterizes these ranch societies as less segregated and repressive.
Apparently in the older ranch counties of the lower Rio Grande Valley
this economic transition was rapid and full of political battles between
ranchers and their political machines and the new reform-oriented farmers and merchants. In the Valley ranchers retreated and created a num-

ber of new counties which preserved their Mexican-based political machines. Montejano attributes this largely to the difference in the pace of change and the "boom style" land schemes in the Rio Grande Valley.

What Montejano seems to overlook in our data is that North Town may be a typical example of his twentieth-century "segregated farm society." The problem with viewing North Town as typical, however, is that our portrayal presents a hybrid of his two ideal types of rural societies. Moreover, we present little evidence that a repressive, apartheid-like labor control system ever existed or worked to control the Mexicano proletariat.

As indicated earlier, North Town agriculture evolved from a semifeudal mode of production to a fully capitalist mode of production over a sixty-year period. We looked at all types of rural production units and found few pure ranchers or farmers. Nearly all landowners had cotton sharecroppers and used temporary crew wage laborers. Even more specialized vegetable farms planted crops and ran cattle, which required a number of permanent, residential workers. Sharecroppers, *vaqueros*, and wage laborers all described this farm society as based on both personalistic *"patronismo"* and racial segregation. Political machines based on the selective controlled participation of Mexicanos emerged. Ranchers, farmers, and merchants all built their political fortunes on controlling the Mexicano vote. Moreover, if there was a period of intensification when growers had an effective repressive labor control system, workers, labor contractors, and growers downplayed it in their accounts. They all, particularly the labor contractors, stressed the autonomy and ingenuity of workers to extract compromises and to go north. This necessitated constantly recomposing the proletariat with Third World labor and, whenever possible, replacing workers with machines. In short, we portrayed these segregated farm societies as being much like Montejano's paternalistic ranch societies until they became more thoroughly capitalist production systems. We were unable to make the sharp distinctions that Montejano does to link types of rural societies with types of labor control systems. We found one emerging, more fully capitalist mode of production replacing the earlier semifeudal, paternalistic mode of production.

Montejano's use of an ideal type society distinction seems to work well for broadly contrasting the nineteenth and twentieth centuries, but this dichotomy overstates the importance and distinctiveness of labor control systems. It also understates the paternalistic character of labor relations in these segregated farm societies. In discussing the contemporary period, Montejano generally tends to characterize the South

307

Texas ethnic political revolts of the sixties and seventies as manifestations of national social movements and structural changes in the state. In his account the urban intelligentsia leads these revolts and makes "forays" into the countryside. This tends to underestimate the grassroots, local character of leadership and the power of the Mexicano proletariat. Greenberg's theory of capitalist racial orders tends to privilege the study of elites and their system of labor control. This type of class analysis studies class recomposition from the top down rather than from the bottom up. This is especially true if few secondary studies of social movements at the community level exist.

Studying social movements from the bottom up, we were struck with the fact that North Town and Aztlán City had no traditional Mexicano elite. The Winter Garden region had no tradition of a racially mixed ruling elite such as exists in the lower Rio Grande Valley. The new Winter Garden Mexicano middle class lacked, therefore, a history of collaboration and compromise between the races. The perceived class differences between Anglos and Mexicanos were apparently sharper in the Winter Garden than in the Valley. This difference is more related to historical patterns of racial incorporation over a long time period than to differences in the labor control systems of the regions. This broad general difference in the accommodation and incorporation of elites makes the Winter Garden region more susceptible to political revolt, *if* autonomous, "organic intellectuals" develop to lead the restless proletariat. José Angel Gutiérrez and lesser-known North Town leaders do exactly that under ethnic populist and cultural nationalist ideologies. This new petty bourgeoisie is genuinely homegrown, and they have emerged out of the class recomposition taking place in these communities. In other words, a class analysis of ethnic politics and capitalist development remains more open and dialectic if it avoids ideal typologies.

[1] Almaguer, Tomas. "Interpreting Chicano History: The World System Approach to Nineteenth Century California." *Review* 4, no. 3 (Winter 1981): 459–507. Barrera, Mario. *Race and Class in the Southwest: A Theory of Racial Inequality.* Notre Dame: University of Notre Dame Press, 1979. De la Garza, Rodolfo. *The Chicano Political Experience: Three Perspectives.* Boston: Duxbury Press, 1977.

[2] Barrera, Mario. *Ibid.* Almaguer, Tomas. *Ibid.* Montejano, David. *Anglos and Mexicans in the Making of Texas, 1836–1986.* Austin: University of Texas Press, 1987.

[3] Acuña, Rodolfo. *Occupied America: A History of Chicanos.* 3d ed. New York: Harper & Row, 1986.

4 Green, James. "Culture, Politics and Workers' Response to Industrialization in the United States." *Radical America* 16, nos. 1 & 2 (January–April 1982): 101–129.

5 Offe, Claus. *Contradictions of the Welfare State*. London: Hutchinson, 1984. Wolfe, Alan. *Limits of Legitimacy: Political Contradictions of Contemporary Capitalism*. New York: Free Press, 1977.

6 Warner, Lloyd, and Allison Davis. "A Comparative Study of American Castes." In Edgar Thompson (ed.), *Race Relations and the Race Problem*, pp. 219–240. Westport, Conn.: Greenwood Press, 1968.

7 Taussig, Michael. *The Devil and Commodity Fetishism in South America*. Chapel Hill: University of North Carolina Press, 1980. Willis, Paul. *Learning to Labor: How Working Class Kids Get Working Class Jobs*. New York: Teacher's College Press, 1981. Novaes da Mota, Clarice. "Jurema Told Us: Kariri-Shoko and Shoko Mode of Medicinal Plants in the Context of North Eastern Brazil." Ph.D. dissertation, University of Texas at Austin, 1987.

8 Peña, Manuel H. *The Texas-Mexican Conjunto: History of a Working-Class Music*. Austin: University of Texas Press, 1985. Limón, Jose. "Western Marxism and Folklore: A Critical Introduction." *Journal of American Folklore* 329 (January–March 1983): 34–52. Limón, Jose. "*Agringado* Joking in Texas-Mexican Society: Folklore and Differential Identity." In Ricardo Romo and Raymund Paredes (eds.), *New Directions in Chicano Scholarship*, pp. 33–50. Santa Barbara: University of California, Center for Chicano Studies, 1984.

9 Clarke, John, Charles Critcher, and Richard Clark (eds.). *Working Class Culture: Studies in History and Theory*. London: Hutchinson, 1980.

10 Wolfe, Eric. *Europe and the People without History*. Berkeley and Los Angeles: University of California Press, 1982.

11 Montejano, David. *Ibid.*

12 Greenberg, Stanley B. *Race and Class in Capitalist Development: Comparative Perspectives*. New Haven: Yale University Press, 1980.

INDEX

Absentee owners, 3, 4, 9, 26, 63, 74–75, 76, 79, 83
Acuña, Rodolfo, 300, 301
Agriculture. *See* Farming; Ranching
Alcoholism, 113, 124–125, 127, 131. *See also Cantinas*
Alonzo, Mr. (Ciudadanos/Raza leader), 157, 214–215, 216, 223, 225, 266, 267–270
Alurista, 301
Anglo attitudes in the 1980s, 284–285
Anglo counter-mobilization, 144–146, 151–154, 160, 263, 266
Athletics. *See* Sports
Aztlán City, 2, 64, 85, 105, 112
  farming in, 70–71, 79, 81
  politics in, 141, 142, 148, 151, 156–157, 159, 165, 167, 169–171, 200, 210, 211, 214, 265, 274–277

Bailes (dances), 13, 42, 50, 52, 89
Barrios, 105, 116–117, 147
BGL (Better Government League). *See also* Elections; Luna, Benito; Politics, Anglo
  and Ciudadanos, 155–168, 172–173, 193, 200–201
  in control of local government, 179–181, 202–203, 220, 238
  ideology of, 151–153, 154, 155–156
  internal dissension in, 178, 196–199
  membership of, 151, 153–154

moderates in, 155, 156, 200, 230–234
  and Raza Unida Party, 154, 155, 157, 160, 163, 178–179, 182–184, 188–189, 200–201, 214–216, 222–223, 227, 229–230
  recruits Mexican-Americans, 191–196, 202
Bilingualism, 14, 23, 39, 68, 83, 100, 111, 119–120, 149, 164, 169. *See also* Language difference
Birth control, 61, 73, 112
Boll weevils, 3, 7, 17, 70
Border Patrol, 5, 18, 67
Braceros, 80, 87, 132, 273, 281. *See also* Labor
Briscoe, Dolph, 101
Brown Berets, 141
Businessmen. *See* Merchants
Busing, 35, 38–39, 65

Cameron, Mr. (city manager/marshal), 23–25, 92–93, 100, 101, 134
Cantinas, 23, 24, 115, 124–125, 131, 134. *See also* Alcoholism
Cattle. *See* Ranching
CCC, 71
Celebrations, 13, 109, 124, 179. *See also Bailes*; *Diez y Seis*; Entertainments; *Fiestas*; Weddings
Chamber of Commerce, 266. *See also* Civic organizations
Chicano movement
  and American politics, 270–273

311

Discrimination against Mexicanos, 14, 23, 24–25, 28–29, 40, 41, 65, 90, 95–96, 146, 148, 190, 195, 239, 240. *See also* Schools; Segregation
Dobieville, 203, 204
Doctors. *See* Medical care
Drainage. *See* Civic improvements

Economic inequality, 15–17, 29, 33, 45–47, 48, 51, 67, 68, 90, 91, 131, 137
Economic Opportunity Development Corporation. *See* EODC
Education, 14, 18, 33, 34–35, 36, 39–40, 68, 73, 91, 95, 96, 98, 109, 110, 271, 293, 297. *See also* Schools
Education Act of 1965, 140
Elders, respect for, 52, 57–58, 60, 61, 122–123
Elections
city council, 96–97, 139, 143–144, 156–161, 163, 183, 201–202, 220, 263
city manager/marshal, 92–93
county, 19, 25, 64
county judge, 95, 203–205
school board, 64, 112, 139, 143–144, 160–161, 163–165, 201–202, 220
sheriff, 145–146
state, 141
student, 189
voting practices and irregularities in, 99–100, 146–147, 158–159, 160, 161–163, 172, 214–215, 223
and voting reform, 234–235
Employment. *See* Labor
Enganchadores 5, 18. *See also* Labor —contractors
Entertainments, Mexicano, 58–59, 60, 61, 116. *See also* Celebrations
EODC (Economic Opportunity Development Corporation), 139, 140, 178, 181, 185, 203, 225, 227, 230, 232, 236
Esposito, Mr. (school board member), 139, 164, 165, 166, 169

Family, Anglo, 13, 32, 35, 63, 64, 73, 79
Family, Mexicano
changes in, 305
and children, 13, 29, 33–39, 42, 43, 53, 54, 56–58, 89, 116–117, 122–124, 125, 126, 129, 131, 133, 140
extended, 53, 59, 62, 63, 66, 87, 88, 116–117
marriage and courtship in, 52, 60, 61, 122, 126–128, 129, 130, 131–132. *See also* Social relationships, Mexicano-Anglo—mixed marriages
migrant, 73–74, 87, 88, 89, 91
roles in, 13, 53–60, 110, 117–118, 120–121, 122, 125–128, 129, 131. *See also* Women
and sex, 126, 128, 129, 130, 131
size of, 6, 10, 40, 47, 49, 61–62, 73–74, 90, 116, 131
and solidarity, 32, 52, 59, 62, 66, 87–91, 116–118, 124
Farming. *See also* Ranching
and agribusiness, 133
cotton, 3–7, 10–12, 16, 17, 63–64, 70, 71, 74–77, 79, 83–85, 87, 89–90
crops, 291–292
hardships of, 11–13, 14, 32, 48, 49, 62, 71, 78, 89
irrigation and water for, 3, 5, 7, 8, 32, 72, 75–79, 81, 82, 294
livestock, 10, 76–77, 291–292
peanut, 72, 74–77
and politics, 21–22
spinach, 9, 63, 70–71, 79, 84, 85
tenant (sharecropping), 6–7, 9, 10, 13–17, 50, 53, 62, 70, 73–74, 89, 290
vegetable, 4, 5, 7–8, 9, 11, 12, 16, 17, 63–64, 70–72, 74, 75, 78–81, 84, 85
Federal assistance, 272, 276. *See also* Social welfare programs
Federal government, 17–18, 62, 66,

71, 81, 82, 84, 91, 92, 94, 95–96, 133, 139, 140, 155
FFA, 37, 40, 83
FHA, 37, 40
Fiestas, 50, 109
4-H Clubs, 37
"Free wheelers," 84, 85, 87, 90. *See also* Labor—migrant
Future Farmers of America, 37, 40, 83
Future Homemakers of America, 37, 40

Galván, Mr. (county-judge candidate), 203–205
G.I. Forum, 95, 96
Gilmer-Aiken Act (1949), 95
Goodman, Mr. (mayor), 92, 93
Graft, 5, 24, 26, 27
Grand jury, 161–163, 172, 178
Green, James, 302
Greenberg, Stanley B., 279, 284, 306, 308
Guerra, Mr. (city council member), 94, 98, 99, 213
Gutiérrez, José Angel, 175, 182, 202, 275, 277, 301, 308

Head Start Program, 178, 185–188
HEW (Department of Health, Education, and Welfare), 227, 230
"Hilltopper Anglos," 98
"Homecoming affair," 190
Hospitals. *See* Medical care
Housing, 10, 18, 78, 80, 87, 90, 93, 94, 105, 131, 139, 160, 181
HUD (Department of Housing and Urban Development), 232

Immigration, 4–5, 8–9, 12, 17, 18, 19, 66, 73, 132. *See also Mojados*
Integration, 95–96, 105, 107, 113, 132–134, 136, 139, 140. *See also* Segregation
Internal colony, 301–303
Interracial groups and dating, 171, 242. *See also* Social relationships —Mexicano-Anglo

Irrigation. *See* Farming—irrigation and water for

Judges, county, 2, 19, 20–21, 25–27, 65, 94–95, 99, 146, 203–205

Kornblum, William, 277
Ku Klux Klan (KKK), 17, 18, 66, 280

Labor
child, 9, 13, 34–35, 53, 54, 78, 87, 89–90, 91, 109
contractors, 5, 8, 18, 73, 75, 80, 84–88, 99, 102, 136
and cooperation, 6–7, 9, 52, 53, 63, 65, 67, 77, 118, 132, 134
exploitation of, 9, 14, 15, 16, 18–19, 51, 62–63, 66, 67, 68, 74, 86–87, 89, 90
Mexican (from Mexico), 4–5, 8–9, 12, 13, 17–19, 23, 66, 70, 78, 80, 82, 84, 134, 150
Mexicano (in U.S.), 8, 9, 12–13, 14, 16, 66, 71–72, 73–74, 77–78, 80–81, 82–85, 93–94, 192, 241
migrant, 2, 3, 9, 73–74, 80, 83–91, 109, 116, 118–119, 132, 136, 273, 281
relations, 6, 9, 13–16, 48–49, 60, 74, 77–78, 83, 118, 122, 132
reserve, 281
unions, 18, 68, 132
wages, 10, 15, 78, 80, 81, 88, 89, 113, 119, 131–133, 140, 144–145
Language differences, 2, 14, 38, 39, 113, 131, 147, 149. *See also* Bilingualism
Local government, 17–19, 22, 27–29, 65, 92, 101–102, 151. *See also* City government; County government; Elections
LULAC (League of United Latin American Citizens), 95–99, 101, 112, 136, 139, 145, 149, 221, 225, 263
Luna, Benito (mayor), 230–234, 263–264, 266, 267, 270

314